# GUNFIGHTERS

# GUNFIGHTERS
## THE OUTLAWS AND THEIR WEAPONS

### EDITED BY
## CHRIS MCNAB

THUNDER BAY
P·R·E·S·S
San Diego, California

**Thunder Bay Press**

An imprint of the Advantage Publishers Group

5880 Oberlin Drive, San Diego, CA 92121-4794

www.thunderbaybooks.com

ISBN-13: 978-59223-507-0
ISBN-10: 1-59223-507-7

Library of Congress Cataloging-in-Publication Data available upon request.

Printed in China
1 2 3 4 5  10 09 08 07 06

**Credits**

Project Editor: Shaun Barrington
Designer: John Heritage
Picture Researcher: Carla Penagos
Production: Kate Rogers
Index: Steve Theobald
Reproduction: Anorax Imaging Ltd.

**Additional Captions**

Page 1: Handcuffs and a deputy sheriff's badge made from the back of a pocket watch.
Page 2: Captain John Jarrett, a former guerrilla and later member of Jesse James's gang. Said Cole Younger, "He never knew fear."
Jarrett was married to the Younger brothers' sister Mary Josephine, "Josie."
Page 3: A Colt single-action Army revolver, with $7^1/_2$-inch barrel, .46 caliber.
Page 5: Confederate Army revolvers: a Le Mat Second Model revolver (top); T. W. Cofer revolver (bottom).

# CONTENTS

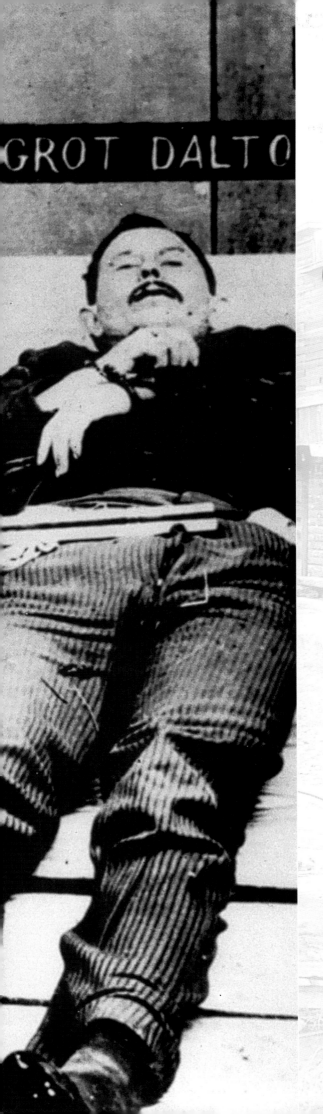

# Chapter One

## THE GUN-SMOKE FRONTIER:

# GUNFIGHTERS OF THE WILD WEST

Soon the cry "The Daltons! The Daltons!" echoed up and down the street. Armed citizens were soon on hand, hiding themselves and laying in wait for the gang. Bob and Emmett successfully robbed the First National Bank, but when they rode to join their companions they were met by a hail of bullets.

LEFT: The Dalton gang, like so many Western career criminals, ended their lives full of lead. Here Tim Evans, Bob Dalton, and Grat Dalton lie dead and handcuffed outside the Coffeyville jail on October 5, 1892. Their attempt to rob two banks at once had failed in bloody fashion.

# THE GUNFIGHTER

The gunfighter is as much a part of American folklore as are the cowboy, the Indian, and a host of other legendary characters whose exploits have enthralled a worldwide audience for generations. Unlike the majority of those folk heroes, however, the gunfighter evokes a sinister image, one that stirs emotions, arouses controversy, and generates conflict. For many, he represents a knight-errant fighting the dragon of crime and corruption, but to others he is the personification of evil, a character who, regardless of the circumstances, reacts to any situation with violence. In short, he is a professional killer both behind and in front of a badge.

Emphasis on the gunfighter's killer instinct has provoked some alarming reactions among today's pundits. Any civil unrest or violent behavior involving firearms is seized upon by the media as a return to the "Wild West" and its so-called lawlessness. Yet set against the harsh realities of the modern world with all its foibles and faults, such reasoning seems ironic and misplaced. Such cynicism is in stark contrast to the nineteenth-century view, when morality, religion, and family, coupled with a sense of duty, took precedence over the individual's civil rights. Most people at that time yearned for law and order, and those who transgressed soon learned that justice could be swift and terrible. Nowadays, the emphasis is on the lawbreakers rather than the lawmakers, a view that is hard to discourage.

Such an extreme divergence of opinion is only fully appreciated when one remembers that America has been preoccupied with firearms since revolutionary times. The Constitution gave the individual the "right to bear arms," which has been interpreted to mean to "possess and to use them in defense of home, family, and possessions." Others claim that the right to bear arms really meant in defense of the Union in time of war or civil unrest. Not surprisingly, a

people's champion or a kind of Robin Hood in buckskins has enormous appeal. Although the cowboy fits this image, it was the man who lived and died by the gun who exerted most influence. He can only be understood when one examines the circumstances that gave birth to the character we now call the gunfighter. The war with Mexico spawned him, and his adolescence witnessed the California gold rush and the Kansas–Missouri border wars of the middle- and late-1850s. By the time of the Civil War, he had reached maturity and was prominent among the guerrillas on both sides. His adult life was spent in the postwar cattle, rail, and mining boomtowns.

As a class, gunfighters did not conform to the stereotyped image of the motion pictures. Generations of Western fans have seen them portrayed as cowboys, gamblers, and occasionally in the guise of a frontier scout complete with buckskins, but the cowboy image dominates. From the earliest appearance of the Western movie, the dress and manner of the gunfighter has been reflected in the image of the cowboy. The huge sombrero, neckerchief, double or single gun belt, knee-high boots (worn with pants tucked in or pulled down over them), and jingling spurs all served to create a false image of the man behind the gun. In reality, most gunfighters dressed normally, according to the current fashions of the time, and would probably be missed in a crowd. Only when they openly carried pistols would they

**ABOVE: Sam "One Arm" Berry (left) and Sue Mundy (Marcellus J. Clarke) were two infamous Kentucky guerrillas who rode with William Clarke Quantrill's "Raiders" during the American Civil War. Both individuals were involved with the brutal plundering of the town of Hickman, Kentucky, in the final year of the war. While Berry survived the war, Mundy was hanged in Louisville in 1865.**

command much attention. In fact, the editor of the Kansas City, Missouri. *Journal* on November 15, 1881, made a point of describing the "man-killer" or "civilizer" that today we call the gunfighter:

> The gentleman who has "killed his man" is by no means a *rara avis* ... He is met daily on Main Street, and is the busiest of the busy throng. He may be seen on "change and in the congregations of the most aristocratic churches. He resides on 'Quality hill', or perhaps on the East Side ... This ubiquitous individual may be seen almost anywhere. He may be found behind the bar in a Main street saloon; he may be seen by an admiring audience doing the pedestal clog at a variety theatre; his special forte may be driving a cab, or he may be behind the rosewood counters of a bank ... He is usually quiet in demeanor, sober [and] ... he may take a drink occasionally, but seldom gets drunk ... He is quiet—fatally quiet ... Your gentleman who has dropped his man is, therefore, no uncommon individual.

The editor's graphic portrait of the typical gunfighter refutes the loudmouthed, troublemaking "shoot at anything that moves" Texas cowboy of the 1860s and early 1870s. There were cowboy gunfighters, but they were the exception. Most of the men who lived and died by the gun were indeed a breed apart. Some were honest, law-abiding individuals who became peace officers sworn to uphold the law. Others, equally honest but by no means as dedicated, took to the badge to avoid starvation or to fill in between other occupations. The likes of Bill Tilghman and Bat Masterson came within the first category, while Wild Bill Hickok and the Earp brothers were part of the second group. Few of these men were trained peace officers. They were motivated

**ABOVE RIGHT:** William "Bill" Tilghman, an upright individual who earned his reputation in the Kansas cow towns such as Dodge City and furthered it in early-day Oklahoma Territory. Later, having been a State Senator, Tilghman became a marshal again, to be killed in the line of duty in 1924—at the age of 70!

**RIGHT:** Wild Bill Hickok, dressed for his appearance with Buffalo Bill Cody's theatrical troupe in 1873. Apart from his long hair, he looks a typical eastern dandy attired in the latest fashion.

economically or politically rather than by any great sense of justice. Aligned against them were the likes of the James brothers, Billy the Kid, and others for whom the gun symbolized power and the ease with which one could acquire wealth and instill fear in honest citizens whose only ambition was to survive in a very harsh environment.

The views of mid-nineteenth-century Europeans regarding the penchant for the pistol in certain parts of the United States make interesting reading. In England, for instance, the *Daily Telegraph* of October 22, 1869, remarked:

> Duellists, travellers, and the rowdy bullies of the New World, enjoy the doubtful honour of having brought the pistol to its present sanguinary perfection. It is the weapon of the self-dependent man; and those who can find a "final cause" of good rattlesnakes and poisonous drugs might cite a great many instances to prove that the pistol has furthered civilisation, and has been especially the arm of progress . . . Unhappily, the drunken bully and gambler of America and Mexico has found the six-shooter convenient, and carries it more regularly than his tooth-pick. Some day, we hope, the Government of The United States, remembering what Thucydides says about the barbarity of a people who "wear iron," will make it a punishable offence to carry a "Derringer" or a "Colt." But these

bloodthirsty scoundrels complain of the revolver. It kills, but not immediately; its bullet is too small to paralyse; the victim dies by internal bleeding, but not before he has time to discharge his own battery. Hence those extraordinary encounters in the Western and Southern States, where a whole volley of shots is discharged before one of the wretched combatants succumbs.

This view neglected to examine (or perhaps was ignorant of) the West itself.

The gunfighters, or perhaps their gunfights, loom large in America's folklore and remain the subject of debate a century or more since they last squeezed a trigger. Some died with their boots on, and others in bed, but so fascinating is the subject that it has inspired a modern six-shooter cult that dwells primarily upon how fast on the draw certain individuals might have been rather than their accuracy and what first provoked them to kill.

**BELOW: The revolver became the defining firearm of the American West, with Colt being a preeminent name from the mid-nineteenth century onward. Here we see a Colt single-action Army revolver accompanied by its double-loop holster and belt. A box of .45-caliber cartridges is seen in the foreground.**

The gunfighter arose out of the turbulent conditions that existed in the frontier West, when a man's best friend and hope of salvation was a gun, for there were many remote parts of states or territories where law and order was either over extended or unheard of. The classic gunfight of fact, fiction, and the silver screen, which depicts two or more individuals facing each other down in a high-noon duel, is now an accepted part of Western folklore. In reality, the gunfight was loosely based upon the old-time *code duello*, but it lacked the rules of the original and instead relied on the cold-blooded science of getting the "drop" on an opponent. The importance of the "drop" was paramount. "One must always have the drop on an antagonist," noted the *Topeka Daily Commonwealth*, on September 23, 1871, "or nothing more than an exercise of the vocal muscles ensues. The code of chivalry seems to be to fight only a smaller man who is unprepared and unsuspecting. Shoot him in the back, bite his

ear or nose off as a memento, and your reputation as a fighting man is made." Among men of reputation, however, such brawling was rare. A man's "honor" was set above everything else, and it was a trait that can be traced right back to earlier times when duelists fought hand-to-hand encounters that would have appalled some of the latter-day six-shooter virtuosos who depended upon the "drop" and the killer instinct for survival.

Men have fought each other all through history, using rocks, clubs, and swords, right down to firearms. The individual's preoccupation with personal supremacy has been motivated by debts of honor, sexual betrayal, or public humiliation. In Europe, where dueling was considered the province of the aristocracy, young men were schooled in the art of fencing and knife fighting. These weapons remained popular on the Continent until the nineteenth century, but in England, by the late eighteenth century, the dueling pistol

LEFT: "I am a shootist," declared Clay Allison in 1878; he meant "gunfighter." Feared killer that he was, this photograph, made in about 1868, is ironic—for Allison died in a wagon accident in 1887.

RIGHT: Saloons were as much places of sudden violence as centers of entertainment. Here one Ed Dale lies booted and dead in Morgan's place.

was coming into its own. Some regarded dueling as a sport, others considered it a retrograde step in human relations, and in England it was outlawed in the early years of the nineteenth century. Ireland, however, regarded the individual who would not fight a duel for his honor as a coward, and young men of breeding were expected to own a case of dueling pistols. Thus, the Irish *code duello* formed the basis for similar rules and behavior in other English-speaking countries, notably America.

Dueling in the northern states was uncommon, whereas in the South, with its homegrown aristocracy based upon the European variety, it flourished. A man's honor or his wife's reputation meant everything to him, and if it was necessary to carry weapons to protect or assert either he would do so.

Many cited the famous English legal expert William Blackstone's definition of self-defense as "the mutual and reciprocal defense of such as stand in the relations of husband and wife, parent and child, master and servant," which enabled him to "repel force by force." By the mid-1850s, however, with the arrival of the revolver, the old-fashioned rules of dueling disappeared. For every individual who relied upon his weapon for protection, there were many others who saw it as a means to an end. The day of the pistoleer had arrived.

Despite revision and review by historians, the old myths and fables concerning the American West and its gunfighters are perpetuated. While historians strive for the truth, they often find that people prefer legends. It is much more

# THE COMING OF THE
# THE RAILROADS

The railroads were central to the story of the American Wild West. Without the railroads, the widespread settlement of the North American interior would not have been possible, and the enormous commercial growth of the United States would have been curtailed. Alternatively, the railroads provided new escape routes and fresh targets for gunfighters and bandits, and they also fueled the construction of some of the most lawless towns in all of America.

Construction of the U.S. rail network began early in the nineteenth century around Boston, and during the first half of the century a sprawling network of lines coalesced around the eastern seaboard and spread out to the area around and to the south of the Great Lakes. More southerly routes tracked down as far as New Orleans. Most of the early railroad construction focused on linking two proximate cities or providing links from cities to good harbors or agricultural areas. However, in 1844 a trader from New York City, Asa Whitney, proposed the construction of a transcontinental railroad. The idea matured slowly, the plans for the line complicated by myriad territorial disputes and political tensions. In 1854 the Corps of Topographic Engineers began the Pacific Railroad Survey, an effort to determine the most viable route for a transcontinental line. By the end of the decade the engineers had their route. The Central Pacific line would be built along the 41st parallel eastward from San Francisco to near Salt Lake City, while the Union Pacific line would connect with the Central Pacific and link up with the rail network in the eastern United States.

Construction work began the year after the Congressional Pacific Railroad Act of 1862. The respective lines were placed in the hands of two huge commercial organizations, the directors of which were to become enormously wealthy not only through overinflated stock prices but through the rights to land that ran alongside the thousands of miles of track. Immigrant workers, mainly Irish, African American, Hispanic, and Chinese, who lived on terrible wages, did most of the construction. Construction bosses worked them night and day at a fanatical pace; on April 28, 1869, one gang on the Central Pacific laid ten miles of track in the day. Only seven years after the rail-laying had begun, and despite four years of Civil War, the two lines met at Promontory Point, northwest of Salt Lake City.

America now had its first transcontinental railroad, and in 1870 a large connecting line was built between Kansas City and the Union Pacific. By the end of the century America had two more great transregional railroad lines, the Southern Pacific and Northern Pacific, and hundreds of smaller lines in between. The American West was truly opened up to settlement, and the railroad companies themselves ran resettlement offices, taking thousands of families out to the West on (much exaggerated) promises of good land and healthy living.

So what effect did the railroads have on the world of the gunfighters? For the criminal fraternity, the railroads presented a new and highly lucrative target for robbery. Train robberies were mainly a post–Civil War phenomenon. The end of hostilities in 1865 left gangs of heavily armed men wondering what to do next with their lives, and some saw the railroads as easy pickings. Trains carried gold shipments and payrolls, usually contained in safes in the express car. The train robbers used several methods to bring a train to a stop. Sometimes they mounted the train engine from horseback and forced the driver to either stop immediately or take the train on to a remote location where it would be robbed. Alternatively, the bandits would, in the style of the Hole-in-the-Wall gang, hijack the train at some isolated depot or actually pose as passengers on board the train before springing the raid at a suitable spot. More rarely, the gang might destroy track in advance of the train to force an emergency stop.

The Reno brothers conducted the first of the major train robberies on May 22, 1868. They robbed the Adams Express Company on the Jeffersonville Railroad, at Marshfield, Indiana, netting around $100,000. The scale of the raid awakened the authorities to train robbing, and from then on the outlaws were in a constant battle of wits with the Texas Rangers, U.S. marshals, and the formidable Pinkerton agency. The rail companies had deep pockets, and by the end of the century rail robbing had been virtually stamped out, most of the bandits being either dead or incarcerated.

**ABOVE LEFT: The completion of the Pacific railroad as locomotives of the Union and Central Pacific lines meet at Promontory Point in 1869.**

**RIGHT: Railroad construction at Topeka, Kansas. Railroad workers lived brutal lives and for fourteen-hour days, seven days a week, they were paid around $30–$35 a month.**

**ABOVE:** James Daniels was a hardened criminal who stabbed a man to death during a card game in Helena, Montana, in 1866. He was arrested, but released. However, he didn't escape the hands of the local vigilantes, who lynched him shortly after his release.

filmmakers and novelists. For whatever one may think of the men who used firearms for good or evil, their exploits still fascinate and command a large following.

Although the heroic image of the gunfighter is not contemporary to his time, it is true that a man who could handle a pistol better than those who used them for gain or power was much in demand. But unlike his fictional counterpart, he was held responsible for his actions, if need be in a court of law.

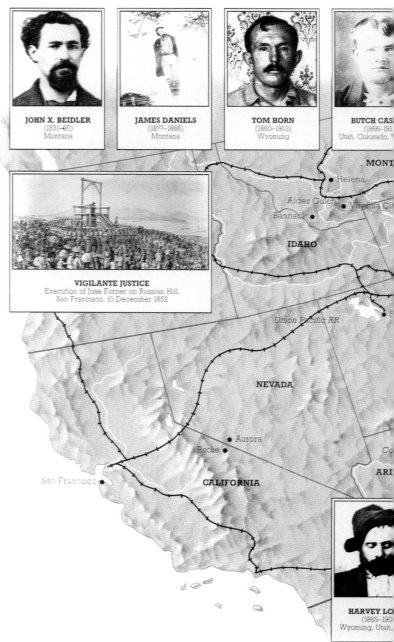

exciting to read that Billy the Kid killed twenty-one men—one for each year of his life—or that Wild Bill disposed of "considerably over a hundred bad men," than to be told that the Kid killed perhaps six people and Wild Bill's tally was closer to ten than a hundred. In each instance, legend took care of the remainder and it is the legend that appeals to most people and not the facts.

In this book, we intend to depict the gunfighter's role in society, its reaction to him, and how he was accepted or rejected, rather than the time-warped image so beloved by

## The Beckoning West

The frontier West in the early nineteenth century was unknown territory, a wilderness inhabited by nomadic tribes of Indians, vast herds of buffalo, and other forms of wildlife. It was widely believed that much of the land was a great desert and unfit for habitation. But following on from the early explorations of Lewis and Clark and later Pike, by the late 1840s there began a mass migration that was to turn that wilderness into a civilized country. In the process, however, many people perished; wars were fought and reputations made or lost. For it was also the age of the entrepreneur, the visionary, the civilizer, and the man with the gun.

The most enduring part of the gunfighter legend is the belief that he played a part in civilizing the West, that his pistol pacified the lawless and strengthened the resolve of the law-abiding souls who sought to tame the wild land and provide a new life for themselves and their families. In fact, it was mass migration and not the individual with a gun who

JOHN BROWN
(1800–1859)
Kansas

JAMES H. LANE
(1814–66)
Mexico, Kansas

QUANTRILL'S
GUERRILLAS
Kansas, Missouri

BILL ANDERSON
(1839–64)
Missouri, Kansas

JESSE JAMES
(1847–82)
Kansas, Missouri

BILL DOOLIN
(1858–96)
Kansas, Oklahoma

LUKE SHORT
(1854–93)
Kansas, Texas

COLE YOUNGER
(1844–1916)
Kansas, Missouri

THE DALTON GANG
(Bob 1868–92, Emmett 1871–1937, Grat 1865–92)
Oklahoma, Kansas

JOHN ARMSTRONG
(1850–1913)
Texas

JOHN WESLEY HARDIN
(1853–95)
Texas, Kansas

tamed the West. Perhaps the most important contribution was the railroad. As its silver rails spread like tentacles out across the country, in its wake came people anxious to settle somewhere on its route. And once the tracks moved on, in place of the chaos and confusion of tent cities that had housed hard-working, hard-drinking tracklayers, graders, and others bent upon pushing the rails West, permanent structures sprang up that became townships and cities.

As they advanced, the railroads also posed their own problems, for the tracks frequently outpaced civilization. Most of the embryonic townships in their wake lacked government and witnessed bouts of lawlessness that deterred rather than encouraged would-be settlers. More hardy folk, however, were prepared to face up to the violence and fight for what they believed in. It was their self-reliance and spirit that conquered the frontier West.

The West and its land was no place for the weak, the timid, or the hesitant. Rather, it was there for the taking by those who grasped at the opportunities regardless of the odds. Of the thousands who invaded the region, no one will ever know how many failed to reach their goal. Perhaps understandably, it is not the hard-working, dedicated farmer, homesteader, or storekeeper that appeals to today's audiences and readers but the outlaw, scout, mountain man, cowboy, and soldier. All of them exuded an aura of romanticism that

inspires a mixture of adulation and nostalgia for an era that created legends.

The Easterner, living as so many of them did in overcrowded cities and ghettos, faced with a growing immigrant population that threatened his existence and employment prospects, yearned for the West where, if he believed the stories, there was greater freedom, more room to move around, and a future. Only when they gave serious thought to the hazards to be faced did the less venturesome think twice about moving West. Westerners were people used to making on-the-spot decisions and who were contemptuous of the Easterners' obsession with legal formalities, an attitude that in some areas still survives. Westerners held similar views over law and order. What suited the Easterner, used to courts and due process, meant little to a man in the wilds of Wyoming or the Great Plains who had stock rustled. If he could get his hands on the culprit, he would deal with him himself and if need be kill to recover his property. This simplistic view was not in contempt of the law but because of the lack of it. Where no law existed, or it was too extended to rely upon, people tended to take care of their own problems. Cattle rustlers and horse-thieves risked being shot or hanged, while less dangerous or petty

criminals might endure a severe thrashing. But whatever the crime, if caught, punishment (if not always justice) was swift. Time and the influx of more people, as well as the establishment of local government, schools, churches, and the essentials of civilization, eroded the need for expedient justice and replaced it with both state and federal law.

A part of the frontier tradition was that the line between the outlaw and the lawman was thinly drawn; it was not unknown for a man to have a reputation on both sides. Indeed, some of the better-known gunfighters had pasts that included court appearances or perhaps prison sentences. Yet with a change of circumstances—a public need—they were reinstated to society. Once they were no longer needed, and they were out of a job, there was the threat of being charged with vagrancy, "for having no visible means of support." Wild Bill Hickok suffered this indignity at Cheyenne in 1875 when he wandered in and out of the place for some months.

Perhaps the most prominent frontier tradition was that of the vigilante. No study of the era can ignore either the significance or the effect of those who followed this course. Two places in particular illustrate the power of the vigilante movement, for both exemplified the manifestation of "people power" that followed the centuries-old belief that if there was

**ABOVE LEFT:** An El Paso County tombstone evokes the violent West. Harkens was a 55-year-old laborer killed by Mexican bandits in 1863.

**LEFT:** The early settlers of the American frontier moved into virgin territories with little or no formal structures of law, apart from guns.

**RIGHT:** Nevada City, seen here in the 1850s. The city was founded in 1849 by A. B. Caldwell and initially served local mine workers.

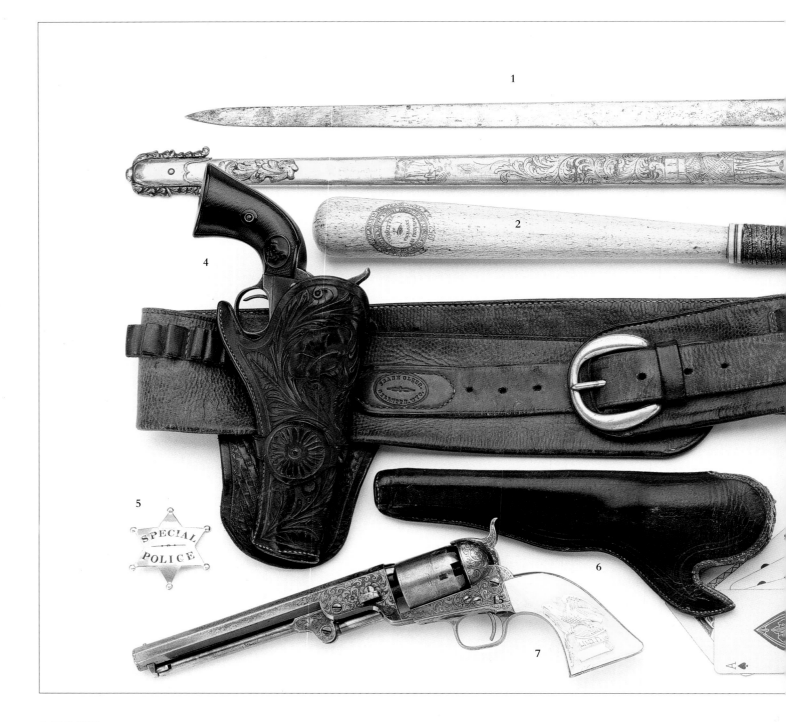

## LAWMEN

Tools and emblems of office carried by those who enforced the law in the West varied in quality and formality. Accounts of San Francisco vigilantes suggest disorganized mobs and rampant ruffians, but these vigilantes were well organized and carried almost fraternal-like accessories. Some law agencies actually specified the use of uniforms, especially in cities. But usually, the Texas Ranger, local sheriff, or U.S. marshal chose weapons to suit individual taste.

Pistols carried by old-time gunfighters are prized. Bat Masterson faked notches in secondhand pistol butts to fool gullible collectors. Inscribed guns are also prized. The Navy pistol shown here (7), said to have once belonged to Wild Bill Hickok, has an interesting history. In 1937 it was exhibited at the premier of Gary Cooper's film about Hickok, *The Plainsman*. At that time the back-strap inscription read "J.B. Hickock 1869." When it appeared again in 1975, the second "c" had been skillfully removed.

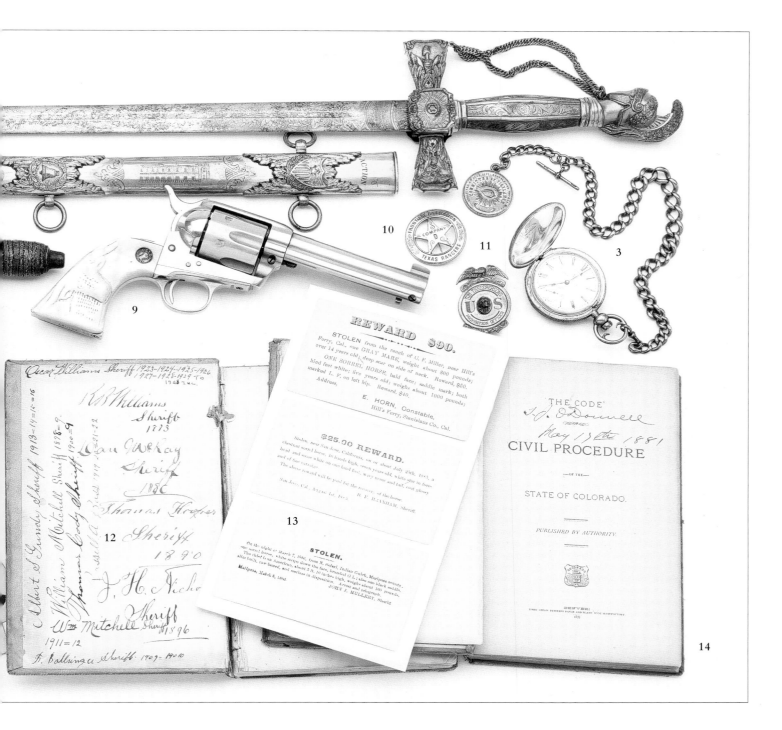

1. San Francisco vigilante sword, silver plating, gold wash, precious stones, with the vigilante symbol of the "all seeing eye" engraved on the scabbard.
2. Ivory club carried by Samuel P. Hill in the San Francisco vigilantes, dated 1852.
3. Silver pocket watch carried by Bartholomew Williamson. The silver fob has the "all seeing eye" of the San Francisco vigilantes—a different kind of badge indicating membership in the group. (Items 1, 2, and 3 are from the collection of Greg Martin.)
4. This holster, belt, and Colt revolver belonged to George Gardiner, a some-time cowboy, Wild West performer, and law officer in the 1890s and later.
5. Law badge worn by George Gardiner in Sheridan, Wyoming.
6. Plain, finely lined holster with the initials "JB" scratched on the back. Of the quality made by E. L. Gallatin in Cheyenne, Wyoming, the holster accompanies the Hickok Navy (7).
7. This factory-engraved ivory Colt 1851 Navy bears Hickok's name on the

back strap. Serial No. 138813 chillingly reflects the "Aces and Eights" of his last poker hand.
8. "Aces and Eights," or the "Dead Man's Hand," held by Hickok when he was murdered by Jack McCall in Deadwood.
9. Colt single-action Army .45 carried by Texas Ranger Tom Threepersons after the turn of the century.
10. Tom Threepersons's Texas Rangers badge.
11. Prohibition officer's badge, made from a silver dollar and used by Tom Threepersons.
12. Sheriff's manual signed by successive sheriffs in Central City, Colorado, after 1882.
13. Reward notices for horse thieves.
14. Another source governing the activities of Colorado law officers—published Civil Procedure.

(Artifacts courtesy of Gene Autry Western Heritage Museum, Los Angeles.)

no law to take care of culprits, then the vigilantes would. San Francisco, California, in the midst and wake of the gold rush, formed a group of vigilantes that became world famous, while in Virginia City, Montana, the vigilantes proved that ordinary citizens could only take so much before retaliating against outlaw domination and terror.

California, following the discovery of gold in 1848, became the most popular place on earth. Thousands flocked there, and the population grew so much that the citizens petitioned the government for statehood. This was granted in 1850. However, the huge influx of would-be miners and the usual gamblers, prostitutes, and "speculators" presaged any but the most basic attempts at establishing law and order or local

**BELOW: Hydraulic mining was an incredibly destructive form of gold digging. A hillside would be blasted to pieces with pressurized water jets, the resulting slurry being channeled down into a processing plant where gold would be extracted.**

government. Although California had established law and order by 1851–1852, with the aid of vigilantes who flourished despite complaints of a "Reign of Terror" and talk of a "Committee of Public Safety" reminiscent of the French Revolution, state laws made little impact upon the lawless element. The vastness of the country and lack of population in the more remote areas proved to be a haven for outlaws and desperadoes. However, when justice caught up with malefactors, it was swift.

In 1848, it was the small port of Yerba Buena, with a population of less than 1,000, but following the discovery of gold its name was changed to San Francisco and it became the home of thousands of would-be gold seekers. Destroyed several times by fire, the young city nevertheless managed to improve with each new building, and by the mid-1850s the "tent city" of the early days was largely constructed of bricks and mortar. By 1853, the "Queen of the Pacific," as she was affectionately called, boasted a large number of hotels,

ABOVE AND LEFT: These views of San Francisco, dated 1851, graphically depict the almost deserted look of the place and the ships—all abandoned by men in search of gold.

churches, schools, hospitals, banks, and several fire companies, together with saloons, gambling halls, and brothels. Access to the place was via the overland route from St. Louis or via ship from eastern seaboard ports to the Isthmus of Panama (the canal had yet to be built), Nicaragua, or "round the Horn" at risk of violent seas and storms. Communication overland was slightly better after 1853 when a 200-mile telegraph link was installed between San Francisco and Marysville. This was later extended to Salt Lake City, Utah, and with the arrival of Western Union in 1861, East was linked to West.

Back in the early 1850s, however, there were genuine fears that law and order would be slow to reach not only the "diggings" but also California in general. Consequently, the vigilantes were accepted as a necessary evil. A number of men

were hanged, following a trial; the first of these was a man named Jenkins, a persistent criminal who hailed from Australia. Not surprisingly, a number of former convicts or men who had been transported to Australia from England for various crimes headed for California if given the chance. The Americans named these characters "Sydney Ducks" or "Sydney Coves." Some of them even established a "Sydney Town" at Clark's Point on the outskirts of San Francisco. Although the vigilantes, in hindsight, contributed much toward law and order, they were powerless to stop the increase in violence brought about by the use of firearms.

The growth in the population of California and the increasing use of firearms aroused much concern. By 1857, the *Chronicle*, according to *The Illustrated London News* of

RIGHT: Aurora, Nevada, was founded in 1860 as a gold-mining town, its citizens extracting $27 million of gold over the subsequent seven years. Today Aurora is nothing more than a haunting, derelict ghost town.

BELOW: Bodie, California, seen in 1880. Bodie was a gold town named after W. S. Bodie, who discovered gold in the nearby hills in 1859.

ABOVE: William Walker, the noted early California "lawyer-duelist" and editor of the *San Francisco Herald*. Walker's 1850s-style dress is in sharp contrast to that of his latter-day rivals of the 1870s and later.

## PERCUSSION COLTS

Samuel Colt's idea of the revolver caught on quickly. Texans understood the value of the weapon, and with the coming of the Mexican War, one of them, Samuel Walker, helped to influence the government in ordering a newly designed .44-caliber monster. The Walker Colt and many of its successors (all of the latter made in Hartford, Connecticut) had images of dragoons fighting Indians on the cylinder. Sam Colt understood the value of his product to the Western market,

and he exploited this for all it was worth. Until after the Civil War, a variety of Colts in different sizes, calibers, and models were produced and widely used throughout the West.

Along trails, in western gold fields, gambling dens, and elsewhere, there were other types of handguns, but none was ever as popular as the Colt. The .44-caliber Army and dragoon models served military and civilian needs alike. Premium prices were also paid in the West for the lighter .36-caliber models.

1. The massive Walker-model revolver, .44 caliber, popular in the Mexican War. One of one hundred civilian models that were made after the completion of the 1847 government contract.
2. First model Dragoon revolver, .44 caliber, made in 1848.
3. Model 1860 Colt Army revolver, .44 caliber, experimental model, serial number 4 with fluted cylinder. Thousands saw use in the hands of civilians and Western cavalry in the 1860s and early 1870s.
4. Third model Dragoon revolver, with attachable shoulder stock, .44 caliber, carried by dragoon and cavalry troops in the pre–Civil War West.
5. Model 1851 Navy Model, .36 caliber, cutaway demonstration model.
6. Cased 1851 Navy, with London markings.
7. Model 1848 pocket revolver, known as the "Baby Dragoon," lightweight, easy to carry, and popular throughout the West.
8. Model 1849 pocket revolver, .31 caliber, five shot, cutaway demonstrator made in 1857.

9. Prototype of the Wells Fargo–model 1849 pocket revolver, serial number 1, .31 caliber, with separate loading tool—easily concealed, but all business.
10. Experimental pocket revolver, unfinished, .36 caliber.
11. Model 1862 pocket Navy revolver, made in 1863, stagecoach holdup scene engraved on the cylinder.
12. "Trapper's" model 1862 Police revolver, experimental prototype without serial number.
13. Model 1862 Police revolver with accessories, inscribed "H.A. Bridham/U.S.A." with rare casing in the form of a book.
14. Cased model 1855 side-hammer revolver with accessories, .28 caliber, made in about 1856, the cylinder roll engraved with a scene of an Indian fight.
15. Standard model 1855 side-hammer revolver, cutaway demonstrator.

(Artifacts courtesy of Gene Autry Western Heritage Museum, Los Angeles.)

September 15, was bemoaning the demoralizing effects caused by the "universal and cowardly practice of carrying revolvers." Personal disputes invariably led to shoot-outs, and the press paid much attention to the situation. Yet historians have tended to ignore the fact that California, Nevada, and Montana were as violent and had their share of "bad men" who were the equals of their better-known Midwestern counterparts. The reason, of course, was a lack of publicity. Apart from William B. Secrest's *Dangerous Men: Gunfighters, Lawmen and Outlaws of Old California*, John Boessenecker's *Badge and Buckshot: Lawlessness in Old California*, and *Gunfighters, Highwaymen and Vigilantes: Violence on the Frontier* by Roger D. McGrath, little recent attention has been paid to the subject. Roger McGrath, however, confines his subject to only two places: the gold and silver camps of Aurora and Bodie.

Contemporary reports of the San Francisco vigilantes caused some consternation, but Aurora and Bodie had similar organizations. The law being practically nonexistent, the citizens provided their own (after a fashion) and soon emulated their San Francisco cousins by setting up lynch mobs or "regulators" and "committees of safety," which for the most part was the best that could be done. If nothing else, a number of murderers were "jerked to Jesus" in the approved manner, which convinced others of the error of their ways. Gangs of outlaws were common. Aurora boasted the John Daly gang, many of whom perished from lead poisoning or rope burns and in their time ranked with the James brothers and the Daltons. One suspects, however, that Bodie's reputation at least was helped in later years by a story published in the *Sacramento Daily Bee* in 1880 entitled "The Bad Man from Bodie." But the eyes of the nation were fixed upon San Francisco in the early years, and by 1851, when the gold rush was at its height, a number of individuals were already making their mark within the city. Secrest recorded the exploits of several men who, for a variety of reasons, are now a part of California's folklore. Among them was Will Hicks Graham, a lawyer who had come to California in June 1850. He worked for Judge R. N. Morrison who was (so he and other clerks thought) unjustly criticized by the editor of the *San Francisco Herald*, William Walker, a noted duelist.

Hotheaded action by the clerks led to Graham drawing the short straw and challenging Walker to a duel.

At that time, dueling was a popular means of settling disputes in California. Condemned by some but attended by crowds, news of the challenge soon spread and on January 12, 1851, the pair met, watched by a vast crowd that included judges, policemen, and other officials. The *Alta* noted that "The weapons used were Colt's revolvers, and five [shots] were to be fired, unless one of the parties was hit before. Two shots were exchanged. At the first fire, Mr. Walker received his adversary's ball through the leg of his pantaloons, and at the second was shot through the fleshy part of the thigh. The wound was of a very trifling character." Both men were ten paces apart. Walker conceded his opponent's victory, and the affair closed. Graham was charged with aggravated assault and for engaging in an unlawful duel, but was later found not guilty. By this time, reported Secrest, he was involved in another duel when he learned that the love of his life was having an affair behind his back. Graham challenged his rival,

George Lemon, to a duel, but Lemon was not anxious to swap lead. When they did eventually exchange shots, Graham missed with every one and, backing off, tripped and fell. Lemon then rushed up and shot him through the mouth, the bullet splitting his tongue and loosening several teeth before lodging in his throat. Amazingly, Graham recovered and again challenged Lemon. This time Lemon was seriously wounded, and honor was satisfied. Graham survived a number of duels, served as a vigilante, and practiced law. Yet he did not relish his reputation as a gunfighter. Such a reputation he thought was a curse and only encouraged every "reckless fool who wants to get his name up as a desperado," as he put it in a letter, to force one into a fight. For such an individual, his constitution was frail, and he died in bed with his boots off in 1866.

Another of the lesser-known California gunfighters was James ("Jim") McKinney, a bad man who plagued the state in later years. Some recalled that when sober he was a fine man, but when drunk he was treacherous and deadly. A

**ABOVE LEFT:** Hydraulic mining in the rubble-strewn landscape at Alder Gulch, Montana Territory, in 1860–1871. By this time, much of the earlier pick and shovel work had been replaced by machinery.

**LEFT:** A Bannack street scene in the 1860s. Depicted are a number of the buggy-type carriages that proved to be popular in most Western areas. Note the false-fronted buildings on the street.

compulsive gambler, he was involved in a number of shooting scrapes that brought him to the law's attention. He served some time in San Quentin Prison, from which place he was released in 1895. He was soon in trouble, and by 1900 was again on the wanted list. In 1901 he killed a man named Red Sears in a duel in Bakersfield, and in 1902 shot it out with the local law in Porterville after getting blind drunk in the Mint saloon in company with an equally obnoxious character named Scotty Calderwood, who owned a beer and eating establishment called Scotty's Chop House. McKinney shot Willis, the local marshal, in the mouth, and when a friend named Billy Lynn tried to intercede, Jim fired both barrels of a shotgun into his stomach. McKinney survived constant chases and committed several more murders before being blasted to death by a shotgun held by the brother of a man he had just killed. So passed one of California's deadliest and most-feared old-time gunmen.

Montana's gold rush was overshadowed to some extent by that which took California by storm, but it was nonetheless as important. Gold deposits had been found as early as 1851, and again in 1858, but it was 1862 before the first big discovery was made at Bannack. This was followed on May 26, 1863, by a strike at Alder Gulch. One William Fairweather, accompanied by six others, made the strike. Once the news reached Bannack, hundreds and then thousands moved into the area, and within weeks, Virginia City was teeming with would-be gold seekers, and the fourteen-mile-long gulch would eventually yield more than $100 million in "dust." On May 26, 1864, exactly one year after the gold strike, the Montana Territory was created. In July another strike was made at the "Last Chance Gulch" where Helena was established.

All manner of people arrived in the region: deserters from the Union or Confederate armies, speculators, gamblers, prostitutes, and a number of professional people, among them doctors, lawyers, newspapermen, and a few priests. Rarest among them were genuine miners, but regardless of profession, most were prepared to dig and hoped to prosper. Inevitably there also appeared numerous individuals whose exploits could at best be called colorful or at worse "murderous." These were professional thieves, road agents,

ABOVE: John X. Beidler, the chief hangman of the Montana vigilantes, who "jerked a number of noted bad men to Jesus" in the interests of law and order, if not necessarily in the name of justice.

and others devoted to the accumulation of wealth at someone else's expense.

The list of those associated with the lawless element is long and contains the names of individuals who are now immortalized in folklore. There was Henry Plummer, sheriff of Bannack, who was later discovered to be the leader of the road agents: George Ives, Haze Lyons, Frank Parish, Boone Helm, George "Club Foot" Lane, and Jack Gallagher, among others. Of this motley crew, perhaps Plummer and Helm were the best known. Of Plummer, it was said that he spent much time perfecting his marksmanship, and, according to Thomas Dimsdale, author of *The Vigilantes of Montana*, he could draw "his pistol and discharge the five loads in three seconds." Modern fast-draw fanatics might scoff at such a was different. He came from Illinois, had fought in the Mexican War, and had achieved a good reputation as a line superintendent for Russell, Majors, and Waddell. He was also regarded as one of the best shots on the plains, and was never loath to demonstrate his skill. Indeed, Mark Twain's description of his accuracy has both a touch of the humorous and the macabre:

> Slade was a matchless marksman with a Navy revolver. The legends say that one morning at Rocky Ridge, when he was feeling comfortable, he saw a man approaching who had offended him some days before—observe the fine memory he had for matters like that—and, "Gentlemen," said Slade, drawing, "it is a good twenty-yard shot—I'll clip the third button on his coat!" Which he did; the bystanders all admired it, and they all attended the funeral too.

Slade's weakness was drink, and when liquored up he was dangerous. Having warned him several times of his behavior, the vigilantes finally called a halt, and on March 10, 1864, they hanged him. His distraught wife rounded upon his slayers and berated them for not having the guts to shoot him rather than hang him like a dog. Indeed, some of those who had been involved were later reported to have wept openly as the box was kicked away and Slade choked to death. But right or wrong, legal or unlawful though the vigilante movement was, its role in containing violence prior to the establishment of courts and other due processes cannot be ignored, for without such drastic action, there would have been only one alternative—anarchy.

## Bleeding Kansas

If California and Montana exemplified the era of the vigilantes, then it was Kansas and Missouri that presaged the era of the guerrilla, whose penchant for the pistol was well known. On May 30, 1854, President Franklin Pierce signed the Kansas–Nebraska Act, opening up a territory some 200 miles long by 700 miles wide. Most of it was grassland inhabited by various Indian tribes and roaming herds of buffalo and other animals. The act established the boundaries of Kansas on the west of the Missouri state line to the continental divide and a part of the Rocky Mountains and

ABOVE: Captain James Williams was one of the mainstays of the Montana vigilante movement. People-power counted for an awful lot in the early days when law and order was more or less nonexistent.

comment, but Dimsdale made it very clear that it was not just a case of drawing and pulling the trigger; Plummer also took aim. Sadly for Henry, his skill with a gun could not save him from the inevitable, for allied against him and his cronies were Captain James Williams and some very determined characters, among them Neil Howie, John Fetherstun, and the inimitable John X. Beidler, who acted as "hangman" when the occasion demanded it. And among the so-called "good bad men" who flocked to the place was the notorious Joseph Alfred "Jack" Slade, who was, according to Mark Twain, "more feared" in some parts than "the Almighty." The murderous activities of Plummer and his gang eventually led to their deaths at the hands of the vigilantes with no remorse or regrets from any quarter, but in the case of Jack Slade it

## CALIFORNIA
# THE GOLD RUSH

The California gold rush of the mid-1800s was a landmark event in United States history, a social and commercial earthquake that resulted in one of the greatest human migrations in American history and the creation of the wealthiest state in the Union. On January 24, 1848, one James Marshall and a gang of laborers were completing the construction a sawmill along the American River near Coloma. Marshall spotted a small piece of gold in the earth, and soon the laborers were unearthing dozens of other samples. Once the identity of the metal was confirmed, a businessman named Sam Brannan vigorously promoted the discovery of gold, displaying a container of gold dust on the streets of San Francisco. Brannan's promotion was his highly successful attempt to sell huge amounts of mining gear—he earned $36,000 in nine weeks—but it was also the spark that sent gold fever through the United States.

Once the major American newspapers reported the discovery of gold in California, a huge exodus began as men left homes, families, and jobs for the glittering prospects of the gold rush. Many underwent traumatic journeys of thousands of miles by boat, horse, or foot. Some from the East attempted a 2,000-mile overland journey, one where lack of water led to some Californian entrepreneurs trading single glasses of water for a dollar. Around 80,000 people arrived in

California in 1849 alone, and they quickly acquired plots of land to pan for gold.

Gold was certainly to be found in the California hills. Indeed, during the gold rush years, around $2 billion worth was extracted. However, this figure did not translate into personal wealth for many. The first two years of gold prospecting were the boom years, with individuals making personal fortunes either through gold itself or through ancillary industries, such as equipment sales or through providing transportation. The humblest "forty-niner" (a name given to the gold diggers, after the major year of migration into California, 1849) could make around twenty-five dollars a day from his efforts, money that might have taken a month to earn on some Midwest farm. However, the alarming food and lodging prices, with records of single eggs being sold for around eight dollars in gold towns such as Deadwood, offset the earnings. Moreover, by 1851 the gold was becoming much harder to find, and many men turned away from their toils for the lures of gambling and drink. The gold rush settlements and gold towns became centers of criminality and violence. Mining did continue, but mainly via companies that used more advanced, and environmentally damaging, mining techniques. Eventually the landscape was well and truly scoured of its gold. However, San Francisco had been transformed into a city of enormous wealth and a huge population, and California would never be the same again.

ABOVE: Gold towns sprang up throughout California during from the early 1850s and were generally violent, lawless places.

OPPOSITE: The grim working conditions experienced by gold miners are evident in this photograph taken near Nevada City in 1852.

LEFT: Gold prospectors and their pack horses take a break near Camp Verde, Arizona. Arizona's gold rush began in earnest in 1858 after one Jake Snively discovered gold along the Gila River in the southwest of the state.

## MINERS

Discovery of gold in California at Sutter's Mill in early 1848 was the beginning of "Gold Fever." Men left their families, and soldiers and sailors deserted to head west, drawn by the all-consuming quest for easy riches. Justice, if there was any in the gold towns that sprung up overnight, was self-imposed by vigilante miners' courts. The huge Comstock Mine in Nevada brought big business into mining and the tools of the small-time entrepreneur shown here gradually became outdated.

1. Heavy iron-bound wooden stave utility barrel for general camp use.
2. Metal and glass lantern, oil-fueled, for camp and mine use.
3. Hand-forged metal pry bar, about six feet overall, from the Old Gold Reef mine.
4. Tin cash or valuables box.
5. Shallow pan, the primary tool of the gold seeker.
6. Small hammer and pick combination tool.
7. Standard pick with the wooden haft.
8. Heavy sledge hammer with wooden haft.
9. Colt Model 1849 pocket revolver, .31 caliber, a type carried West during the Gold Rush.
10. Colt holster Model Paterson revolver, .36 caliber. Note the folding trigger that extends when the revolver is cocked.
11. English percussion double-barreled shotgun, made by W. & O. Scott, 12 gauge.

12. Wooden brass-tipped ramrod for shotgun.
13. Blunt and Syms standard frame saw-handled under-hammer percussion pepperbox pistol, .31 caliber, a popular type of weapon in rough mining camps.
14. Iron-bound, wooden stave whiskey barrel, a fixture in many isolated, primitive mining camps.
15. Weight scales, brass, iron, and wood construction, a common instrument in the assayer's office.
16. Brass weight for the above scales.
17. Allen and Thurber dragoon-size percussion pepperbox, .36 caliber, another popular multishot weapon that was carried West in some quantity.
18. Mucking boots with wooden soles and leather uppers, worn by miners standing in damp areas for prolonged periods.
19. All-purpose tin cup, used for drinking or holding candles down in the mine.

20. Fancy leather-trimmed vest of the kind worn only on special occasions.
21. Silver dollars—the end result of many a miner's hard work and one of the standard mediums of exchange.

(Artifacts courtesy of Buffalo Bill Historical Center, Cody, Wyoming.)

present-day eastern Colorado. The act also provided for popular sovereignty, which meant that the people themselves would decide whether or not the territory would achieve statehood as a "free" or "slave" state.

The issue of slavery, that "peculiar institution" that pervaded southern thoughts and actions, had long been a subject of debate. Under the Missouri Compromise of 1820, states were admitted to the Union on the basis that there should be an equal number of "free" or "slave" states in the Union. In simple terms, the "Missouri Compromise" permitted slavery in that state, but she was forbidden to exclude free Negroes and mulattoes. West of the state,

RIGHT: In 1859, proslavery Missourians kidnapped Dr. John Doy. Tried in St. Joseph, he was found guilty of "slave-stealing." Jayhawker (abolitionist) friends rescued him from jail and were photographed with him in Lawrence.

however, slavery was outlawed from all U.S. territories north of the 36° 30' parallel, Missouri's southern boundary. In 1850, California was admitted to the Union as a free state, which meant that the next admission—Kansas Territory—would be slave-owning. However, since the act allowed for a free vote, conflict was inevitable.

Once the act became law, pro-slavery Missourians were poised to invade the territory and claim it for the South. In the meantime, the government had forcibly moved several Indian tribes farther south to Indian Territory (present-day Oklahoma). It was now the calm before the storm.

The early months of 1854 proved to be quiet. Some

## DERINGERS 1859–1875

Between the late 1850s and the 1870s, rimfire ammunition became available and deringer-type single- or multibarreled pistols were in great demand. In the 1870s, single- and double-barreled versions proved popular. The carrying of such deadly weapons inspired much thought. Some relied upon boot tops, sleeve cuffs, waistbands, or even inside hats. Ladies of easy virtue even carried them in a "crotch pouch."

1. A Sharps & Co. .32 caliber four-barrel pocket pistol. By depressing the button at the front of the frame, with the pistol at half-cock, the barrel could be pushed forward to load or eject the cartridges.
2. A later version of the Sharps four-barrel model with a bird's-head grip.
3. William Marston's three-shot pocket pistol.
4. Later version of the Marston pistol.
5. Remington's .41 "Double Derringer." Made in .41 center- and rimfire.
6. Late Sharps four-barrel pocket pistol with bird's-head grip.
7. Frank Wesson's two-shot pistol. Center "barrel" sometimes contained a small "dirk."
8. .22 caliber long-cased rimfire ammunition.
9. Two .32 caliber rounds.
10. Remington-Elliot .32 caliber rimfire four-barrel ring trigger deringer, sometimes called "pepperbox."
11. Remington double deringer (s.n. 99745) shown opened.

12. A Sharps four-barrel pistol with checkered walnut stock.

13. Similar pistol but with gutta-percha grips.

14. Version of the Marston three-barrel pistol.

15. Eben T. Starr's four-barrel pepperboxes were rivals to the Sharps version.

16. Remington's "Saw Handle" deringer (c.1865) was produced in rimfire calibers from .30 to .41.

17. David Williamson's .41 rimfire deringer was modeled upon Henry Deringer's original. Unique in having a percussion insert when fixed ammunition was not available.

18. Colt's first model deringer based upon National No. 1.

19. A left-hand view of a similar pistol.

20. Jacob Rupertus single-barreled pocket pistol.

21. Union single-shot deringer.

22. Rollin White pocket pistol with a unique swivel breech.

23. A J. T. Stafford single-shot .22 caliber pistol with original holster.

24. Colt's No. 3 deringer in .41 rimfire.

25. Dexter Smith patent single-shoot, .22 caliber breech-loading pistol.

26. Two .41 short rimfire cartridges.

27. Rupertus single-shot .38 caliber breech-loading pistol.

28. .32 rimfire cartridge.

29. F. Schoop patent two-shot "harmonica" .30 caliber rimfire pocket pistol.

30. Merwin & Bray .30 caliber single-shot pistol.

31. American Arms Co., Wheeler patent .32 caliber rollover pocket pistol.

32. Dickinson .32 caliber single-shot pistol. The ratchet is the extractor.

33. The Hammond I Bulldog pistol.

34. Brown Manufacturing Co. "Southerner" with a pivoting barrel.

35. Marlin Repeater I cards, "made by Miss Annie Oakley."

36. Marlin's "O.K." Model deringer.

(Artifacts courtesy of Buffalo Bill Historical Center, Cody, Wyoming.)

Missourians crossed the border to establish pro-slavery towns, among them Leavenworth, Kickapoo, and Atchison, while free-staters set up places such as Topeka, which eventually become the state capital. Word filtered back East describing the lush grass and farming land awaiting settlement. Soon the trickle of immigrants became a flood.

The territory had six governors between 1854 and 1861, none of whom lasted long in office. Andrew Reeder, appointed in October 1854, set the first territorial election, which was a fiasco, for November 29, 1854. Militant Missourians crossed the border and intimidated the electorate, forcing them to join the pro-slavery vote. The same thing happened at the next election on March 30, 1855. Patience was fast running out, and it was only a matter of time before there was violence.

It is traditional to assume that the free-state element consisted of the heroes and the proslavery Missourians the villains in the Kansas-Missouri disputes, but that is erroneous. A large number of the immigrants were God-fearing folk, anxious to settle in the territory and start a new life. Others, however, had different ideas. Politically as well as racially motivated, they sought power and prestige. Among them was the radical John Brown, whose abolitionist views were religiously motivated. On the Missouri side, a similar

**BELOW: John Brown, whose "soul goes marching on." Fanatic, madman, saint—many words can be found to describe this violent individual, but no one will ever forget John Brown of Kansas. No man starts a war alone, but Brown comes closest.**

**BELOW: General James H. Lane, the "Grim Chieftain." His "Tree State Army" played a major role in the Kansas-Missouri border wars. He committed suicide in July 1866 following a bout of depression.**

**RIGHT: This sketch of a Border Ruffian would also aptly describe the feared and often loathed Civil War guerrilla—feather in cap, plain or fancy shirt, knee-boots complete with Bowie knife, and armed with two pistols.**

situation existed, for not every Missourian was a slave-owner. Many of them were more concerned with survival than slavery, and did not necessarily share the view of their vociferous neighbors that the Kansans were a bunch of "Abolitionist nigger-stealers."

In Washington, the government was seriously concerned at the developments in Kansas. Troops were dispatched in an effort to cool tempers by keeping the warring factions apart. Then in June 1855 the free-staters held a convention at Lawrence, repudiating bogus election results. Their aim was the abolition of slavery. Prominent among them, however, was James H. Lane, a former congressman from Indiana who had fought in the Mexican War, and who had come to Kansas in the belief that he could organize a Democratic party. When this was rejected, he changed sides and joined the free staters, becoming one of their best-known leaders. It was James Lane's "Free-State Army" that pitted itself against the Missouri "Border Ruffians."

On May 21, 1856, the Border Ruffians attacked Lawrence. John Brown swore to avenge the attack and set off for Pottawatomie Creek, where he knew a number of proslavery Missourians were camped. On the 24th, aided by four of his sons, he went to the homes of five men, dragged them out, and murdered them in front of their families. The murders outraged the territory, and Brown was forced to flee. In May 1858, as a reprisal for the Pottawatomie raid, Missouri Border Ruffians murdered five free-state men on the Marais des Cygnes.

Following the Brown outrage in 1856, additional troops were rushed to the area. Missourians, led by David R. Atchison, caught up with Brown and fought him, but he escaped. Federal troops then engaged the Missourians. Lane, anxious to join the fight, was prevented from doing so by troops from Fort Leavenworth.

Daniel Woodson succeeded Governor Reeder as acting governor on August 16, 1855. Woodson, a pro-slavery man,

organized companies of militia in the belief that the territory was in open rebellion. Wilson Shannon replaced him on September 7, but the pair alternated as governor until September 9, 1856, when Governor John W. Geary was sworn in. Geary promptly disbanded the militia but was unable to prevent Colonel James A. Harvey's company from fighting a minor engagement with the proslavery men at Hickory Point. Harvey had deserted his wife and family in Chicago to seek adventure in Kansas. Following the Hickory

**LEFT:** Captain John Jarrett, a former guerrilla and later member of Jesse James's gang. He was present when the James-Younger gang robbed the Russellville, Kentucky, bank on March 21, 1868.

**OPPOSITE:** Col. Charles R. Jennison, leader of the 7th Kansas Cavalry—"Jennison's Jayhawkers"— from a rare Civil War portrait. Many of the men who rode with him later became members of the "Red Legs."

Point fight, a number of them were arrested by federal troops and lodged in jail at Lecompton. Backed by Federal troops, Geary persuaded Atchison and his men to leave the territory.

The influx of people into the territory and the danger of attack proved to be a bonus for arms makers and dealers in weapons. The Colt Navy, Dragoon, and Pocket models were much in favor, but there was also a demand for rifles and carbines, the most popular arm being the Sharps. Christian Sharps, a native of New England, had worked at the government arsenal at Harpers Ferry and later set up on his own. His breech-loading pistols, rifles, and carbines proved very popular, but it was the carbine that attracted most attention. In 1853, the British government purchased 6,000 of them. But the most famous or notorious model was the so-called "Beecher's Bible" version. The Connecticut Kansas Colony, organized by a group of abolitionists in New England, among them the Reverend Henry Ward Beecher, shipped in a number of these weapons to the colony in boxes marked "Bibles." The colonists later built a church that they named the "Beecher Bible and Rifle Church," which still stands. John Brown is also reported to have purchased 200 Sharps carbines that were shipped to him in Kansas. Many of them were recovered following Brown's abortive raid on the Harpers Ferry arsenal, for which he was tried and hanged on December 2, 1859.

The individuals who formed part of the free-state forces (or "Jayhawkers," as some called them) were much on par with their Missouri counterparts. The Pottawatomie and Marais des Cygnes massacres, horrible though they were, were minor events when compared to the antics of the guerrillas in Missouri, Arkansas, and parts of Kansas in the Civil War.

## The Guerrilla Wars

History records that the American Civil War was fought for the most part in the eastern states, where victories, defeats, and appalling casualties captured the interest of the world. Yet there was another war going on at the same time where murder and mayhem were constant companions. This took place in southwest Missouri, eastern Kansas, and much of Arkansas. It was a guerrilla war where no quarter was given,

none asked, and those that survived it carried the scars for life.

When the Civil War erupted following the firing on Fort Sumter, South Carolina, there was a lull in the Midwestern states while in the East and South men rushed to join the Union or Confederate cause. Kansas, which had been admitted to the Union in January 1861, was relatively quiet, but in Missouri, where the Union army had immediately gained control of St. Louis, the railroads, and other places where their military influence was felt, many of the inhabitants were pro-Southern. Most people considered the state to be a part of the Confederacy, and the suggestion that she had been "invaded" encouraged resistance among much of the population. Several attempts had been made by the Confederacy to take over the state, but apart from a number of noted victories—Wilson's Creek in August 1861 and the

occupation of Springfield—they had not been too successful. The Union regained Springfield, and its forces continued to occupy important strategic places right through the war. Among the population were many thousands of young pro-Southern men whose families occupied homesteads behind Union lines, where they lived at peace with Unionists. Some of them slipped south and joined the Confederate army. Others, however, remained behind. This left a confusion of loyalties. Many of the Missourians, caught between both sides, tried to remain loyal to the Union, resentful though they were of federal intrusion. Some others thought that they could serve the South better by direct action, and many a former Border Ruffian simply changed tack and henceforth acquired a new name—guerrilla.

By the fall of 1861 there were a number of guerrillas operating in Missouri, foremost among them the infamous William Clarke Quantrill. His acts of terrorism in the name of the Confederacy aroused bitter hatred, even among some Southerners who felt that the wholesale destruction of persons and property was unjustified. And when, in August 1863, his band attacked Lawrence, Kansas, and murdered 150 civilian men and boys, the Union was determined that he should be destroyed.

The earliest attempts to stop Quantrill were made in late 1861 or early 1862 with the formation of the equally infamous Kansas "Red Legs" (so-called because of the red-dyed sheepskin toppings to their boots), formed from men of Colonel C. R. Jennison's 7th Kansas Regiment known as "Jennison's Jayhawkers." The Red Legs survived until 1863, by which time they had degenerated into a band of thieves and murderers. They were disbanded, and orders were given that anyone seen wearing the familiar red boot topping would be shot on sight.

William "Bloody Bill" Anderson, Quantrill's able lieutenant and eventual successor, vied with his chief to be even more vicious and on several occasions proved it. He was eventually killed by Union troops (ironically, so was Quantrill himself, a month after the war ended). Others, however, many of them now lost to history, fought in the woods and forests of Missouri and Arkansas. In scenes reminiscent of revolutionary France in the 1790s, no one was sure whether his neighbor

RIGHT: Noted guerrilla George Maddox, dressed in the approved fashion, also sports a pair of Remington's 1863 New Model Army pistols. The chambers of the left-hand pistol are clearly seen to be loaded and ready for action. Despite his fancy duds, Maddox was a cold-blooded killer. Some historians have erroneously confused him with one Dick Maddox, who also followed the "black flag" of Quantrill.

ABOVE OPPOSITE: The aptly named "Bloody Bill" Anderson was with Quantrill at the Lawrence, Kansas, massacre in 1863. Note the bullet holes in his forehead and cheek.

OPPOSITE: John Nichols, seen in jail just before he was hanged as a "bushwacker" in September 1863. He and his gang were greatly feared. Note the ball and chain and the guard's Navy pistol barrel.

# THE TEXAS
# RANGERS

The Texas Rangers—still in existence today as the United States' oldest law enforcement agency—were much feared by the gunfighting criminals of the nineteenth century. They were formed in the early 1820s, in then Spanish province, what is today Texas. At this time, Texas was populated by several hundred colonists attempting to scratch out a hard living from the land, while simultaneously trying to survive banditry, horse and cattle rustling, and the hostilities of Native American tribes. In 1823 Stephen F. Austin, one of the men who had enabled the settlement of families in the Spanish province, suggested that in the absence of army protection he form and lead a small group of ten

armed volunteers to act as a de facto law enforcement agency. He applied the name "Rangers" to them, based on the fact that they were required to "range" across the country.

The Rangers continued on an informal basis until November 24, 1835, when, with the state on the eve of independence, they were formed into a dedicated force known as the Texas Rangers. This organization, placed under

**ABOVE: Two units of the Texas Rangers pose for group photographs. The photograph above shows Company D pictured at Realitas, Texas, in 1887. Second from the left on the back row is the infamous gunfighter Bass Outlaw.**

the overall jurisdiction of the army, consisted of fifty-six men and ten officers with a major as its commander. Their service during the 1830s and 1840s was frequently inglorious, often being used in guard and menial duties, although in actions against both the Mexicans and the Indians they were tough and resolute fighters. The numbers of Rangers were expanded by Congressional policy in 1838, and the Rangers rose to distinction during the Mexican War of 1846, acting as hardened reconnaissance scouts to General Zachary Taylor's army as it advanced to the Rio Grande. The Rangers fought with distinction in battles such as Palo Alto and Resaca de la Palma, and were feared hunters of Mexican guerrillas. Names of Ranger leaders such as Jack Hays and Samuel Walker became revered throughout the states.

Following the end of the Mexican War in 1848, the Rangers' profile dipped low, as the U.S. government now had formal responsibility for protecting the Texan frontier. In 1861, the Rangers entered the Civil War fighting for the Confederacy, and consequently they were disbanded following the Union victory in 1865. The state police and U.S. Army took over policing duties in the West during Reconstruction, the former being a generally incompetent and corrupt agency of around two hundred men that was disbanded in 1873. Texas, faced with appalling lawlessness and banditry in the aftermath of the war, needed a strong legal arm, and Governor Richard Coke reinstated the Rangers. They were divided into two units—the Frontier Battalion and the Special Forces—and together totaled around sixty men. The Rangers took on all manner of adversaries, from Indian tribes and train robbers to Mexican bandits, and law-breaking gunfighters. They had superb scouting skills and would track their adversaries for days across all terrains. They were also not afraid to use their guns to impose justice.

The Rangers went through a number of further mutations during the nineteenth century, losing the Special Forces and Frontier Battalion distinctions (the American frontier was effectively consolidated by the beginning of the twentieth century, removing the need for the Frontier Battalion) and generally contracting in numbers. Only twenty-four Texas Rangers remained in 1901, but following World War I there was a renewed growth in their activities. The Rangers were

**ABOVE:** James B. Gillett joined the Texas Rangers at the age of nineteen in 1875 and served with distinction until 1881. In 1876 he joined Major General John B. Jones's Company A, Frontier Battalion, and was selected to be one of an elite unit that set out to clean up the Dublin gang in Kimble and Menard Counties. Gillett killed Dick Dublin after a running pursuit. Gillett was one of the men involved in the killing of the outlaw Sam Bass in 1878. Why does he look like he works in a bank? Well, he became a bank director and wrote his autobiography in 1925, when this photo was taken.

made part of the Texas Department of Public Safety in 1935 and today are a professional and flexible element of Texan law enforcement. It remains a small group (118 members in 2000) but tackles crimes ranging from bank fraud to murder. In 2002 alone, the Rangers made 1,805 felony arrests.

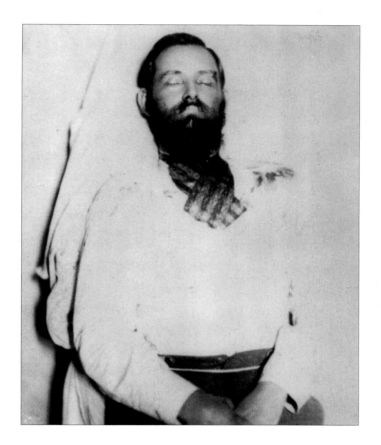

**LEFT AND ABOVE: Two striking photographs of the infamous Jesse James, obviously taken at very different points in his career. James began his gunfighting life as one of William Quantrill's guerrillas, thereafter graduating to bank and train robbery. He was finally killed on April 3, 1882, and was photographed (above) to show the West he was finally gone.**

might betray him, or if the late-night visitor was a friend or foe. Worse still, the arrival of a military detail in the uniform expected sometimes turned out to be the enemy in disguise, who lost no time in looting and killing. Many a family was woken in the night, their menfolk dragged away and their bodies found hanging or lying shot dead in the woods.

The sort of men who perpetrated these crimes claimed that they did it for "the cause." Even in old age, many of them skated around the atrocities and instead remembered only the excitement and the thrill of battle. Invariably they would bring out their prized Navy revolver, which had been the principal weapon of the guerrilla on either side. Quantrill's men were reputed to have carried as many as eight such pistols spread around their belts or in saddlebags. Other

weapons were used, of course, and the Colt New Model Army of 1860, a .44 caliber weapon intended for cavalry use, proved very popular. It had been designed to replace the existing 1848 model Dragoon and weighed just a few ounces more than the Navy model (upon which it was based). At the same time, Colt introduced their New Model Navy, which resembled the Army model in that it had a round barrel and instead of the old hinged lever ramrod of the original Navy pistol; it was now operated by a ratching system, and in appearance was more streamlined than its predecessors. But any Colt revolver was at a premium in the South, as indeed were other northern-made arms, particularly the Remington.

Eliphalet Remington Jr. produced his first gun at Ilion Forge, New York, in 1816, and by the late 1850s the family firm had grown enormously. They entered the revolver market in 1858 with a pistol based upon a design by Fordyce Beals who assisted with other models. Then in 1863 the company produced the famous New Model Army pistol, a solid-frame .44 caliber percussion revolver that remained in production until 1875. Despite the lapse during the latter part of the war, when a number of the pistols blew up, the majority of them were welcomed and much appreciated by soldiers and civilians alike.

The total disregard for human life displayed by the guerrillas during the war culminated in a period of retribution once hostilities ended, and a man was liable to keep quiet about his war activities. Only in later years, when nostalgia figured in most reminiscences, did the old-timers admit to their past, by which time reunions of surviving ex-guerrillas had become an annual event, some such gatherings occurring until the 1920s. And among those survivors were some of the men who continued their association with the gun by becoming outlaws.

## The Owlhoot Trail

The legend of the outlaw or social misfit has long had mass appeal, especially if it can be claimed that the individual was wronged and only turned to outlawry in order to fight injustice by righting the wrongs of others. This theme has permeated folklore for centuries, and is a familiar part of the

Robin Hood myth. Similarly Jesse James, "America's Robin Hood" would seem to be a natural successor. There the similarity ends, for the real Jesse James bore little resemblance to his legend. He was a product of an era that spawned many like him: survivors of the Civil War who had experienced the power of the pistol—when fighting on either side—men who found it difficult to adjust once the war ended. In Jesse's case, it has been claimed by his descendants that because of his record he was refused a pardon. Instead, he was shot and wounded when he tried to surrender, and this changed his whole life. His best biographer, William A. Settle, discovered that there is no record of Jesse ever attempting to surrender, and the story of his wound is not corroborated, although he does admit that Jesse may have been wounded about this time—perhaps from a late-war engagement. Whatever the truth, the James brothers lived a rootless existence, moving from place to place. Jesse and Frank kept low for some time, but on February 13, 1866, they robbed the Clay County Savings Bank and became wanted men.

Jesse Woodson James was born on September 5, 1847, in Clay County, Missouri, the youngest son of Robert James, a Baptist minister, and Zerelda, a strong-willed lady who in later years proved to be a formidable opponent of those whom she thought had persecuted her sons. Frank James, Jesse's elder brother, was born on January 10, 1843, and although four years older than his brother, in later life Frank was dominated by Jesse.

Robert James succumbed to gold fever in 1850 and left for California, where he contracted a proper fever and died. The widow James then remarried, but this was not a success, and at her third attempt she married a quiet but prosperous man named Reuben Samuel. By the time the Civil War broke out in 1861, the family boasted several Negro slaves and were

**BELOW: The James Farm, Missouri, childhood home to Franklin and Jesse James. Jesse and Frank's father died when the boys were young, and their mother subsequently twice remarried, although the middle marriage only lasted a few months.**

ardent in their support for the Confederacy. Frank is reported to have joined Quantrill, and later claimed to have been on the Lawrence raid. Most historians state that the James or Samuel family suffered at the hands of Union sympathizers,

**RIGHT: Thomas Coleman "Cole" Younger, one of the gang's deadliest members. He rode with Quantrill and was present at the Lawrence, Kansas, massacre. He, too, rode with the James gang.**

**BELOW: James Younger, the least experienced of the gang; following his imprisonment after the Northfield raid, he was later paroled but committed suicide in St. Paul, Minnesota, 1902.**

**BELOW RIGHT: Robert "Bob" Younger was the baby in the family, and followed his brothers when they joined Jesse James. Captured at Northfield after the abortive raid, he died of consumption in prison in 1889.**

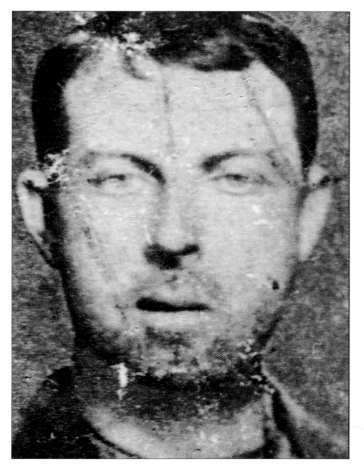

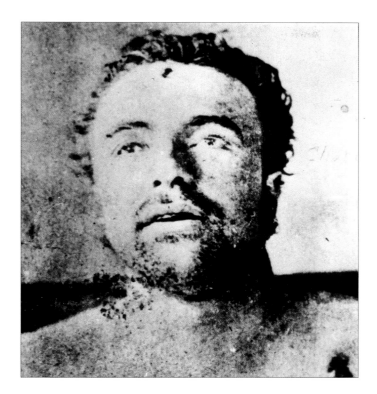

**ABOVE:** Clelland "Clell" Miller was a member of the James gang and said to have worshipped both Jesse and Frank. Miller was shot dead in the street during the Northfield Bank raid in September 1876.

**ABOVE:** James Copeland was said to have terrorized the entire southern states during the 1840s and the early 1850s. His hanging was well attended, when, according to court records, "the drop fell and a brief struggle ended his blood stained career."

**LEFT:** The infamous Richard "Dick" Liddell, who was involved in the plot to kill Jesse James. As a result, he earned the undying hatred of Jesse's family. He is armed in this photograph with a Whitney Navy pistol.

and on one occasion Reuben was dragged to a tree, a noose tied around his neck and he was lifted off his feet in an effort to persuade him to impart information that he did not have. Sixteen-year-old Jesse witnessed this and swore revenge against the Yankees. By 1864 he was reported to have joined Quantrill and for a time rode with "Bloody Bill" Anderson. Some have suggested that it was his relationship with Anderson that eventually prevented his pardon. Be that as it may, a taste of killing and robbing had its effect, and the robbing of the Clay County bank was only the start of a career of robbery and murder that was to last almost fifteen years, by which time his reputation as a latter-day Robin Hood was assured.

Jesse James was an enigma. He married and had a family yet continued his career of outlawry. Claims that his latter exploits were directed at the "robber barons" who ran the railroads and cheated people out of their property by claiming that they had "right of way" to build tracks across their land were widely believed by those who were anxious to discredit the corporations behind the railroads. Similarly, "crooked" banking houses were also targeted. It was claimed by some that it was the railroad and banking concerns that hired the Pinkerton Detective Agency to hunt down the James gang. In this latter respect, the activities of the Pinkertons do not inspire confidence. William Pinkerton's Civil War exploits have come into some criticism, but it was the attack on Jesse's mother's home on January 26, 1875, that calls their role into question.

According to most sources, the Pinkertons set fire to the family home in an effort to drive them out. A fireball of burning cotton was discovered in the kitchen, and when it

# THE WESTERN
# MOVIE

The popular understanding of life in the Wild West has generally been derived from Western genre movies. The dime novels (see pages 64–65) established Western narratives as a highly popular genre, so with the emergence of film technology at the very end of the nineteenth century, it was natural for filmmakers to gravitate toward the cowboy and gunfighter as core characters. In 1898, the Edison Company, beginning the great age of the silent Western, treated theater houses in the eastern United States to the short feature *Cripple Creek Barroom*. *Cripple Creek Barroom* was an understandably crude production, but Edwin S. Porter's ten-minute *The Great Train Robbery* of 1903 had more of the classic ingredients of Western narratives and cleaner editorial control.

By the second decade of the twentieth century, the Western movie industry was flourishing, mainly located in California, a location providing ready access to ideal western landscapes. D.W. Griffith was a seminal figure in the silent Westerns, shooting panoramic landscapes and creating vivid characters, including "Bronco Billy," played by G.M. Anderson, one of the movie industry's first Western superstars. Other great names of this period include actor William S. Hart and director John Ford; Hart used his own life experience to create Westerns with a degree of realism. Some of Hart's best-known films are *Hell's Hinges* (1916) and *Tumbleweeds* (1925), and his films have been critically characterized as "serious" Westerns. The serious Western was set against the gross fictionalization of the Wild West in the multitude of "B" movies (meaning budget) that appeared on American screens.

Another exponent of the serious Western was the great John Ford. Ford's career in Westerns, first as an actor (he began his Hollywood career in 1915, acting in D.W. Griffith films), then as a director, spanned five decades, successfully making the transition from the age of silent movies to the age of "talkies" (the first film with a sound track was released in 1927). Ford's West was one of panoramic landscapes, great heroes, and equally great villains. His film *The Iron Horse* (1924) was an acclaimed representation of the building of the transcontinental railway, and in 1939 he released *Stagecoach* featuring a rising star named John Wayne. Ford would be a dominant force in Western movies well into the postwar years, with Wayne starring in many of the best. (Wayne had made his entrance into the Western genre in Raoul Walsh's poor *The Big Trail* in 1930, a film that nearly killed Wayne's career and reduced studio interest in Westerns throughout much of the 1930s.) Great Ford titles include *The Searchers* (1956), *My Darling Clementine* (1946—featuring Henry Fonda and Victor Mature), *Fort Apache* (1948), *Wagonmaster* (1950), and one of the greatest Westerns of all time, *Who Shot Liberty Valance* (1962). Apart from Ford, other significant Westerns of the pre–World War II period included George B. Seitz's *The Vanishing American* (1927), *The Virginian* (1929) by Victor Fleming and starring Gary Cooper, and *Billy the Kid* (1930) by King Vidor.

The love affair with Western movies continued following the end of World War II, although the tone and content of many of them shifted. While there was a continuance of the light-hearted "singing cowboys" Westerns, a genre pioneered by actors such as Roy Rogers and Gene Autry, other Westerns became more psychologically complex and dark. Turbulent characters, sexual tension, harder violence, and ethical gray areas characterized the "adult Western." Landmark films of this period include Fred Zinneman's *High Noon* (1952), George Steven's *Shane* (1953), and Henry King's *The Gunfighter* (1950). The latter film, starring Gregory Peck as a weary gunfighter trapped by his past, bravely attempted to strip the gunfighter character of his glamour.

The 1960s saw the advent of the "Spaghetti Western," low-budget Western productions produced abroad in countries such as Spain and Italy. The greatest director of this genre was undoubtedly Sergio Leone, who brought Clint Eastwood to the movie screen with *A Fistful of Dollars* (1964) and *The Good, the Bad and the Ugly* (1966). The Spaghetti Western contained lead characters living by the gun in a world with no room for the weak, and the genre steadily spun out morally ambivalent Westerns such as *High Plains Drifter* (1974), also starring Eastwood.

Which are more realistic, the morality tales of the 1950s or the predatory, amoral universe of Leone? Neither. The great *Shane* includes moments of transcendental, messianic spirituality as well as an ugly, contemptuous murder in a muddy street. As Alan Ladd says: "A gun is a tool . . . no better or no worse than any other tool, an axe, a shovel or anything. A gun is as good or as bad as the man using it."

The genre flagged in popularity during the 1970s and 1980s but revived in the 1990s with Kevin Costner's *Dances with Wolves* (1990) and Clint Eastwood's *Unforgiven* (1992), both of which won Academy Awards. While the genre is unlikely to revisit the popularity of the 1950s, Westerns will still make periodic strong showings at the box office.

**LEFT: Emmett Dalton photographed prior to the Coffeyville raid. The lady is believed to be Eugenia Moore, his brother Bob's sweetheart. It has been claimed by some that Eugenia rode with the gang to Coffeyville.**

was pushed into the fireplace, it exploded, killing Jesse and Frank's nine-year-old half-brother and so seriously mangling his mother's hand that she had to have it amputated. The local press was incensed, and the Pinkertons were widely condemned for the attack and were described as "fiendish." Claims that the device was only a "smoke bomb" were dismissed with contempt. Only very recently has it been discovered, following some research at the National Archives in Washington, that the ordinance department authorized the issue of a bomb containing what has been described as "Greek fire" to the agency, thereby confirming that there was an attempt to destroy the whole family.

Sympathy for Jesse, however, would be misplaced, for he cared little for those who might get in his way. He never trusted anybody, was ever watchful and suspicious of strangers. Some recalled that his eyes were constantly on the move, and he blinked all the time. Others credited this to a complaint known as "granulated eyelids," but it was far more likely that he suffered from trachoma, which was common at the time, that could cause pain and discomfort. It did not necessarily endanger the sight, but did require treatment.

By the early 1870s, the James brothers and the Youngers (James, John, Robert, and Coleman) had teamed up and were including train robbery in their itineraries. No one knew for sure where they would strike next. In September 1872, Frank and Jesse were reported to have held up the cashier's office at the state fair and escaped with the takings. Later, when a young reporter gave them a glowing write-up in a Kansas City paper, describing them as "heroes," he received a "visit" and a present of a gold watch. He refused this, thinking it was stolen. "Perhaps you can name some man around here you want killed?" He politely declined.

The final showdown came on September 7, 1876. Eight members of the James-Younger gang tried to rob the Northfield, Minnesota, First National Bank. The staff resisted, and during a bloody battle in which local people joined in, several of the gang and some citizens were killed. Missourians might feel supportive when the James gang robbed banks or hit at the railroads, but in Minnesota there was no such support, and the killing of innocent people only strengthened their resistance. Jesse and Frank escaped, but a seriously

wounded Bob Younger was captured. Cole and Jim, who were both wounded, refused to leave their brother, and they too were captured. Bob died later in prison, but Cole and Jim were paroled in 1901. Cole later teamed up with Frank James in an unsuccessful "Wild West" show.

Jesse James was murdered by one of his own gang, Robert Ford, on April 3, 1882, in St. Joseph, Missouri, where he was living under the alias of "Howard." Ford shot him in the back as he stood on a chair to adjust a picture. Ford, it was believed, had connived with the state governor, Thomas T. Crittendon, to murder Jesse and had been promised the $10,000 reward. Crittendon was later to deny any knowledge of such a plot but admitted that he was aware that Bob Ford was with Jesse when he was killed; the governor later became closely associated with the James family. As for the reward, it was divided up among several "deserving parties." The governor received one quarter of it—he had been instrumental in raising the money from the railroad companies—and one eighth went to Richard "Dick" Liddell, a notorious member of Jesse's gang who sought to redeem himself at their expense and who suffered public humiliation when Mrs. Samuel called him a "traitor." Other officials received their cut of the reward, which left one-eighth for Bob and Charlie Ford. So the man who killed Jesse James received only a little more than $600 and with it a reputation as a back-shooting coward. Ed Kelly in turn shot Ford dead in 1892.

Frank James, following several court appearances and aborted trials, escaped jail and survived until 1915, dying in bed at the old James farm.

## Mississippi Misfits

Apart from a cursory glance at the outlaws of California or the roughs and toughs who proliferated along the banks of the Mississippi and Missouri rivers, not much attention has been paid to Southern outlaws. One of the most notorious of these was James Copeland, who terrorized parts of southern Mississippi during the 1830s and the 1840s. So infamous was Copeland that he became a household name from Mobile Bay to Lake Pontchatarain as a man of violence, a robber, and a killer who created trouble wherever he went.

Like many of his kind, Copeland was born to respectable folk, his father a veteran of the War of 1812. He was born in the Pascagoula River Valley near the Mississippi Gulf Coast, about ten miles from the Alabama border. John Guice, who rediscovered the *Life and Confession of the Noted Outlaw James Copeland* by Dr. J. R. S. Pitts, published originally in 1858, in his introduction to the 1980 facsimile edition wrote that Copeland began his life of crime at the tender age of twelve. Copeland claimed that his mother upheld his "rascality" when he was accused of stealing pigs from a neighbor. She and a man named Gale H. Wages, a notorious character from Mobile, convinced the boy that if the local courthouse were burned down, evidence against him would no longer exist!

From then on, Copeland, aided by Wages, turned to crime. Arson continued to be a favored means of acquiring wealth, together with grand larceny. So began a career that took Copeland from the ranks of a petty criminal to serious crime. These were the days before Colt's revolvers were readily available, and great reliance was placed upon single-shot pistols, shotguns, and knives. But lack of firepower did not impair Copeland's rise to infamy. In 1841, accompanied by Wages and some other companions, he took a trip to Texas. From there the gang moved to Ohio, Louisiana, and back to Mississippi, following a lucrative tour. During his nefarious career, Copeland attempted just about every crime in the book, including counterfeiting, rustling, and the illegal sale of Negro slaves. But the net was closing. In the winter and spring of 1848, a man named James A. Harvey, who was himself murdered by Copeland, shot Wages and another gang

**ABOVE: A sequence of photographs gives a panoramic view of the Coffeyville streets. The building in the center of the middle photograph is the Condon Bank. The wide streets must have provided good fields of fire to outlaws and lawmen alike.**

member. In 1849 Copeland was arrested and charged with larceny and sentenced to four years in the Alabama penitentiary. On his release in 1853, he was promptly rearrested by the Mississippi authorities and charged with grand larceny. Following two years in the state prison, he was handed over to the sheriff of Perry County, who placed him in jail to await trial for the Harvey murder. Two years later, in 1857, he was put on trial, found guilty, and sentenced to hang. On October 30, the morning of his execution, a large crowd gathered, some out of morbid curiosity, and others concerned at the news that he had dictated his memoirs to

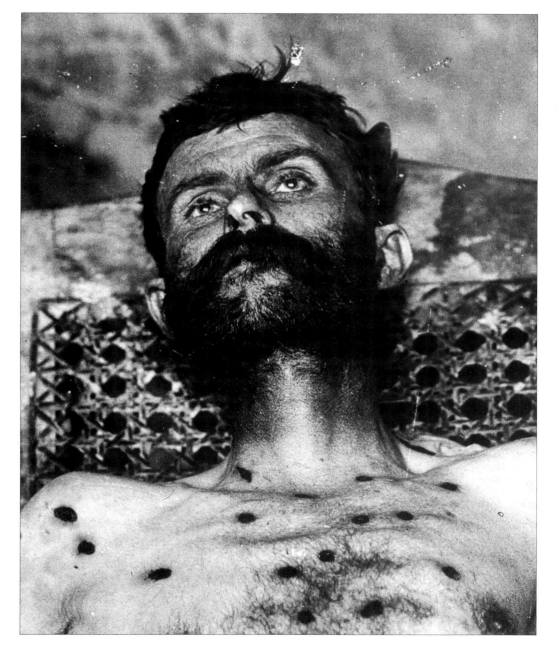

LEFT: William M. "Bill" Doolin lies dead on a mortuary slab riddled with bullets. He was the leader of a gang of outlaws known as the "Oklahombres." He was killed by a posse in Lawson, Oklahoma, in 1896.

OPPOSITE: The Condon Bank at Coffeyville, photographed at the time of the raid. It has changed little in one hundred years (today it is known as the Perkins Building), and neither have other landmarks made famous by the Daltons' bloody visit.

Pitts and that he had threatened to name accomplices. The effect was such, noted Dr. John Guice in the introduction to Pitts' *Life and Confessions of the Noted Outlaw James Copeland*, (1859) that for "Mississippians who trace their roots to the former haunts of the Copeland clan, the mention of the *Confession* draws an emotional response to this day."

## The Daltons

Copeland was typical of the breed that harbored criminal instincts from childhood, and his like could be met almost anywhere. The James brothers, on the other hand, came from a stable background but blamed the Civil War for their eventual outlawry. Another famous outlaw family, however, had no such excuse, for they started out law-abiding, and some of them actually served the law. Then, for various

reasons, things went wrong and they, too, rode the Owlhoot Trail. These were the Dalton brothers, whose exploits have long intrigued historians, novelists, and filmmakers alike.

The Daltons were a very large family: fifteen children (ten boys and five girls, although two of the children died when young) born to Lewis and Adeline Dalton. Most of the children were born when the family lived in Cass County, Missouri, where Lewis was a saloon owner. Adeline was the true backbone of the family. While she devoted herself to caring for the children, Lewis attempted to get through life doing as little as possible, apart from heavy drinking and indulging his love of gambling on the horses. Adeline herself was small in stature but tough in personality. She was related to the Youngers, but unlike the infamous brothers, she had a highly moralistic personality fed by fundamentalist Chris-

**LEFT: Roy "Arkansas Tom" Daugherty, a well-known gunfighter from Missouri who teamed up at one time with the Doolin gang. His attire makes him look more like a successful banker than an outlaw.**

**RIGHT: Emmett Dalton, survivor of Coffeyville, in a Hollywood role.**

tianity. Although she attempted to impart her values on her children, four of them would turn to criminal careers: William (Bill), Robert (Bob), Emmett, and Grattan (Grat).

In 1882, the family moved to the edge of Indian Territory and settled on a farm close to Coffeyville, Kansas. The eldest son, Frank, served as a deputy U.S. marshal attached to the formidable Judge Isaac Parker's court in Fort Smith, Arkansas, that for judicial purposes included Indian Territory as a part of its district.

Indian Territory (Oklahoma) at that time was considered one of the most dangerous places within the United States.

More law officers were killed there than anywhere else, yet despite the hazards there was no shortage of would-be deputy marshals. Frank Dalton, eldest of the Dalton boys, was highly regarded as a deputy U.S. marshal and revered by his younger brothers. Then came tragedy. On November 27, 1887, while attempting to serve a warrant on one Dave Smith for horse stealing and the illegal sale of whiskey in Indian Territory, he was killed in the ensuing gun battle. Deputy U.S. Marshal James R. Cole, who accompanied Frank, was wounded six times but not seriously. Frank had been shot in the chest by Smith (who had immediately been

shot and killed by Cole) and was then approached by William Towerly. Looking up at him, and the Winchester pointing at him, Frank begged him not to shoot again: "Please don't fire; I'm preparing to die." Towerly ignored him, and placing the muzzle of his rifle into Frank's mouth, he fired. A second round in his head finally killed him. A $1,000 reward was issued for Towerly for Frank's murder, and Towerly's freedom was short-lived. With every available deputy on his trail, he was a marked man.

Deputy marshals Moody and Stokley finally caught up with him at Atoka. Towerly killed Stokley, but Moody in turn killed Towerly. Just before he died, he admitted shooting Frank as he lay wounded. Moody, however, did not live to enjoy the reward; he was killed soon afterward by Billy Bruner, an Indian.

Writing in 1918, Emmett Dalton recalled that Frank's death appalled his family, and when an invitation came from the U.S. marshal for the Indian Territory for Grat to become a deputy, he leapt at the chance. Soon Bob joined him. The Dalton brothers were at first very successful and respected in their roles as deputy marshals, but, according to Emmett, when the brothers discovered that they were being short-changed by the administration (alleging that fees owed were not paid or were deferred through lack of funds), the brothers decided that they had had enough. "Grafting as we of today

**BELOW: Henry Newton Brown, flanked by William Smith and John Wesley (the tall form of Ben Wheeler is to their left), is captured on film hours before he and his gang were done to death by furious townsfolk.**

**ABOVE: A Western stock yard. Cattle, alongside mining and sheep, became a principal industry of western America. Most gunfighters at some point during their lives worked on a farm or with livestock.**

know the term was a mild, soothing description of what occurred," wrote Emmett. "The government was fleeced by the men in authority, and the men in the ranks were fleeced as well." Both Bob and Grat slipped into criminality, their official status (Bob even reached the rank of police chief) acting as a wholesome cover. People journeying through the Dalton's territories were often made to pay on-the-spot fines simply to allow their passage, and the Daltons were also implicated in the murder of a man who was dating their cousin Minnie (the Dalton's claimed that the killing occurred when the man was resisting arrest). The citizens of Indian Territory were further outraged when the Daltons shot down an Indian boy after he was accused of stealing by a local storekeeper. Later, rumors that Emmett and Grat had been mixed up in cattle rustling on the side reached the ears of the court, and they, too, were fired. Whatever the cause, the Daltons were beyond the law and so began a brief but hectic career of outlawry.

The Dalton brothers drifted in various directions to conduct their criminal activities and to evade the long arm of the law. They first popped up in Santa Rita, New Mexico. There they robbed a casino of its takings, apparently in disgust at the fixing of the gambling tables, during which raid Emmett was shot in the arm. With their notoriety increasing, the Daltons separated out. Emmett went back to Oklahoma to hide out, while Bob and Grat went south to California to join their brothers Littleton and Bill. The Californian authorities, however, had soon issued warrants for the arrest of the Daltons following an armed robbery of a Southern Pacific train on February 6, 1891, at the Alila village depot. During this raid, conducted by Bob and Grat

THE **JESSE JAMES STORIES**

ORIGINAL NARRATIVES OF THE JAMES BOYS

THE ORIGINAL PORTRAIT

Issued Weekly. By Subscription $2.50 per year. Entered as Second Class Matter at New York Post Office by STREET & SMITH, 238 William St., N.Y.

No. 1.                    Price, Ten Cents.

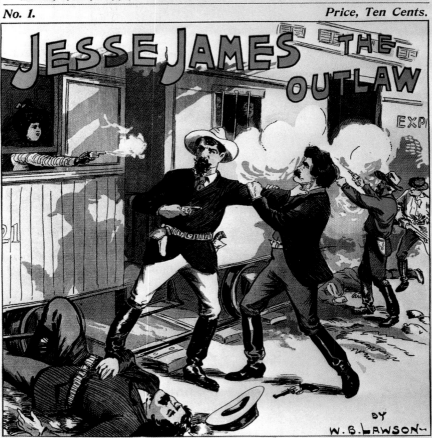

JESSE JAMES THE OUTLAW

BY W. B. LAWSON

# DIME
# NOVELS

The mythologization of the Wild West began well before the advent of the Hollywood movie Westerns of the twentieth century. In the 1860s, a new publishing phenomenon was created—the dime novel. Dime novels were a similar type of literature to the "Penny Dreadfuls" of Victorian Britain. They were serialized works of adventure fiction aimed at a mass-market readership that craved stories of violent daring deeds, colorful cowboy personalities, heroes, villains (the latter often being Indians), and romance.

Selling for only ten cents, the dime novels achieved an unprecedented popularity. The first publisher of the new literature was Erastus Beadle, who launched his first dime novel in June 1859, a 128-page work entitled *Malaeshka, the*

**ABOVE: A classic dime novel cover for *Jesse James the Outlaw*. The James narratives were issued weekly and cost the reader $2.50 for an annual subscription (the individual price was ten cents). Issue no. 1 was released in 1901.**

*Indian Wife of the White Hunter* by Anne Stevens. The story is essentially revealed in the title, and in its first year in print, it sold 300,000 copies. Beadle's titles sold over five million units by 1865.

Dime novels were sensationalist in nature, and they blurred fact and fiction without compunction to tell the most exciting story possible. Although dime novel genres ranged from romantic tales for women to stories of enterprise and self-improvement, the most popular genre was the Western. The Western dime novels featured embellished tales of cowboys fighting to project home and family, of lawmen hunting dangerous bandits, and of gunfighters drawn to fight on the dusty street. The following extract typifies the style of the dime novel. It is taken from *Jesse James, the Outlaw*, the first volume of a series entitled *The Jesse James Stories: Original Narratives of the James Boys,* published by Street and Smith, New York, in 1901, and describes a train raid in classic dime-novel style:

Throw up your hands! Down from that engine, or my bullet's in your heart! Where's the express messenger?"

The words were sharp and explosive. The voice was that of Jesse, the outlaw. Our train had just been balked by a false signal in the Red Cut. By peering out of the car windows we could see the robbers, some dismounted, some still in the saddle, thronging both sides of the track, with the steep bluffs of the cutting at their backs. The dusk of evening was rapidly deepening.

Quick—you chaps that I named!" called out Timberlake, in a hoarse whisper. "To the front, Lawson! Craig will attend to the rear."

Our car had long before been especially altered for just this sort of an emergency. Timberlake arose while speaking, and pressed a spring over his head. A trapdoor in the roof of the car noiselessly opened. He shinned up through it like a cat, more clumsily followed by the six constables. In the meantime, while Craig headed a part of our remaining force toward the rear door, I stole forward, followed by Gorham, Ford, George Sheppard, and my personal satellites, Sloane and Chipps. As I slid back the door, Cole Younger confronted me,

revolver in hand. Others were at his back, still others were breaking into the express car, right ahead, and there was the customary pandemonium of curses, yells, and pistol-shots being raised on every side, for the purpose of creating a panic.

In many instances, the fictional character of a dime novel was based on a real person, and often the real individual became defined by his dime-novel persona. The character of "Buffalo Bill," created by writer Edward Z.C. Judson (who worked under the name Ned Buntline), was developed out of a meeting between William F. Cody and Judson at Fort McPherson, Nebraska. At the time, Cody was an army officer employed against the Sioux, and using Cody's character as a basis, Judson wrote "Buffalo Bill, the King of the Border Men" in *New York Weekly*. The stories, and an offshoot theatrical production, turn "Buffalo Bill" into a household name, and Cody embraced the image of himself created in the fiction, eventually putting together his own Wild West show. The depiction of Cody largely laid the groundwork for the noble cowboy characters depicted from the 1880s to this day. Other legendary individuals to feed off their dime novel publicity included Calamity Jane and Wild Bill Hickok.

William—William tended to provide the "intelligence" for the operations rather than participate in them—but also local hard cases such as "Black Faced" Charlie Bryant, Dick Broadwell, "Bitter Creek" Newcombe, Charley Pierce, Bill Powers, and Bill Doolin. For about eighteen months, the Kansas-Oklahoma region was under the shadow of the Dalton's activities, which seemed mainly focused on train holdups.

An infamous Dalton holdup occurred the morning of July 15, 1892, at the train depot in Adair, Oklahoma. Bob and seven other members of his gang took over the depot at gunpoint at 9:30 a.m., laying in wait for the 9:42 train. The train arrived on time and was hijacked.

As often occurred, the occupants of the express car holding the safe refused to open the door; a few gunshots through the side of the wagon soon changed their minds, and the bandits were admitted. While several gang members looted the safe, the remainder were quickly caught up in a gunfight with train guards and local law enforcement officers. Three lawmen were injured, and stray bullets hit two doctors observing the gunfight from a local drugstore, one of them dying from his injuries.

Train holdups and other crimes kept the Daltons busy until they planned what was to be their final heist—two banks at Coffeyville, Kansas, to be robbed at the same time. The decision was a controversial one among the group members. Some felt that a less ambitious, but therefore more viable, plan was to rob the single bank in Van Buren, Arkansas. After much arguing, Bob, Emmett, Grat, Bill Powers, and Dick Broadwell all opted for the Coffeyville raid, while the cautious Bill Dalton and Bill Doolin did not want a part in the action. (Doolin had had previous dealings in Coffeyville. In 1891 a gunfight had ensued after police officers attempted to break up one of Doolin's illegal beer parties, resulting in two lawmen killed. After this incident, Doolin joined the Daltons.)

and associates, a fireman, George Radcliffe, was shot and killed after he attempted to flee the scene. Nor did the Daltons manage to break the safe in the express car, and they fled the scene with the authorities in hot pursuit. Bob headed back to Oklahoma, but Bill and Grat were both arrested. Bill was quickly found innocent and released, but Grat received a twenty-year prison sentence. However, with classic Dalton bravado Grat escaped from a train taking him to the penitentiary and headed up to join his other brothers in Oklahoma.

The Oklahoma Daltons had already established their notoriety by the time that Grat reached them. The Daltons, with Bob as their leader, formed themselves into one of the most active criminal gangs in the history of the American West. The gang not only included Grat, Bob, Emmett, and

RIGHT: John Wesley Hardin from a tintype believed made at Abilene in 1871. Wes is "all dressed up" for the occasion, but his bemused expression does not suggest that he was too happy about the experience.

On the morning of October 5, 1892, Bob, Grat, and Emmett, accompanied by Dick Broadwell and Bill Power, set out for Coffeyville. David Stewart Elliott, editor of the *Coffeyville Journal* who later published an account of the battle, wrote that as the five horsemen reached the edge of town, all of them disguised with beards or moustaches, a local farmer "took them for a Deputy United States Marshal and posse, who frequently came up from the Indian country in such numbers, similarly equipped. No arms were visible on any of them. Their coats were closely buttoned and their broad-brimmed black slouch hats set forward on their foreheads."

The plan was for Bob and Emmett to rob the First National Bank, while at the Condon Bank, Grat and Broadwell would make a similar large withdrawal. Unfortunately for the gang, a passerby, a little more curious than most, recognized Bob and Emmett, and soon the cry "The Daltons! The Daltons!" echoed up and down the street. Armed citizens, led by city marshal Charles T. Connelly, were soon on hand, hiding themselves and laying in wait for the gang.

The bank raids soon went wrong. Bob and Emmett successfully robbed the First National Bank, netting some $21,000. However, escape from the bank was not going to be easy, as they faced heavy gunfire. They left the bank through a back entrance into an alleyway, and on their journey to the street where their horses were they killed three local men who had armed themselves against the gang.

Meanwhile, the slow-witted Grat was having trouble in the Condon Bank. The bank staff had told Grat that the safe would take ten minutes to open; incredibly, Grat decided to wait the time period out even as his fellow bandits were beginning to trade gunfire with the townsfolk. Broadwell was shot in the shoulder, and finally Grat decided to make a break, rushing out into the street with Broadwell and Powers, who were both hit by the gunfire.

Hopelessly outnumbered, the gang fled into what is now known as Death Alley, where the furious citizenry hounded them as they tried to reach their horses. When they first arrived in town, they found that work on the street had made it necessary to place their horses at the farther end of the

**BELOW: El Paso, Texas, in its early days. The wooden false-fronted buildings are typical of the period, and some remained long after bricks and adobe dwellings became common. Note the canvas billboard.**

**LEFT:** Texas Ranger John Armstrong, who pursued Wes Hardin to Florida following a tip-off. He owed his survival to the fact that when Wes went for his gun it was caught in his suspenders!

alley, where they hitched them to an iron pipe. Leading the attack was John J. Kloehr, a liveryman considered by many to be the hero of the aborted raid. Powers was shot dead as he tried to mount his horse. Grat managed to kill the town marshal, Charlie Connelly, but was wounded twice before Kloehr finally dispatched him with a Winchester round through the throat. Bob and Emmett were also down in the alley, but Bob was mortally wounded. Seeing that Bob still moved, Emmett—who had successfully mounted his horse and could possibly have ridden an escape—galloped to him and reached down to try and get him into the saddle. There was a convulsive shiver as he opened his eyes and muttered, "Good-bye, Emmett. Don't surrender: die game." At that moment, Emmett, already wounded, was hit again by a load of buckshot and passed out. Broadwell managed to get a mile from town but fell dead from his horse. The Dalton gang's final raid had taken place.

John Kloehr refused to accept that his behavior had been in any way heroic and always played down his part in the affair. In 1900 he was elected chief of police. When the Winchester company said that they wished to present him with an inscribed weapon, to avoid any mention of his own name, he told them his real name was Jim Spears, which is what appears on the weapon that now holds pride of place in the local museum, just below Kloehr's photograph taken when he was chief of police. As for the victims and the villains, on display in the museum is the local undertaker's burial book. In there is the bill for the outlaws' funerals sent to the mayor for payment. Their mass grave was unmarked for many years except for a piece of the iron pipe to which they hitched their horses (it is still there). Many years later, Emmett personally paid for a stone to mark the spot.

Emmett's survival was miraculous. He later stood trial and, following conviction, was sentenced to life imprisonment in the Kansas State Penitentiary. Fourteen years later, he was pardoned and thereafter led a blameless life. The Western writer and former cowboy Earle R. Forrest, who knew Emmett very well, told this writer that he once invited him to dinner, which terrified his wife, but she found him to be a charming and a very erudite man. Emmett became involved with motion pictures and in 1909 returned to Coffeyville to act as adviser when a film of the raid was made on the original location. Now available on video, it is an uncanny glimpse into the past. His own "star" quality was recognized by an appearance in several early one-reel Westerns playing a heroic role. Later, however, he became an adviser for the movies and wrote several books and articles denouncing crime and criminals. He died in 1937.

### The Good Bad Man

The theme of many a Hollywood Western is the "good bad man," who either goes from bad to good in a scene of heart-warming reformation, or, rarely, goes from good to bad and ends up dead. William S. Hart, a Shakespearean actor turned

Western star, specialized in such roles in the early days of films, but even he might have blanched at some of the characters that crossed or recrossed the thin line between good and bad. One of the most notorious of these was Henry Newton Brown, marshal of Caldwell, and former sidekick of Billy the Kid, who is remembered not for his association with the Kid but for an attempt at bank robbery while a sworn police officer.

Henry Brown was born at Cold Spring Township, Missouri, in 1857, and had one sister. They were orphaned when quite young and reared by an uncle on his farm near Rolla, Missouri. The boy grew up full of tales about the pre-Civil War skirmishes between the Jayhawkers and the Missouri Border Ruffians, and the even more lurid escapades of the Civil War guerrilla bands that infested the state. Yearning for adventure, he left home aged about seventeen and worked as a cowboy, buffalo hunter, and later became involved in the Lincoln County cattle war, at first on the side of Murphy and later with Chisum, joining Billy the Kid in some of the more bizarre incidents.

Following a brief career in law enforcement, during which time Brown earned a reputation as a man always looking for a fight, he ended up at Caldwell, Kansas, where he was appointed a deputy city marshal. This was in 1882, two years after Caldwell got into the cattle trade with the arrival of the Cowley, Sumner & Fort Smith Railroad. Brown was soon promoted to marshal, and he in turn appointed as his deputy Ben Robertson, a Texas hard case who went under the name of Ben Wheeler. The pair did such a good job that in 1883 Brown was presented with a brand new Winchester rifle. The appearance in Liverpool, England, during the 1950s of a Colt .45 Peacemaker with Wheeler's name and Caldwell inscribed on the back strap suggests that he, too, was rewarded with or perhaps purchased the pistol himself and had it inscribed.

Brown married in 1884 and was regarded as a solid officer and citizen. However, he and Wheeler, together with two cronies from Oklahoma Territory, had other ideas. On April 30, 1884, the four attempted to rob the bank at Medicine Lodge, Kansas, having convinced the mayor of Caldwell that they needed some days off to pursue a murderer headed for Indian Territory. The robbery was a failure. The gang killed

**ABOVE: Bass Outlaw, who hailed from Georgia and was well educated. He served as a Texas Ranger and won rapid promotion. Found drunk on duty, he was forced to resign. He was killed by John Selman in 1894.**

several citizens before being pursued and captured by the infuriated townsfolk. Brought back to town, they were photographed before being lodged in jail where Brown wrote to his wife telling her that it was "all for you," but "I did not think this would happen." The four men were then remanded to await trial. Later that same evening, a number of men appeared at the jail where, despite some resistance, the four men were dragged outside. Brown tried to escape and was blasted to death with a shotgun. Wheeler was also wounded, but his pleas were ignored: the mob dragged him, William Smith, and John Wesley to a tree and hanged them all. Greed and the criminal instinct, with its short-sighted view of life, only led to misery. People-power had again taken a hand: there was just so much that they would accept without taking drastic action. Brown and Wheeler should have known better. Instead, they risked all for nothing.

## The Misfits

Social misfits, habitual criminals, and so-called rebels or anarchistic individuals thrived in the Old West. John Wesley Hardin, whose parents had named him after the father of Methodism (his father was also a Methodist minister), could not possibly have imagined that he would grow up to be one of the most feared gunmen in Texas. Whether Hardin was the homicidal maniac some claim or a psychotic killer is a matter for debate, but his violent tendencies are reflected in his numerous encounters, most of which were the result of alleged insults directed at him or blood debts to cousins or close kin. As a result, he built up a reputation as a notorious gunfighter.

Hardin was born on May 26, 1853 in Bonham, Texas. A tendency towards violent aggression emerged in Hardin at an early age. When he was eleven years old he stabbed a boy twice during a knife fight. His first known killing was that of a former slave named Mage, during a visit to his uncle's plantation at Moscow, Texas, in November 1868. He and the former slave fell out during a wrestling match, and Mage is reported to have threatened Hardin. Soon afterward, as Wes was preparing to return home, Mage appeared carrying a large stick.

Without hesitation, Hardin pulled a pistol and shot the man three times. He died several days later. The murder was reported to the Union Army, and three soldiers were ordered to bring Wes Hardin in. He ambushed and killed all three, two with his shotgun and the third with a handgun. Former Confederate sympathizers hid the dead bodies, and Hardin escaped.

So began a long, bloody gunfighting career, despite the best efforts of his family to reform him. He drifted through a variety of jobs and towns, each episode usually terminating

**BELOW: A photograph believed to depict George Scarborough and Jeff Milton (on the left). Jeff Milton was said to be a skilled man with a gun and was considered one of the Old West's truly great lawmen.**

**ABOVE:** The lifestyle and frequent economic hardship of the nineteenth-century West bred tough men who, as this photograph shows, were reliant upon the gun. The group here is a Texas trail herd gang photographed in Miles City, Montana.

in a murder and flight. By 1874 Hardin had killed around thirty people, and even marriage and fatherhood in the 1870s did not quiet him—he was involved in three more shootings shortly after tying the knot with Jane Bowen and had to be rescued from jail by criminal associates. One of the men he killed was Deputy Sheriff Charles Webb, and this led to a $4,000 bounty on his head and pursuit by the Texas Rangers. Hardin tried to avoid his inevitable fate by settling down with his family in Florida and Alabama for around three years, working in jobs that included saloon worker, logger, and livestock trader.

**LEFT:** John Selman, whose main claim to fame is that he killed John Wesley Hardin in 1895. But his own exploits beyond that included periods on both sides of the law. He was killed by George Scarborough in 1896.

In examining the killings credited to John Wesley Hardin, it is apparent that he concocted devious schemes to get the drop on any opponent, rarely facing down a man in the traditional manner. For someone reputed to be a wizard with a six-shooter, and who could have earned a living in a circus as a trick shot, he seems to have been surprisingly reluctant to engage in face-to-face conflict. For example, in September 1871 in Smiley, Texas, Hardin was informed that two state policemen were looking for him in the town. With ruthless determination Hardin sought them out in a local store, where he found them eating a light snack. Hardin approached them and asked if they had even seen their quarry. When they replied no, Hardin responded "Well you see him now," before drawing his guns and killing one officer and wounding another. Such was typical of Hardin's ruthlessness, and there

are many occasions accounted when he killed people for no necessary reason other than opportunity. Hardin was finally cornered on a train at Pensacola, Florida, on August 23, 1877, by the Texas Rangers who had received a tip off that he was posing as J. H. Swain Jr. and that he would be on the train. Hardin went for his pistol, but it jammed in his suspenders. James Mann, a nineteen-year-old companion who sat next to Hardin, managed to pull his pistol and put a bullet through Ranger John Armstrong's hat. Armstrong promptly shot him in the chest.

The boy jumped from the train, staggered, and died on the platform. Hardin was disarmed after a short struggle, during which he was hit over the head with a six-shooter. Back in Texas, he was put on trial and sentenced to the state penitentiary in Huntsville.

Unlike many who were similarly sentenced, Hardin studied law and eventually passed his bar exams. Shortly before he was due for release in 1894, his wife died. This had a devastating effect on him. Hardin opened a law practice in

**BELOW: Wichita, Kansas, in 1871. Main Street was still a collection of false-fronted wooden shacks with the occasional two-story structure. Note the dusty street and hitching posts for horses.**

Gonzales, Texas, where he spent some time with his children. Later, he moved to Junction, Texas, where on January 8, 1895, he married Callie Lewis, a girl said by some to have only been fourteen at the time. She was captivated more by his reputation than the man, and within hours of the marriage she had fled.

Hardin next showed up in El Paso where he again hung up his shingle, but with little success. Too many people recalled his erstwhile reputation, and he gradually drifted into a life of dissipation. A fracas in a saloon over a game of cards in which he was accused of robbing the pot at gun point did not endear him to the hardcore faction, and they shed no tears when, on the night of August 19, 1895, as he stood at the bar of the Acme saloon, he was shot down from behind by John Selman, a gunman and part-time policeman from El Paso. Selman apparently wanted to boost his own reputation. The previous year he had killed Bass Outlaw, another hard-

drinking, hot-tempered individual with a reputation and a past. Selman, however, himself became another notch on the pistol of George Scarborough, who killed him during an argument in 1896.

Hardin's present reputation is not good; many believe that had he been born in a more peaceful era, and his aggressive instincts been channeled toward the law at an earlier age, he might have ended up a much-respected advocate. Instead, he is remembered as a killer who boasted of "forty notches."

Bass Outlaw himself is worthy of some reflection. Brought up in a good family in Tennessee and Arkansas, Outlaw grew to be a man of diminutive stature, being only five feet, four

**BELOW: The embryonic Dodge City in about 1872, looking west. Built close to the Santa Fe Trail and to Fort Dodge, it attracted much attention in the press. Today it is remembered as the "Cowboy Capital."**

RIGHT: This photograph is reported to be of William L. "Billy" Brooks, one of the West's most famous good bad men. No valid proof has been found, however, to verify the claim that it actually is Brooks.

inches tall. Bass joined the Texas Rangers, where he was a popular and competent officer. A fellow officer described him as a man who "could laugh louder, ride longer, and cuss harder than the rest of us; but he could be more sympathetic, more tender, more patient than all of us when necessary." Bass rose up the ranks of the Rangers, becoming a sergeant in 1892.

Outlaw, however, had one fatal flaw—alcohol. With a few drinks inside him, his personality was transformed, and he became violent bordering on psychopathic. In fact, in 1885

he had killed a man in Georgia, and flight from this crime took him to Texas, whereupon he joined the Rangers. Gunfights dogged Outlaw wherever he went. In 1889 in Sierra del Carmen, Coahuila, Mexico, Outlaw—who had been drinking heavily—became involved in an argument with a Mexican mine worker. The Mexican man inadvisably pulled a knife, whereupon Outlaw drew his gun and shot him dead.

Outlaw's potentially fine career in the Rangers was ended when he was fired after being found drunk on duty. Outlaw

**LEFT: Henry Brown (left) with Fred Waite, before Brown became a cowtown lawman. Both men were involved with Billy the Kid in the killing of Sheriff Brady in Lincoln, New Mexico, in 1878.**

**RIGHT: James Courtright, known as "Long-haired Jim," served as Fort Worth's marshal and later opened his own detective agency. His death in a gunfight with Luke Short was a sad end for one who deserved better.**

spent a couple of years working in various semilegal roles, including acting as a bandit-hunter. However, in 1894 he found new employment as a United States marshal. It was in this capacity that he found himself in El Paso on April 5, 1894. He was due to appear in court as a witness, but first he went on a drinking spree around the town's bars. He ended up in Tillie Howard's brothel with two colleagues, Constable John Selman and Frank Collinson, and there he for some reason fired a shot from his revolver. The gunshot, and the alarm whistles blown by Howard's staff, brought Texas Ranger Joe McKidrict to the scene, who met Outlaw in the street outside. Challenging Outlaw as to why he fired the shot, Outlaw responded by shooting McKidrict through the head and once again in the back as he lay on the ground.

Selman drew his gun, but at a distance of only a few feet from Outlaw, he received a powder blast in the face from Outlaw's gun. Although the bullet missed Selman, the blast burnt his face. A blind shot from Selman hit Outlaw in the chest. Outlaw staggered back and managed to put two more rounds into Selman, critically injuring him. Outlaw then staggered out into the street, where he surrendered to another Texas Ranger. He was dying from Selman's shot, which had penetrated his chest just above his heart. The Ranger, Frank McMahon, took Outlaw to the Barnum Show saloon, where he was eventually placed on a prostitute's bed and left to die, the doctor declaring that there was nothing he could do. Four hours later, Outlaw died. Reportedly, his last words were "Oh God, help! Where are my friends." Selman

survived the shooting, although with impaired eyesight, and he had to walk with a cane. His later killing of Hardin, however, showed that he lost none of his grit and ruthlessness.

Possibly one of the most intriguing characters who went from bad to worse was William ("Billy") Brooks, who achieved considerable fame as a gunfighter, peace officer, stagecoach driver, and finally as a horse thief. According to an 1870 census, he was born about 1849, somewhere in Ohio. Whether he grew to adulthood there or migrated with his parents to Kansas soon after his birth is not known, but by 1870 he was already possessed of a reputation as a tough character. He is also reported to have been a noted buffalo hunter and to have been dubbed "Buffalo Bill" (which

confused him with William F. Cody, the best known, or William Mathewson, the original Kansas "Buffalo Bill" who was known as Buffalo Bill as early as 1860). Whatever the truth, by 1870 Brooks had a growing reputation as a gunfighter. In appearance he was about five feet, eight inches tall and was reported to wear his hair shoulder-length in the manner of Wild Bill. Indeed, his custom of carrying a pair of Colt's Navy pistols was reminiscent of Hickok. But the only alleged photograph of Brooks depicts him with short hair and sporting a narrow-brimmed high-crowned hat. Around his waist are a cartridge belt and one single ivory-stocked Colt revolver that must have been a conversion from percussion to rim- or center-fire.

Brooks appeared in Wichita in 1870, two years before the railroad arrived and with it the cattle trade. Nevertheless, Wichita already had an unenviable reputation as a tough town. Employed as a driver by the Southwestern Stage Company, Brooks drove a six-mule team with great skill. For a while he settled at El Dorado, and when the railroad reached Newton, the stage company switched routes; Brooks then drove his stagecoaches between Wichita and Newton.

Here Brooks found that the cattle trade was in full swing. It would be short-lived, however, for soon Wichita would take over. In the meantime, it was badly in need of law enforcement. Early in 1870 the place was incorporated as a third-class city, and the city council wasted no time in appointing a police force. Brooks's reputation as a tough character led to his appointment as town marshal on April 1, and as his assistant he had Charles Baumann, of German origin and a quiet but determined individual.

Baumann's term in office was short: a fight with the notorious half-blood Indian, Dan "Cherokee Dan" Hicks, who had got himself drunk and shot up a saloon, left Baumann with a severe leg wound, and he was dismissed. Hicks was killed later in a fight with saloon owner Harry Lovett. Brooks was now on his own.

On June 9, a bunch of cowboys raised a ruckus in Edward

LEFT: This view of main-street Silver City, New Mexico, dates from the early 1870s. Ox trains were a common sight. Many Texas longhorns ended up teamed with oxen, and proved very durable.

## HANDGUNS AND HOLSTERS

Not everyone in the West carried a gun. Those who did needed some kind of container or holster to make carrying the gun comfortable and to ensure that the firearm would be protected and easy to draw when needed. Single-shot percussion or flintlock pistols prior to the 1830s could be carried in a belt sash or might have a metal clip on the side to hook the gun onto the belt. In the 1830s it was common for both military and civilian personnel to drape a pair of pommel holsters over the front of the saddle to carry pistols and holsters on horseback. Civilian use of pommel or saddle bags that had built-in holsters continued until well after the turn of the century.

As the number of handguns proliferated, holster styles rapidly developed and changed. Earlier civilian styles reflected military influences in the use of flap covers. Saddle makers manufactured holster styles that in the 1860s and 1870s were formfitting and held the revolver snuggly in place.

1. U.S. military-issue pommel holsters for 1855 pistol carbine on one side and Colt Walker on the other, about 1855.
2. The Colt Walker's massive weight made it impractical to carry on the person. Pommel holsters were desirable for such revolvers.
3. Standard military-issue flap holster used with Colt dragoon and army revolvers, 1850s–1860s.
4. Civilian half-flap holster with an 1851 Colt Navy revolver, complete with belt and attached steel for starting fires.
5. Civilian half-flap holster for an 1861 Colt Army.
6. Formfitting civilian holster, open top for 1860 Army.
7. Inexpensive civilian holster of the 1860s.
8. Mail-order Montgomery Ward holster for Colt single-action Army revolver.
9. Typical Colt .45, also available by mail from Montgomery Ward.
10. Left-handed holster, about 1880, from Dodge City, Kansas, by S. C. Gallup.

11. Colt .44–40 frontier revolver.
12. Colt .45 single-action, 1880s.
13. Experimental Bridgeport devise, tested by the army. An enlarged hammer screw on the revolver slid into the metal plate, holding the gun so that it could be pivoted and fired.
14. Typical civilian tooled holster for the Colt single-action.
15. Belt holster for the Colt Lightning double-action revolver.
16. Patented pocket holster for concealing double-action revolver.
17. This 1860 .44 caliber Colt Army revolver and its matching holster have been cut down to create a powerful but concealable belt gun.
18. Colt single-action Army .45 of the 1890s.
19. Shoulder holster for the Colt single-action Army, 1890s.
20. Smith & Wesson hammerless double-action revolver.
21. Shoulder holster.

(Artifacts courtesy of Gene Autry Western Heritage Museum, Los Angeles.)

T. "Red" Beard's saloon, and Brooks was sent for. He persuaded them to leave the place and escorted them to the edge of town. Suddenly, one of them pulled his pistol and shot Brooks in the right shoulder. They then fled toward the stockyards. Brooks gave chase, and in a running gunfight that lasted for ten miles, he was shot twice more. The Texans escaped, and Brooks returned to have his wounds seen to. On June 14, the *Wichita Eagle* declared that "Bill has sand enough to beat the hourglass that tries to run him out." Brooks, however, had had enough. For the seventy-five dollars per month they paid him, he did not think it worth laying his life on the line. He next appeared in Ellsworth, where he was employed as a policeman. He soon moved on to a place that would one day become world famous—Dodge City. The place was situated on the tracks of the Atchison, Topeka, and Santa Fe Railroad and close to Fort Dodge on the Santa Fe Trail. At first the haunt of buffalo hunters, it gradually attracted people and merchants who dabbled in the hide business—it was reported that some two hundred thousand hides were shipped east in the winter of 1872–1873. When Brooks arrived, the town was thriving. It was also a very violent place. J. B. Edwards, of Abilene, who spent some time in Dodge in its early years, recalled that there was no organized law at the time. It was also a time when the local Boot Hill became very populated. "I helped bury a few of the first ones killed there on Boot Hill."

Confusion rages over who was the first so-called marshal of Dodge. Jack Bridges, himself a noted character and police officer, is thought by some to have been the first marshal. They point out that he was already a serving deputy U.S. marshal. This would have had no effect on any civil appointments, but it would count when the city fathers considered candidates. We know that he and his wife Ella and his daughter were living in Dodge at the time, where he was engaged in a federal offensive against horse thieves. In any event, it was some time before Brooks's status as an "assistant marshal" was mentioned. By then, his reputation was against him. Henry H. Raymond, then a young buffalo hunter, recalled many years later that one of the first sights to greet him when he first arrived was a crowd around a table playing cards in a saloon. "The man sitting with his back to the door

as I entered wore two big revolvers, whose ends showed beside the stool on which he was sitting. I learned afterwards that he was Bill Brooks, a gambler and all-round crook."

Brooks (some called him "Bully Brooks," but not to his face) became a notorious character in Dodge, and his name was linked, but only in hearsay, with several unexplained killings. Brooks was reported to be involved in a possible saloon-owning partnership with a man named Sullivan who was himself involved in allegations of cheating, and on November 21, 1872, it was reported in the *Newton Kansan* that some Texans had tried to walk off with the ante in protest. Sullivan pulled a pistol and struck one of them over the head with it, the hammer spur piercing his left temple and into his brain, from which wound he died. His friends rushed to his aid, but Brooks opened fire killing one of them. Sullivan then joined in, seriously wounding another. Later, a Matthew Sullivan (who may or may not have been the same

LEFT: Tom Horn photographed standing in the door of his cell. He busied himself making lariats. Some even claim that he spliced his own "necktie."

RIGHT: Luke L. Short, noted gambler and gunfighter, dressed like a New York dandy. As author Stuart H. Holbrook pointed out in his 1957 book *Wyatt Earp: US Marshal*, it was said of Luke Short that he was the undertaker's friend, for he "shot 'em where it didn't show."

man), described as a saloonkeeper, was killed when someone shoved a pistol through a window and shot him dead. For some reason, Brooks was believed responsible. The *Topeka Daily Commonwealth* of December 31 even stated that "It is supposed that the unknown assassin was a character in those parts called Bully Brooks, but nothing definite is known concerning the affair, or what led to it." Brooks was later involved in a shootout with a Mr. Brown, former yardmaster at Newton. According to the *Wichita Eagle* of January 2, 1873, "'Bully' Brooks, ex-marshal of Newton, and Mr. Brown . . . fired three shots each, Brown's first shot wounded Brooks, whose third shot killed Brown and wounded one of his assistants. Brooks is a desperate character, and has before, in desperate encounters, killed his man." Later, it was reported that Brown was not killed and that the reason for their fight was that a nineteen-year-old prostitute named Jessie or "Captain Drew" had deserted Brooks for Brown and had also nursed him back to health.

Much of Brooks's subsequent career is a mixture of hearsay, alleged gunfights, and tall tales. But on one occasion, when he ran foul of the buffalo hunter Kirk Jordan, it could have been his last. On March 4, 1873, Jordan rode into Dodge looking for Brooks, a long-barreled buffalo rifle in the crook of his arm. He lay in wait for Billy, and when he stepped from a saloon, up went the barrel. Brooks, however, saw the glint as the sun flashed along it and threw himself behind a water butt as the huge ball thudded into it. His only "injury" was a dousing from the water that splashed down his neck. Various stories claim that the pair were persuaded to shake hands, or that Jordan skipped town, but Billy's reputation suffered from the implied criticism of his action in hiding rather than defending himself against Jordan.

By 1874, Brooks had turned to outlawry and horse thievery full time, and it comes as no surprise to learn that Sheriff John G. Davis and posse, following a siege near Caldwell, had arrested him and several cronies. Taken to Wellington, Brooks was placed in jail. But late on the night of July 30, he, Charlie Smith, and L.B. Hasbrouck, by profession a lawyer who had somehow gotten himself embroiled with the outlaws, were removed from the jail by a large gang of silent men who took them to a tree on the main road between Caldwell and Wellington. Despite pleas

LEFT: Following the death of Allan Pinkerton, the founder of the famous Pinkerton Detective Agency, in 1884, the agency was run by his two sons, William (pictured here) and Robert. They gained notoriety by employing their agents in several high-profile labor-dispute and strike-breaking cases during the 1880s and 1890s.

**ABOVE: The Craddock Ranch, Kansas. Although pistols have been identified as the archetypal gunfighter's weapon, rifles—such as the one seen here on the right—were the weapons most suited to daily use for farmers and cowboys.**

**RIGHT: Tom Horn photographed shortly before he was hanged for the murder of Willie Nickell. Convicted on circumstantial evidence and an alleged confession when drunk, many believe he was railroaded.**

for mercy and a fair trial, the three men were hanged. Brooks is reported to have begged for mercy. The *Sumner County Press* report, published within hours of the hanging, remarked, "The distorted features of Brooks gave evidence of a horrible struggle with death. The other men looked naturally, and evidently died easily."

For the many who gawked at the bodies as they were laid out in a storeroom prior to being wrapped in blankets and hastily buried in their unmarked graves, it was both a

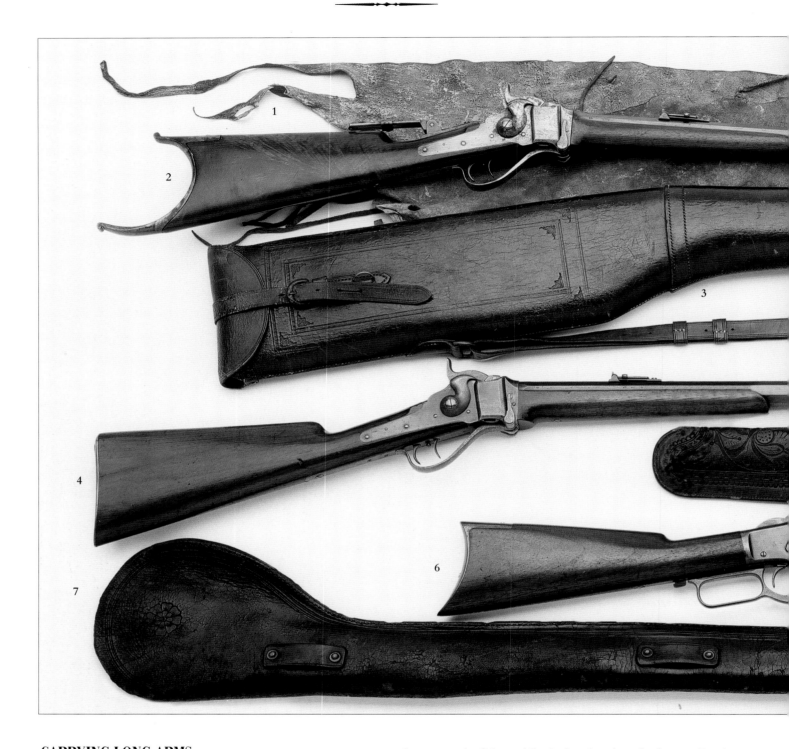

## CARRYING LONG ARMS

Any hunter, lawman, cowboy, or gunfighter carrying a rifle or shotgun would want his weapon to be protected from the elements and also to be easily at hand. At the same time, such weapons were heavy and bulky. A quality scabbard helped to protect the weapon and made it easier to carry.

Buckskin scabbards, often embellished with fringe or beading, could be easily made or purchased from Indians or traders. Sheathed in such covers, rifles could be carried across

the pommel of the saddle, in hand and ready for use. By the 1870s, leather scabbards, both plain and fancy, could be purchased from saddle and harness makers with buckles and straps to attach them to the saddle. Personal taste dictated which side of the horse the scabbard was attached to, and different opinions held whether the butt of the gun should face to the front or the back.

Long-range rifles and sporting shotguns could be fitted to more rigid cases and boxes that could be stored or carried in

<table>
<tr><td>5</td></tr>
</table>

wagons or other conveyances. Most gunfighters, however, were more concerned with pistols than long arms, although many of them owned such weapons and on occasion owed their lives to them, for out on the plains there lurked many dangers. A pistol was of course the weapon of choice for close-range shooting but of little use when confronted by hostile Indians whose ambition was to get up close. A rifle made sure they kept their distance. In that sense, the long arm was more worthy of the name "Peacemaker."

1. Indian tanned antelope skin scabbard of about 1875, which was used by "Antelope" Ernst Bauman.
2. Sharps rifle used for market hunting by "Antelope" Ernst Bauman on the eastern plains of Colorado in the late 1870s.
3. Rare factory-supplied leather case for the heavy 1874 Sharps buffalo rifle.
4. 1874 Sharps hunting rifle, caliber .45, 2 7/8 inches, made on special order from E.Z.C. Judson, better known as Ned Buntline, dime novel author.
5. Scabbard for a lever-action rifle of the 1880s or 1890s, made by F.A. Meanea, Cheyenne, Wyoming; there would have been an extra charge for the fine leather tooling.
6. Winchester model 1873 rifle in .44-40 caliber, bought in Texas and probably used for hunting by a railroad locating engineer.
7. Standard rifle scabbard of about 1880 purchased for use with the above Winchester '73, a plain but serviceable weapon.

(Artifacts courtesy of Gene Autry Western Heritage Museum, Los Angeles.)

warning and a revelation. Brooks inspired little comment in the press. Only long after his death would he be remembered for what he had done in the early days before civilization overtook and engulfed the short-lived wilderness that had spawned him.

Lawmen who turned bad were by no means in the minority, and Henry Brown and Ben Wheeler were not typical. Neither for that matter was Timothy Isaiah Courtright, better known to his cronies and to history as "Long-haired Jim." Born in Iowa in 1848, he came to prominence in the years following the Civil War in which he served briefly toward its end. Hearsay records that he led a checkered career as a military scout, mine guard, ranch foreman, and later as a lawman. Others contend that during

this period and later he was also a racketeer, having his hand in several ventures that bordered upon or were outright crooked. But it was as marshal of Fort Worth, Texas, from 1876 to 1879 that he is best remembered. In *Fort Worth: Outpost on the Trinity*, Oliver Knight recorded that Courtright was known as a man of ice nerves and with a "capacity for inspiring loyalty." He was the first city marshal

to serve more than one term. In appearance he was quite tall and, in common with some other gunfighters and Indian scouts, sometimes wore his hair shoulder-length. His right hand was "slightly crippled," which may account for him carrying two six-shooters, butts forward in the approved plains manner. Dr. Will Woody, who had been a small boy when Courtright ruled the roost at Fort Worth, told Dr.

**LEFT: The infamous Tom Horn (white shirt, center) is here seen surrounded by his captors after a brief escape from a Cheyenne jail in 1903. Horn was awaiting the outcome of an appeal when he attempted the escape, but was hanged on November 20.**

**BELOW: Joe LeFors, the shadowy lawman who tracked Tom Horn down to his Denver lair and got him drunk enough to "confess" to the murder of Willie Nickell. Only LeFors knew the truth about the "confession."**

**ABOVE:** William P. Longley cuts a striking figure following his capture. Original prints of this photograph have not been found; the only known copy is this badly retouched version. Longley stares hard at the lens.

**ABOVE:** Sheriff Ed Smalley was involved in the capture and ultimate execution of Tom Horn in Cheyenne, Wyoming, November 1903. Before long, a name such as Horn's would seem an anachronism in the twentieth century.

Knight in 1949 that Courtright did not use a cross draw, but "drew from the right hip with the right hand, claiming it was faster that way. When indoors, he carried his pistols in a sash." Courtright was obviously well versed in the use of the plains or reverse draw that not only proved to be quick but was also perhaps the safest means of drawing and firing a pistol.

Jim Courtright proved to be a good officer, but he was not as rigid in his attitudes to his deputies, turning a blind eye when they occasionally drifted into variety houses or brothels when they should have been patrolling the streets. Here he epitomizes the conflict between duty and devotion that so beset the old-time peace officers. Sworn to do their duty according to city and state statutes or ordinances, they

sometimes had problems when it came to enforcing gambling and prostitution laws, especially if it meant offending someone who might prove helpful in a crisis. He himself was a gambler, and Knight reports that he was once hauled into court for playing pool. Courtright went to Silver City, New Mexico, when his term as marshal of Fort Worth ended. Here he did his stint as a guard at the American Mining Company. He and fellow guard Jim McIntyre of Wichita Falls were implicated in the deaths of several Mexicans who were alleged to have attempted to rob a train carrying silver. Later, when two ranchmen were murdered and questions were asked, the pair fled to Texas.

Back in Forth Worth, Courtright opened his T.I.C. (for his

initials) Detective Agency. Somewhere along the line, "Tim" had been corrupted into "Jim." For some weeks, things remained quiet, but Courtright was aware that he might well have problems following his New Mexico exploits. This came about on October 17, 1884, when two Texas Rangers and the chief of police of Albuquerque called upon him. To allay his suspicions, they invited him to their hotel to examine photographs of wanted criminals. Courtright, not entirely duped, asked a friend, deputy sheriff James Maddox,

**BELOW: The Wild Bunch dressed to kill; note the assortment of single- and double-breasted waistcoats or "vests." Robert Leroy "Butch Cassidy" Parker is the smiling figure on the right. "Sundance" is on the left.**

to accompany him, but on a pretext Maddox was kept in the hall while Jim entered the room. He was then arrested, and they decided to keep him hidden until the 9:00 p.m. train arrived, when they would smuggle him on board. Unfortunately for the lawmen, when the train arrived, a passenger reported that the Rangers had arrested McIntire in Wichita Falls and were after Courtright.

The news flashed around town. Maddox then remembered the hotel visit. When Courtright failed to return, he had gone home. Once it was learned that Jim was indeed confined in a room on the second floor of the Ginnochio Hotel, a mob besieged the place. There were many who sympathized with him, influenced by his previous good name and reputation. The officers slipped through the crowd

at the rear of the hotel, and shoved him into a waiting carriage, and sped to the jail, where he sat in the sheriff's office awaiting events.

The *Fort Worth Gazette* of October 20, 1884, reported that Courtright expressed the opinion that because of the "bitter feeling between Americans and Mexicans, I am convinced that I could not have a fair trial. The assertion that I am wanted as a witness is only made to allay the public feeling in this city." This was later confirmed. On the evening of October 19, prior to the publication of the above statement,

Jim had been having a meal in the Merchants Restaurant, escorted there under guard. When he dropped his napkin and asked the guard if he would like to pick it up, the guard snapped, "Pick it up yourself!" Jim stooped to retrieve it and came up instead with a brace of pistols. As he shoved back his

**BELOW: A posse of detectives who tracked the Wild Bunch pose for a photograph by the side of a Union Pacific railcar. They are (from left to right) George Hiatt, T. T. Kelliher, Joe LeFors, H. Davis, Si Funk, and Jeff Carr.**

chair, he lined them up on the guards. "It's my turn now," he said quietly. Minutes later, and mounted on a swift horse, he was away, accompanied by the shouts and cheers of his supporters. The county attorney, W. S. Pendleton, infuriated by the escape and the apparent reluctance of the guards to lock him in a cell and feed him, was reported by the *Gazette* on October 20 to have bemoaned the fact that his friends had served him "boiled fish, quail on toast, and pistols under the table for dessert."

Courtright succeeded in escaping by rail and ship to New

York from where he kept in touch with friends in Fort Worth. He returned later to New Mexico, where he was cleared of all charges. Oliver Knight reports that when he did return to his wife and family in Fort Worth, he was met by a large crowd that gave him a rousing welcome. He then reopened his detective agency.

Luke Short, fresh from his dispute with Dodge City, had set up in business in Fort Worth, and his presence irritated Courtright, or at least that is the impression one gets from some sources. Others, however, point out that Jim's activities as a racketeer were hidden behind his detective agency and he acted as a front man for others. On the evening of February 8, 1887, Courtright appeared at the White Elephant saloon run by Short and Jake Johnson. Courtright spoke for some minutes to Johnson who then called Luke out, and the trio walked down the street and stopped outside the Ella Blackwell shooting gallery. Later reports suggest that Courtright wanted money that Luke was not prepared to pay. The pair was standing about four feet apart when, according to Johnson's statement published in the *Gazette* on the February 10, the trouble started, "Luke had his thumbs in the armholes of his vest," Johnson said, "then he dropped them in front of him, when Courtright said, 'You needn't be getting out your gun,' Luke said, 'I haven't got any gun here, Jim,' and raised up his vest to show him. Courtright then pulled his pistol. He drew it first, and then Short drew his and commenced to fire."

Courtright failed to pull the trigger. Luke fired, and Jim fell. Luke then put another four shots into him. It was later discovered that Jim's cylinder was jammed. Short was given a preliminary hearing and released on a $2,000 bond but never faced trial. Courtright was given a fine funeral, for he still had many friends in town. His wife and children later moved to California. Just how crooked Courtright really was or if in fact he was maligned is a matter for speculation. But his demise and reputation exemplify the manner in which such men hovered on the edge of social acceptance or stigma, often on the whim of hearsay, prejudice, or downright hypocrisy.

Another so-called bad man whose exploits have long interested the public was Tom Horn. His involvement in the

## OUTLAW GUNS

As is the case with more law-abiding citizens, breakers of the law tended to favor the most reliable weapons they could get their hands on. Hence, Colt or Remington revolvers are common. Winchesters, the Sharps, and other shoulder arms served best for long-distance work. Ultimately, the sawed-off shotgun was considered the most deadly of weapons—a tool to demand respect and compliance with such orders as "put up your hands" or "surrender your money."

Some outlaw guns have survived because they were given as gifts or were captured. Frank James presented his revolver, belt, and holster to Dr. A. H. Conkwright in Sedalia, Missouri, before surrendering to the authorities. Black Bart's shotgun was captured at the time he was tracked down, following the evidence of laundry marks present on garments left at the scene of the holdup. (Black Bart made something of a habit out of holding up Wells Fargo stagecoaches, but the company got even: they hunted him down and kept the gun as a souvenir.)

The revolver that belonged to Belle Starr was given away by a granddaughter in the 1940s. Pancho Villa gave his Colt to a friend, while Harvey Logan of the Wild Bunch presented his revolver to a younger member of the gang who kept it until the 1970s.

1. Leather cartridge belt with .44–40 cartridges worn by Frank James. The matching holster held the outlaw's Remington revolver.
2. Remington model 1875 revolver, caliber .44–40, carried by Frank James.
3. Belle Starr's .45 caliber Colt single-action Army revolver carried by her near the end of her career.
4. Invitation to a hanging.
5. Colt Bisley, .44–40, which belonged to Pancho Villa, and was carried by General Jose Ruiz.
6. William "Bill Kick" Darley was a youngster when he joined the "Wild Bunch." Harvey Logan, better known as "Kid Curry," gave him this Colt 45 with nickel finish. Abrasions on the barrel are from twisting barbed wire around it.
7. This Wells Fargo wanted poster for Black Bart included descriptions of the outlaw and his various holdups.
8. Loomis IXL no. 15 shotgun with a short barrel. Charles Boles, alias "Black Bart" carried it during numerous holdups of stages in California.

(Artifacts courtesy of Gene Autry Western Heritage Museum, Los Angeles.)

Graham-Tewskbury war and later the Johnson County war, together with a reputation as an army scout, gave him a status that kept him in the public eye. He was born on November 21, 1860, in Memphis, Missouri, and, like many others, drifted from job to job. He is reported to have worked on railroads, driven stagecoaches, been a teamster, and generally worked his way westward before securing employment as an army scout in 1875. He became highly proficient and also learned to speak fluent Apache. This brought him to the attention of Albert Sieber, chief army scout at the San Carlos reservation, and Horn worked for him on and off until about 1886 when, according to Horn, he was responsible for arranging Geronimo's surrender to General Nelson A. Miles.

Horn was also an adept horseman, taking part in several early rodeos, winning the steer-roping contest in Phoenix in 1891. He is also reported to have gone to Cuba with the Rough Riders as a mule-pack-train operator during the Spanish-American War. But it was his western exploits that brought him the most attention. Between 1890 and 1893, he worked for the Pinkerton Detective Agency, and then he hired himself out to the Swan Land and Cattle Company, where his reputation as a killer was founded. It was claimed that he ambushed would-be or alleged "rustlers" using a high-powered rifle. It is also reported that his trademark was a couple of rocks placed beneath his victim's head to guarantee his $600 fee.

How true many of these stories were has never been satisfactorily explained, but in his book *Tales Never Told Around the Camp Fire*, Mark Dugan introduces material that provides a more balanced view of Horn's activities. He certainly was a killer, yet he had his share of courage. His weakness, however, was his tongue, and when drunk he said things that were boastful.

When two local ranchers, William Lewis and Fred Powell, were murdered, Tom Horn was blamed on hearsay evidence. Lewis was generally disliked by his neighbors, who were convinced that he was rustling cattle. Arrested and indicted, he managed to evade trial on legal technicalities, and when he finally came to trial the jury acquitted him, Lewis promptly sued for costs. On July 31, 1895, as he was loading a skinned calf into a wagon, three .44 caliber slugs from a rifle

slammed into him, and it was three days before his partly decomposing body was found. Although a reward was offered for information on the killing, local press reports indicate that "all the people within a radius of fifteen miles of Lewis's place say they are glad he is dead." No one, it seems, had any sympathy for him.

Fred Powell, if anything, was worse than Lewis in his

LEFT: The cabin shown is called the Ghent cabin, after Alexander Ghent, a Hole in the Wall resident who rode with the Currys and other gang members. It was moved by the present owner of the Willow Creek ranch up Buffalo Creek to a spot nearer the original Hole in the Wall ranch buildings, which had been washed away by floods in the early part of the century. In the early 1970s, the cabin was acquired for Old Trail Town, and in the spring of 1973 was reconstructed and restored there. The roof and floor boards had to be repaired and new windows were installed. (Courtesy Bob Edgar, Old Trail Town, Cody.)

attitude to his neighbors and their possessions. Dugan cites a number of instances that illustrate how detested the man was, including this anonymous letter addressed to Powell and published, following his death, in the *Cheyenne Daily Leader-Sun*, September 11, 1895: "Laramie, Wyo., September 2, 1895 Mr Powell—This is your third and last warning. There are three things for you to do—quit killing other people's cattle

or be killed yourself, or leave the country yourself at once."

Before Powell could make any decision, however, he too was the victim of an unknown rifleman at 7:30 on the morning of September 10. His hired man stated that they were alone on the ranch when the shot was fired, hitting Powell in the chest. He gasped out "Oh! My God!" clutched at his breast, then fell dead. Again, speculation was rife over

who killed Powell. His wife Mary, herself a very tough lady, later claimed to have known who killed her husband, and she was adamant that it was not Tom Horn.

Horn's nemesis was an equally shady character named Joe LeFors, a lawman put on his trail late in 1901 following the killing of a fourteen-year-old boy named Willie Nickell on

**LEFT: William Ellsworth Lay, aliases "Elzy" and "William McGinnis," rustler and train and bank robber. This photograph was taken when he was captured. Reformed, he went straight and died in 1934.**

**RIGHT: Harvey Logan in a relaxed pose. Known as "Kid Curry," he was considered to be one of the most dangerous members of the Wild Bunch. He met his end in 1904.**

**BELOW: Logan wrecked this train on June 8, 1904, but got away with little money. He and his companions were pursued and surrounded. Rather than be captured, Logan took his own life.**

July 18. John Coble, owner of a large ranch north of Laramie, Wyoming, had employed Horn earlier in the year. Horn had reached that stage in his life when he looked to the future. He had also become friendly with a local schoolteacher named Glendolene Kimmel. Her family were involved in a feud with Kels P. Nickell, and since Coble also had a dispute with him, it seems Tom got involved. When news of the boy's killing was made known, rumors spread that it was identical to the Powell and Lewis killings. Once again, Horn came under suspicion. However, he was in Denver by this time, where he used to go just to let off steam. Unfortunately, when he got drunk he said many things that were just bravado. LeFors tracked him there, became friendly, and got him drunk. On the basis of that "confession," Horn was arrested and put on trial. He denied killing the boy and the others, but despite pleas on his behalf by Miss Kimmel and some of the cattlemen (who paid for his defense), he was sentenced to hang. An attempted break out from jail was foiled, and he then spent the remainder of his time in writing a one-sided account of his adventures.

On the eve of his forty-third birthday, November 20, 1903, Tom Horn was hanged. Years later, when Dean F. Krakel came to write his book *The Saga of Tom Horn*, the first edition had to be withdrawn and some names omitted. Even after fifty years, there were those who still did not wish Tom Horn's alleged involvement in the Nickell murder to be discussed. Horn, however, continues to intrigue those who seek to understand the "good-bad" characters that populated the Old West.

John Wesley Hardin's rise to fame amid claims that he had been forced into killing and outlawry by circumstances can be matched by another Texan of similar ilk. Indeed, many thought him Hardin's equal. But unlike Hardin, he did not live long enough to prove it. This was William Preston Longley, who was born October 16, 1851 (two years before Hardin). Bill Longley also used the "Reconstruction" of Texas

**LEFT: Robert Leroy Parker, more famously known by the name Butch Cassidy, was more of a career criminal than a gunfighter. Unlike hardened killers such as Jim Miller and Wes Hardin, Cassidy probably killed no one during his life on the run.**

as his excuse for violence. However, his apparent ease when it came to squeezing the trigger suggests that there were other factors involved. Born on Mill Creek in Austin County, he grew to manhood with a local reputation as a tough character. Before he reached the age of twenty he is reputed to have shot several men. Working as a cowboy, horse-breaker, and with some farming experience, he spent most of his formative years in Evergreen, Texas, where the family had moved when he was two years of age. His first killing is alleged to be that of a Negro soldier (again the similarity with Hardin). Soon he was wanted for other crimes. He left home and eventually joined up with the infamous Cullen Baker's gang. Baker's death on January 6, 1869, in Arkansas at the hands of a posse, forced Longley to change his base, and he returned to Texas and to Evergreen. Before long, he resumed his murderous career and was eventually captured in Louisiana and returned to Texas. Put on trial at Giddings, he was sentenced to hang. He complained to the governor of the state that his alleged "crimes—if such they were" compared with those of John Wesley Hardin, yet Hardin was only given a sentence in the penitentiary, whereas he, Longley, was to hang. What justice was that?

On October 11, 1878, Bill Longley was hanged at Giddings, just five days short of his twenty-seventh birthday. Many legends have grown up around the event. Some claim that when he was hanged, his legs touched the ground. He was not immediately hauled up again as reported but cut loose and smuggled away. And so the stories go on. Some recent writers have dubbed him "Wild Bill," a name, his family has assured this writer that was never used in his own lifetime.

Individuals who went bad were common, but when a number of them joined forces, then heaven help those who encountered or opposed them. The notorious "Wild Bunch" led by Robert Leroy Parker, alias "Butch Cassidy" was a fine example. Parker, their leader, was born near Circleville, Utah, in 1866, to devout Mormons. The young man, however, who was raised on a ranch, was more concerned with material rather than spiritual pursuits, and he became infatuated with a cowboy-turned-rustler named Mike Cassidy, who persuaded him to leave home. It was not long before Robert turned rustler himself, adopting his mentor's name as his own alias. Soon he graduated to other levels of crime, doing so in the company of fellow outlaws Matt Warner and the brothers Bill and Tom McCarty. On July 24, 1889, the gang robbed a bank in Colorado, their last crime as a gang. Unlike others of his ilk, Butch was never known to kill anyone. Captured in Wyoming in 1894, he was sentenced to the state penitentiary. In 1896, however, on the alleged promise that he would "never worry Wyoming again," he was paroled. Many believe this story to be hearsay.

Brown's Hole, bordering the states of Wyoming, Utah, and Colorado, and the nearby "Hole in the Wall" region, proved to be ideal for outlaw activities. Its remoteness deterred most pursuers. Here Cassidy met up with such diverse characters as George "Flat Nose" or "Big Nose" Curry, Harry "The Sundance Kid" Longabaugh, Benjamin "The Tall Texan" Kilpatrick, Harry Tracy, Harvey "Kid Curry" Logan, and others who formed the infamous Wild Bunch. Apart from Cassidy, the two individuals who would become most famous within the group were Sundance and Kid Curry.

Longabaugh was born around 1861 in Mont Clare, Pennsylvania, and by his teenage years had already entered a life of crime. He served two years in prison from 1887 to 1889 for horse stealing and then narrowly escaped justice in 1892 for his part in an attempted train robbery. He joined the Wild Bunch around 1897.

Harvey Logan was also a former horse and cattle rustler when he joined the Wild Bunch, and his "Kid Curry" moniker was borrowed from the leader of his former gang. Unlike many of the others in the Hole-in-the-Wall gang (as the Wild Bunch was also known), Curry was a hardened killer. Cassidy never killed anyone, and Sundance only one man in his career, but Curry would kill lawmen in three states and a host of other individuals.

The Wild Bunch's first raid occurred on August 23, 1896, a successful, though minor, robbery at a bank in Montepelier, Idaho, that netted Cassidy and two others (Elza Lay and Bob Meeks) a total of $7,165. After the bank raid, the same trio would rob a mining payroll at Castle Gate, Utah. Pretending to be laborers looking for the work, the gunmen held up officials as they transferred the payroll from a train to the office. Once again the three made an escape, this time clutching $8,800 in cash.

It wasn't long before the Wild Bunch became far more ambitious in scope, and their raids began to net ever-larger hauls. A bank raid at Belle Fouche, South Dakota, took $30,000. The same amount was taken during a train robbery near Wilcox, Wyoming, on June 2, 1899. They stopped the train on the Union Pacific Railroad by blowing out a bridge. Using dynamite, they first blew off the doors of the express car then blasted open the safe.

Despite a vigorous pursuit, the Hole-in-the-Wall gang once more evaded arrest. It was a close call, however. The gang's exploits received a great deal of nationwide publicity and attracted large rewards and the attention of the Pinkerton and other agencies. Soon the gang started to feel the pressure. Lawmen surrounded the gang as they camped at night after the Wilcox raid, resulting in a morning shoot-out that saw Kid Curry kill Sheriff Joe Hazen. The law had its partial revenge when Lonnie Logan, Kid Curry's brother, was shot dead while sitting on the toilet, it being believed that Lonnie was also involved in the criminal activity.

On July 11, 1899, Kid Curry, Lay, and Sam Ketchum robbed a train near Folsom, New Mexico. The raid was a disaster. Not only did the express car contain only fifty dollars, but also, during the subsequent chase, both Lay and Ketchum were badly wounded. Ketchum died later, and Lay was captured and sent down for life.

Cassidy, aware that the noose was tightening around the gang, now attempted to make a deal with the Union Pacific Railroad. He offered to become an express-car protection officer if they dropped all charges against him. The deal fell through. Cassidy turned to his other plan—flight to South America. He, Sundance, and others conducted several large-scale robberies to finance this venture. They took $32,000 in a bank raid at Winnemucca, Nevada, on September 19, 1900. Inadvisably, the gang had a now famous group photograph taken to celebrate, and this was ultimately circulated throughout the West, destroying their visual anonymity. The Wild Bunch committed one more major crime together—a train robbery in Montana that yielded $64,000—but in 1901 the gang split up to go their separate ways. Many members of the gang would later end up being arrested or worse.

Kid Curry certainly avoided the quiet life. In December 1901, he was involved in a shoot-out with the law after a fight broke out over a poker game in Knoxville, Tennessee. Logan's bullets seriously wounded three patrolmen, but the Kid himself took a bullet in the shoulder. He still managed to escape but only made it ten miles out of town before a posse with dogs tracked him down and captured him. He was sent to prison in Knoxville but made a breakout on July 27, 1903 (he was due to be transferred to a high-security prison in Columbus, Ohio). The breakout was a classic example of

Curry's ingenuity. He made a lasso using some wire he had taken from a prison broom and wrapped it around a guard's neck as the lawmen walked too close to the cell bars. He used the guard's keys to open the cell door, armed himself with two pistols, then walked out of the prison using the terrified guard as cover. Logan then mounted the sheriff's own horse and rode out of town.

Curry stayed on the run for nearly a year. Instead of lying low, however, he continued in the criminal life. On June 7, 1904, he and his gang robbed a train near Parachute, Colorado. Having dynamited the safe door open, they found

**LEFT: Reuben "Rube" Houston Burrows. His early life was blameless; he married and had a family and was involved with the Masons. But he later met his end at the hands of a railroad detective in 1889.**

only a few dollars, and a huge posse pursued Logan. The chase ran through the night and ended up in rocky terrain near Glenwood Springs. The inevitable shoot-out followed, during which Logan was hit and badly injured. He decided his time had come. Instead of surrendering to the authorities, he shot himself through the forehead with his own .45 revolver (the two other gang members made an escape). His body was at first unceremoniously dumped into a common grave, but it was later exhumed for formal identification.

So ended the career of "Kid Curry" Logan. Meanwhile, Butch Cassidy and Sundance, accompanied by Sundance's girl, Etta Place, decided upon a sea voyage. It is claimed that the trio went to England, where one of them had relations living in Preston, Lancashire, before returning via New York to Latin America. For a time they lived in Brazil, close to the Chilean border, where they aroused no interest. Etta, unwell, returned to the United States in 1906, followed by Sundance, who returned on his own some time later. Etta then disappeared. In 1911, Butch and Sundance, following a series of bank robberies, were reported to have been killed by Bolivian soldiers during a gunfight in a remote village. Butch's sister, who died in recent years, claimed that he escaped the troops and returned home where he lived in obscurity. Another claim was that he changed his name to William K. Phillips and died in 1937 in Spokane, Washington. Longabaugh is also said to have returned, sought out Etta, married her, and lived under an assumed name until his death in 1957: he is reported to be buried in Casper, Wyoming. In 1992, human bones were removed from a grave in the village where the two "American desperadoes" were killed and buried in 1911. These were dispatched to the United States for forensic study. The evidence produced early in 1993, however, suggests that they are not the bones of Butch and Sundance.

The infatuation some people have with outlaws and outlawry has intrigued historians and sociologists for years. It is not enough to suggest that their lives were exciting. Rather, one must examine the implications of their acts. For even the most cursory study will reveal the fact that it was often rebellion against authority, organized existence and so-called "normal" living that prompted some to kick over the traces. Others, however, would have gone bad no matter what the circumstances, for they were convinced that the world owed them something and its riches were theirs for the taking. Some matured, reformed, and led respectable lives. Others continued their nefarious existence and paid the price. The likes of the James brothers, the Daltons, and a host of other noted characters may have relished their reputations, but they well knew that they did not have the freedom of their more honest neighbors.

Living in fear of betrayal from other gang members, recognition by someone who might have witnessed a crime

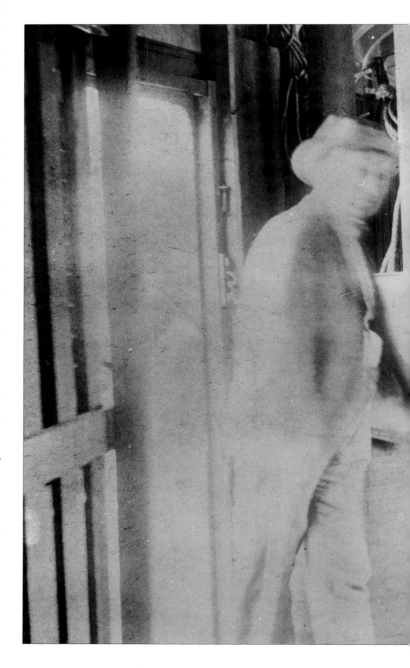

or known them in former years, induced a state of tension that was hard to live with. Jesse James came to realize that his only hope of survival was to disappear, but he did not get the chance. His brother Frank, however, was more fortunate. He managed to evade jail on legal technicalities and live a nearly normal life boosted by a reputation that kept him in the public eye for the remainder of his life. But he was by no means a happy man.

The same could be said of many others who rode the Owlhoot Trail: the spoils might be good, but the prospect of a tight noose or a bullet made for a poor investment. Also,

public reaction to outlawry was mixed. When the James boys appeared to be getting back at the railroad barons, they were the darlings of the dispossessed and others who had lost their homes to the advancing iron rails. Government intervention and legal wrangling eventually controlled the speculators, and the growing need for law and order over six-shooter advocacy also turned public opinion against the lawless. It was then the turn of the dime novel, the movie, and, much later, television to perpetuate the myth of the outlaw as a Robin Hood, an attractive figure living by his wits rather than a social misfit wrecking people's lives.

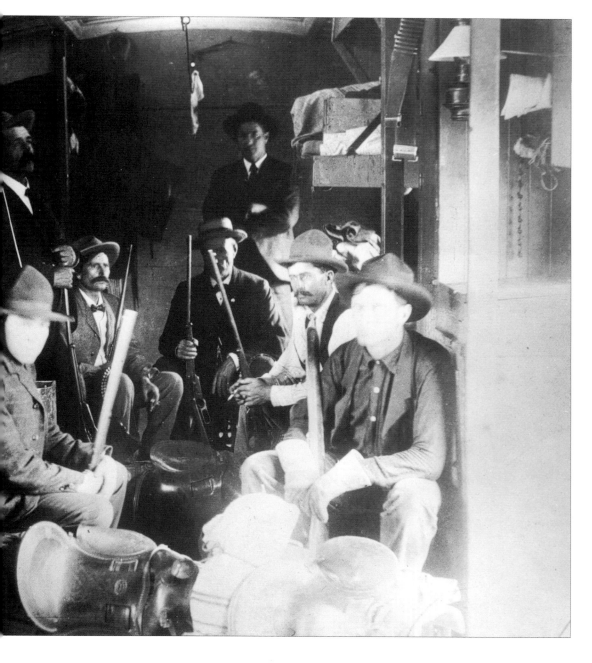

**LEFT:** The Union Pacific organized a squad of hard cases to pursue the Wild Bunch. Here, looking relaxed but alert and armed with an assortment of weapons, they sit among saddles and equipment.

**FOLLOWING PAGES:** A modern representation of a typical frontier cabin. The .45-caliber Colt handgun is placed handily on the bedstead, ready for quick use in case of a nighttime raid or emergency.

# WILD WEST
# REENACTORS

The Wild West is a vivid slice of human history, so it is unsurprising that many people wish to reenact its life and culture. Modern Wild West reenactment societies have reached an extraordinary level of historical veracity and educational value. Typically they will travel around public venues depicting scenes from cowboy life or gunfighter stories. Among the best groups, the clothing, equipment, mannerisms, and transport of the Wild West are meticulously researched for authenticity.

The basis of the research is usually photographic documentation. Outside of books, major locations for photographic research include the Library of Congress Photographic Archive, the National Archives, the

**ABOVE: A group of highly authentic looking reenactors—ranging from a U.S. Army soldier to a Mexican bandit—pose for a group photograph outside Yuma Territorial Prison, Arizona. The group specializes in representing the period 1870–1880.**

Smithsonian Institute, the National Cowboy and Western Heritage Center, and a host of private organizations.

Over the last twenty years, the reenactment groups have been sought out by the film and television industries for historical consultancy or to provide historically grounded extras for Western movies or documentaries. For example, the Ghostriders organization, based in Tulsa, Oklahoma, have collaborated in the production of documentaries such as the U.S. Department of the Interior/National Parks Service's *It Took Brave Men: Deputy U.S. Marshals of Fort Smith*, while its members have appeared in films ranging from *The Patriot* to *The Alamo* (2003). (See www.ghostriders.org., where you will quickly be informed "The GhostRiders is not a comedy act.")

The most spectacular element of Wild West reenactment is the shooting displays. Firearms used in the displays are authentic to the period, and many groups even go as far as loading their own cartridges according to documented nineteenth-century powder-charge weights. The displays have even evolved into a sport, Cowboy Action Shooting (CAS), which originated in the 1980s and is currently being presided over by organizations such as the Single Action Shooting Society (SASS) and the National Congress of Old West Shooters. CAS is a competitive event in which the shooters, all dressed as cowboys and competing under a Western alias, have to demonstrate their shooting skills in a number of different target environments, known as "stages." Usually the cowboy will shoot with three different firearms at each stage—a single-action revolver, a long rifle, and a shotgun—and fire off ten pistol rounds (for safety the six-shot revolvers must only be loaded with five rounds to keep an empty chamber under the hammer), nine rifle rounds, and up to eight shotgun rounds. The targets are typically metal plates or clay disks.

For those who want a more extreme Wild West shooting experience, they could always try Cowboy Mounted Shooting. In this event, the shooters are mounted on horses and while under a gallop fire at balloons with black-powder single-action revolvers. Under Cowboy Mounted Shooting Association rules, however, live ammunition is not used. Instead, a special brand of blank is employed that consists of a black-powder charge firing nothing more than ground corncob or ground walnut shells, this "ammunition" breaking the balloons at ranges of up to fifteen feet. For more information, see www.cowboymountedshooting.com.)

**LEFT: A group of reenactors create an authentic impression of a nineteenth-century camp out West. Many reenactment groups have become commercial enterprises as well as pastimes, providing historical imagery for education and the media.**

# Chapter Two

## DEATH ON THE RANGE:

# THE WESTERN FEUD

The cattle-sheep dispute triggered the Graham–Tewksbury feud, but prejudice and hatred fanned the flames that kept it alive. It was a hatred that passed from generation to generation, even though the majority of the original combatants were long dead.

LEFT: A dramatic image of a cattle drive in Texas. The cattle trails could cover enormous distances, sometimes exceeding 1,000 miles. Such distances meant that the frequently isolated herds were vulnerable to bandits and cattle rustling, and the cowboys had to be as good with a gun as with a rope to ensure that their stock reached the railheads.

# EARLY FEUDS

As soon as men and women began to settle the western frontier, there were feuds. The events that led to these feuds were the timeless ingredients of social rivalries: arguments over land, political infighting, ethnic mistrust, and bloody murder. In the West, feuds and range wars reached their peak during the 1870s, the violence intensified by the legacy of the Civil War, but they were a feature of Western life from the very beginning of the century.

Some of the early Western feuds had the qualities and scale of minor civil wars. Between 1839 and 1844, for example, Harrison and Shelby counties in East Texas were held in the grip of the "Regulator-Moderator War." In theory, the "war" was fought between two clear sides. On the one side were the "Regulators," a group of men devoted to combating cattle rustling around the borderlands of Texas and Mexico. Arraigned against them were the "Moderators," a band who set themselves against the perceived excesses of the Regulators, and whom the Regulators would claim were nothing better than cattle-rustling outlaws. As always with the Western feud, this simple description masks the fact that neither side had the monopoly on legal or moral right, and

the feud degenerated into a sickening and largely futile slaughter.

The war heard its first gunshots in 1840. The "Neutral Ground" area on the Texan-Mexican border had long been a source of land disputes, usually revolving around fraudulent head-right certificates being used to claim territory. Sheriff Alfred George was at this time locked in a bitter dispute with a local man, Joseph Goodbread. In an attempt to solve his problems, George called on the help of one Charles W. Jackson, a gunman then on the run from state authorities in Louisiana. Hired by George, he shot Goodbread dead in

**RIGHT:** Ellen Watson, aka "Cattle Kate," was a successful rancher who was lynched on July 20, 1889, by rival cattlemen on the charge of cattle rustling. Her and her husband were strung up from cottonwood trees along the Sweetwater River in Wyoming.

**BELOW:** A scene from a courtroom in Tombstone, Arizona. The law struggled to maintain order in Tombstone, as the cattle industry and the nearby gold mines filled the town with hardened men quick to resort to the gun to settle their problems.

Shelbyville before muscling in on local territorial opportunities by forming his own gang, the Regulators. The Regulators were soon monitoring land distribution and allocation in the area, exercising their muscle over land transactions. In response, three men—Edward Merchant, John Bradley, and Deputy Sheriff James Cravens—organized a counterforce, the Moderators, to control the Regulators' accelerating power.

Guns would soon be drawn between the two sides. On July 12, 1841, Jackson was put on trial for the murder of Goodbread. The trial had an additional antagonism—the judge, John M. Hansford, was a friend of the Moderators. Regulator men were soon riding through Shelbyville to show that they ruled the roost, even burning down a few local homes. The courtroom itself filled up with Regulator supporters; Hansford was so intimidated that the court did not sit and Jackson was acquitted.

Shortly after the abortive trial, Jackson and another man named Lauer were shot dead. Charles Watt Moorman, a man who, according to the following account written by his brother-in-law, did not follow the usual profile of a hardened gunfighter, stepped into Jackson's shoes:

Watt could shoot straighter than any man I ever saw. He was a good scholar, wrote poetry that was real funny, and he had a comical laugh. He would not confine himself to any kind of business, was the ideal of his father and mother, played billiards and ten pins, bruised fellows' heads with billiard cues, rode his friends' horses, spent their money and wore their clothes. He gave away his own clothes if had more than his share, had the most respectable men for his friends, and anything he wanted that they had was at his service.

Despite the clean-living impression given here, Moorman was actually wanted by the law in Mississippi on forgery charges. He led a posse to hunt down Jackson's killers, the McFadden brothers (a McFadden home had been burned by

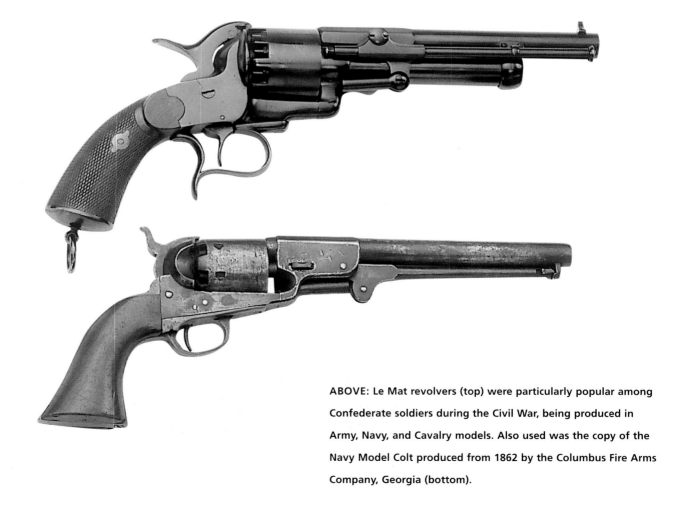

**ABOVE: Le Mat revolvers (top) were particularly popular among Confederate soldiers during the Civil War, being produced in Army, Navy, and Cavalry models. Also used was the copy of the Navy Model Colt produced from 1862 by the Columbus Fire Arms Company, Georgia (bottom).**

the Regulators during the trial riots), who were captured twenty-five miles north of Crockett. In October 1841, all except one of the McFadden brothers were hanged for the Jackson-Lauer killing.

## A Broken Truce

With blood already on the ground, the Regulator–Moderator war began to turn up the heat as relatives and associates of the deceased looked to settle scores. In 1842, a man named Hall was shot dead in Shelbyville by another gunman named Stanfield (Stanfield had accused Hall of hog theft). Stanfield happened to be boarding at the home of a Regulator, and quickly the Moderators were on the trail of revenge, this time

BELOW: The feuds of the nineteenth century often had their origins in the internecine bloodletting of the Civil War. Here we witness the destruction of the city of Lawrence, Kansas, by Confederate guerrillas on August 21, 1863.

with a new leader, John M. Bradley. The law only became involved in the escalating gunfire to take sides, and the Regulator-Moderator war became an impossibly complex web of violence and counterviolence.

Matters took a dramatic turn in the summer of 1844. During a meeting at Bells Springs, the Moderators renamed themselves the Reformers. A change of name also brought a change in leadership, and James J. Cravens replaced Bradley. At the same meeting, the Moderators laid down plans to occupy Shelbyville and seize it from the grasp of the Regulators. Meanwhile, the Regulators still had their sights set on killing Bradley. Bizarrely, on July 24, 1844, the Regulators and Moderators signed a truce, claiming that this protected all "good and unoffending citizens." Few people in the two groups fell into these categories, and four days after the signing of the truce Bradley was shot dead at a Baptist meeting near San Augustine. A Regulator named Louis Watkins was murdered in return.

The militia arrested ten key individuals, and eventually both sides signed a government agreement to disband their respective groups. It was the practical end to the Regulator-Moderator war, although Moorman was shot and killed as a violent aftershock. The irony was both sides eventually came together to fight for the United States in the Mexican War.

## The Civil War and the Feuds

The Regulator-Moderator war shows that the feud was a significant pre–Civil War problem in the West. However, the

**ABOVE: Sam Houston, president of the Republic of Texas, took an active role in stopping the Regulator-Moderator war of the 1840s. Houston completed his second term as president in 1844, dealing with the war shortly before leaving office.**

Finally, in August 1844, the feuding between the Regulators and Moderators reached the level of almost open warfare. What occurred came to be known as the Church Hill Battle. Some 225 Moderators rode to Shelbyville and attacked a group of 62 Regulators, who had some reinforcement from groups of sympathetic civilians. Fusillades of shots were traded, and remarkably, considering the number of people present, only one man was killed. The Regulators then launched their own assault on the Moderators; once again there were thankfully few casualties.

By now the state and federal authorities of Texas were becoming alarmed at the escalation of matters in East Texas. On August 15, 1844, President Houston ordered a militia force to enter the region and clamp down on the ringleaders.

end of the war in 1865 was the catalyst for a horrific epidemic of feud violence that swept the territory from the 1860s to the 1880s. As with all civil conflicts, the American Civil War tore communities apart and bred lasting enmities, while also creating the social disorder, economic upheaval, and the massive distribution of firearms that fueled general lawlessness. Many men returned home from the war with ideas of settling wartime scores in a peacetime context. Furthermore, in America's deep South hundreds of thousands of former Confederate soldiers had to live under jurisdiction of Union authorities and often those who had supported the Union cause.

A typical example of the post–Civil War feud occurred between the Early and Hasley families between 1865 and 1869. The feud began in Bell County, Texas, with a hostile encounter between Home Guard soldier John Early and an old man named Drew Hasley. Early had become a Yankee man in the later stages of the war, so when Hasley's son, Sam, came home after fighting the war in the Confederate army, it was inevitable that there would be trouble. Bitterness began

**ABOVE: Cowboys had to ensure that the herd stayed as tight as possible. Any cattle wandering off were in danger of being rustled or (if they were not branded) being claimed as the possessions of other ranches under so-called maverick laws.**

to ferment between the two families, the Hasleys gathering to themselves tough men such as Jim McRae. On July 30, 1869, McRae was shot dead in an ambush by the Early followers, the Hasleys responding by killing one Dr. Calvin Clarke in Arkansas. With the two men dead, the feud effectively burned itself out, but it illustrates how Civil War mentalities could return to haunt the postwar world.

The 1870s were a peak decade of feud violence in the West. Many of the landmark feuds, such as the Lincoln County war and the Sutton–Taylor feud, are described below. In the time of outlaws and vigilantes, few people came out innocent. Lynchings, assassinations, theft, and corruption characterized the activities of the feuding families and individuals. However, despite the fact that there was some renewal of feuding in the 1890s, the worst of the feuds petered out by the 1880s. The increased reach of federal authorities, better local policing, and more rigors in land documentation took much of the fire out of the feuding way

**RIGHT: John Chisum, one of the Old West's legendary cattle barons, whose exploits have inspired novelists and Hollywood in their depiction of the sort of men who created and ruled vast cattle empires.**

ABOVE: James J. Dolan and Lawrence G. Murphy photographed in a typical formal pose at Christmas 1871, at Fort Stanton. Suggested by their expressions, both were ruthless and hardheaded business men.

LEFT: Henry McCarty, alias Antrim, alias William H. Bonney— "Billy the Kid"—has become the archetypal Western legend. His appearance was lethally deceptive; he may look half-witted, but he was both a cunning and very dangerous man to cross— and one who killed in cold blood.

of life. Yet there are individuals alive today who, in the dim and distant memories of childhood from the 1930s and 1940s, can remember feud animosities of the nineteenth century persisting well into the early decades of the twentieth century.

## The Lust for Land

Greed, power, and the lust for land: they were the ingredients that led men to fight each other in a bid for supremacy in the race for possessions in the West. Range wars and feuds took their toll, adding to the hazards of frontier life. Probably the most famous, or infamous, of these was the Lincoln County war of 1878–1881. Its present-day fame is very much a part of the Billy the Kid myth, although the "Kid" himself was only a minor character.

Some writers believe that the "war" was really a conflict between individuals rather than a social or blood feud between divided factions. In fact, the actual war came at the end rather than the beginning of what had been an increasingly anarchical dispute for more than a decade. New Mexico at that time was a melting pot for the races. Inhabited for centuries by the Pueblo Indians and various Navajo and Apache tribes, it had witnessed Francisco Vasquez de Coronado's march northward in the 1540s and in the years following had been "invaded" many times by exploring parties from Spain and later by the French. Then, in 1848, following the Treaty of Guadalupe Hidalgo, which ceded California to the United States, New Mexico was included. It was not until 1850, however, that a formal territorial government was organized. The area was vast and led to disputes with Texas, a state of affairs that was only resolved when the state accepted $10 million to surrender its claim. In 1853, a niggling dispute with Mexico over an international boundary was settled by the Gadsden Purchase. This particular treaty enabled the United States to push a railroad link to California via southern New Mexico. Finally, the territory of Arizona was formed from land ceded by New Mexico in 1863.

The country had long appealed to cattlemen, and one particular region of it attracted considerable attention— Lincoln County, a rather remote part with a reputation for violence and lawlessness. John Chisum, a typical cattleman of the time, had run cattle in the area since the early 1870s and had a reputation for preempting government lands and for getting what he wanted. This did not sit well with some, in particular Lawrence G. Murphy, a hard-nosed entrepreneur who saw a future not in cattle but in merchandise and property.

PRICE, 25 CENTS.

# BILLY THE KID.

**A ROMANTIC STORY OF LIFE IN THE GREAT WILD WEST.**

Founded Upon the Play by Walter Woods and Joseph Santley.

**ARDA LA CROIX, Author.**

"I LOVE YOU, NELLIE, I HAVE ALWAYS LOVED YOU."

As Played by **LEROY E. SUMNER,** Young America's Favorite Actor.
Management of CHAS. H. WUERZ.

**ABOVE: Popular culture's fascination with Billy the Kid has led many to iron out the sheer ugliness of his character. In the poster for this stage play, the actor playing the Kid looks positively angelic when compared to McCarty.**

Chisum believed that control lay in government beef contracts and provisions, which would include meat for Indian reservations and lucrative eastern and western markets. However, his plans were thwarted by the so-called Santa Fe Ring, a political group of prominent Republican businessmen based at Santa Fe. They supported Murphy and, with their help, he acquired many of the government contracts that Chisum had his eyes on. The ring sought control of the economics as well as the politics of New Mexico. They were so determined that they even supported Democrats who shared their aims, which is how James J. Dolan and others came to join Murphy to virtually monopolize the economy of the territory. Their power did not stop there: control and influence extended even to the law enforcement, and lucrative positions were reserved for those who supported their views and ambitions.

John Chisum, whose baronial empire included vast herds of cattle, felt threatened, and he determined to sidestep the Murphy-Dolan faction and seek government contracts on his own. Meanwhile, a former Kansas lawyer named Alexander McSween had arrived. Initially he joined the Murphy camp. Later, he changed his mind, and in 1876 he joined forces with an Englishman, John Tunstall, and formed a rival merchandise outfit that not only rivaled the Murphy-Dolan partnership but aligned itself with Chisum.

Murphy eventually sold out to his partners, Dolan and James H. Riley, who found themselves unable to compete with the Tunstall-McSween business. The ring then supported Dolan and Riley and began to bring political and economic pressure on Tunstall and McSween. This soon led to public utterances and local ranchers began taking sides.

Meanwhile, Chisum's preempting of public lands continued, which served to alienate many of the smaller ranchers, some of whom changed their allegiance to Dolan. It was no comfort to the Tunstall-McSween partnership to know that many of those who expressed allegiance to Dolan did so out of sufferance, for they were in his debt for patronage or simply because they owed him money. On the other hand, a lot of the Spanish-speaking homesteaders and small land owners rallied to Tunstall simply because he represented the opposition to the unpopular Dolan group.

Rumors began to spread that Dolan was dealing in stolen cattle. Proof was not forthcoming, because, so it was claimed, as soon as the cattle were rustled they were slaughtered or the brands were altered if they were moved on the hoof. Whether this was malicious gossip or part fact was not explained, but it was also believed that no action was taken simply because Dolan controlled the local law enforcement.

Historian Philip J. Rasch discovered an unpublished affidavit by one Andrew Boyle claiming that when Tunstall hired Richard M. "Dick" Brewer as his foreman, he sent him out to buy stock at below the going rate, making it clear that he was not too concerned about their origin just so long as

LEFT: Billy the Kid's friend Tom O'Folliard, who was killed in a gunfight with Garrett's posse. Tom hailed from Texas, and this photograph is thought to depict him in his late teens or early twenties.

# THE SLAUGHTER OF THE
# AMERICAN BUFFALO

The massacre of the buffalo was one of the most shameful environmental disasters in North American history, the result of direct government policy, unfettered commercial exploitation, and the refinement of firearms technologies. At the beginning of the nineteenth century, there were an estimated sixty million buffalo in North America. The creatures had been integral to the lives of the Native Americans since prehistory. Buffalo not only yielded meat and hides, the latter used for making both clothing and shelters, but also provided fuel from their dung, tools from their bones, and glue from the hooves. Francis Parker, a

Bostonian writer who actually lived with the Sioux tribe in the 1840s, wrote that: "The buffalo supplies the Indians with the necessities of life; with habitations, food, clothing, beds and fuel, strings for their bows, glue, thread, cordage, trail ropes for their horses, covering for their saddles, vessels to hold water, boats to cross streams, and the means of purchasing all they want from the traders. When the buffalo are extinct, they too must dwindle away."

Parker's insight would prove cruelly prophetic. By the 1850s the buffalo were being slaughtered in unprecedented numbers by white hunters on the American plains. They

**LEFT AND ABOVE: Scenes of the great American buffalo, c.1880. Large-scale herds (left) became increasingly uncommon as the century drew to a close. A hunter with a single rifle (above) could kill over one hundred buffalo a day.**

were mainly killed for the commercial value of their hides, but the sheer numbers also allowed killing for pleasure, as *Harper's Magazine* pointed out in an article dated December 12, 1874: "The vast plains west of the Missouri River are covered with the decaying bones of thousands of slain buffaloes. Most of them have been slaughtered for the hide by professional hunters, while many have fallen victims to the sportsmen's rage for killing merely for the sake of killing. These people take neither hide nor flesh, but leave the whole carcass to decay and furnish food for the natural scavengers of the plains."

An individual hunter would be quite capable of killing a hundred buffalo in a day, and there are many records of individuals shooting over 250 in a single hunt. William "Buffalo Bill" Cody personally killed some 4,280 buffalo in his hunting career, and the hunter Bill Tilghman racked up a tally of 7,500 buffalo with a single gun. That gun was the Sharps rifle, and the Sharps was one of several large-caliber,

long-range hunting rifles that came into being in the mid-1800s. Firing bullets typically of .45 and .50 caliber, with ranges in excess of 1,000 yards, the rifles allowed hunters to occupy comfortable high-ground vantage points and spend a morning steadily working their way through the animals beneath them. Alternatively, horsemen would actually ride in among the buffalo, shooting individuals at close range.

While the shooting of buffalo was a profitable enterprise, it also had its political motivations. The United States military in particular recognized that by slaying the buffalo herds, the Native Americans would be forced into compliance with resettlement policies, as their primary source of food and other subsistence essentials would be cut off. Lieutenant-General Philip Henry Sheridan, the commander of the Military Division of Missouri, is quoted as saying about the buffalo hunters, "Let them kill, skin, and sell until the buffalo is exterminated; it is the only way to bring lasting peace and allow civilization to advance."

By 1890, sixty million American buffalo had been reduced to only 750 solitary creatures. Only at this point was it recognized that the complete extermination of a species was impending, and the buffalo received government protection to stop the killing.

## BUFFALO HUNTERS

The original buffalo hunter was the Indian, who used every part of the animal for food, shelter, clothing, and weapons. In the early 1880s the herds were still vast. The building of the railroads was the beginning of the end for the buffalo, because the railroad workers subsisted largely on their meat provided by hired hunters. Young William F. Cody earned his nickname supplying the Kansas Pacific crews with meat in 1867. Tanning methods of hides greatly improved, and slaughter for hides increased after 1870. One and quarter million hides were sent East in 1872 and 1873, and railroads promoted excursion trips for "sport hunters." It is said that buffalo carcasses lined the tracks of the Kansas Pacific for 200 miles. Professional hunters were interested in the hides only, leaving thousands of tons of meat to rot. To accomplish the slaughter, Sharps and Remington rifles in calibers .49–90, .44–90, .45–120, .50–90, and others, were used. About 80 percent of buffalo were killed with such weapons.

Apart from Buffalo Bill, another "shootist" associated with the buffalo trade was Andrew "Buckshot Bill" Roberts, for two reasons: the first was that he worked as a buffalo hunter, possibly with Cody. The second is that when cornered by Regulators at Blazer's Mill without a weapon, it was a Sharps buffalo gun he found with which to kill Dick Brewer.

1. Heavy lined buffalo hide coat with double frog closure.
2. .40–70 caliber cartridges.
3. Winchester Model 1873 lever action rifle, .45–60 caliber.
4. Wood-handled skinning knife.
5. Brass-studded leather sheath of Indian origin for above.
6. Brass-studded leather belt of Indian origin.
7. Rudimentary rawhide-covered pack saddle of probable Indian origin.
8. Rolled tanned buffalo hide.
9. Tanned hide of small buffalo calf, hoofs still attached.
10. Bleached buffalo skull.
11. Spencer rifle altered to a buffalo gun by adding heavy .50 caliber octagonal barrel and set trigger.
12. Rifle cartridge belt, leather with nickel buckle.
13. Sharps Model 1874 sporting rifle, .45 caliber, with nickel finish.
14. Utility side knife with stag horn handle.
15. Leather sheath for above.
16. Colt single-action Army revolver, .45 caliber, with nickel finish.
17. Braided leather quirt.

they did not come from Chisum's herds. Such rumors abounded, and perhaps on the pretext of one of them the Dolan crowd served a notice of attachment on Tunstall's stock. Deputy Sheriff Jacob B. Miller attempted to serve it but excluded some horses.

On February 18, 1878, Tunstall set out to drive the horses to Lincoln. Accompanying him was Brewer, John Middleton, Robert Widenmann, and a young man known variously as Henry McCarty, William H. Bonney, or "Kid Antrim," but since immortalized as Billy the Kid. Two of the group, Widenmann and Brewer, rode ahead looking for wild

**LEFT: Left to right are Pat Garrett, John W. Poe, and James Brent, all of whom were involved in the hunt for the Kid and his gang. Deputy Sheriff Poe later wrote the book *The Death of Billy the Kid*.**

**BELOW: The Murphy-Dolan store from a photograph believed taken in 1884. The row of "Lincoln County Officials" includes John W. Poe (extreme left) and center is Jim Brent, who succeeded Poe as sheriff in 1886.**

turkeys. They happened to glance behind, and in the distance they could see dust and riders. They shouted a warning, and Billy and the others rode to them, taking cover behind some rocks, thinking that Tunstall was with them. Realizing their error, they turned and raced back. But they were too late: Jesse Evans, Tom Hill, Frank Baker, and William Morton had caught up with Tunstall and started an argument. They pulled their pistols on him and opened fire, claiming later that he had "resisted arrest." By the time the Kid and his companions arrived, Tunstall lay dead and the killers were gone. Tunstall's murder sparked off the Lincoln County war.

Following the murder, the justice of the peace, John B. Wilson, unwisely appointed Brewer a special constable with authority to arrest the murderers. Among the posse men was Billy the Kid. Other members of the gang included John Middleton, Frank McNab, Charlie Bowdre, William McClosky, Henry Brown, Wayt Smith, Jim French, and J. G. Scurlock. On March 9, the posse captured Morton and Baker after a five-mile chase. The future for the two men was grimly uncertain. While the posse appeared to be taking them in for formal justice, the prisoners were aware of a

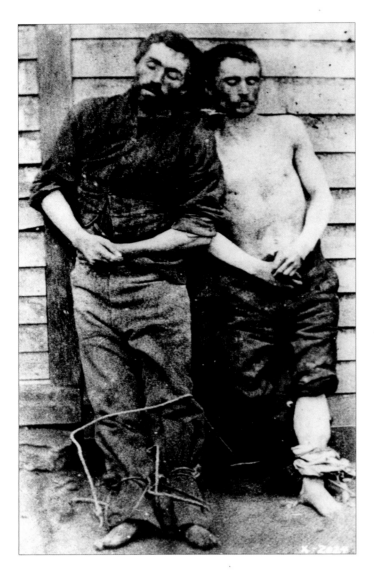

**ABOVE: Silas "Sam" Pond and Arthur Pond (known locally as Billy the Kid) were lynched for having held up a stagecoach. Many cowmen drifted into crime as they attempted to escape the hard life of farming and herding.**

Devine McCarty. (The date was established several years ago by historian Jack DeMattos.) His father is believed to have died in the early 1860s, leaving his mother with Henry, another son Joseph, and a daughter Bridget (she has so far eluded researchers). Catherine moved west, where for a while she lived in Wichita, Kansas, and later went to Silver City, New Mexico. Here she married William Antrim, an alias occasionally adopted by his notorious stepson. Following his

mounting desire simply to execute them. (We know this from a letter Morton posted in Roswell while under captivity.) During the trip, Morton managed to seize McClusky's revolver and shot him dead, the two prisoners then racing off while pursued by the posse. They did not get far, and both were killed.

Billy the Kid's role in what followed was minor, but made major by his reputation as a gunfighter and a man of violence. He was born on September 17, 1859, in New York City, and he was the son of Patrick Henry McCarty and Catherine

mother's death in September 1874, Henry McCarty became a troubled young man and went from scrape to scrape. He soon experienced his first taste of prison life after being convicted for theft, but, with a suggestion of the bravado for which he would become known, he escaped from prison and headed off to Arizona, where he worked as a laborer and cowboy.

Eventually McCarty would achieve a reputation as a man-killer, being credited in legend with twenty-one men—one for each year of his life. The true tally, however, was closer to six, the first of these being gunned down in Fort Grant in 1877. McCarty had found himself in a barroom argument with an Irish blacksmith, F. P. Cahill. Cahill, physically far tougher than the youthful looking "Kid," threw a punch. In response, McCarty pulled out his pistol and shot Cahill, who died the next day from his injuries. McCarty evaded justice and disappeared for a time into New Mexico, reappearing to

**LEFT: The "Maxwell House," where coffee and accommodation was one of Pete Maxwell's specialties. It was here, during the night of July 14–15, 1881, that Pat Garrett sat in Pete's bedroom and shot the Kid in the darkness.**

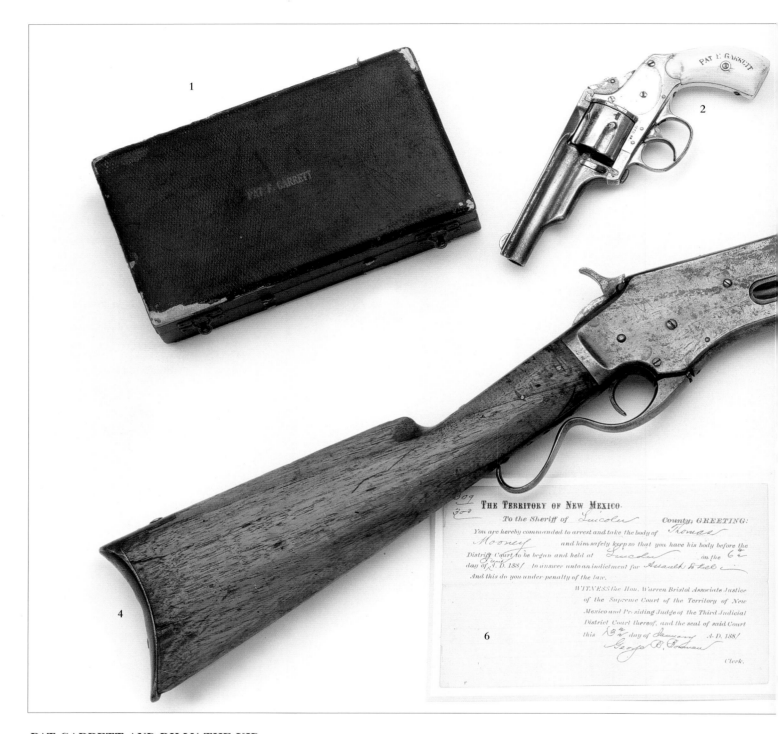

## PAT GARRETT AND BILLY THE KID

Few Western characters have attracted as much attention as Billy the Kid and Pat Garrett. They have been the subjects of books, dime novels, stage plays, and films. Sorting out the real individuals from the myths that have grown around them becomes increasingly difficult with the passage of time. Actual objects that belonged to either man are rare reminders of the drama, tensions, and violence that were played out in the course of their real lives.

It is agreed that Pat Garrett used a .45 caliber Colt single-action to kill the Kid. As a lifetime lawman, however, Garrett owned a variety of guns—many of them presents from admirers. He ultimately was murdered, shot from behind with his own shotgun. Many of the mementos of Garrett's career were kept for years by his son Jarvis.

Billy the Kid carried a variety of Winchester rifles and Colt revolvers during the course of his career. However, it is also claimed that in about 1880 he swapped his Peacemaker for a

Colt .41 caliber double-action "Thunderer." The film actor William S. Hart was once the proud owner of a "Kid" pistol, but unfortunately it was manufactured in 1887—six years after the Kid's death.

The Whitney-Kennedy lever-action carbine (4) is purported to have been presented by the Kid to deputy U.S. marshal Eugene Van Patten for treating him fairly when in his charge. Van Patten treasured the gift, recalling the part he played in the Kid's life.

1. Box embossed on the lid, Pat. F. Garrett, for Merwin and Hulbert revolver.
2. Merwin and Hulbert revolver, .38, ivory grips with name Pat F. Garrett.
3. Silver-cased pocket watch engraved, "From Grateful Citizens, Lincoln County, September 1881 To Pat Garrett."
4. Whitney-Kennedy lever-action .44-40 caliber carbine given by Billy the Kid to deputy U.S. marshal Eugene Van Patten.
5. Hopkins and Allen, .32 caliber revolver, inscribed, "Patrick Floyd Garrett."
6. Warrant issued to Pat Garrett to arrest Thomas Mooney "for assault to kill," Lincoln, New Mexico, to appear June 6, 1881.
7. Letter from U.S. marshal to Robert Ollinger, conveying warrant to arrest William Bonney, April 5, 1880. The Kid later killed Ollinger with his own shotgun before escaping from jail.
8. Pat Garrett carried out this warrant on March 22, 1882, arresting one Daniel Dedrick and charging the court the sum of $16.12 for his expenses.
(Artifacts courtesy of Gene Autry Western Heritage Museum, Los Angeles.)

become a ranch hand for John Tunstall, an employment that began his gunfighting career.

The McSween-Chisum association continued following Tunstall's murder, and it is reported that their supporters, sometimes called Regulators or Modocs (or indeed the Mexican Party, according to some contemporary accounts), at one point numbered about sixty-three men. Among those who were involved were said to be about thirty Mexicans. Billy the Kid accompanied McSween when he and about fifty men rode into Lincoln on July 15, 1878, and repossessed a store owned by him. Until the night of July 19, the group was under siege. The Dolan faction managed to hoodwink the commanding officer at Fort Stanton into believing that McSween's party were all outlaws, and when troops arrived, their commanding officer showed a marked partiality toward the Dolan faction. When the place was set on fire, the Kid and some of his companions escaped, but McSween was

**ABOVE: Blazer's Mill, the site of the shootout during the Lincoln County war that took the lives of Dick Brewer and "Buckshot" Roberts. Roberts, heavily outnumbered by "Regulators," killed Brewer with a rifle shot but died later of gunshot wounds.**

killed, shot down while unarmed and attempting to surrender.

During this conflict, the McSween faction had not been entirely blameless. On April 4, the Kid, Dick Brewer, and about eleven others had ambushed and killed Andrew "Buckshot Bill" Roberts, a member of the Matthews posse who was involved with the Tunstall murder. Roberts is one of those classic figures of the American West whose life inextricably mingles fact and legend to create a apocryphal biography. His birth date and the place of birth are unknown, although the strongest evidence points to Texas around 1833. The stories suggest that he was a soldier in the Union army during the Civil War, reaching the rank of sergeant before leaving to become a buffalo hunter, possibly serving under the legendary William Cody. Legend also suggests that he served for a time with the Texas Rangers before actually becoming a fugitive from them after an illegal killing.

Roberts' "Buckshot" nickname is accredited to the presence of shot in his body from a gunfight with the Rangers, or alternatively to his preference for using a shotgun or a rifle rather than a pistol. Both are possibly true, as Roberts had been partially crippled by gunshot wounds and was only able to fire from the hip, making a shotgun the ideal weapon, its shot spread compensating for any loss in accurate shooting.

Roberts moved to Lincoln County in 1873, and after (possibly) a short return to military service (from which he deserted) he set up his own ranch and made friends with Murphy and Dolan and put himself on the road to his own violent end. But Roberts would prove hard to kill in what was later remembered as the "Gunfight at Blazer's Mill." Roberts had involved himself in the hunt for the Regulators, enticed by large reward monies and deciding to make a preemptive strike before the Regulators came looking for

LEFT: Despite its damage, this photograph, taken in about 1879, is a good likeness of Robert "Bob" Ollinger (standing), whose murder by the Kid in 1881 aroused much anger. Ollinger was killed by his own shotgun, which fell into the Kid's hands during a successful escape from a Lincoln courthouse. Dwarfed by the tall lawman is the famous outlaw hunter James Dolan.

**ABOVE: Robert Beckwith, one of the Kid's followers, who was killed in the fight at McSween's store. When McSween refused to surrender, both he and Beckwith were cut down in the fusilade that followed.**

**LEFT: Charlie Bowdre and his wife Manuela Herrera. His garb depicts the fashion of the time: button-over shirt front, fancy necktie, and a "waist armory" that includes a Colt Peacemaker in a hand-tooled holster and a Winchester lever-action rifle.**

him. On April 4, 1848, Roberts rode into Blazer's Mill, New Mexico. Unfortunately for him, a group of fourteen Regulators were already there waiting to dine and included among their ranks John Middleton, Charlie Bowdre, Frank and George Coe, Billy the Kid, Billy Bonney, Henry Brown, and Doc Scurlock. Roberts entered into a debate with Frank Coe, Roberts's former friend, but the rest of the gang decided to move in and arrest him. Bowdre, raising his rifle, ordered Roberts to surrender. Roberts replied by beginning one of

the most dramatic gunfights in the history of the Wild West. He flipped up his own rifle, and he and Bowdre both pulled their triggers almost simultaneously. Roberts received a serious wound through his chest, while Bowdre was uninjured, although Roberts's bullet ricocheted of a cartridge belt and hit George Coe in the hand, severing two of his fingers. Roberts then shot John Middleton in the chest and managed to injure Doc Scurlock, while Billy the Kid had his hat taken off by one of Roberts's shots.

Badly injured, Roberts managed to escape inside Blazer's Mill, where he took refuge. He had now lost his rifle and was out of ammunition, but a search around the interior of his shelter yielded a Sharps buffalo gun and cartridges. The highly rattled Regulators surrounded the house and called for Roberts's surrender. Brewer—positioned behind a log pile—lifted his head up to gain a better view. Roberts promptly shot him in the head, the large Sharps bullet taking off the top of his skull and killing him instantly. Roberts then permitted a doctor to enter into the house, and the doctor reported to the Regulators that the gunman would soon die of his wounds. Seeing no reason for further deaths or injuries, the Regulators retreated. Roberts died the following day. He was buried in the same coffin as Brewer.

Sheriff William Brady (who also held a commission as a deputy U.S. marshal) was also implicated in the Tunstall killing, and as a known partisan of the Dolans, he was on the hit list of the Kid. Billy and four other gang members set up an ambush for Brady in Lincoln, New Mexico, hiding in wait behind an adobe wall overlooking Lincoln's main street. Brady appeared, walking down the street with Deputy George Hindman and three other men. They walked into a storm of gunfire from the Kid and his associates. Both Brady and Hindman were cut down and killed, although one of their followers, Billy Matthews, slightly injured the Kid and another attacker with gunfire and forced them into a quick retreat. However, vengeance had been exacted.

The killings and the publicity convinced territorial governor Samuel B. Axtell (a known supporter of the ring) that he should not get involved, and he kept a very low profile. He was later replaced by General Lew Wallace, who at that time was engaged upon his life's work—the novel *Ben*

RIGHT: The Tewksbury cabin, scene of the bloody shoot-out on September 2, 1887. The hogs feeding in the yard are probably those alleged to have chewed at the bodies of John Tewksbury and William Jacobs.

FOLLOWING PAGES: Old Trail Town in Cody, Wyoming, gives visitors an insight into life during the second half of the nineteenth century. It consists of twenty-six buildings constructed between 1879 and 1901. In testimony to the nature of the times, the River Saloon still bears bullet holes in its door from a gunfight.

*Hur,* the epic work depicting conflict in the Roman Empire.

Although violence subsided following the McSween killing, Governor Wallace was anxious to rid the country of the outlaws. He called Pat Garrett, the newly elected sheriff of the county who had known the Kid for some time, ordered him to find Billy, and is reported to have promised the Kid an amnesty if he would surrender. But a series of events determined a different course. The Kid is thought to

have fallen foul of Chisum, whom he alleged had failed to pay him for his support of Tunstall. Some have even suggested that Billy regarded the Englishman as a surrogate father, which might account for his revenge killings. However, to spite Chisum, Billy rustled his cattle. He was also involved in several shoot-outs, which had origins going back prior to the war. When he was finally captured by Garrett in December 1880, any hope of amnesty was long gone. Tried and

While he was away, the Kid requested a visit to the toilet. Bell led him outside, but someone had hidden a pistol in the jail's outhouse, and Billy emerged with it hidden under his shirt. Back inside the courthouse, the Kid produced the gun and ordered Bell to raise his hands. Inadvisably, Bell chose to make a run for it, and he was killed by gunfire, although only by a ricochet off one of the courthouse walls. Ollinger heard the gunshots and rushed across the street. He heard his name called. Looking up he saw Billy sitting in the window of the jail, Ollinger's shotgun in his hands. It was the last thing Ollinger saw; cold-bloodedly, Billy fired both barrels and cut him down. Almost casually, he escaped, breaking open the leg irons with a pickaxe handle and taking a horse from outside.

Billy the Kid's meteoric career as an outlaw-cum-gunfighter was finally stopped by Sheriff Pat Garrett at Fort Sumner during the night of July 14–15, 1881. The events of that night have gone down in Western legend. The Kid had been hiding near Fort Sumner but decided to venture out to see an old girlfriend, Celsa Gutiérrez. The Kid stayed in Celsa's room until it was dark before hunger drove him to his friend Pete Maxwell's house in search of some food. By this time, Pat Garrett and two other officers—Tip McKinney and John Poe—were in Fort Sumner closing in on the Kid's whereabouts. Arriving at Maxwell's house, the Kid came upon McKinney and Poe outside, neither of whom recognized that it was the Kid. The Kid did not know that Garrett was inside, talking with Maxwell in the darkened bedroom. In the darkness outside, the Kid, now with his .41 pistol drawn, called out "*¿Quien es?*" ("Who is it?"), and not receiving an answer backed himself into Pete Maxwell's bedroom. Inside the bedroom, the Kid asked Maxwell, "Pete, who are those fellows outside," but then saw that there were two shadows in the room. Garrett sat on Maxwell's bed, but such was the darkness that the Kid could not see the lawman's features. He leaned close to Garrett, and once again asked "*¿Quien es?*" Garrett immediately went for his gun and fired two shots, the first of these hitting the Kid squarely in the chest and killing him instantly. Both Maxwell and Garrett then fled the room, and it is a measure of the respect held for the Kid that the lawmen would not go back into the house to see if he was dead. Eventually, a boy brought a candle to

sentenced to death, Billy the Kid was due to hang on May 13, 1881.

Aware of the feeling for and against him in the territory, his guards—J. W. Bell and Bob Ollinger—were extra vigilant. The Kid had been placed in ankle irons and chained to the wall of a room in the upper floor of the courthouse. Around noon on April 28, Ollinger left Bell in charge as he went across the road to a local restaurant to get something to eat.

look through the window, and the corpse of Billy the Kid was seen stretched out on the floor. He was buried that night in the local graveyard with little ceremony.

Despite the death of Billy the Kid, the violence of the Lincoln County war continued and included a number of racially orientated disputes. But with the death of Chisum in 1884 and Dolan's departure from the area, the war was effectively over. As for the infamous Pat Garrett, he had many more years of law enforcement ahead of him. Typical of his profession, however, a bloody and dusty death awaited him in the future. In 1908, Garrett leased a tract of land in New Mexico to Wayne Brazel. A dispute arose between Garrett and Brazel over the grazing of a herd of goats. On February 29, 1908, Garrett, Brazel, and another man involved in the dispute, Carl Adamson, were riding together to Las Cruces in an attempt to thrash out a settlement. During a toilet stop on the road, Garrett was shot in the back of the head and once

in the body as he urinated. He was dead before he hit the ground.

Responsibility for the killing is very difficult to ascribe. Brazel was initially charged with the killing, indeed he confessed to the act as self-defense. An investigation conducted by the Territorial Mounted Police, however, concluded that another man did the killing. While some still hold Brazel responsible, others pointed to Adamson. However, another candidate would be Jim "Killer" Miller. Miller had become embroiled in the goat-herding land dispute, and there is evidence that he was hired by a long-standing enemy of Garrett's, W. W. Cox, to kill the lawmen,

**BELOW: A mass of sheep cluster along the Powder River. The competition between cattle herders and sheep farmers was a regular source of territorial tension, with both types of creature requiring good sources of pasture.**

RIGHT: Thomas Graham, leader of the Graham faction who tried vainly to keep the feud from escalating into a bloodbath. His own murder in 1892 heralded the end of the war in the inaptly named "Pleasant Valley."

**ABOVE:** Tom Pickett was born in Texas and first became involved in rustling age seventeen. He joined the Kid in 1880, and was later involved in the Graham–Tewksbury feud. He died at Pinetop, Arizona, in 1934.

**LEFT:** Anne Melton Graham, the long-suffering wife of Thomas Graham who was to testify that Ed Tewksbury and John Rhodes murdered her husband. In court she shoved a gun into Rhodes's back, but it misfired.

laying in wait with his .45 until Brazel engineered the toilet stop. Whatever the case, it was an ignominious end to one of the greatest law enforcers of the Wild West.

Jim Miller himself provides an interesting character study of a Wild West killer. He was born on October 25, 1866, in Van Buren, Arkansas. His parents died when he was young, and Miller was sent to live with his grandparents. He would grow up to be a psychopathic murderer, and evidence of his violent tendencies begins when he was very young. In 1874,

**ABOVE: The Graham ranch, nestling in Pleasant Valley in central Arizona, was the scene of a large gunfight on September 21, 1887. Following a series of fatal shootings, a twenty-five-man posse attacked the ranch and killed John Graham and Charles Blevins.**

his grandparents were murdered; the eight-year-old Miller was actually arrested for it but never charged. He was then sent to live with his sister and his brother-in-law, John E. Coop, and worked as a ranch hand. That relationship ended when, in July 1884, Miller crept up on Coop as he was sleeping on his porch and blasted him to death with a shotgun. Although he was arrested and sentenced to life imprisonment, a legal technicality kept him out of prison and he began a murderous career.

Jim Miller was also known as "Deacon Jim" because of his impeccable social manners and his apparently genuine devotion to church-going and Bible reading (his religiosity seems to have begun with his marriage to one Sallie Clements in 1891). During some of his subsequent spells in prison, he was even known for arranging prayer meetings and scripture studies among the inmates. At the same time, he was a truly vicious killer who not only murdered for money contract-style, but also appears to have killed out of pure enjoyment. Miller himself claimed to have killed fifty-one people in his lifetime, a claim that does not appear to have been an exaggeration.

After the Coop murder, Miller drifted around the Texas-Mexico border country, and in the early 1890s even became a deputy sheriff (in the late nineteenth century, employer background checks into a man's life were almost unheard of). His time as a lawman appears to have involved much killing of Mexicans. and he bragged that, "I have lost my notch stick of Mexicans I killed out on the border." Subsequent careers included saloon owner, hotel keeper, and gambler, but his work as a killer, hired or otherwise, was a constant throughout his life.

A typical Miller operation, and his last, occurred on February 26, 1909, in Ada, Oklahoma. A rancher, Gus Bobbit,

**LEFT:** John Tewksbury, the handsome victim (along with William Jacobs) of Andy Cooper's ambush. The bodies of the two men lay in front of the Tewsbury ranch for some time, where pigs started to eat them, as Ed and Jim Tewsbury were unable to leave the ranchhouse because of gunfire. John's death only intensified the hatred that boiled over and led to further bloodshed.

the citizens of Ada decided to end Miller's career once and for all. A lynch mob broke into the jail on April 19, 1909, and took Miller and the three cattlemen to a local livery stable. Miller was hanged last, the crowd intent on making him watch his fate as they strung up the others. However, Miller seemed to remain unmoved, his final words apparently being "I'm ready now . . . you couldn't kill me otherwise. Let her rip." Miller died as violently as he had lived, and seen in hindsight there is little doubt that the West was better off without him.

### Sheep versus Cattle

Arizona, bordering on New Mexico, witnessed much of the troubles of its near neighbor, but it also had feuds of its own, perhaps the most notorious being the Graham-Tewksbury feud (1886–1892). This feud is memorable for its passion rather than politics or greed. Yet that aspect has long been overshadowed by the belief that it was a battle for survival between cattlemen and sheepmen. The cattle-sheep dispute triggered the war, but prejudice and hatred fanned the flames that kept it alive. It was a hatred that passed from generation to generation even though the majority of the original combatants were long dead.

The Tewksburys and the Grahams settled in the ironically named Pleasant Valley in the Tonto Basin. Both families initially got on well together, and their sons rode for neighboring outfits. The quarrel developed over cattle, and there were rumors that both families were stealing strays from other ranchers, splitting up the cattle and applying their own brands. It was also alleged that one of the Grahams actually registered a brand in his own name without consulting his partners, the Tewksburys. Members of both families were arrested and charged with stealing cattle. Soon both factions were bitter enemies, which was not helped when the

was locked in a feud with local cattlemen. Miller accepted a contract to kill Bobbit and covertly studied the area around Bobbit's house for a suitable ambush point. When Bobbit and a ranch hand, Bob Ferguson, rode back onto the ranch in the evening, Miller sprang the trap, leaping up and blasting Bobbit with his shotgun. Bobbit lay dying in his wife's arms as Miller galloped away from the scene.

Miller was not long on the run from his crime. He and the three cattlemen who had contracted him to do the killing were soon arrested and held in the jail in Ada. Miller seemed unconcerned. Throughout his life he had survived numerous trials, using top lawyers to clear him on legal technicalities while impressing juries with his apparently pious character. For the Bobbit case, Miller had hired the formidable talents of litigator Momon Pruitt, a man who had managed to save all of his 300-plus clients from execution in murder trials.

Aware that Miller was likely to escape justice once again,

RIGHT: Commodore Perry Owens, in a pose reminiscent of an earlier era, cuts a striking figure. He wears his hair in a rather anachronistic "frontier style," and his double cartridge belt for rifle and pistol ammunition supports a reverse draw holster. During the Pleasant Valley war, Owens killed three men in a gunfight in the Bucket of Blood Saloon in Holbrook, Arizona.

Grahams became more involved with their neighbors to the exclusion of the Tewksburys. Understandably, the Tewksburys became bitter, and in 1886, when the foreman of a local rancher accused Edward Tewksbury of horse theft, Ed promptly shot him. Then, to add insult to injury, the Tewksburys introduced sheep into the Tonto Basin, which until then had been exclusively cattle country. This aroused bitter feelings, especially among those who resented the fact that the Tewksburys had Indian blood in their veins, making them "half-breeds."

In the early stages of the dispute, cattlemen confined their violence to sheep killing, their activities held in check by Thomas Graham, who was against killing men. But when a Navajo shepherd was brutally murdered in February 1887, both sides were faced with the grim reality that their feud was not only out of hand, but others were now involved as well. In *Arizona's Dark and Bloody Ground*, Earle R. Forrest came down on the side of the Tewksburys and told the author that he had reached that conclusion from talks he had had with surviving participants and from an examination of available documentation. In more recent years, however, researchers have discovered that the real villains were the Tewksburys. In an article published in the *Journal of Arizona History* in its spring 1977 issue, it was alleged that "an important pioneer settler never before associated with the killing had been exposed as the leader of the vigilantes who quenched the last embers of the feud by hanging the survivors." One obvious choice for such a role was the Blevins family, who were shadowy figures flitting in and out of the story. They arrived in the valley in 1884 and established a cattle ranch on the boundary of Graham land. Once the ill feelings between the Grahams and the Tewksburys developed into a full-blown feud, it was impossible not to take sides, and the close proximity of the Blevins to the Grahams left them no choice but to align themselves with the Grahams.

One of Old Man Blevins's sons, Andrew, or Andy Cooper as he liked to call himself, was a hard case. He was wanted in Oklahoma Territory for selling whiskey to the Indians and in Texas for rustling and perhaps murder. Soon the Grahams had an assortment of "hands," men who seemed more at home with a gun than a rope or a branding iron. Andy,

LEFT: A restaged photograph of the aftermath of the Dewey-Berry gunfight in Kansas in 1903. The Dewey-Berry feud was essentially the last range war in Kansas. The gunfight was the result of a dispute over a water tank and led to the deaths of three men and the wounding of two others.

**LEFT: Josiah Horner was better known as Frank M. Canton, a name he adopted after escaping from prison in 1877 following a conviction for armed robbery. As occurred with many gunmen, Canton later became a lawman.**

**BELOW: The land on which vast herds of cattle or sheep were run was comparatively flat, well-grassed, and watered. For the time it was as valuable as oil is to the present generation, hence the bitterness over which it was fought.**

meanwhile, had persuaded some of his Texas friends to hire on as hands with the Aztec Land & Cattle Company, better known as the Hashknife Outfit on account of the shape of its brand. Formed in 1883, the Hashknife Outfit covered a wide area and led to a mutual contact with the local ranchers. The Hashknife Outfit was never part of the feud, but some of its riders joined forces with the Graham-Blevins group. Mr. Forrest noted that many of these men were "as wild and

lawless a bunch as ever rode for one brand. Always looking for trouble, they simply could not keep out of a good fight."

The Grahams had driven the sheep out by the summer of 1887, and many thought that the cattlemen had won, but beneath the surface tempers simmered and it would not take much to provoke a fight. On August 10, Hampton Blevins, accompanied by five men, some riders for the Hashknife, apparently had a verbal run-in with Jim Tewksbury, who is alleged to have taken a shot at them as they rode away. The cowboys later claimed that the attack was unprovoked, but Tewksbury claimed they had drawn their pistols on him. As more detail came to light, it was obvious that things were now becoming very serious. It appears that Blevins, John Paine, and the cowboys rode to the Tewksbury ranch and invited themselves for supper. Jim Tewksbury told them he did not keep a boarding house, "especially for the likes of you." There then followed a frenzied gunfight, the first major battle of the war. No one inside the place was hurt, but

Hampton Blevins and Paine were both killed. Both sides now realized that there was no turning back.

Thomas Graham, however, continued to do what he could to keep the lid on the feud, despite his own growing exasperation and anger. And when one of his men tried to track down Jim Tewksbury and was killed in the attempt, everyone knew it was just a matter of time before things got out of hand.

Beneath the facade of feuding families, there lurked what historians now regard as the real reason for all the bloodshed—horse stealing on a grand scale. Though it now seems evident that the Graham family were not directly involved, many of their partisans were, and no amount of denial on the family's part could convince folks otherwise. On August 17, only days after the killing of Hampton Blevins and Paine, eighteen-year-old Billy Graham was murdered by James D. Houck, a deputy sheriff of Apache County, as he returned home from a dance. Houck, however, claimed self-defense, since the boy had drawn on him. Billy's death brought the Blevins and the Graham families even closer together.

On September 2, 1887, Andy Cooper and some unidentified companions ambushed John Tewksbury and William Jacobs as they were rounding up some horses within sight of their ranch. Both men died without any chance to defend themselves. Inside the house were Edwin and James and their father John D. Tewksbury, together with Jim Roberts, a neighbor who had joined them. Cooper and his friends kept the family pinned down until the next day, leaving the bodies of the murdered men in the yard where wild hogs started to chew at them. It is a part of folklore that John's wife Eva begged permission to bury them to prevent further desecration by the hogs, and it was agreed to cease firing while she dug shallow graves. In reality, the bodies lay where they fell, while Cooper and his band kept up a siege until the law finally arrived. Only then were the bodies buried.

Andy Cooper met his end only days later at the hands of the infamous Commodore Perry Owens, sheriff of Apache County, on September 4, 1887. Owens would become a legendary lawman during the 1880s. He was born on July 29, 1852, in Tennessee, his name given in memory of

Commodore Matthew C. Perry, who had won a great victory over the British fleet at Lake Erie during the War of 1812 (Owens's birthday was the fortieth anniversary of the battle). Owens grew up to be a tough youth and young adult, working on a ranch as a cowboy during his teen years (he had run away from home when he was thirteen to work on ranches) prior to becoming a stage station employee. He had the classic—actually extremely outdated—"frontier" image, with long blonde hair, a fringed buckskin jacket, a wide-brimmed sombrero, brass-studded chaps, and a torso wrapped

**BELOW: Ella Watson, better known as "Cattle Kate." Her features appear quite plain, but she evidently had other charms that endeared her to many—except the men who decided to lynch her for alleged rustling.**

with ammunition belts for his rifle and .45 long-barreled Colt. This appearance was a source of suspicion for many, and some authors point out that this was a feeling compounded by Owens's habit of taking a bath once a week, a practice that in those days bordered on the effeminate.

Yet there was no weakness in Owens, nor were his guns just for show. He was a phenomenal shot with both pistol and rifle. He wore two .45 pistols in hip holsters, a layout necessitating a cross-handed draw when both pistols needed to be employed. He was also reputed to have shot and killed

**BELOW: James Averill, who, along with Cattle Kate, shared a fate that aroused much anger. Albert Bothwell, who lynched the pair, escaped prosecution but not the anger and loathing of the homesteaders.**

a squirrel with a Sharps rifle at one-mile range in Keams Canyon. In 1881, Owens moved to Arizona, and by 1887 he had already proven himself to be a calm killer of Native Americans in his job as a herd enforcer. His strong presence led him to become the sheriff of Apache County after an incident in 1886. While protecting a herd of horses, a group of Native American horse rustlers charged the herd, attempting to put it into a stampede. On his own, Owens engaged the rustlers in a gunfight, killing two of them and putting the last man into flight.

Owens was after Cooper on a matter quite unrelated to the Tewksbury affair, but knowing his man, he prepared for the worst. Following the siege at the Tewksbury ranch, Cooper fled to Holbrook where he stayed at his mother's home. John, Andy's brother, saw Owens arrive and warned his brother. Owens, carrying his Winchester rifle and with a holstered pistol on his hip, strolled toward the house and climbed the porch. He looked through a window and saw Cooper and three others. He ordered Cooper to come out. Moments later, the door opened slowly. Andy was using his left hand. In his right was a pistol—aimed dead center on Owens. At that moment, Johnny Blevins emerged from a side door, so that Owens was now in the middle. With great coolness, he told the rustler that he had a warrant for him on charges of theft. In reply Andy fired, as did Owens, both shots sounding as one. Andy missed but Owens did not.

With Andy dead, Mose Roberts, the third man in the house, joined in and was also shot dead. Johnny Blevins took a shot at the sheriff but missed. Again Owens's Winchester cracked, and the bullet smashed Blevins's shoulder. At that moment his younger brother, Samuel Houston Blevins (aged about sixteen), grabbed a pistol and leaped into the street and aimed it at Owens. He fired once again and the boy fell, dying in his hysterical mother's arms.

The bloodletting at Holbrook was so egregious that Owens was treated as something of an outcast. He did not seek reelection to the post of sheriff, and in 1888 became a train guard on the Sante Fe line. Owens returned to the position of lawman when, in 1895, he was appointed sheriff to Navajo County. He later became a saloon owner, and he died on May 10, 1919, at the age of sixty-six.

# THE WESTERN
# HORSE

The horse was as integral to the life of the nineteenth-century West as the car is central to the modern world today. A good horse was both an urban and an agricultural asset. In the town they served as public and private transportation and enabled the transfer of goods to shops, while in the country they were used to draw plows and gather stocks. The nineteenth century was a time of massive population growth in the United States, and this expansion in turn affected the employment and breeding of horses. Horse-drawn farming equipment became more efficient

from the 1820s onward and at the same time the acreage of farms tended to expand to feed the increasing number of American mouths. (In 1800 an average farm was around 120 acres; by 1860 it was in the region of 200 acres.) Horses, therefore, were hard worked, and from around 1840 stronger and heavier European draft stock was imported into the country to cope with the burden.

Alongside expanding crop production came a huge development in the American appetite for beef. Cattlemen had to drive herds across great distances from the ranch to the railheads, the cattle then being transported to the major population centers out east. The horse became the cowboy's principal tool of work, used for rounding up the cattle, driving them to market, and traversing the long distances of range and trail. Ability to handle a horse well, particularly talents in roping from horseback, could bring a horseman promotion and respect, so it is little wonder that an intensely symbiotic relationship could exist between a cowboy and his horse.

The most well known of the Western horse breeds was the mustang. The Spanish introduced these tough animals into the Americas in the late fifteenth century, and they became the favored animal of Native Americans. As such, they initially attracted the opprobrium of the Anglo-American settlers, and they were killed in the hundreds of thousands. Between 1838 and 1840, for example, around 40,000 wild horses were killed in California, the settlers seeing them as competitors for grazing land earmarked for cattle and sheep. Railroad passengers were encouraged to shoot at horses from the carriages to alleviate the boredom of a long journey. Animal cruelty such as this was reduced following the creation of the American Society for the Prevention of Cruelty to Animals in 1866; Henry Bergh founded the organization mainly as a response to mistreatment of working horses. Although the treatment of wild, and many domestic, horses would remain horribly variable during the nineteenth century, the cowboys soon recognized that the mustang was the ideal workhorse.

The mustang was very strong and agile, it was intelligent and responded well to instructions, and it also demonstrated loyalty to its rider. New developments in saddle design meant that the cowboy could get the best from his animal. Improved tanning processes made the leather softer and therefore more comfortable for the hours spent on the range. Fastenings were strengthened so that a calf could be roped securely to the saddle.

The importance of the horse to the cowboy meant that the animals naturally became the target of horse rustlers. Horse rustling was as big a problem as cattle rustling in the mid- to late nineteenth century, and even Western luminaries such as Butch Cassidy and Billy the Kid were periodic horse thieves. A Kansas newspaper editor wrote in 1869 that "hardly a day passes without one or more cases of horse-stealing coming to our ears. At the penitentiary one-fourth of the convicts are in durance for offenses connected with the horse, and many more are outside than are in." A conviction for horse theft could easily result in a capital sentence, depending on the state and the territory.

**LEFT: A herd of wild horses moves through a stunning landscape in Wyoming. Wild horses went from being persecuted creatures to valued transportation in the nineteenth-century West.**

**RIGHT: The rodeo developed out of informal competitions held between cowboys at the ends of trail rides.**

RIGHT: The main street of Helena, Montana. The town was founded in October 1874 following the discovery of gold in the region. Indeed, only twenty years after this photograph was taken, Helena was one of the richest cities in the United States, with fifty resident millionaires. Note the number of horses and mules required to pull what may be a heavy gold wagon.

The feud itself dragged on until the final survivors were Thomas Graham and Edward Tewksbury. At first it seemed that they had buried the hatchet, but in 1892, Tom was murdered, some claimed by Ed Tewksbury and John Rhodes. Tewksbury was tried for murder but acquitted on a technicality.

Ironically, Ed Tewksbury ended his days as a lawman in Globe, Arizona, where he died in 1904 from tuberculosis. Jim Roberts, who was to emerge as the strong man of the feud, outlived all of them and was known as "the last man of the Pleasant Valley war."

**RIGHT:** Major Frank Wolcott, a pompous martinet who imagined himself above the law. When his army of "Regulators" invaded Johnson County, Wyoming, they found that they themselves were the hunted.

**BELOW:** A rare view of some of the so-called Regulators, who embarked upon a reign of terror among the homesteaders. Prominent among the group is Frank Canton (no. 34), who led the group into action.

THE INVADERS
JOHNSON COUNTY CATTLE WAR. TAKEN AT Ft. D.A. RUSSELL
(FRANCIS E. WARREN) MAY 4th 1892

| NO.1 TOM SMITH | NO.8 A.R. POWERS | NO.15 W.C. IRVINE | NO.22 Y.U. CLARKE | NO.29 J. BARLINGS | NO.36 JEFF MYNETT |
|---|---|---|---|---|---|
| 2 A.B. CLARKE | 9 A.D. ADAMSON | 16 BOB TISDALE | 23 L.H. PARKER | 30 FRANK M. NALLY | 37 BOB BARLINGS |
| 3 H. LESLIE | 10 C.A. CAMPBELL | 17 JOE ELLIOTT | 24 TISCHMACHER | 31 MIKE SHONSEY | 38 S. SUTHERLAND |
| 4 E.A. WHITCOMB | 11 FRANK LABERTEAUX | 18 JOHN TISDALE | 25 B.C. SCHULZE | 32 DICK ALLEN | 39 BUCK GARRETT |
| 5 S.D. BOONE | 12 PHIL DUFRAN | 19 SCOTT DAVIS | 26 W.H. TABOR | 33 FRED HESSE | 40 G.R. TUCKER |
| 6 W.S. WALLACE | 13 MAJOR WOLCOTT | 20 FRED DEBILLIER | 27 J.J. GARRETT | 34 FRANK CANTON | 41 J.M. BENFORD |
| 7 CHAS FORD | 14 W.E. GUTHRIE | 21 | 28 | 35 | 42 WILL ARMSTRONG |

LEFT: Nate Champion (in the light coat) stares impassively at the camera. His courage and subsequent death when besieged by the Regulators is now a part of Wyoming's folklore.

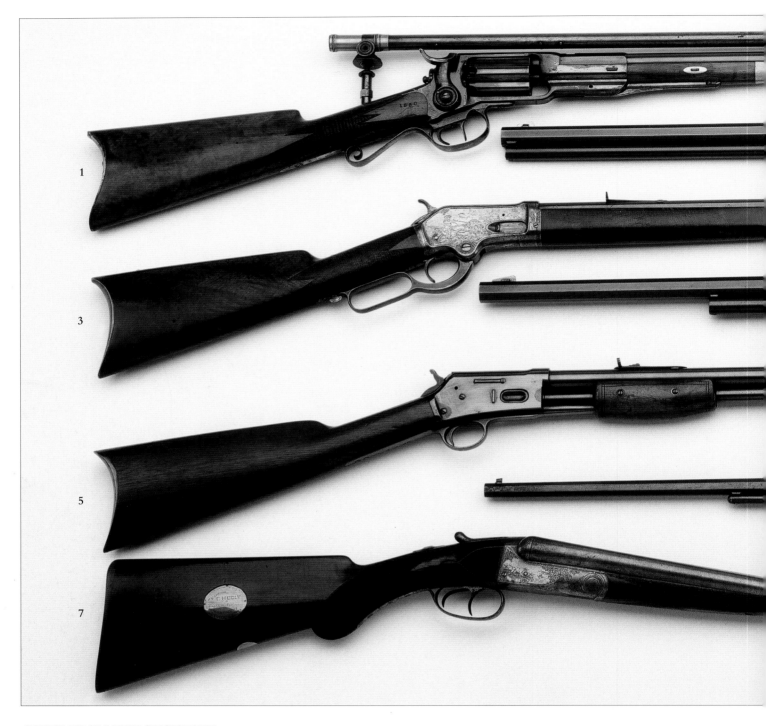

## COLTS FROM THE SHOULDER

Westerners throughout the nineteenth century favored a wide variety of shoulder arms. The trapper's Hawken rifle, the buffalo hunter's Sharps, the soldier's Springfield, and everyone's favorite the Winchester all saw heavy use. Miscellaneous other manufacturers added a variety of patented actions and other features to the mix and all had their proponents.

Prior to the American Civil War, Samuel Colt had included revolving cylinder rifles, carbines, and shotguns in the company's lineup. Many of these were not practical, however, and it was not until the proliferation of metallic cartridges after the war that Colt began to develop and produce more successful shoulder arms. Single-shot military rifles sold worldwide helped to keep the firm in business through tough economic times. Hammer shotguns and rifles in the late 1870s gave way to the 1883 hammerless double-barrel shotgun and the Burgess lever-action rifle. In 1884, the first slide-action Lightning rifles were shipped, and until just after

1900, Colt tried to compete with the more successful rifles manufactured by Winchester. The Burgess lever-action .44–40 was introduced in 1883 to compete with Winchester's 1873 and 1876 models, who countered with several prototypes for revolvers, thus forcing Colt to abandon this particular line.

1. This half-stock Colt revolving sporting rifle of the Model 1855 is equipped with a sighting scope and has special finish and set triggers. It was the top of the Colt company's rifle line at the time.

2. Lever-action .44 caliber Colt Burgess rifle, manufactured between 1883 and 1885. Fewer than 7,000 were made.

3. Colt Burgess, deluxe engraved, inlaid with gold, presentation inscribed from the Colt factory to William F. "Buffalo Bill" Cody in 1883, the first year his famed Wild West show traveled to the East.

4. Lightning slide-action rifle, large frame, caliber .40-60-260, half magazine, peep sight.

5. Lightning slide-action rifle, medium frame, .44-40 caliber, purchased about 1898 for the San Francisco Police Department.

6. Lightning slide-action rifle, small frame, .22 caliber, 1890.

7. This hammerless model 1883 Colt shotgun was a presentation from Samuel Colt's son Caldwell in about 1891.

(Artifacts courtesy of Gene Autry Western Heritage Museum, Los Angeles.)

### Cattlemen and "Nesters"

Sheep and cattle may have inspired feuds and wars, but the eternal fight between cattle barons and homesteaders (known as "testers" if they settled illegally on alleged cattle land or "sodbusters" if they claimed land under the Homestead Act) probably accounted for more disputes and sudden deaths than the former, for the acquisition of land and water rights proved a crucial factor in the ongoing battle for supremacy or survival. Such a situation arose with the outbreak of the much publicized Johnson County cattle war of 1892.

No Western movie or novel is complete without some reference to cattle barons or "kings" and the rustlers who plagued them. Johnson County, situated some 250 miles northwest of Cheyenne, was ideal for cattle-raising. It became so popular that many of the cowboys quit working for the big outfits and set up on their own, establishing small herds on a homestead. They claimed the right under the 1860 Homestead Act that allowed individuals to claim public land up to 160 acres; after working it for five years, they could register it and claim title. Should a man wish to claim title prior to that date, after a minimum of six months from date of possession he could do so by paying $1.25 an acre and receive title to it. But even those rights might not be enough to protect him if he took up land in the middle of a cattle empire.

The large cattle outfits claimed that many of the so-called homesteaders were too handy with a long rope and a branding iron to have worked long and hard to build up a herd. Rather, they stole cattle from their former employers and rebranded them. But proving it was something else, and even with the courts on the side of the cattlemen, evidence of theft was not easy to find. Another thing was the general dislike of the absentee barons who either never showed up at

**BELOW: The Deringer handgun had no purpose other than shooting people. Cowboys and farmers would carry revolvers and rifles on the range, but the Deringer could be slipped into a pocket for those potentially dangerous trips into town.**

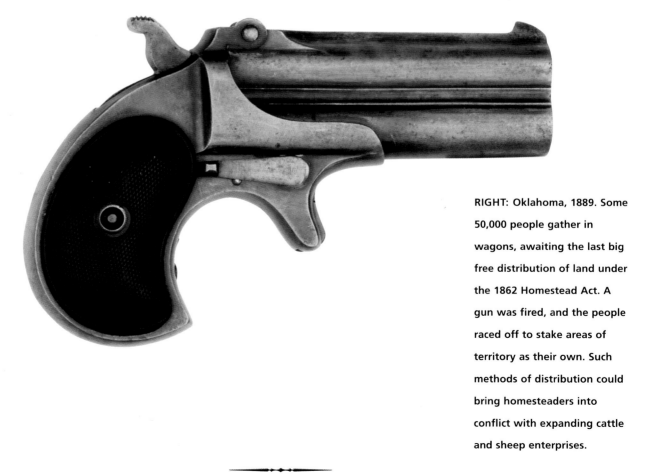

**RIGHT: Oklahoma, 1889. Some 50,000 people gather in wagons, awaiting the last big free distribution of land under the 1862 Homestead Act. A gun was fired, and the people raced off to stake areas of territory as their own. Such methods of distribution could bring homesteaders into conflict with expanding cattle and sheep enterprises.**

all or only occasionally surveyed their domains. This had a great affect upon juries who, despite the legality of the charge, were inclined to support the homesteaders. So began a reign of terror caused by the "detectives" hired by the ranchers to spy on their neighbors and, where possible, catch would-be rustlers in the act.

Until 1886, most of the large cattle outfits had profited from the cattle business, and some (although they might not admit it) had also indulged in the same practices that they now accused their small-time rivals of doing. But in 1886 came disaster. The ranges were overstocked; there was a widespread drought, and many of the cowboys found themselves out of work. Then, to add to their misery, came the great blizzard of 1886–1887, one of the worst in Western history. It killed an estimated three quarters of Wyoming's cattle, and when it was over the cattlemen realized that to survive they would need to stock the lands with only enough cattle to make the best use of available space and to make provision for winter feeding. They were then faced by another problem: sodbusters, large numbers of whom had moved in to claim what had previously been open range. Resentment boiled over and the cattlemen protested to the

# CATTLE
# RUSTLING

Cattle rustling was a crime of the Wild West and is still a problem even today. As recently as the mid-1990s, inspectors for the Texas and Southwestern Cattle Raisers Association were recovering, on average, 4,000 stolen cattle each year within their territory alone. Back in the nineteenth century, however, the problem was on an entirely different scale. In South Texas, the authorities claimed that 145,298 cattle were stolen by Mexican rustlers between 1859 and 1872. The total number of cattle stolen was raised by those taken by Native Americans and white rustlers, the latter actually being the most prolific cattle thieves in the American West. Texas was, and is, the most vulnerable state in terms of cattle rustling, its sheer expanse and proximity to the Mexican border allowing for the easy disappearance of large herds of cattle.

Cattle rustling was at its height during the second half of the nineteenth century, and it was an attractive crime for

**ABOVE: Although the brands could appear as a permanent mark of ownership, castle rustlers could change them using heated wire bent into another shape. Brand inspectors would travel around to ranches trying to spot evidence of modified brands.**

those not wanting to work for a living or for those cattle owners who wanted to inflate the ranks of their own herds without the financial outlay. The huge territories of cattle owners often resulted in dispersed herds that were easy pickings for rustlers. Cows and their calves would either be driven or stampeded off the owner's territory to the rustlers' own corral or taken straight to market. Alternatively, sometimes the cattle were moved to a remote location where they were killed and butchered on the spot, the meat then being taken for sale.

Branding proved to be one of the greatest challenges for the rustler. If the stolen cattle were already branded, then the brand would be modified or rebranded to make it "belong" to the rustler's herd. This would usually be done using a "running iron"—a rod featuring a curved branding section on the end—or a more easily concealable length of strong wire that could be bent into the required branding shape.

The problems of rebranding cattle, however, meant that the rustlers' generally preferred to steal unbranded calves. Here the major problem was to keep the calf and its mother separated until the calf was weaned onto grass—a reunion between a branded mother and a stolen calf would betray the theft. Measures for preventing the reunion ranged from penning the calf and temporarily injuring it so that it could not walk to shooting the mother.

Although rustling by Mexican farmers and Native Americans was commonplace, the largest portion of the rustling fraternity consisted of cowboys looking to make easy money. Rustling was a cause of much violence and feuding in the West primarily because the size of the law enforcement agencies was generally inadequate to the scale of both the problem and the territory involved.

Groups such as the Texas Rangers did reduce the instances of rustling and apprehended many of the outlaws engaged in the occupation, but often the ranch owners took the law into their own hands.

As the nineteenth century drew into its last years, the problem of rustling was increasingly tackled through fencing. Barbed wire—at the time a revolutionary new fencing material first patented in 1867—underwent a rapid fall in price between the 1870s and 1890s. In 1875, a hundred-

ABOVE: A highly romantic perspective on cattle rustling. In reality, cattle rustling was a violent business that often involved the mutilation of animals and led to bloody feuds, interranch wars, and killings.

pound roll of barbed wire cost in the region of twenty dollars, but by 1897 that price had fallen to $1.80. This price plunge meant that even the largest ranches could be encircled with barbed wire—the XIT Ranch in northwest Texas, for example, enclosed three million acres of land with four-strand barbed wire running a total distance of 1,500 miles.

During the 1880s there was a virtual stampede for ranches to purchase and fence as much land as possible as the days of the open range came to an end. (Many ranchers illegally fenced in government land, and it took until the presidency of Theodore Roosevelt to shake the last pieces of that from private hands.)

Fencing prevented cattle wandering and so gave the rustlers far fewer opportunities for theft, although it was straightforward, but often hard, work to cut a fence to access a herd. Ironically, the enclosing of ranches spawned a whole series of "fence wars" between territorially competitive ranchers and settlers, and many of these were as bloody as the wars over cattle rustling.

RIGHT: A peaceful Western scene as two cowboys watch over the grazing herd near Miles City, Montana, in 1894. The tough nature of the cowboy life meant that many cowboys lived to excess when they reached the towns. The cocktail of alcohol, gambling, prostitutes, and guns made the urban areas dangerous places in the night.

powerful Wyoming Stock Growers' Association whose one hundred members included wealthy cattle barons and high-powered politicians. They invoked the "maverick law," which allowed every unbranded calf found upon a member's land to become his property. Ostensibly, they claimed that this was to prevent rustling, but many of the mavericks were later sold at prices too high for the average homesteader or small-time cattleman to afford. This tactic also helped pay the wages of the high-priced gunfighters who acted as detectives and who could command $250 for every rustler they caught and who was convicted.

The chief of this unsavory bunch was the notorious Frank Canton, whose real name was Josiah ("Joe") Horner. Horner was one of those figures of Western history sporting an unusually dramatic and involving life, shifting between the worlds of criminality and the law on several occasions. He

**LEFT: John Wesley Hardin from a photograph believed to have been taken around the mid-1870s. The print is an excellent version of this famous plate. Wes's arrogant expression suggests that he was even then ready for a fight. He died in El Paso at the age of forty-two after a life of inveterate violence.**

**RIGHT: John H. Selman's main claim to fame was his killing of Bass Outlaw on April 5, 1894, and for his shooting of John Wesley Hardin in 1895. Despite having rid the world of Hardin, Selman was living on borrowed time, and he was gunned down by George Scarborough in April 1896.**

was born in 1849 near Richmond, Virginia, moving to Texas while still young. He was destined for a life among cattle, working as a cowhand during the 1860s. However, the 1870s brought a change of vocation, as from 1871 he began his criminal career, mainly involving himself with bank robberies and cattle stealing. The exact extent of his activities is unclear, but he was soon making killings. On October 10, 1874, Horner found himself in a saloon in Jacksboro, Texas. Many black soldiers who had served at Fort Richardson frequented the saloon, and Horner found himself in a violent argument with some of them. In the subsequent gunfight, Horner shot dead one soldier and injured another. He went on the run again, but in 1877 his luck ran out when he was finally caught by the law. He was jailed for a year for his part in a bank robbery in Comanche, Texas, and in 1878 Horner seems to have given up on criminality and returned to cattle

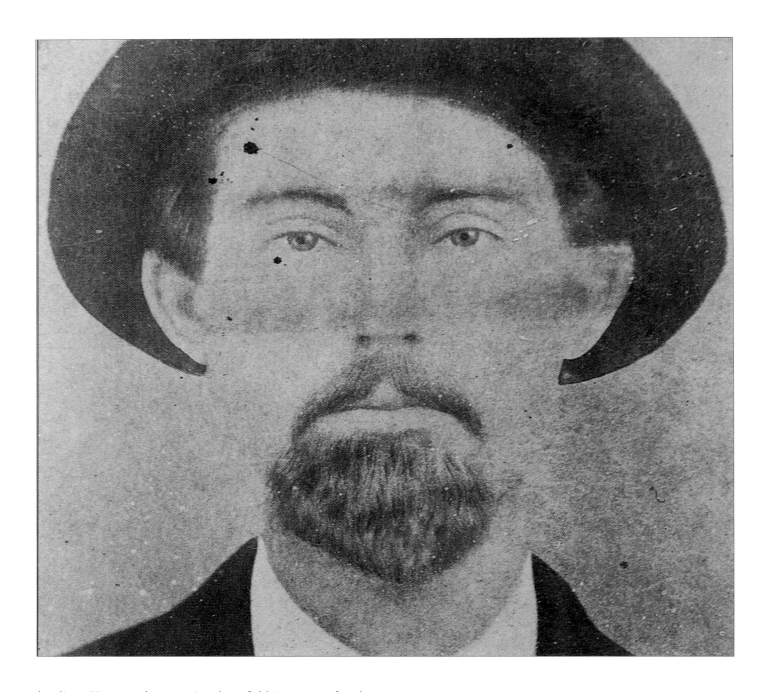

herding. He was also appointed as field inspector for the Wyoming Stock Growers' Association and at this time changed his name to Frank Canton. Canton settled his own ranch in Buffalo, Wyoming, in 1880, and, as a mark of his newfound respectability, between 1882 and 1886 he was even elected sheriff of Johnson County, a position he used to battle against the rustlers.

In 1886 Canton retired from being a sheriff and returned to the association where he again joined the fight against rustlers. It is also reported that he was commissioned a deputy U.S. marshal. Canton joined the cattlemen in the Johnson

**ABOVE: Philip Taylor, known as "Doboy." A veteran of the Texas Revolution of the 1840s, he was very active during the early days of the Sutton-Taylor feud. The son of Creed Taylor, he was murdered in 1871.**

County war, his various legal guises giving a veneer of respectability to some unsavory activities. In the years following the conflict, he was to climb higher up the social and political scales and eventually achieved an enviable reputation as a scourge of outlaws and rustlers.

Perhaps one incident more than any other led to the

RIGHT: James "Jim" Taylor, Wes Hardin's cohort during the Sutton-Taylor feud. It was Jim who shot dead Bill Sutton as Sutton and his wife boarded a steamer. He was finally killed by the Sutton faction in December 1875.

# THE EL PASO
# SALT WAR

Violence among the settlers of the American West was not only caused by land, livestock, and gold. A more unusual catalyst for violence, in the case of the infamous Western town of El Paso, was salt.

El Paso was given its name in 1859, and the community would become known for its regular gunfights and outright lawlessness. One of the town's principal industries was salt mining, there being extensive salt flats to the northeast of the town that covered around three hundred acres. The salt found in the plains was almost 100 percent free from impurities, and local citizens mined it for both personal and commercial use without charge. Citizens from southern New Mexico,

western Texas, and Mexico were all dependent upon the plains for their salt, and so it was inevitable that the area would become the source of territorial dispute.

Problems arose during the late 1860s when a group of Republican leaders began a legal action to claim land rights over the salt plains, the intention being to charge citizens for their access to the salt. The principal figures of the so-called

**ABOVE: Salt was a highly valuable commodity for the people of El Paso. Not only did it have commercial value in its sale, but it was also an important preservative (it was good for preserving meats through the summer heat).**

Salt Ring were Albert J. Fountain, W. W. Mills, Judge Gaylord Judd Clarke, A. H. French, and Ben F. Williams. Fountain subsequently broke away from the Salt Ring when he was elected to the United States Senate, becoming the leader of the "Anti-Salt Ring." The move sparked hostilities among the competing parties, and in true Wild West style violence was quickly forthcoming. On December 7, 1870, Judge Clarke and another man were shot dead during a confrontation in El Paso. Fountain feared that his own life was in danger, and he moved to Mesilla in New Mexico. (Fountain would subsequently be murdered in 1896, his body never being recovered.)

The 1870 shoot-out was just the beginning of the El Paso Salt War. In 1872 the Democratic lawyer Charles Howard made his own move to claim title on the salt plains, using the name of his father-in-law, Major George B. Zimpleman, to make the claim. Initially Howard was supported in his efforts by immigrant businessman Louis Cardis, but the two soon became bitter enemies, especially when Howard attempted to stop public access to the salt lands. Cardis, alongside the priest of San Elizario village, Father Antonio Borrajo, was an advocate for local people's rights to mine the salt, while Howard even went so far as to arrest two men who were determined to continue salt gathering. San Elizario was the main habitation for the salt gatherers, and it soon become the focal point for the war. Howard's actions against the two "illegal" salt gatherers resulted in his house arrest by a riotous mob, his life being bought by a retraction of his legal claim to the land. Howard moved out to Mesilla as Fountain had done before him, from where he plotted his revenge. He personally killed Cardis with a shotgun in a store in El Paso on October 10, 1877.

Now the salt war evolved to an entirely new level. A force of Texas Rangers, incompetently led by one Lieutenant John B. Tays, was assembled to investigate the bloodshed. Although the Rangers were initially tasked with bringing Howard to full legal process over the Cardis killing, they actually became a de facto escort of Howard, and on December 1, 1877, they rode with Howard into San Elizaro. Howard was there to press charges against the "trespassers" who had been collecting salt from "his" land. It was an act of appalling

ABOVE: El Paso is located in the hardest of natural environments in the far western tip of Texas. The area had been explored since the sixteenth century, but only with the arrival of the railroads in the 1880s did El Paso truly become part of the modern world.

provocation, and the citizens of San Elizaro, headed by one Chico Barela, roused themselves into a vengeful mob.

Howard and the Rangers soon found themselves under siege in the town's Ranger quarters. They watched as the mob killed storekeeper Charles Ellis, who was hacked to death in the town square owing to an allegiance with Howard, and the following day Ranger Sergeant C. E. Mortimer was killed by a sniper. After a few more beleaguered days, the Rangers surrendered to the townsfolk, leaving Howard to face his fate. He was led to a local field and shot, then his body was mutilated. Two more of his civilian associates faced the same fate.

Over the next few days, the El Paso valley became a cauldron of violence and score-settling. The town started to empty its civilian inhabitants, as rape and casual killing became commonplace. They headed off across the Rio Grande into Mexico where some built new lives and others awaited normality to return across the border. Only the arrival of a substantial U.S. military force restored some semblance of order in El Paso. The salt war was legally resolved by a congressional investigation, and the contentious chemical became a government property. Ultimately the salt war was as much about personal vendettas as about salt.

Johnson County cattle war: the lynching of Ella Watson (known as "Cattle Kate") and James Averill. Kate hailed from Ontario, Canada, but had moved to Lebanon, Kansas, as a child. As a young woman, she had a failed marriage with William Pickell, a farmer, after which she slipped into a life of prostitution and domestic work. She was reported by the cattle faction to be running a bawdy house in Sweetwater, Wyoming Territory, where she soon established a rapport with the local cowboys. In return for her favors, they paid her with beef. As an extra, she also laundered clothes for them. James Averill, a justice of the peace and her friend and alleged partner in a thriving cattle-rustling business, was himself unpopular with the cattlemen because of his outspoken views. On April 7, 1889, the *Casper Weekly Mail* carried a comment by him to the effect that he regarded the cattlemen as speculators and land grabbers. This remark particularly angered Albert Bothwell, a cattle baron who had laid claim to the land upon which Kate and Averill's properties lay. In July, Bothwell and some friends decided to take the law into their

own hands and dragged Kate and Jim from their homes and hanged them from the same tree, alleging that they were rustlers. Since no attempt was made to prosecute or even question these high-handed actions, anger erupted and matters came to a head—war was declared between the cattlemen and the homesteaders.

The cattlemen then drew up plans to invade the county and wipe out the nesters and cattle-rustlers once and for all. A list of suspects was drawn up, and members of the association were invited to nominate those they thought should be included. It was later alleged that most of the names on the final list were fugitives from justice anyway and that they were wanted in several states, but why it was thought that they were masquerading as homesteaders was

**BELOW: German immigration into the United States peaked during the 1860s and 1870s. The Europeans sought a new life in the States for varied reasons, including freedom from Europe's perennial wars and persecutions and financial opportunity.**

never explained. Neither was it explained who organized a meeting of a large number of known gunfighters in Paris, Texas, with the promise of monetary reward if they would volunteer their services as "Regulators" in Johnson County.

On April 5, 1892, forty-six of these so-called Regulators or invaders (some preferred "vigilantes") assembled in Cheyenne. Fully armed and well provisioned, they (and their horses) were then entrained and headed for Casper. This motley crew was under the command of Canton and Major Frank Wolcott, a pompous individual who saw himself as the leader of an army of retribution. In Casper the force detrained and prepared for action. They had soon located two of the men on their "list," both of whom were killed. But by this time word was out and they soon became the hunted rather than the hunters. Before they were intercepted, the invaders had laid siege to a cabin in which were two of the alleged suspects, Nick Ray and Nate Champion.

Nate Champion was the main target. Born in Williamson County in 1857, Champion was a veteran cowboy who had worked in both Texas and Wyoming. His cattle-rustling reputation came from his appropriation of stray cattle on his land, and it was for this "crime," and the straying of Champion's cattle onto the large ranchers' land, that the big ranchers in the area labeled him "King of the Rustlers." It is debatable whether Champion had committed any crime at all, but this didn't matter to the rival ranchers. To them, Champion was the enemy.

Prior to the 1892 shoot out, Canton had met Champion on a previous occasion. On November 1, 1891, Canton and three other Association men—Joe Elliot, Tom Smith, and Ray Coates—set out to capture Champion on charges of cattle rustling. Their destination was the Powder River in

**BELOW: Preparing to start a new life in the Oklahoma territory. "Unlike Rome, the city of Guthrie was built in a day. To be strictly accurate . . . in an afternoon. At twelve o'clock on Monday, April 22nd, [1889] the population of Guthrie was nothing; before sundown it was at least ten thousand." (Harper's Weekly)**

LEFT: Lynchings were a public event in the West during the nineteenth century and could be used for either summary justice or simply to dispose of enemies. Here, George Tetherell is hanged in the Main Street, Pueblo, Colorado, in 1888. He had previously served sixteen years for murder, but the murder of another man forced the local community to act.

Wyoming, where Champion had a log cabin that he shared with a colleague, Ross Gilbertson. Canton and his gang moved into position surrounding the cabin during the night and waited for daybreak. With the sun up, the Regulators stormed the cabin, bursting through the door to find Champion in his bunk and Gilbertson nearby. The Regulators issued a challenge for the two men to surrender, to which Champion famously replied, "What's the matter then, boys?" Like lightning, Champion then grabbed his revolvers from the side of the bunk. The interior of the cabin saw a ferocious exchange of gunfire at almost point-blank range. Champion received a powder burn to the face, but in return he slightly wounded two of his attackers. Canton and his gang were soon deterred, and they made their escape, although Joe Elliott prevented Champion following the gang by using suppressive gunfire.

Champion evaded death on this occasion, but it was to catch up with him when the Regulators established their siege around the KC ranch on April 9, 1892. Champion was inside the property with Nick Ray and two other men, Bill Walker and Ben Jones. As dawn broke, the men were completely unaware that they were surrounded by around fifty Regulators. Jones went out to get water and was captured, and the same fate befell Walker half an hour later when he went out to see why Jones was taking so long.

The Regulators were not to be so restrained when Ray stepped into the open minutes later. A ripple of gunfire cut him down just outside the door. Badly wounded, he crawled slowly back into the cabin while Champion, now aware of the threat, opened fire from the cabin door to provide cover. Ray made it inside the cabin, but after a couple of hours died of his wounds, despite the efforts of Champion to save him. Champion, meanwhile, continued to fight. For the rest of the morning until midafternoon he held the attackers at bay with pistol fire. Realizing that no progress was being made, Canton and the Regulators decided to force the issue. They commandeered, at gunpoint, a passing wagon and filled it with hay and pitch. The cart was set on fire and pushed up against the cabin to burn Champion out. When Champion could no longer stay put, he burst from the house firing his guns. Champion somehow managed to get fifty yards before

being riddled with bullets (twenty-eight individual bullet impacts were counted on his corpse). After his death, a document came to light which was alleged to have been written by him during the siege, in which he had noted the names of some of his attackers, among them Canton. The whereabouts of that document (if it still exists) is unknown.

When word reached Casper that the invaders had killed Ray and Champion, the sheriff organized a posse and set off in pursuit. He caught up with the band at a ranch some thirteen miles south of Buffalo and surrounded them. In the state capital, Cheyenne, the acting governor was appraised of the situation and promptly ordered the cavalry to intercede before any further bloodshed could make the situation worse. It was demanded that Wolcott and his men should face trial in Buffalo, but instead the cavalry escorted them to Cheyenne. Here, with the help of some high-powered lawyers, they were freed at their trial in January 1893 when no one appeared against them. Rumors were rife that anyone foolish enough to offer testimony would simply "disappear."

The outcome of that trial split the state for years, but it did break the power of the barons, many of whom were bankrupted both by the cost of the invasion and legal fees. The federal government, anxious to contain the situation still further, sent in deputy U.S. marshals to tackle the rustlers ,and eventually a semblance of peace was restored. But resentment and distrust continued to simmer on both sides for years.

Ironically, it was Nate Champion, alleged rustler who withstood a twelve-hour siege against nearly fifty gunmen, who is remembered by people with respect and admiration. As for Wolcott and Canton, the architects of the whole fiasco, they were regarded as craven cowards. Yet this incident did not stop Canton from going on to pastures new within the law and business. In 1893 he and his family (he had married in 1885 and had two daughters) moved away from Johnson County to Nebraska, where he worked for the Nebraska City Packing Company. The life of commerce was not suited to Canton's personality type, and he took up the post of deputy U.S. marshal in Oklahoma Territory. In this role he was soon back in action again. For example, in 1893 in Pawnee, Texas, Canton and Deputy Sheriff George Hanner were caught up in a brawl with local hard man Lon McCool following the arrest of one of McCool's associates for murder. McCool took the inadvisable option of hitting Canton, whereupon Canton pulled out a .44 Derringer and shot McCool through the head (McCool remarkably survived).

Two years later, during actions against Oklahoma's outlaw gangs, Canton was part of a posse charged with arresting two men, Bill and John Shelley, who had broken out of jail and were on the run. They were tracked down to a cabin on the Arkansas River, a chase conducted through a bitter winter snowstorm, and in a daylong siege over eight hundred rounds were fired at the cabin in an attempt to gain the brothers' surrender. In the end, Canton reapplied the burning cart technique he had used against Nate Champion, although this time the fire simply flushed the brothers out to be arrested rather than gunned down.

Canton's law-enforcing activities may have increased his social standing, but they also gained him many enemies. On November 6, 1896, one of those enemies, gunman Bill Dunn, stopped Canton on the boardwalk outside Pawnee Courthouse. Dunn informed Canton, "I've got it in for you," and went to draw his gun. Unfortunately for Dunn, he should have gone for his weapon first instead of delivering an address, as Canton managed to pull his .45 from his waistband and shot Dunn through the forehead, killing him instantly.

Canton stayed restless for the remainder of his life. In 1897 he became a deputy U.S. marshal in Alaska, where he tackled criminal individuals and gangs in a hard wilderness for a period of two years. After becoming snow-blind, he returned to Oklahoma, this time as sheriff of Comanche county. In the twentieth century, he became adjutant general in the Oklahoma National Guard from 1907. Having lived an unusually full and morally questionable life, Jo Horner/Frank Canton died in 1927.

## The Blood Feud

The range feud may command more publicity and lend itself to folklore, but family and personal disputes that became feuds were every bit as dangerous and damaging both to individuals and communities alike. In his classic *I'll Die Before I Run,* C. L. Sonnichsen pointed out that feuds took all manner of forms from "blood" to "vendettas" among rivals. They often started over trifling misunderstandings or over something really serious like a killing. And as generation followed generation, the reasons were often forgotten, but the "feud" existed simply because it was a tradition.

Texas was a hotbed of "feudists," and their activities could be traced back as far as the time white folks settled into the region in the 1820s. But it was in later years that the more memorable clashes took place. In the 1840s there was a particularly vicious encounter between Charles W. Jackson and Joseph Goodbread, in the hills along the Sabine River. Dr. Sonnichsen noted that the region had long been a no-man's land where innumerable counterfeiters, horse-thieves, "nigger-stealers," and others congregated and prospered. Jackson determined to expose this den of thieves, and when he killed Goodbread the deceased's friends decided to take action. Jackson promptly organized a band of "Regulators" who set to work on the transgressors with a vengeance. They were so successful that the outlaws organized a band of Moderators in opposition. For four years, both sides hounded each other; crops were ruined, families bereaved, and in general it was mayhem. Finally, Sam Houston himself put a stop to it. The aging president of the Republic of Texas called in the militia and with their backing forced the warring factions to surrender and disperse.

Closer to the typical "Wild West" feud beloved of novelists and filmmakers was Texas's classic interfamily fracas between the Suttons and the Taylors. It is made more interesting because John Wesley Hardin, the most homicidal of Texas's gunfighters, took an active part on the side of the Taylors. DeWitt County, the center of the Sutton-Taylor feud, was situated about halfway between San Antonio and the Gulf Coast, its predominant economy centered upon cattle. The abundance of cattle following the end of the Civil War and a

**RIGHT: The Texas Rangers had been so ruthless and lethal in the Mexican War that the fearful populace called them "los diablos Tejanos." Here they are armed with the ubiquitous Colt revolvers and Winchester rifles.**

shortage of labor led to difficulties with the erstwhile Negro slaves, who were largely unemployed and wandered the countryside in search of work. When asked to work they were inclined to demand rates far higher than the norm. Worse, many of them were armed, dangerous, and "insulting their former masters." And the Union army did not help. They tended to take the sides of the former slaves, which did not endear them to the white population, especially when they also liked to disarm anyone they wished, regardless of their reasons for carrying weapons. However, a crop failure and an abundance of cattle inspired rustling, and many of those animals found themselves on the long march to the Kansas cow towns.

The Sutton-Taylor feud got off to a blazing start when Billy Sutton killed a horse-thief named Charles Taylor whom, the Taylors later protested, "weren't no kin of our'n." But later, in 1880, it was grudgingly admitted that he had been a "distant relative." There then occurred another and much more provocative incident: Buck Taylor, the son of William R. Taylor, was killed. Many considered him the leader of his particular part of the clan and feared the worst.

Buck's demise came about on Christmas Eve 1868 when a large party was planned in Clinton. During the evening there were sounds of shots and, as people rushed into the area near the courthouse, men were seen streaming out of a saloon. Word spread that the fight started because Buck had accused

Billy Sutton of being involved with some recently stolen stock. When Billy suggested that they step in to the street and settle it, Buck readily agreed and stalked out of the saloon where ambushers opened up on him from the darkness. Hearing the shots, Dick Chisholm, an innocent bystander, rushed from the saloon and was also cut down in the crossfire.

Later reports claimed that the feud started long before both families even ventured into the area, but they were dismissed as hearsay. By 1874, however, the killings were mounting and attracting statewide attention. When John Wesley Hardin aligned himself with the Taylors, things really heated up. In July 1873, Wes had a run-in with Jack Helm, sheriff of

DeWitt County, and believed by most people to be a shining light in the Sutton faction. Hardin claimed that Helm's gang, which included Bill Sutton, had murdered a number of men. Helm had also made an enemy of Hardin. When Helm tried to shoot Jim Taylor, he reckoned without Wes, who promptly blasted him with a shotgun. Jim Taylor then finished him off with his six-shooter. Wes, adept at finding excuses for his actions, wrote, "I received many letters of thanks from the widows of the men whom he had cruelly put to death. Many of the best citizens of Gonzales and DeWitt counties patted me on the back and told me that was the best act of my life." Hardin's role in the feud is not easily defined, but some claim that a large number of his alleged "forty notches" were for killings in the feud. As it was, he was related to the Taylors by marriage, which would explain a lot.

In his autobiography, Hardin devotes a lot of space to the Sutton-Taylor feud and imparts the impression that he masterminded some of the action. "In April 1874, Bill Sutton prepared a herd for market at Wichita, and planned on setting out by rail to await its arrival. We had often tried to catch him, but he was so wily that he always eluded us," Wes recalled. "Jim Taylor had shot him and broken his arm in a saloon in Cuero. He had a horse killed under him in a fight on the prairie below Cuero and he had another killed while crossing the river below there. He was looked upon as hard to catch, and I had made futile efforts to get him myself. I had even gone down to his home at Victoria, but did not get him."

Hardin informed his brothers and friends that "Bill Sutton was my deadly enemy" and advised them that he understood he was to go to Kansas via New Orleans, but if they could get to him before he left Indianola, "I could tell Jim Taylor to go at once to Indianola to kill him, as it was a life or death case whenever either I or Jim Taylor met him." Word filtered back that Sutton, his wife, and one Gabriel "Gabe" Slaughter had boarded the steamer *Clinton*; close behind them were Jim

**LEFT: A long shot of Tombstone, Arizona. "The Town too Tough to Die," Tombstone was the scene of several major feuds, most famously between the Earp brothers and their longstanding enemies the McClaury and Clanton brothers.**

356      FRANK LESLIE'S ILLUSTRATED NEWSPAPER.      [JANUARY 22, 1881.

COLUMBIA WELCOMES THE VICTIMS OF GERMAN PERSECUTION TO "THE ASYLUM OF THE OPPRESSED."

A. T. Stewart & Co. | THE "LONGFELLOW JUG." | THE SUN for 1881.
Will offer during the next        Everybody reads THE SUN. In the editions of this

**LEFT: Columbia welcomes the Jewish victims of German persecution to "the asylum of the oppressed," an engraving in *Frank Leslie's Illustrated Newspaper*, January 22, 1881. A few years earlier, the welcome was not so warm, as the Anglo-Texans resented the newcomers' taking advantage of the Fisher-Miller Land Grant.**

and Billy Taylor. Within minutes the shooting had started, and Jim Taylor shot Sutton through the head, while Billy took care of Gabe. In the middle of the confusion, the pair ran down the gangplank and headed for the cattle pens where friends had horses waiting for them. Minutes later they were riding hard for Cuero, which was about sixty miles from Indianola. Mrs. Sutton, who was pregnant, took charge of Bill's body and had it shipped home to Victoria, where she gave birth to her child, raised it, and survived to a very great age, embittered not only by her husband's violent death but by the fact that she and other innocents had been as much a victim as the feudists themselves.

The Sutton-Taylor feud persisted long after Hardin's involvement ceased, and by the time it was generally agreed to be over (some thirty years later), most of the original participants were long dead. As time passes, such blood feuds as this dissolve into insignificance, but their importance on the broad canvas of the West cannot be discounted.

### Spiraling Feuds

In many cases feuds began over a single issue, but they would quickly spiral out into complex conflicts mixing issues of politics, ethnicity, blood vengeance, livestock, and land. One of the most famous, and convoluted, of these feuds was the

Mason County war of the mid-1870s, also known as the "Hoodoo" war ("Hoodoo" was a local term for bad luck).

The roots of the Mason County war actually lay in patterns of immigration into Texas during the first decades of the nineteenth century. Germans formed one of the major immigrant ethnic groups into the area.

By the thousands, the Germans settled communities on and beyond the frontier, taking advantage of the free land established between the Llano and Colorado Rivers by the Fisher-Miller Land Grant. The land grant and the presence of the Germans attracted much hostility from the Anglo-Texans, despite the fact that most of the German settlements did not initially infringe on Anglo-Texan territorial ambitions. The situation was soon to change. The Land Grant was eventually repealed and during the 1840s, Anglo-Texan settlers flooding into the area were dismayed to find that much premium land had already been claimed by the immigrants.

The Germans were in a vulnerable situation not helped by their generally Federal loyalties in an area that, during the Civil War, would be staunchly Confederate. Persecution of the Germans became violent during the four years of conflict. For example, on August 10, 1862, a total of thirty-two Germans were killed and nine wounded out of a party of immigrant men attempting to flee to Mexico to avoid conscription into the Confederate army. The war ended in 1865; the hostilities remained. In fact, the animosity was strengthened by claims and counterclaims of cattle rustling that flew between the two social groups. The German immigrants were indeed particularly hard hit by rustling. Their herds tended to be smaller than those of the Anglo-Texans (the immigrants were often more reliant upon crop foods), and few were able to afford substantial fencing. Furthermore, the huge influx of outlaws and degenerates into Texas in the aftermath of the Civil War created a whole new subclass for whom rustling was a way of life.

Mason County was dominated by German officials, and in 1872 a man named John Clark was elected Sheriff and one Dan Hoester was made the County Brands Inspector. The Brands Inspector had a particularly difficult job. Cattle rustlers would stamp wandering unbranded cattle (usually young calves) as their own or take cattle and modify the stamp to make it appear as their own. Both men, however, were tough individuals, and they set out with determination to clamp down on the rustlers.

In February 1875 the Mason County authorities sent a posse to examine cattle held on ranches to the northwest of Mason. Led by John Clark, the posse found many branding anomalies in the cattle "owned" by the brothers Pete and Linge Baccus. Seven men in total were arrested and taken back to Mason for trial. However, the people of the town, whose blood had been raised over cattle rustling during the preceding years, had other plans for the men.

On the evening of February 18, Deputy John Worhle was at home when a gang of men broke in and forced him to give them the jailhouse keys. The gang gained access to the prison and began dragging the prisoners out for summary justice. John Clark and a local Texas Rangers officer, Captain Dan Roberts, were quickly on the scene but were unable to control a large crowd of vigilantes, who managed to escape out of town on horseback with five of the prisoners.

About half a mile out of town, the vigilantes began to hang the prisoners. As they did so, Clark, Roberts, and a large party of Rangers arrived. There was chaos and gunshots, and the vigilantes dispersed into the night. Four of the prisoners were hanged, and two, Pete and Linge Baccus, were already dead.

The two other hanged men, Aber Wiggins and Tom Turley, were cut down still alive. Wiggins, however, had also been shot in the head and he died of his injuries the following day. One of the men, Charlie Johnson, actually managed to make his escape.

Having nearly been killed did not buy Turley clemency, and he remained imprisoned for cattle rustling. There was now injected an element of infighting into the escalating situation. Tom Gamel, a member of the Clark posse, began suggesting that the lynching was actually sanctioned by members of Clark's team, something that Gamel had wanted nothing to do with.

The accusations brought threats down on Gamel, and there were even some rumors that he, Turley, and another detained cattle rustler, Calb Hall, would soon be the targets are another lynch mob. In terror, Hall and Turley escaped from jail and left the area entirely. Gamel, however, went to face down Clark, backed by cowboys, all heavily armed. Clark, probably wisely, left Mason as the Gamel gang rode into town, but he returned quickly with his own posse of sixty men. What could have been a bloodbath was averted by negotiation and a truce, besides agreeing that due legal process would have to take place before any more executions.

Violence would return to the Mason County war from another direction. The man whose death would kick-start the killing was Tim Williamson, a thirty-three-year-old cowboy who had been arrested for cattle theft.

Williamson, who worked a large local ranch owned by Carl Lehmberg in Llano County, had been released on bail. However, Clark later turned up at his home with an order to collect unpaid taxes (Clark was the county tax collector and had placed Williamson's home in an unrealistically high tax category). Williamson was not at home, so his wife was threatened instead. This incensed Williamson, and he confronted and verbally challenged Clark.

On May 13, Wohrle rode to Lehmberg's ranch and informed Williamson that he was to be taken back into custody and that he would have to ride immediately with him back to Mason. Lehmberg said he would go with them, offering to pay the bail once they arrived at the jailhouse. However, roughly ten miles from the ranch the three men were ambushed by a large group of masked men. Williamson had his horse shot from beneath him, and he was killed on the spot; Worhle and Lehmberg managed to escape. Williamson was reportedly killed by Peter Bader, one of the immigrant farmers.

Mason County now became a place of violence and fear. The Anglo-Texan community were incensed by the Williamson killing. Furthermore, no one was brought to trial over the murder, so the Anglo-Texans began to take matters into their own hands. Three German men were ambushed around their campfire at night near Willow Creek, one being injured and another later dying of gunshot wounds. Shootings became commonplace, and people on both sides had to travel in groups for their own protection.

## Enter Scott Cooley

In early August 1875, with the Mason County war seemingly at its height, an individual named Scott Cooley rode into Mason. Cooley was a tough cowboy with a lively and checkered past. He worked on the frontier most of his life and had even been a Texas Ranger. After he left the Rangers, he worked as a cowboy and ran herds up to Kansas for a man with whom he was a close personal friend. That man's name was Tim Williamson. Cooley and Williamson had been friends since they were children, with Williamson's mother helping the young Cooley recover from typhoid fever.

In Mason, Cooley made several discreet inquiries. On August 10, Wohrle and another man were digging a well in the west of the town. Cooley rode up to Worhle as his helper,

named Harcourt, was at the bottom of the well. They talked amicably for a few minutes, and Worhle even gave Cooley a leather thong to help bind his rifle holster to his saddle. Then Worhle turned back to his work, pulling Harcourt up from the bottom of the well with a rope. At that moment Cooley drew his pistol and blasted Worhle in the back of the head. Worhle died instantly, and Harcourt fell to the bottom of the well and was injured. Cooley took total vengeance by getting off his horse and emptying his revolver into Worhle's body, then scalping him with a knife. He rode off, but Cooley's reign of terror was only just beginning.

After killing Worhle, Cooley gathered around himself a group of unpleasant hard men. These included gunman George Gladden, tough cowboys Moses and John Baird, and

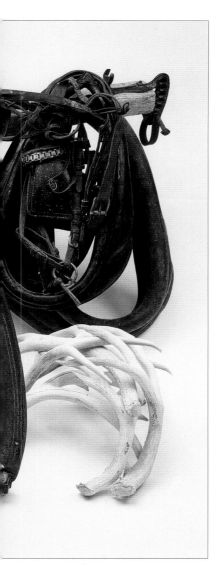

LEFT: In the twenty years after the Civil War, more land became cultivated than in the previous 250 years. This feat was accomplished by farmers who faced not only bitter cold, intense heat, flood, and droughts, and huge swarms of locusts but also the animosity of the cattlemen. The invention of barbed wire in 1874 by Illinois farmer Joseph F. Glidden accelerated the closing of the open range. This collection of "sodbuster's" equipment includes a bow-saw, tightened by twisting rawhide, an iron-bladed plow, and a mule headstall and collars.

the notorious Johnny Ringo. Ringo was a particularly brutal addition to Cooley's gang. Details about Ringo's past are hard to come by. He is thought to have been born in the 1850s in Ringoes, New Jersey, or possibly in Missouri. Although a well-read and likeable man, Ringo was prone to drinking and was quick to use a gun to solve his problems.

Cooley and his gang soon set about terrorizing Mason County, and they became very assured of their position. In one saloon the bartender asked Cooley for payment and was presented instead with Worhle's scalp. Needless to say, drinks were on the house. There was also the matter of Peter Bader left undone. On August 19, Cooley and his men went to the Bader farm in Llano County. There they found Carl Bader, Peter's brother, working in a field. Whether they mistook his identity or whether they felt he was a suitable surrogate for Peter is not known, but Carl was gunned down in the field where he stood.

Back in Mason, news of the killing galvanized Clark and his men into action. Clark used a gambler named Jim Cheney to arrange for George Gladden and Moses Baird to come to Mason, the intention being to launch an ambush on them. Near Keller's store east of Mason, Gladden and Baird were shot down. Baird died instantly of gunshot wounds, while Gladden was critically wounded.

Mason was now in a state of virtual civil war, and the newspapers were full of very public concern that their society was degenerating into anarchy. A petition was sent to Governor Coke requesting that state forces be deployed to protect the citizens. In September 1875, a company of the Frontier Ranger Battalion, commanded by Major John B. Jones, arrived in Mason. Their arrival, however, did not immediately stop the steady escalation of violence. On September 24, Ringo and associates had gone to the home of Jim Cheney. Cheney had been implicated in the Keller Store ambush, but he did not know the extent of Ringo's knowledge. Cheney invited both men into his home for breakfast. After breakfast, while Cheney was shaving, Ringo shot him through the head.

The same day, Cooley was also out looking to settle old scores. He had ridden to Mason with a small gang to confront Irish store owner David Doole, a man who openly traded with the German immigrants. Doole confronted Cooley from inside his store with a rifle, so Cooley and his men instead went to sit in Tom Gamel's saloon. While there, they saw three prominent Germans—Dan Hoester (the County Brands Inspector), Peter Jordan (Hoester's brother-in-law), and Henry Pluenneke—riding up the main street toward the saloon. Cooley and his men left the back of the saloon to prepare an ambush. As the three Germans rode in front of a barbershop, they suddenly came under the heavy rifle, shotgun, and pistol fire. Hoester was struck by a shotgun blast and killed, while Jordan and Pluenneke managed to escape across the street and return fire.

Cooley and his men rode out of town, and shortly afterwards Major Jones and his soldiers arrived in Mason and attempted to impose some order. They sent out a posse after Cooley and managed to capture Bill Coke, one of the men who had been involved with the Hoester killing. Coke subsequently disappeared and it is likely that either the soldiers or the mob killed him. More murders occurred, and Jones found himself quite unable to impose any framework of law on the anarchic county. Furthermore, he was facing some internal problems. It appeared that some of his Rangers were less than committed in their pursuit of Cooley; Cooley had, after all, been a Ranger himself, and many of Jones' men had a scarcely concealed hostility for the Germans.

However, in December 1875, Ringo and Cooley were finally captured by Sheriff A. J. Strickland in Burnet County, and the Rangers started to make progress on apprehending other outlaws. It was the beginning of the end for the Mason County war, although there were still killings to come. In

**BELOW: On July 14, 1882, the notorious John Peters Ringo was found by teamster John Yoast, dead, leaning against a tree outside the town of Galeyville, a .45 Colt in his hand. The coroner's verdict was suicide. Ringo died with his boots off, strips of an undershirt wrapped around his feet.**

January 1876, Gladden and John Baird killed Peter Bader—the two men ambushed him on the road between Llano and Castell and shot him dead without mercy.

The key figures of the Mason County war subsequently either disappeared or met appropriate sticky ends. Sheriff John Clark left Mason County after having been indicted over the disappearance of Bill Coke. Scott Cooley and Johnny Ringo both escaped from jail and returned to cattle rustling. In 1876, Cooley died of illness at the age of twenty-

**BELOW: Eventually the cowboys on the open range would be beaten by market forces. By the early 1870s, wheat and alfalfa crops were actually more profitable than ranching. By 1899, California was the largest producer of grapes, and the turn of the century saw steam power turn barren plains into granaries.**

one, his body buried in Blanco County. George Gladden and Johnny Ringo were both captured in November 1876 and charged with murder. Gladden received a ninety-nine-year prison sentence but was released in 1884. Johnny Ringo was acquitted. Yet on July 14, 1882, Ringo was found with a bullet hole through his head in Morse's Canyon. Although some theorized that the gunman Buckskin Frank Leslie had shot him, others felt that the position of the body—propped against a tree—suggested that Ringo had killed himself, haunted to suicide by a life of violent deeds.

Those who lived either among feudists or were indirectly affected by their activities must have existed in a nightmare world, never knowing if or when they would become embroiled in the conflict. It was a time for silence—better a silence of the tongue than the deathly stillness of the grave.

# BUFFALO BILL'S
# WILD WEST SHOW

Buffalo Bill's Wild West Show was an important ingredient in the mythologizing of Western history and in the subsequent hero worship given to the cowboy figure. It should be remembered that for much of the nineteenth century, the term "cowboy" had negative connotations, suggesting someone rough in manners and slippery in morals. The Wild West Show replaced this character with a rugged but noble frontiersman, risking his life among romantic landscapes and against terrible enemies.

In the early 1870s, William F. "Buffalo Bill" Cody was well on his way to immortalization through Ned Buntline's dime novel representations of his life. Buntline extended his

ABOVE: Buffalo Bill's Wild West Show provided an amazing spectacle for the public, as is evident from this photograph of Indian cast members. William Cody served as a prairie scout during the Indian Wars.

ABOVE: William Frederick Cody was born in Iowa in 1846 and was given his "Buffalo Bill" nickname when he was twenty-two— he supplied buffalo meat to Kansas City Railroad workers. In 1872 he won the Congressional Medal of Honor for military service.

repertoire by writing a drama entitled *The Scouts of the Prairie,* in which Cody played himself. Cody appeared on stage in New York on December 17, 1872, and in general the play was well received, although one critic commented that Cody was "ridiculous as an actor." The negative review didn't put Cody off an acting career, and he subsequently gathered

himself and several other Western extroverts into the Buffalo Bill Combination troupe.

The Buffalo Bill Combination performed Wild West–themed stage plays until 1882. The shows presented sketches of Western life and highly dramatized accounts of the battles that took the West from the Native Americans. In 1882, Cody created the Wild West, Rocky Mountain, and Prairie Exhibition, but this unwieldy title mutated into the Wild West Show in 1883. The show relied not on actors but on genuine cowboys and Western figures recruited from ranches. Using horses, wagons, buffalo, and dozens of Native American actors, they re-created the Western experience, presenting everything from cattle drives to the Battle of Little Big Horn. The show was a spectacular, and it gained an international reputation. In 1887 it even crossed the Atlantic and was a headline feature of Queen Victoria's Golden Jubilee celebrations. (Cody would make a subsequent European tour in 1889.)

Cody was not the only star of show. Annie Moses—better known to history as Annie Oakley—stunned audiences with her sharpshooting skills. She was nicknamed "Little Sure Shot" by one of the show's other leading characters, the Lakota Sioux Chief Sitting Bull. Cody's relationship with the Indian cast members has attracted controversy and debate. On the one hand, in the battle scenes the Indians were shown ultimately as defeated peoples. In one show scene Cody himself would ride into a battle and take an Indian scalp, pronouncing it as vengeance for the killing of Custer (the Indian called Rains in the Face, possibly the man who killed Custer, actually starred in Cody's shows). But Cody was also known for his respectful treatment of the Indian cast and even went on record to accept that the killing of Custer and his men was the natural act of warriors protecting their people.

Buffalo Bill's Wild West Show ran on into the early twentieth century, the most famous of the many Western shows running in competition. However, the market for Western themes declined during the early 1900s, and in 1909 financial pressures forced Cody to merge the show with that of a competitor, Pawnee Bill.

Finally, in 1915, Cody's long-running theatrical venture went into bankruptcy. By this time, however, Cody had done the groundwork for the veneration of the cowboy seen in future generations.

**LEFT:** Buffalo Bill had a strong sense of the theatrical, but he also became an important voice for political causes. He vigorously opposed exploitation of Indians, women, and America's shrinking buffalo herds.

**RIGHT:** The figure whose exploits and death inspired one of Buffalo Bill's most successful reenactments, the Battle of the Little Big Horn, George Armstrong Custer was as theatrical and publicity-hungry as Buffalo Bill himself—though Custer's courage, arrogance, and savagery were real enough.

# Chapter Three

## HARD LIVES, TOUGH TOWNS:

# THE AGE OF THE COWBOY

Overall was the ever-present odor of cattle, bellowing their protests as they were driven from pen to freight car, the shriek of locomotive whistles, and the eternal crash of shunting cattle trucks moving into or out of the yards. Only when darkness fell did other noises replace the daylight din.

LEFT: Wichita was the archetypal cow town. It was founded in 1864, its creation spurred by the run of the Chisholm cattle trail and the development of nearby railheads. By 1872, Wichita was a cattle shipping center, and so it was regularly filled with a through-traffic of cowboys—some good, some bad.

# THE COW-TOWN ERA

The end of the Civil War and the period before Reconstruction, when the Union army would impose itself upon the defeated South, witnessed a depression. In the North, where its machine-orientated economy had dictated the outcome of the war and where thousands had been employed in the war effort, there was a sudden halt. Manufacturers found themselves with a surplus of war goods, and even the government had difficulty in disposing of them. Unemployment was rife, while in the South many people faced starvation. It was then that eyes turned toward Texas, where before the war cattle raising and marketing were thriving businesses.

Andalusian cattle were introduced into the New World by Cortez, and by the early nineteenth century their descendants were spread all over what was to become Texas and parts of Mexico. Cortez also introduced the horse in 1540, and they, too, abounded.

The Spanish influence was to continue and with it the traditional *vaquero* or cowboy. There was an influx of white settlers into Texas in the 1820s who brought with them cattle and other livestock, which led to interbreeding. By the fall of the Alamo in 1836, there were an estimated 100,000 head of cattle running wild during the battles that led to independence from Mexico.

Although the "Texians" were to acquire the knowledge and skills associated with the cattle business, they grudgingly admitted that they learned much of it from the "Mexican greasers," who in turn lost no time in reminding the "gringos" that they had been there first. The origin of the word "cowboy" is disputed. Some claim that it can be traced back to the American Revolution when loyalist or Tory fighters in New York's Westchester County stole the cows of patriots. It has even been suggested that the notorious Stamp Act and Anti-Rent Rebellion in 1766 fostered the term when Dutch colonists called their rebellious tenants "cowboys."

Early pre–Civil War drives took cattle to as far away as New York State, where their meat was considered inferior to existing local stock. Some herds were driven west to California, and others due north to Missouri. The existence of "Texas fever," caused by a tick carried by the longhorn cattle, aroused much concern. The Texas cattle were immune to it, but domestic cattle that came in contact with the herds were at risk. In 1868, the English scientist John Gamgee was

persuaded to come to the United States, where he diagnosed the problem and suggested a solution, by which time a number of Texans had suffered at the hands of ex-guerrillas and Jayhawkers in reprisal for the loss of stock.

The outbreak of the Civil War brought the drives to a halt along the Shawnee Trail, established by Texans to Kansas City. In 1866 the drives were resumed as far as Baxter Springs, Kansas, on the border with Missouri, or on to Sedalia, where the Missouri Pacific Railroad could transport them east. But

trouble with Indians, ex-Jayhawkers, and others brought this venture to a halt. That same year Charles Goodnight and Oliver Loving managed to get a herd as far as Fort Sumner and on to Colorado. Loving died soon afterward following

**BELOW: Abilene, looking south from Third and Cedar Streets, about 1882. Its rip-roaring cattle-driving days behind it, the place had now settled into a peaceful existence, farmers and others having replaced the cowboys, gunfighters, and other frontier "types."**

infection from a wound caused when a band of Comanches attacked him, but Goodnight survived to become one of the richest of all cattlemen. Tired of Indian attacks and local disputes, the Texas cattlemen reckoned that a direct route north with a railroad link to the East would be their salvation. So began the era of the cow towns.

The cow town has a mystique all of its own. The word conjures up a vision of dusty streets, false-fronted buildings, hitching posts, cattle pens, railroad tracks, and innumerable mounted cowboys. Purists will argue that the correct term was "cattle town."

In *The Cattle Towns*, Robert Dykstra made the point that no self-respecting shipping point would call itself a "cow town"—a somewhat derogatory term that appeared in the mid-1880s. But cow town has a romanticism that the more formal "cattle town" lacks, which may explain why cow town prevails.

Early in 1867, Joseph G. McCoy, a partner in the firm of

William K. McCoy and brothers, conceived the idea of establishing a cattle trade with the Texans. He had learned of the large herds running wild in Texas from Charles Gross, a former Union army telegrapher who had seen them personally. The problem was how to get them to market.

Following a number of setbacks with the presidents of various railroads, McCoy finally persuaded the Union Pacific Railway Company (Eastern Division) building west across Kansas to construct a switch or siding at a little place called Abilene. He then purchased land and built huge shipping and holding pens. Word was then sent down the trail to Texas to drive the herds north to the railhead at Abilene.

**BELOW: A group of cowboys take a rest during the roundup of cattle near Lone Cone, Colorado, in 1884. The era of open-range cattle farming declined two years later, caused by new federal land laws, overgrazed trail pastures, and a drop in the price of beef.**

RIGHT: Charles Goodnight who, in 1866 in partnership with Oliver Loving, blazed the Goodnight-Loving trail to Fort Sumner and on to Colorado. Goodnight's tough, almost aristocratic features say it all.

LEFT: Jesse Chisholm, photographed shortly before his death. The original was a tintype that was copied by the Leavenworth photographer E. E. Henry. Jesse's trail is legendary.

Although Kansas had a quarantine law in force, there were so few settlers in the region that there was little opposition to the trade, especially when it was learned that McCoy had convinced the governor of the state that the trade would be good for the economy. Handbills were printed and distributed, and a route was decided upon. This followed a trail established between Texas and Wichita by a mixed-race trader named Jesse Chisholm.

The "Chisholm trail" ran from the tip of Texas right up through Austin, Waco, and on to the Nations or Indian Territory, which is now Oklahoma, and on to Wichita, where it ended officially.

From there, the trail to Abilene was known either as "McCoy's Extension," or the "Abilene Trail." The first herd of cattle reached Abilene late in August, and on September 5 a twenty-car train loaded with longhorns left for Chicago. Abilene, the first of the Kansas cow towns, was in business, and for four years it would be the focus of attention and the scene of cowboy violence.

Many of the men who drove the cattle up the trails from Texas in the immediate postwar years were inexperienced. Among them were returned veterans of the late war, some totally "unreconstructed" in their attitudes. *The Kansas Daily Commonwealth* of August 15, 1871, described the typical cowboy as "unlearned and illiterate, with few wants and meager ambition," who seemed content to live on a "diet of Navy plug and whisky." His principal vice was gambling, and wherever he went he sported a pair of revolvers, "which he will use with as little hesitation on a man as on a wild animal. Such a character is dangerous and desperate, and each one generally has killed his man. There are good and even honorable men among them, but run-away boys and men

ABOVE RIGHT: The Kansas Pacific Railway issued several editions of this guide to the Texas cattle trails in which they included detailed and vital information on grass and and water locations and a map of the trail.

K. P. DEAD LINE.

KANSAS PACIFIC RAILWAY,

THE OLD ESTABLISHED AND POPULAR

**Texas Stock Route**

GRAZING GOOD, WATER PLENTIFUL. SHIP-PING FACILITIES PERFECT, YARDS FREE, RATES LOW.

2 Fast Stock Express Trains Daily from Ellis, Russell, Ellsworth, Brookville, Salina, Solomon and

**ABILENE TO**

**KANSAS CITY** & **LEAVENWORTH**

Connecting with the following Roads :

ST. LOUIS, KANSAS CITY & NORTHERN; MISSOURI PACIFIC; CHICAGO, ALTON & ST. LOUIS; CHICAGO & ROCK ISLAND; TOLEDO, WABASH & WESTERN; HANNIBAL & ST. JOSEPH, AND KANSAS CITY, ST JOE & COUNCIL BLUFFS.

The only route by which Shippers have the choice of all the following Markets :

Denver, Colorado, Russell, Ellsworth, Leavenworth, Kansas City, Quincy, St. Louis and Chicago.

Drive to the KANSAS PACIFIC RAILWAY, and avoid hauls over new roads of 300 and 400 miles without transfer or rest.

**Edmund S. Bowen,**
Gen'l Supt

T. F. OAKES, Gen'l Freight Agt.,
KANSAS CITY, MO.

CATTLE DROVERS, NOTE LOCATION OF

AND GOVERN YOURSELVES ACCORDINGLY.

who find it too hot for them even in Texas join the cattle drovers and constitute a large proportion of them. They drink, swear, and fight, and life with them is a round of boisterous gaiety and indulgence in sensual pleasure."

It was this view of the cowboy that remained uppermost in the minds of the public. To them he was a ne'er-do-well. And as late as 1896, the cowboy's penchant for the pistol was noted in an amusing comment in the Oberlin, Kansas, *Herald* of March 5, which reported that cowboys in Arizona, on waking in the morning, invariably shot at each other to "increase the circulation of the blood." However, one of them, it was noted, "shot himself in the foot."

Similarly, the cowboy had his own lingo, as explained by the Garden City, Kansas, *Finney County Democrat* of March 26, 1887:

The cowboys have a language intelligible only to the initiated. They call a horse herder a "horse wrangler," and a horse-breaker a "broncho buster." Their steed is often a "cayuse," and to dress well is to "rag proper." When a cowboy goes out on the prairie he "hits the flat." Whisky is "family disturbance," and to eat is to "chew." His hat is a "cady," his whip a "quirt," his rubber coat a "slicker," his leather overalls are "chaps" or "chapperals," and his revolver is a ".45." Bacon is "overland trout" and unbranded cattle are "mavericks."

Anticowboy feeling was by no means confined to Kansas. Back in Texas, the editor of the *Denton Monitor* had pointed out that the addition of Mexican spurs, six-shooters, and pipes only inspired the young men toward a career of thievery, when they should be encouraged to stay home and learn a trade. As it turned out, they did learn the hard way how to handle half-wild and totally unpredictable longhorn cattle. As for those who had survived the horrors of the late war, the indignity and shame of defeat made them understandably resentful of the so-called Northern or Yankee involvement in the cattle business. Yet they accepted their lot in much the same manner as they had survived the long years of war when food was scarce, clothing became rags, and only a blind faith in the fight for "Southern rights" kept them going. Ironically, in their new role they fared little better. Poor food and all-weather existence for an average wage of thirty dollars a month only added to their frustration. Many of them also succumbed to disease and suffered from rheumatic problems. In later life, hernias and slipped disks were common. One old-time cowboy told this writer that "hanging three pounds of loaded Colt and a belt full of cartridges around my hips did not help much either!" So much for the romantic outdoor life of the cowboy on the trail.

On the trail itself, most of the Texans managed to control their prejudices against the Mexicans and the African Americans who also rode the cattle trails. Philip C. Durham and Everett L. Jones state in their book, *The Negro Cowboys*, that according to available figures, an estimated 35,000 cowboys followed the herds north between 1868 and 1895, and "about one-third were negroes and Mexicans." They concluded that the Mexicans, although better vaqueros, were bitterly prejudiced against the Texans, few of whom spoke Spanish, whereas the blacks proved more adaptable. And besides, abolitionist feelings still ran high in the cattle states. The Texans regarded the Mexicans as foreigners and treated them as outcasts. A number of blacks achieved status on the trail, a few were even employed as trail bosses, but they were the exceptions. In later years, however, when the encroachment of settlement, quarantine laws, and the introduction of barbed wire severely curtailed the routes, many African Americans replaced the whites on the trail drives.

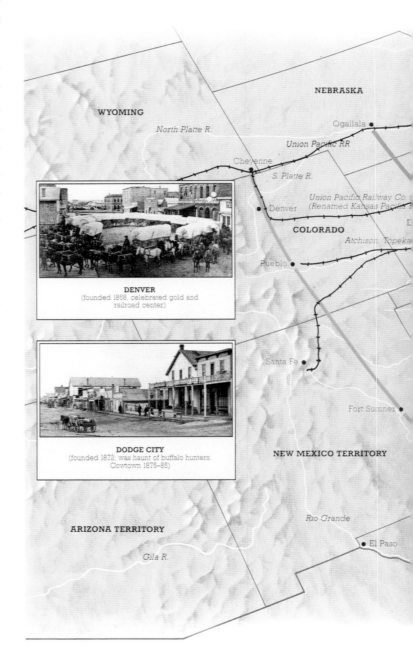

DENVER
(founded 1858, celebrated gold and railroad center)

DODGE CITY
(founded 1872; was haunt of buffalo hunters. Cowtown 1875–85)

In the immediate postwar years, however, young "unreconstructed rebels" made no secret of their dislike for blacks. One of the most virulent of these men was cowboy William Preston Longley, also known as "Wild Bill" (see also Chapter 1). Longley would become known as "the nigger killer" on account of his regular tendency to shoot African Americans. His first black victim was a Negro soldier, killed when Longley was only fifteen. He encountered the soldier on the road near his family farm in Evergreen, Texas, in 1867. The two men became locked in argument, and the black soldier unwisely fired a pistol shot at Longley. The boy was no child when it came to shooting—he devoted most of his youth to learning how to shoot with pistol and rifle. Longley quickly whipped out his revolver and shot the soldier through the head, killing him instantly. He pulled the body into a ditch.

Longley's first killing only seems to have fueled an appetite for the murder of black men. Later in the same year, in Lexington, Texas, Longley and another man, Johnson McKowen, rode through a Negro street dance, firing wildly

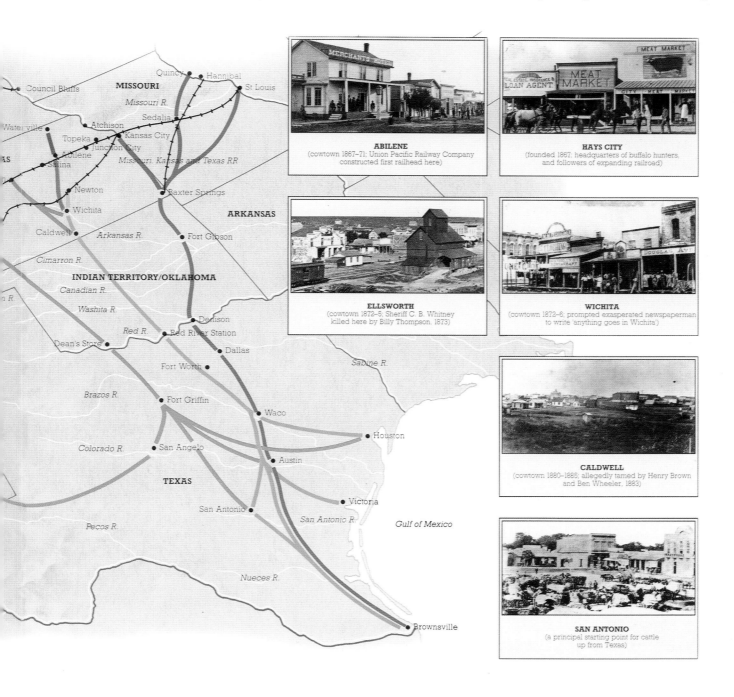

**ABILENE**
(cowtown 1867–71; Union Pacific Railway Company constructed first railhead here)

**HAYS CITY**
(founded 1867; headquarters of buffalo hunters, and followers of expanding railroad)

**ELLSWORTH**
(cowtown 1872–5; Sheriff C. B. Whitney killed here by Billy Thompson, 1873)

**WICHITA**
(cowtown 1872–6; prompted exasperated newspaperman to write 'anything goes in Wichita')

**CALDWELL**
(cowtown 1880–1885; allegedly tamed by Henry Brown and Ben Wheeler, 1883)

**SAN ANTONIO**
(a principal starting point for cattle up from Texas)

# THE COWBOY
# LIFESTYLE

The nineteenth-century dime novels and the early Western movies of the twentieth century presented cowboys as figures of romantic individualism, hard men with a love of their freedom and a penchant for breaking into song around the campfire, while breaking hearts as they passed through cow towns. The actual lifestyle of the cowboy, however, was singularly unromantic.

During the 1860s and 1870s, the heyday of the cattle drives, there were an estimated 50,000 cowboys riding the trail, with around 35 percent of those being Hispanic or African American. Usually working for large corporate cattle enterprises, the cowboys were generally poorly paid, working for around twenty-five to thirty-five dollars per month. The work itself was exceptionally hard. A cowhand was exposed to the full range of elements, from blistering summer heat to

**ABOVE: A group of cowboys entertain themselves by shooting craps. Boredom could be one of the biggest problems of the cowboy lifestyle, and goes a long way to explaining the excesses cowboys indulged in when they hit the towns.**

Arctic blizzards, twenty-four hours a day while on the drive or out on the ranch. Much of his time was spent on monotonous or backbreaking tasks, including tracking down lost cattle, branding, and mending fences. Foods tended to be very plain, mainly nonperishable fare such as cornmeal, beans, molasses, and biscuits supplemented by the occasional buffalo steak, turkey, or bacon.

There was much danger in cattle work. The cattle themselves could weigh 1,000 pounds each and were belligerent animals prone to stampede. The severe Western climates threatened either heatstroke or hypothermia depending on the season, and there remained a perennial danger from violent cattle rustlers. Little wonder, therefore, that most cowboys were aged in their late teens or early twenties; the physical punishment of the cowboy tended to weed out older men through their own preference or through injury.

Rather than being individualists, cowboys had to be cooperative members of a tightly knit team. Leading the drive was the trail boss. He would be a master of all aspects of cowboy work: able to read the landscape and the climate, navigate the herd to its destination (making sure that the cattle moved between sources of water and pasture), and handle financial transactions. The trail boss would usually select all of his own crew and hence was the highest paid.

Another important member of the cowboy team was the cook. He would man the chuckwagon (the position was especially suited to injured cowboys who could no longer ride on horseback) on which was stocked all necessary foods for the journey, although he would also be responsible for picking up perishable food items during passage through towns. Outside of food preparation, the cook would be a jack-of-all-trades, even acting as the team doctor, treating some of the many injuries and illnesses incurred with the job.

After the trail/ranch boss came the various levels of cowboy. These included the "ranahan" (the head rider), point riders (they rode at the head of the herd to give it direction), the tail or "drag" riders (they followed at the rear), and the "night wrangler" (someone who cares for horses and saddlery at night). Altogether the cowboys formed a team of hardened men with little time for complainers.

BELOW: Being a cowboy meant having greater skill with a rope than with a gun. The lariat required much practice to use confidently—here a mounted cowboy has roped a cow within a corral, where activities such as branding were often conducted.

RIGHT: Hungry cowboys line up at the chuck wagon for some food. The chuck wagon was often piloted by an old or injured cowboy who was no longer suited to the rigors of horseback. It could carry not just provisions but also weapons.

**ABOVE:** A cowboy proudly shows off his horse. Cowboys thrived on simplicity—the stock saddle stemmed from proven designs originating with the Spanish and Mexican ranchers, while personal clothing was based on durability and function.

into the crowd and killing two people and wounding several others. In December 1868, Longley pursued three African Americans, with whom he had argued, back to their camp near Evergreen, Texas. One of the men spotted Longley approaching and fired off a rifle shot. Longley replied by shooting the man in the head—he died later.

It was all too much for the state authorities, and Longley fled his home and moved to Karnes County, where he found work as a cowboy on the ranch of John Reagon. The employment didn't stabilize the young man, however, and in 1869 in Yorktown, Texas, he murdered an army sergeant at close quarters after the soldiers mistook him for Charles Taylor (of the Sutton-Taylor feud fame) and attempted to apprehend him. Longley escaped, but there was now a large reward placed upon his head.

Longley fled again and now fully embraced his deviant nature by joining a gang with outlaw Cullen Baker. They proceeded to rob, rape, and murder their way through eastern Texas and Louisiana, and Longley was soon racking up killings (and only the ones we know about) at a terrifying rate. In late 1869, he was employed on a cattle drive to Kansas and ended up shooting and killing the trail boss after an argument. He then moved to Salt Lake City before heading off to Leavenworth, Kansas, where in 1870 he shot

**ABOVE: A pull of the canteen by Frederic Remington, 1888. Around one quarter of all cowboys were African Americans (one third in the 1880s), although they are distinctly underrepresented in the popular iconography of the Wild West.**

dead a soldier in a saloon. Interestingly, it appears that Longley also joined the army on June 22, 1870, and was stationed at Camp Brown in Wyoming, working in charge of pack mules and horses and bringing his inveterate corruption to the quartermaster's stores. Unsurprisingly, he deserted within only two weeks, was captured, and returned to duty. The army may have wished it had let him run. Longley's partner in the false accounting of army stores was the quartermaster himself, a man called Greggory. Greggory

discovered that his partner in crime had sold some mules for $200 more than the price he had said. A wild man, Greggory set out to kill Longley, and Longley hid at the post corral. There, Longley ambushed Greggory, shooting the man through the head—he died the following day. Longley was subsequently arrested for the shooting. He served nine months army penal service and was due to be transferred to Iowa State Prison to begin thirty years of incarceration. However, on June 8, 1872, he escaped and once again headed back to Texas.

Killing followed the young man wherever he went. In Parkersville, Kansas, he shot a man dead after at argument at a gambling table. He also redemonstrated his violent antipathy towards African Americans. While in Comanche County, he learned that a black man had supposedly insulted

a local woman, a Mrs. Forsythe. Longley found the man and simply walked up to him and put two bullets through his face. Such was the low status of blacks in America at this time that Longley just used cash to buy his way out of custody following the offense.

The murder of African Americans seemed to incur little

**LEFT: The cow towns were places of frequent violence, especially in the saloons. Here two soldiers lie dead on a saloon floor, victims of a gunfight. Tensions between soldiers and cowboys could run high, especially in the days after Civil War.**

**BELOW: A splendid photograph of a group of Mexican cowboys. Mexican cattle drivers were known as *vaqueros*, and they were essentially the first cowboys of the American West. By 1890, approximately one in three cowboys was a Mexican.**

serious penalty, but in 1875 Longley committed two more murders that would elevate his status on the wanted posters and which eventually brought about his downfall. On April 1, he shot and killed one Wilson Anderson in a field in Bastrop County, who had shot dead Longley's cousin, Cale Longley. The following November, Longley was involved in a furious horseback gunfight in the attempt to kill a man named Bill Scrier. By the time the gunfight was over, Scrier had thirteen bullets embedded in his body. Longley survived, but the price on his head now rocketed up to around $250. The authorities in every county realized that Longley simply could not be left at large.

As much as we know, Longley would murder once more in 1876; in his last days of life he would claim in an article for the *Giddings Tribune* to have killed thirty-two people—a plausible figure given his known track record. However, on June 6, 1877, the net finally closed around him. He was working on a small plot of land in De Soto County, Louisiana, which he had rented in an attempt at anonymity. He had been diligently tracked down by two law officers, who arrested him down the barrels of their shotguns in the middle of his cotton field. They took him back over state lines into Texas, where he was hanged on October 11, 1878. Apparently Longley underwent a Christian conversion en route to the gallows, although he would require an unusual level of divine grace to purify his violent short existence.

**Pistoliferous Pranks**

Although Longley seemed to find black Americans a favorite target, as a general rule cow-town violence was usually directed against other whites or the Mexicans. Typical of those who sought confrontation with either group was John Wesley Hardin. When, in 1871, he came up the trail to Abilene as trail boss with Columbus Carroll's outfit (perhaps one of the youngest ever to hold that position), he killed eight men, most of them Mexicans. In his posthumously published autobiography, Hardin claimed that his herd came into contact with one driven by Mexicans. When he protested that they were in danger of mixing, there was a row. The Mexican boss then took a shot at him with a rifle from one hundred yards (knocking off his hat, so Hardin alleged),

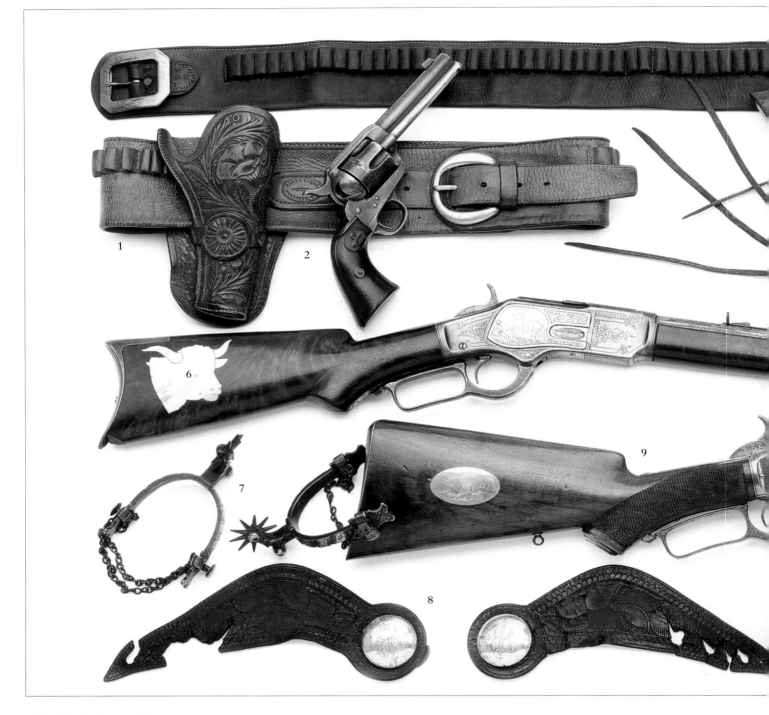

## COWBOY GUNMEN 1870s–1880s

Many cowboys carried revolvers for a variety of purposes. They were used to put injured animals out of their misery, but they were rarely used in range wars and other conflicts. Revolvers were handy for dealing with snakes and rabid animals and with a really lucky shot could help to put meat on the dinner table. Revolvers were also worn for reasons of status, but the truth is that they were also heavy and got in the way. Many cowboys kept their guns in saddle bags or in the chuck wagon, bringing them out as they needed or maybe just for the chance to go to town and to wear while having a picture taken. Down on their luck and out of a job, some cowboys joined the ranks of the lawless, resorting to violence and use of the gun.

Low wages kept most cowboys from having really fancy equipment. They were not without their pride, however, and fancy silver mounted bits and spurs were not uncommon. A Colt revolver with ivory and pearl grips might complement such an outfit along with nicely stitched boots and a

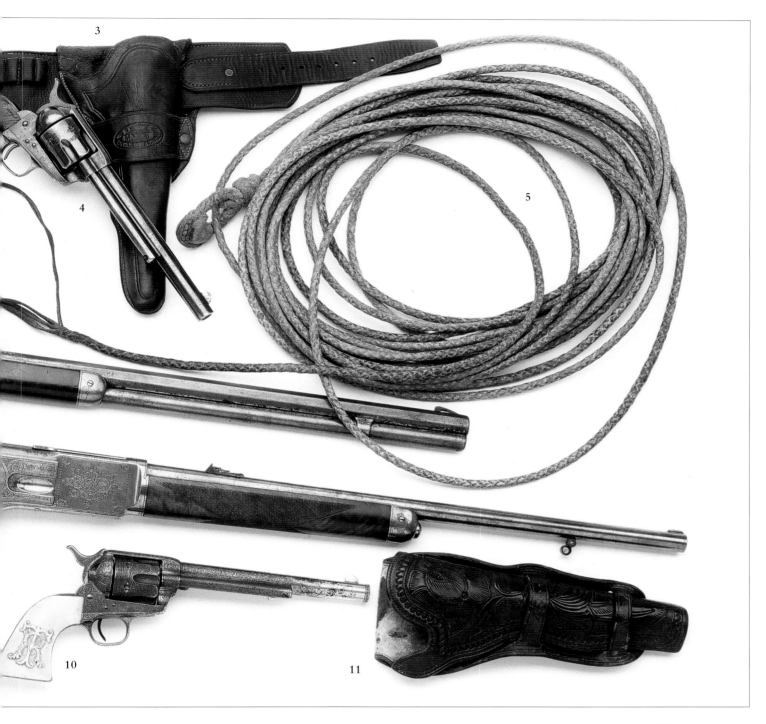

particularly fine shirt and hat. This was rare, and it is not surprising that Dakota cowboys thought rancher Theodore Roosevelt a bit of a dude. He ultimately proved himself and earned their respect, later writing articles and books that showed his respect for them in turn.

1. Hand-tooled holster and cartridge belt that doubles as a money belt, c. 1900, used by George Gardiner, a working cowboy.
2. Colt single action, .38-40 caliber, carried by George Gardiner in the above holster.
3. Typical holster of about 1880, made by R. E. Rice, Dodge City.

4. Colt .44-40 Frontier single-action revolver of about 1885.
5. Rawhide hand-braided riata, late 1800s.
6. Factory engraved and pearl inlaid Winchester rifle model 1873, owned by Charles Goodnight.
7. California-style silver mounted spurs used by Theodore Roosevelt.
8. Spur straps with engraved "TR" conchos, probably made by J. S. Collins in Cheyenne, Wyoming, and used by Roosevelt in the Dakotas, late 1880s.
9. Roosevelt's Winchester model 1876 carbine.
10. Engraved six-shooter with carved ivory grips carried in the West by Roosevelt. It represents his vision of the typical cowboy revolver but does not quite fit the bill.
11. Cheyenne made holster, fitted to T. R.'s revolver in about 1886.

(Artifacts courtesy of Gene Autry Western Heritage Museum, Los Angeles.)

# Ho for Kansas!

**Brethren, Friends, & Fellow Citizens:**
I feel thankful to inform you that the
## REAL ESTATE
### AND
## Homestead Association,
Will Leave Here the
## 15th of April, 1878,
In pursuit of Homes in the Southwestern
Lands of America, at Transportation
Rates, cheaper than ever
was known before.
For full information inquire of
## Benj. Singleton, better known as old Pap,
NO. 5 NORTH FRONT STREET.
Beware of Speculators and Adventurers, as it is a dangerous thing
to fall in their hands.
Nashville, Tenn., March 18, 1878.

One of the many posters calling on southern blacks to leave for Kansas.

# BLACK
# COWBOYS

Approximately one-third of cowboys during the 1880s were African Americans, a fact that has been acutely underrepresented in the mythology of the American West. The African slave trade had shipped into North America thousands of people with cattle-herding experience from their homeland, and the skills, passed on to the children, were of use in the cattle industry of the nineteenth century. Hence, before the Civil War, slaves could be found working cattle in places such as South Carolina, northern Florida, Mississippi, and southeast Texas. Many blacks also made new lives in Mexico, where the vaqueros taught them the skills of cattle herding from horseback.

The Civil War (1861–1865) dramatically increased the numbers of black cowboys as hundreds of thousands of emancipated slaves pushed westward into Texas. The ranches

**ABOVE: A poster calls for Southern African Americans to leave for Kansas. Large numbers of men who took up such a call would become cowboys, and as such they often enjoyed an improved status over those who remained in segregated communities.**

and cattle drives were a major source of employment, and by around 1880 there were an estimated 9,000 African Americans working as cowboys. Blacks were employed in every conceivable cattle-management role except that of trail boss—this leadership position was almost always reserved for whites, even on occasions when every other member of the team was black (there were a few very isolated cases of black trail bosses). As Jim Perry, a black cowboy who worked for the XIT ranch—at three million acres the largest fenced ranch in the world—commented, "If it weren't for my damned old black face I'd have been boss of one of these divisions long ago." (The ranch was separated up into territories called "divisions.")

Famous black cowboys included Perry, Bose Ikard, Jim Fowler, and the legendary Nate Love. Love, who was also known as "Deadwood Dick," was a former slave who moved to Texas following the Civil War and asked a trail boss for a job. The boss told Love that he could have a job if he broke an unmanageable horse named Good Eye. After a crazy ride, Love managed the feat, and he embarked on long career as a cowboy riding through Texas and Arizona.

In July 1876, in Deadwood City, Dakota Territory, Nat Love won a town contest testing the entrants' ability with a rope and rifle. Love won the competition and $200 in prize money and consequently earned his "Deadwood Dick" nickname.

and then made the mistake of walking toward him, firing his six-shooter. Hardin shot him dead. Other Texans then rushed to join Wes, and the fight ended with six Mexicans dead, five of whom were claimed by Hardin himself. Hardin's contemptuous attitude toward Mexicans was typical of many who rode the cattle trails and accounted for much of the trouble that broke out in the early years of the drives.

Abilene was the first true cow town. Although Sedalia, Baxter Springs, and perhaps Kansas City had a prior claim as shipping points, Abilene was the first of such places to be developed solely for the purpose. Named after the Biblical city "The Tetrarch of Abilene" or "City of the Plains," it started life in the early 1860s as a stagecoach stop; by 1867 it also boasted a couple of log huts and a saloon. However, once McCoy began building his shipping pens on 250 acres of

land on the northeastern side of the village, more people arrived. Soon other structures sprang up, including a hotel. This was the celebrated three-story Drover's Cottage (which was demolished later and moved to Ellsworth). Later still, a bank, stores, and more saloons were built on either side of the railroad tracks, which ran east to west. Texas Street initially housed the saloons and some business premises, while to the north a collection of shacks were the province of dance halls and brothels.

Abilene was a typical Western town of the period. It was

**BELOW: Abilene had a well-deserved reputation for violent excess. The *Junction City Union* described how the cowboys who saw "scarcely seen a house, garden, woman or child for nearly 1,000 miles . . . at once fall into the liquor and gambling saloons."**

LEFT: Bader & Laubner's saloon at Dodge City in later years. Gone is the ramshackle rough flooring and green wood effects of earlier times. In its place is cleanliness and comparative opulence.

BELOW: This woodcut originally appeared in Joseph G. McCoy's book on the cattle trade, and depicts Abilene in its early years. The Drover's Cottage Hotel was later dismantled and moved to Ellsworth.

dominated by the railroad, and a person's social standing within the town depended upon which side of the tracks he resided. Most of the buildings and the sidewalks were constructed of wood; much of the timber was still green and affected by changes in the weather. The ankle-deep dust of summer gave way to muddy mire by the fall and winter. Unwary pedestrians who failed to watch their step sometimes tripped over warped planks and stretched their length in the dust or mud. The few permanent residents were mostly storekeepers or the owners or licensees of various saloons or businesses. During the cattle season, however, the population exploded, boosted by Texans and an army of

ABOVE: A number of gunfighters, among them Hickok, Earp, and Masterson, at one time or another hunted buffalo. Here hunters armed with Sharps rifles have set up camp near Sheridan, Kansas.

RIGHT: William "Billy" Dixon (seated left) was a noted shot. It is reported that at the Adobe Walls fight against the Comanches in 1874 he shot a warrior from his horse a thousand yards away. The Civil War had produced a new breed of accomplished sniper, but even so, such a shot stretches credibility.

pimps, prostitutes, gamblers, and others anxious to relieve the cattlemen of their hard-earned cash. And overall was the ever-present odor of cattle, bellowing their protests as they were driven from pen to freight car, the shriek of locomotive whistles, and the eternal crash of shunting cattle trucks

RIGHT: The tall figure in the dark shirt armed with a Sharps buffalo gun is William "Bill" Tilghman, who looks remarkably like the late movie star Joel McCrea. Bill carries his Colt in a reverse draw flap holster, and the cartridges for his rifle are clearly seen. The photograph dates from the early 1870s when buffalo hunting was a profitable business, both for their hides and their bones. With him is James Elder.

moving into or out of the yards. Only when darkness fell did other noises replace the daylight din.

The saloons were open most of the day but really only came into their own at night, when they were rivaled by dance halls and brothels. Abilene's most prestigious saloon was the Alamo, which prided itself on a forty-foot frontage on Cedar Street. Inside there was an impressive mirror extending along its bar. There were also a number of

**ABOVE: Wichita in 1870, when the corner of Main and Douglas Avenue was mere tufts of prairie grass. Within weeks, shacks and tents had sprung up, soon to be replaced by permanent structures, many of them saloons.**

paintings depicting Venetian Renaissance nudes. Its counterpart was the Gold Room at Newton, which was not quite so palatial but did have a large mirror that was bordered

by an impressive display of liquor bottles. Gambling took precedence in the Alamo, and a number of tables were placed just inside the main doorway, which were covered in green baize. Similar establishments were found in other places, notably Dodge City, which had the Long Branch saloon—although in appearance and amenities it was inferior to its Abilene or Newton rivals.

During the day, most of the cow towns appeared almost sleepy. Visitors might be misled into thinking that perhaps the stories of unruly Texans and licentious living were figments of a fevered newsman's imagination, but the permanent residents knew better and dreaded nightfall. In Abilene, which survived two years without any real law and order, the residents grew tired of the cowboy chaos that interrupted their lives or ruined business.

Theophilus Little, an early resident and businessman, recalled that during the early part of the day when the Texans came to town it was quiet enough; but when it came time to leave and they were liquored up, everybody feared the worst, "The signal for leaving town at about 3 p.m. was a few pistol shots into the air, their ponies mounted, a general fusillade all along the line, every pony on the dead run and as they passed my office, it was crack, bang, boom of fifty or a hundred six-shooters into the air. The air, blue with smoke as it curled upward into spiral wreaths."

A similar view was shared by old-timer John B. Edwards, who noted that the Texan of the 1860s and 1870s invariably got "too much tanglefoot aboard" and was "liable under the least provocation to use his navies [six-shooters], of which not less than one or two were always hanging to their belts. In fact, if their fancy told them to shoot they did so, in the air, at anything they saw and a plug hat would bring a volley at any time from them, drunk or sober."

Skillful though he might be with the pistol, like most people the Texan was probably more adept with a rifle. After the war, many cowboys had (illegally) hung on to their

ABOVE: William Smith served as marshal of Wichita and later as county sheriff. Born in England, he emigrated to the United States at an early age. He was rated a good officer and was highly regarded.

LEFT: Scots-born photographer Alexander Gardner visited Fort Marker in fall 1867. This interesting group of employees of the Quartermaster's Department has been joined (on the far left) by Wild Bill Hickok.

service-issue weapons that, under the terms of the surrender at Appomattox, should have been confiscated, or they simply acquired others. These consisted of an assortment of Colt Navy or Army revolvers, Remington Army or Navy pistols, and some copied by Confederate arsenals. Their long arms were a mixture of single-shot percussion or early breech-loading weapons, some of them Sharps or even the Spencer seven-shot repeaters admired by the Union cavalry. And others might have been fortunate to acquire a Henry 16-shot lever-action .44 rim-fire repeater.

Christopher Miner Spencer was born in 1833 and died in 1922. During his long life, he invented a number of things, but he is best remembered for his firearms, in particular the range of seven-shot repeaters that saw service in the Civil War and were adapted for cavalry use during the Indian wars that followed. B. Tyler Henry was chosen by Oliver F. Winchester to manage the newly formed New Haven Arms Company in 1857, which took over the original Volcanic

Repeating Arms Company that had manufactured a lever-operated weapon based upon a system created by Smith & Wesson for pistols. Henry redesigned the ammunition for the Volcanic and also improved the action. The result was the Henry rifle, a weapon infinitely superior and one which saw service during and following the Civil War and was much coveted by troops and plainsmen alike.

The redesigned rim-fire cartridge and action and the fact that the weapon could hold sixteen cartridges in the tubular magazine set beneath the barrel gave the Henry rifle added importance. It proved its worth on a number of occasions, most notably in August 1866 when troops and civilians, armed with .58 caliber Allin-converted Springfield single-shot rifles and Henrys managed to repel an assault of Red Cloud's Sioux at Piney Island until reinforcements arrived with cannon. (For more on the development of Western firearms, see Chapter 5.)

The colorful yet inaccurate claim that the Winchester rifle was the "Gun that Won the West" may have been untrue, but it contributed greatly to its popularity. By the time the trail-drivers were headed for Abilene, Oliver Winchester had redesigned the Henry rifle, and the Winchester Model of 1866, the first to bear his name, became the plainsman's

favored rifle. Basically similar in appearance to the Henry rifle, the new Winchester included improvements to the action and the means of loading. To load the Henry, one had to push the cartridges directly into the tubular magazine. Winchester incorporated a loading slot on the side of the receiver, which was retained in later models. Like the Henry, the new Winchester retained a brass frame, which earned it the name "Yellow Boy." By 1873, Winchester had introduced a modified version with an iron frame and receiver chambered for the .44 caliber center-fire cartridge, which held forty grains of powder.

The riders who came up the trail armed with the latest weapons were also aware that the cattle trade would bring prosperity both to Texas and those connected with it. But the combination of firearms, arrogance, and defiance in the face of authority could no longer be tolerated. By 1869 Abilene was determined to put a stop to the violence. On September 3, a deputation of citizens appeared before Cyrus Kilgore, probate judge of Dickinson County, and presented a petition

**ABOVE: By the fall of 1872, Newton was making great strides. Typically, railroad tracks ran straight through the middle of the town. Social status often depended upon "which side of the tracks" one resided.**

requesting the incorporation of Abilene. The judge granted the request, and Abilene became a third-class city empowered to hold elections. A board of trustees was chosen to act pending an election, and in 1870 the position of town marshal was created. Ellsworth, which would succeed Abilene as a cow town in 1872, had been incorporated since 1867, and by the time the Texans arrived a police force awaited them. The same happened with Newton, Wichita, and Dodge City. In later years when the trail moved on to Caldwell, the place had long been under the influence of the law.

## Pistols, Poker, Pimps, and Perdition

Firearms and their use within city limits were a constant problem. The Texans felt undressed without a pistol or pistols adorning their waist-belts, and the idea that they should disarm was abhorrent. It was by no means a new situation, for although the Kansas Statutes of 1868 decreed that if former Confederate soldiers and others who had been in rebellion were found carrying "a pistol, bowie-knife, dirk or other deadly weapon," they would be fined a maximum of one hundred dollars and face a jail sentence of three months, there were few attempts to enforce the unenforceable. However, the law remained on the statute books for some years and formed

the basis for local legislation. In April 1870, Ellsworth's city council passed "Ordinance No. 1," which made discharging a firearm within city limits an offense, or to be exact: "On the North Bank of the Smoky Hill River East of the Round House on West of a point 600 yards of the East of the Rail Road switch in the eastern part of the town, and south of the North line of the town which is about 100 yards from the foot of the Hills." Failure to obey that ruling could be punished with a ten-dollar fine, and to discharge a pistol in the center of the city meant a twenty-dollar fine. Enforcing such a law, however, proved difficult and dangerous.

By 1871, Abilene's city council had also decided that it was time for the Texans to disarm. On June 8, the *Chronicle* published the following editorial comment:

*Fire Arms.* - The Chief of Police [James B. Hickok] has posted up printed notices, informing all persons that the ordinance against carrying firearms or other weapons in Abilene will be enforced.

**RIGHT: A typical saloon of the 1880s. This one was located in Caldwell, which was much advanced in building techniques and other refinements by the time it received the cattle trade and experienced its "evils."**

That's right. There's no bravery in carrying revolvers in a civilized community. Such a practice is well enough and perhaps necessary when among Indians or other barbarians, but among white people it ought to be discountenanced.

Some chose to ignore that warning, but there were fewer incidences of gunplay in the succeeding months, some claim simply because the Texans feared a confrontation with Hickok and his "posse." In 1872, Wichita was only too well aware of its growing reputation as a "wild and woolly" town, and the fear was that the cattle trade and the violence associated with it would prove a deterrent. "Wichita desires law and order," declared the editor of the *Eagle* on June 7, "with their consequent peace and security, and not bloodshed and a name that will cause a thrill of horror whenever mentioned and which will effectually deter the most desirable class of people from coming among us. Right

speedily will the latter follow if the former are not maintained."

Unfortunately, his words fell upon deaf ears. The city council then tried what they thought was a smart move: they approached the owners of the privately owned Chisholm Trail bridge (which crossed the Arkansas River and linked the city with Delano), who agreed that their toll keepers should be sworn in as special policemen. This empowered them to disarm all those who crossed the bridge. In exchange for their pistols, people received a metal token. This proved to be a failure. A year later, notices were put up that stated: "Leave Your Revolvers at Police Headquarters and Get a Check." Similar tactics were tried at Dodge City and other cow towns with little success. Consequently, the police always wore their pistols prominently displayed, a state of affairs that many citizens, with some justification, found objectionable.

The antics of cowboys and others when drunk were

displays of street firepower, and they set off to confront the man. An alleyway scuffle resulted in the accidental discharge of Graham's revolver, the bullet fatally wounding White in the stomach. Wyatt Earp stepped in and clubbed Graham unconscious with his handgun. Graham did go to trial in Tucson, but the fact that White, as he lay dying, had stated that the shot was an accident led the jury to acquit Graham.

The sensible man would have learned his lesson, but Graham was prone to excess drinking, with all the failures of judgment that entails. On May 25, 1881, Graham was drinking in a saloon in Galeyville, Arizona, with a gang of other hardened cowmen. An argument broke out between Graham and Deputy Sheriff Billy Breakenridge, and Graham followed Breakenridge out of the bar and into the street. Breakenridge mounted his horse then quickly pulled out his revolver and shot Graham through the face. Luck was with Graham that day—the bullet passed through the left side of his neck and exited out the right cheek but hit no vital structures on the way through. It seems that, once recovered, Graham finally saw the error of his ways. He left Arizona and appears to have ditched the wild life, although the Earps pursued him for some time. Wyatt Earp even claimed to have killed Graham in the gunfight; this is not true, and Graham appears to have simply lived out his life in peace.

There were few instances of total domination by "armed transients." Rather, most places were prepared to back their police forces if need be by citizen participation if things got out of hand. The Kansas State Code empowered mayors to order all male citizens aged between eighteen and fifty to arm themselves and help enforce the law should the alarm be rung (the fire station bell or some other means). It was rare, however, for this to be enforced.

Probably the most serious near-riot that afflicted any cow town was the so-called Newton General Massacre. Its cause was deep-rooted, but its effect deadly. It began innocently enough, with the citizens of Newton voting, on August 11, 1871, on a proposal to issue $20,000 worth of county bonds to aid the building of the Wichita & Southwestern Railroad. Michael McCluskie (sometimes spelled McCluskey), a former night policeman employed by the railroad, was commissioned as a special policeman for the election. He was

alarming and occasionally led to fatalities. One such occasion occurred in Tombstone, Arizona, on October 28, 1880, and involved William Graham, otherwise known as "Curly Bill Brocius." Brocius was a cowhand through and through, first working in Texas before moving with the cattle into New Mexico and then Arizona. Graham was a violent bully who preened himself on his gunfighter reputation, although he was actually more of a chaotic sociopath than a skilled and predatory gunman. As the head of a cattle-rustling gang, Graham liked to make virtual takeovers of local towns. After a hard few weeks on the trail, Graham would find a saloon, set himself up there for a few days, and occasionally terrorize the locals by riding up and down the main street firing off guns. In October 1880, Graham found himself in Tombstone, Arizona, on one of his sprees. Tombstone's marshal, Fred White (actually the town's first marshal), assisted by Virgil and Wyatt Earp, had received complaints about Curly Bill's known as a troublemaker, and it came as no surprise when he and another policeman similarly hired, a Texas gambler named Wilson (alias Billy Bailey), rowed over cards. They then pulled pistols, and Wilson died the next day. His infuriated Texan friends set out to find McCluskie, who decided to slip out of town. On August 19, however, he foolishly returned. As it was a Saturday, he spent the evening in Perry Turtle's dance hall. Word soon got around that McCluskie was back, and a number of Texans made their way to Turtle's place. The Emporia *News* of August 25 described the scene of carnage as the Texans wreaked their revenge. Led by one Bill Anderson, they advanced on McCluskie and opened fire. Hit in the neck, he staggered to his feet and shot Anderson through the thigh. "The shooting then became general," reported the editor. "McCluskie was shot in three places and died in a couple of hours. John Martin, a herd boss, was shot through the jugular vein and died." Bill

Anderson's brother John was "shot through the right arm and lungs, Garrett was shot through the lungs and has since died. Patrick Lee, a railroad employee, was shot through the loins and has since died. He was in no way a party to the difficulty." Other innocent people were shot, some of whom died later, and it was also reported that a consumptive youngster named Riley, who had been befriended by

**RIGHT: An unusual photograph of "Chalk" Beeson (left, with watch chain behind his belt buckle) and friend. "Chalk" was not known for his violence, suggesting that he posed for this photograph.**

**BELOW: Cow-town violence was just as much conducted with knives as with guns. Here we see a superb example of a Bowie knife. The scabbard is inscribed "R.P. Bowie to H.W. Fowler, USD" (the recipient was Capt. Henry Walker Fowler, U.S. Dragoons).**

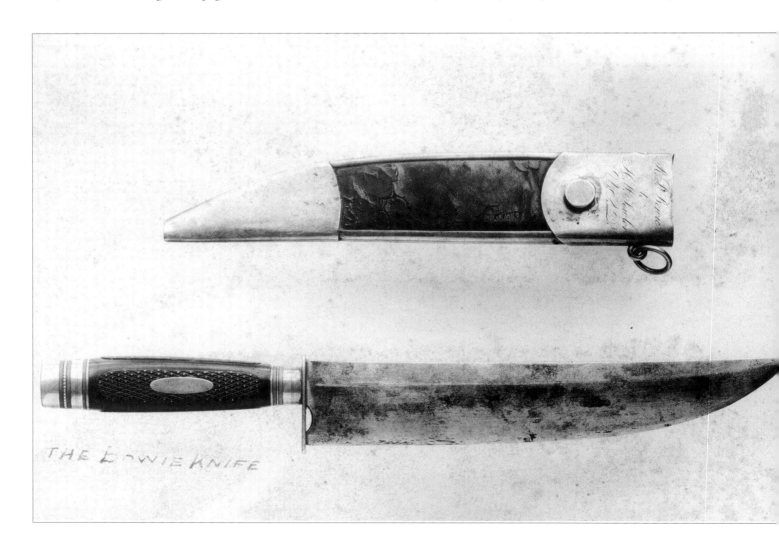

**ABOVE: The St. James saloon, Dodge City, is typical of the time— long bar and a narrow room. The posed look of the place suggests that everyone was on their best behavior despite the boots on the table.**

McCluskie, appeared in the midst of the shoot-out and killed several of the Texans before disappearing. Anderson was arrested, and a coroner's jury decided that he fired the first shot and was guilty of manslaughter. He never went on trial.

Instead, his father came up from Texas and took him home. The "massacre" caused outrage and statewide condemnation, and the *Kansas Daily Commonwealth* on August 22 described the affair as "worse than 'Tim Finnegan's Wake.'" Further cries for a better police force and legislation against firearms were to no avail: the pistol still ruled.

Texans, it seemed, continued to cause, and attract, trouble. The August 20 and 27 *Eagle* described the murder of a Texan by two Mexicans following a gambling dispute. Friends of the deceased pursued the pair, and both were shot and killed "in an attempt to resist an arrest, that at least is what they call it in these parts." It was only one of several incidents that occurred in Wichita that summer and fall. On November 13, 1873, the *Eagle* pinpointed the basic prejudices of the races when it reported that "a dozen Mexican greasers, camped upon the other side of the river, last night attacked Constable Prentiss and beat him with their revolvers most inhumanly. Sheriff [William] Smith is out with a posse this morning and we have no doubt of their arrest and punishment. Some of the people of this city have been laboring under the impression that there was an ordinance in force prohibiting

**ABOVE: The saloons of the Wild West were often basic in the extreme—a single room containing chairs, tables and a bar. This is the Rocky Point Saloon owed by Milton F. Marsh and his wife, who can be seen framing the doorway.**

the carrying of firearms within the city. From the number of revolvers flourishing upon our streets in the last two weeks, we conclude that it was only an impression."

Ellsworth experienced similar problems. On March 7, 1868, the Junction City *Union* reported that one "Chaves," described as a "Mexican bummer" formerly of Kansas City, accompanied by other Mexicans, entered a saloon and announced that "Americans did not like Mexicans." Drawing his pistol, he opened fire, shooting a man in the arm. Despite the shock of his wound, the man drew his own pistol and shot Chaves dead. The unpopularity of the Mexicans was voiced by the Leavenworth *Daily Commercial* of July 7, 1872, when it noted that society at Ellsworth was "of the roughest kind, boiled down. The Greasers are rougher, and the soiled

doves [prostitutes] are roughest." The writer described a "genuine greaser" lounging in a saloon, who was "dressed in a buckskin suit, Mexican spurs, Navy revolvers, bowie knife, and long hair. Across opposite was a Texan similarly dressed." Most of the Mexicans, however, preferred the knife to the pistol and proved to be very dexterous in its use.

In the middle of chaos there lurked a diversion that on one hand provided a social escape and on the other was a direct cause of violence: the saloon. The focal point in any Western movie or novel, the saloon is where strangers are "put upon" to prove their courage or where the villain and the hero exchange words before the inevitable gunfight. In reality, its social attraction counted far more than the occasional violence. It was a place where men could relax, drink, have a meal, play cards, or, if the proprietor catered for it, listen to music. In most camps or settlements, the saloon or beer tent was among the first places to be erected. During the railroad boom, tented saloons followed the tracks from place to place, and companion tents that housed gamblers and prostitutes

often accompanied them. Once a place was settled, however, the saloon took on a distinct life of its own. Later, perhaps, the owner might include "entertainment" in the shape of a "singer" who was usually a practicing prostitute backed by either a piano player, a banjoist, violinist, or, rarely, a three- or four-piece orchestra. The whole was contained in an area that rarely exceeded sixty feet by thirty feet, much of that taken up by the bar, so it was a compact community that endured the aroma of body sweat, liquor, and tobacco smoke.

The fare provided by the average Western saloon varied. Abilene's Alamo Saloon boasted fine liquors, and a selection was displayed along the back bar. In Newton, the Gold Room displayed rows of barrels, each containing beer or selected wines, surmounted by a bar that displayed "clusters of decanters daintily arranged and polished until their shimmer is like that of diamonds," noted the Topeka *Daily Commonwealth* of September 17, 1871. Prices were usually clearly marked, and some idea of the wares available can be gleaned from the following taken from the account book of George M. Hoover, proprietor of a wholesale liquor store at Dodge City: High Mucky Much (a soft drink); Energy; Fire Fly; Orinoco; Ginger Ale, per cask $20. British Bass Ale and Irish "Guinness Stout" were also available for $20 per cask. As for American-brewed beers such as Anhauser, they were $2.50 per case. Jamaica rum was $5.50 per gallon. Port and sherry averaged between one and five dollars a gallon, but Western brandy was $20 per case. Gin, surprisingly, was only $1.50 per gallon. Perhaps the most popular drink was whiskey, home-brewed or imported. This averaged two to four dollars a gallon. Saloon beer prices fluctuated but on average cost two glasses for twenty-five cents. Indeed, it was a dispute over the price of beer that led to the famous shoot-out between Tom Nixon and Mysterious Dave Mather, which is discussed elsewhere.

For those who demanded entertainment with their drinking, the *Times* of November 3, 1877, recommended the Saratoga in Dodge City. An additional attraction was its stove. It was not a "grass valley" stove but the largest stove in town, reaching nearly to the ceiling and shedding its warmth to the remotest corner of the large room. It was shipped from St. Louis especially for the Saratoga." The proprietors, Chalkley

**PREVIOUS PAGES:** The Old Shell Store, of Shell, Wyoming, was established in 1892 and offered a modest but essential stock of general merchandise. The store was also a social place where people would meet and visit for a while or sit around the old wood stove on cold days and drink Arbuckle coffee. There were some years when the storekeeper was also the postmaster and people from the surrounding area would stop to pick up their mail.

**LEFT:** Dodge City has been mythologized as the quintessential violent cow town. Although the town was certainly rough, the murder rate was low compared to gold towns like Deadwood (there were only fifteen murders in Dodge City between 1876 and 1885).

("Chalk") Beeson and W. H. Harris, had provided a "first class" place and did everything they could to make their customers welcome. "The bar, under the charge of Mr. Adam Jackson, furnishes the finest wines, liquors and cigars that can be found in any market. Mr. Jackson is favorably known, and is cordial and polite." An added attraction was the fact that Beeson was an accomplished musician and saw to it that his clientele enjoyed good entertainment, a feature noted by the *Times* on September 29. A particular favorite among those of Irish descent was "The Lakes of Killarney," which always drew "crowds of attentive listeners."

Other aspects of saloon life, however, were not so pleasant. The "facilities" in some places were primitive in the extreme; sometimes a rope, a blanket, and bucket were all that was provided. Others, however, ensured that provision was adequate. Unfortunately, there were those to whom the niceties of social behavior meant little. On July 14, 1879, nine citizens dispatched the following petition to the Mayor and members of the council of Wichita:

Gentlemen

We the undersigned petitioners would most respectfully represent that we are seriously annoyed and our health is greatly endangered by the stench that arises from the filth deposited in the rear of the "Star Saloon" and adjoining buildings and also the rear of Whitworths Block—in some of the following ways—viz: — The filthy condition and positions of the swill barrel of the "Eating Saloon"—the careless manner in which slops of various kinds are thrown into the alley & backyards of above named buildings. Also the conversion of the corner at the rear of the Star Saloon into a place where all the frequenters of Said Saloon & Eating House accustomed, habitually, to urinate—would respectfully ask your honorable body to take immediate steps for the removal of said nuisances and prevent any or all repetitions of a like character.

**RIGHT: It is hard to believe that this is Front Street in Dodge City at about the turn of the century. All gone are the false fronts, hitching racks and other signs of the cowboy era; bricks replaced bullets and Bowie knives.**

Drink was the downfall of many a cowboy's character in the West, often accentuating darker sides of a man's character. A case in point was the notorious rancher Robert A. Clay Allison, (see portrait, page 12), a man who brought his own brand of violent justice to the cow towns while also making for a lively and unpredictable saloon patron. Clay Allison was born on September 2, 1840, near Waynesboro, Tennessee. His father was a livestock farmer and a Presbyterian minister who died in 1845. Childhood was tough for Allison. He was one of nine children in a household with little money, and he also had to cope with a clubfoot disability. When he was twenty-one years old, he joined the Confederate army with the

outbreak of the Civil War and ultimately became a scout under General Nathan Bedford Forrest.

Allison's taste for killing was established during the Civil War years, and not necessarily in the context of military conflict. In March 1862, for example, in Waynesboro, Tennessee, Allison had been sent home from the army on mental grounds. He had suffered a head injury as a child, and unusual behavioral traits had led the army to diagnose him as "of a mixed character, partly epileptic and partly maniacal" and release him from duties (he later reenlisted to become one of Forrest's men). While Allison was at home, a soldier of the Third Illinois Cavalry had attempted to loot the Allison farm: Allison shot him dead after the man broke some of his mother's possessions in the robbery attempt.

In 1865 the war ended, and after spending a few days as a Union prisoner of war in Alabama, he moved to Texas. Near Denison he was involved in a fistfight with Zachary Colbert, a ferryman working on the Brazos River. Allison inflicted a hard beating, and tensions between the Allisons and Colberts would remain high and ultimately led to murder. However, Allison subsequently became a cowhand for Oliver Loving and Charles Goodnight, riding the Goodnight-Loving trail in the 1860s. By this time Allison was enjoying his drink, and his character became less restrained and increasingly violent both

on the trail and in the saloon. Yet despite reckless behavior—in the late 1860s he accidentally shot himself through the right foot while stampeding some army mules—he built up enough business acumen to start his own ranch near Cimarron, New Mexico, in 1870 with 300 head.

Allison would turn his ranch into a lucrative enterprise, but on October 7, 1870, he showed how business responsibilities hadn't curbed his violent excesses. In a jailhouse in nearby Elizabethtown, the accused murderer Charles Kennedy was being held. Allison was at the head of a lynch mob who broke into the jail, dragged Kennedy out, and hanged him in a slaughterhouse. Horribly, Allison then cut off Kennedy's head and displayed it on a spike in a local saloon. Saloon owners soon came to fear a visit from Allison, who became a brawler and even a shooter once he had a few drinks inside him.

On January 7, 1874, Allison's feud with the Colberts came to a head at Clifton House, an inn in Colfax County, Texas. "Chunk" Colbert, Zachary's nephew, had just had an ill-willed horse race with Allison, a race resulting in a draw. The two men, along with Charles Cooper, a friend of Colbert, then retired to Clifton House for some food and drink. During the meal, Colbert slyly reached under the table, drew his revolver, and then leveled it across the tabletop at Allison. With remarkable reactions, Allison instantly went for his gun, and Colbert let off one misaimed shot that buried itself into the tabletop before being shot through the face and killed. He was buried behind Clifton House. Cooper escaped but ominously vanished twelve days later, two days before the charges of murder against Allison were dropped because of lack of evidence.

In early 1874, Allison's saloon behavior seemed to reach new heights of excess. In one incident, Allison engaged in bizarre, drunken tests of manliness with one Mason T. Bowman. These involved a quick-draw competition with their revolvers (although no shots were fired at this stage in the proceedings), then a partially undressed display of

**LEFT: The cow-town saloon may have offered gambling tables, but some Southern steamboats plying the Mississippi also provided offshore gambling with an air of luxury. However, the steamboat ports could be as rough as any cow town.**

dancing that led to both men firing bullets around the feet of the other in an attempt to improve the dance moves. The competition was getting increasingly out of hand, and the saloon owner stopped it at this point.

Less humorously, in early 1875 Allison returned to his enthusiasm for lynchings. On October 30, he and a bloodthirsty gang broke into another jail and seized Cruz Vega, a man accused of murdering a Methodist lay preacher.

There is a strong likelihood that Vega was not the actual murderer, but the mob strung him up from a telegraph pole and shot him. Allison then tied the corpse to his horse and dragged it around the bush until it was badly mutilated. This was not the end of the matter, however. Two days later in Cimarron, Allison bumped into Pancho Griego, Vega's former employer, plus one of Griego's associates and Vega's teenage son, Luis. Allison and Griego had much to talk

about, and so the men went into the saloon of the St. James Hotel. What followed looks like a well-planned ambush. Griego and Allison talked for a few moments, Allison then whipped out his revolver and shot Griego three times, killing him. At that instant the lights went out in the saloon and Allison made a nimble escape.

Allison was becoming a social liability. He took a dislike to anyone who criticized him and even, in January 1876,

vandalized the offices of the Cimarron *News & Press* because of their stories about him (he had to pay damages of around $200). He continued to intimidate saloon patrons, and on

**BELOW: Bodie, California, in its later years following the establishment of the gold and silver mines and, as this photograph shows, a good transport system. The Concord stagecoaches plied all over the West.**

December 21, 1876, he and his brother John attended a dance at the Olympic Dance Hall in Las Animas, Colorado. The two men had refused a request from Deputy Sheriff Charles Faber to check their guns before going into the dance, and they showed their defiance by barging around the dance floor, crashing into other couples.

Faber decided that he had seen enough, and armed with a shotgun, he went to challenge Allison, backed up by two deputies. The deputy sheriff marched straight onto the dance floor and unloaded the cartridge straight into John's chest. Clay Allison was already drawing his guns as the shot was fired, and he opened up on Faber. Faber was killed on the spot, but in his dying moments discharged his second barrel

into John Allison's legs. Clay Allison opened up with everything he had, driving the two deputies from the room before tending to his seriously injured brother. John Allison would later recover from his wounds. Clay Allison was subsequently arrested but was released, justifying the killing on the grounds of self-defense.

Although Allison was implicated in the murder of three black soldiers in spring 1877, the Las Animas incident was his

**BELOW: Ellsworth depot, Kansas; Ellsworth was a typical "end of the line" cow town where violence was commonplace. It was said that "Ellsworth has a man every morning for breakfast." Its fortunes declined as the railway moved on in the mid-1870s.**

last known killing. However, the remainder of his life and career are ample illustration of the chaos and brutality single individuals could impose on the cow towns. At one point a respectable life seemed to be beckoning. In 1878 he moved to Hays City, Kansas, and set up business there as a cattle broker, having sold his ranch in New Mexico. Reportedly, in the same year he inflicted such terror upon Dodge City that even the redoubtable Bartholomew (Bat) Masterson is said to

BELOW: Gambling was the catalyst for many of the cow-town killings. A number of the West's infamous gunfighters at some time earned a living as professional gamblers. Here one man stands and readies his revolver as he accuses another of cheating.

have left the town, only the persuasions of Wyatt Earp causing Allison to get out of Dodge. Two years later he moved back to Texas with his brother and married. His wife bore him two children, and Allison founded a successful ranch in Hemphill County. Allison was as entrepreneurial as he was wild, and in 1886 he established another ranch in New Mexico. During the same year Allison went to visit a dentist in Wyoming at the end of a long cattle drive. The dentist botched the operation on Allison's painful teeth, and as punishment Allison forced the hapless man into his own dentist's chair, whereupon Allison pulled one of the man's teeth out with a pair of pliers.

Most men of Allison's lifestyle in the late nineteenth

## GAMBLERS

"Go West, young man." Well, to do so was a gamble. And it comes as no surprise that, faced with all kinds of hardships imaginable—as well as all kinds of opportunities—for many Westerners, gambling was an integral part of life. For some gunfighters it was also a way of death. Cards, dice. roulette, horse racing, fist fights, and cock fights were all legitimate gambling affairs. Professional gamblers assumed many guises. Few were the slick dandy with the brocade vest and pomade

hair. Most were rough, callous men who didn't stand out: why would you want to stand out from the crowd if you were, as many were, a cheat?

Organized gambling went west via the riverboats heading up western tributaries, but soon every camp, railhead, and cow town had some form of game in the saloon. The inevitable by-product was the dispute that sometimes led to gunplay. Wild Bill Hickok is one of the most famous shootists to die with his cards on the table, but not the only one.

1. Sharps model 1 four shot Pepperbox.
2. Storage case for gaming chips
3. Holder for gaming chips.
4. Red, white, and blue gaming chips, each color indicating a different face value.
5. Roulette table and wheel.
6. Leather shoulder holster for Colt single-action revolver, .45 caliber.
7. Carpet bag.
8. Leather shoulder holster holding a Colt double-action Lightning revolver, .41 caliber.
9. Fancy vest, the white background a good aiming mark in a smoky saloon.
10. Remington double deringer, .41 caliber.
11. Gold and enamel pocket watch.
12. Deck of cards, advertisement for Marlin firearms.
13. Colt first model deringer, .41 caliber.

14. James Reid knuckle-duster revolver.
15. Silver dollars and pocket purse.
16. Knuckle-duster.
17. Josiah Ells third model pocket revolver.
18. Silver-plated, double-doored cigar box.
19. Deck of cards.
20. Unwin and Rodgers knife/pistol combination.
21. Pair of dice.
22. Gaming chips.
23. Minneapolis Firearms Co. palm pistol, "The Protector," .32 caliber.
24. Brass spittoon.
25. Fur-covered saddlebags.
26. Winchester Model 1873 rifle, .44–50 caliber.

century ended their days in a blaze of gunfire, but not so in his case. On July 3, 1887, he was driving a wagon to his ranch when he was thrown from the seat and fell under the wheels. The wagon was stacked high with heavy stores, and Allison suffered a fractured skull and died shortly afterward. Although his family and close friends doubtless mourned him (he was buried in Pecos cemetery), few saloon owners or lawmen could have genuinely been saddened by the death of this wild individual.

**The Pasteboard Pirates**

Rivaling the saloons in the Old West were the gambling places and houses of prostitution. If anything, gambling was the biggest attraction, for it promised more than a "taste-bud tickle" or a "ten second spine tingle." For gambling as a pastime and a passion was common to all the frontier regions. The end-of-track railroad "tent cities" attracted gamblers, as did the mining boomtowns such as Denver, Deadwood, and other places that sprang up during the latter part of the last

BELOW: Tombstone's Oriental Saloon attracted Wyatt Earp, who invested in it. Here the bartender takes justifiable pride in the highly polished bar and maintains the high standards expected by patrons. Despite the name, it is unlikely that Chinese, thousands of whom had worked on the railroad, were welcome.

RIGHT: Bat Masterson lived in two of the toughest cow towns during his life. He moved to Wichita, Kansas, with his family around 1867 then to Dodge City in 1872. Despite his habitats, he was only involved in three known career gunfights and is credited with one kill.

**ABOVE: The "Dodge City Peace Commission" of 1883. Back row (left to right): Harris, Short, Masterson, W. F. Petillon (Petillon added himself to the genuine photo). Front row: C. E. Bassett, Earp, M. F. Mclain, and Neil Brown.**

century. They all followed the pattern of initial capitulation to the pasteboard pirates who flocked there, but time and the inevitable establishment of local ordinances and taxes redressed the balance. Although historians quite rightly have been criticized for spending too much time in "peering into the smoke-filled saloons of the Kansas cowtowns" when assessing the rise and fall of the gambling elite, the fact remains that it was the era of the cow town that added the color and romance usually attributed to the deftly digited denizens who haunted the baize-covered gaining tables, and also it was the cow-town experience that best explains, from surviving records, how the "politics of economics" overcame the resistance to change.

The frontier gambler is as familiar to most Western fans as the cowboy and the gunfighter, and he is often depicted as a combination of all three characters. His origins, however, can be traced back many years before he made his presence felt

RIGHT: Lawrence E. Deger, an early marshal of Dodge City and, in 1883, its mayor. He took over from Alonzo Webster, who had introduced many reforms; some regarded Larry as Webster's "creature."

## DERINGERS 1845–1860

The traditional "hideout" pistol favored by gamblers, gunfighters, or indeed anyone who feared being caught unawares was usually single-shot and less than six inches in length. Henry Deringer introduced his famous range of large caliber pocket pistols in the early 1840s (the second "r" in "derringer" is believed to have crept in when a reporter covering Lincoln's assassination misspelled the weapon used by John Wilkes Booth).

1. Henry Deringer's pocket pistols were the "Rolls-Royces" of their day. This is the medium-size pocket pistol with ramrod.
2. Deringer small-size pistol.
3. German silver was used for trigger guards and as stock decoration.
4. Typical powder flask.
5. The percussion lock was a boon to Deringer and others.
6. Deringer's pistols all followed the same graceful lines. Smaller ones, however, could be hidden in the palm of a hand.
7. Engraving on deringer pistols is mostly confined to the lock plate.
8. A can of American-made percussion caps.
9. A small-size pistol—compare the sizes.
10. A medium-size pistol complete with ramrod.
11. "Baby" of the family, and probably the most famous version. John Wilkes Booth used one of these in .41 caliber to kill Lincoln.

12. Eley Brothers of London supplied millions of percussion caps to American makers (Colt notably).

13. Although clearly marked, Deringer's pistols were widely copied, some even bearing his name.

14. The sights on a deringer were basic and consisted of a blade front sight and a "V" cut into a plate behind the nipple housing. Most users ignored the sights and fired point-blank.

15. Checkering was common to most deringer stocks.

16. A handsome pistol of the larger size minus its ramrod.

17. Ethan Allen's bar hammer pistol that rivaled the deringer.

18. This version of the Allen bar hammer pistol was not as popular as that shown at 17.

19. Typical playing cards of the period.

20. Pair of ivory dice.

21. Another Allen-type pistol but with a conventional center hammer.

22. Powder flasks of this type are often found with Colt's pistols as well as makers of deringer-type arms.

23. A Blunt & Syms side hammer pocket pistol.

24. Unmarked 7 mm pin-fire single-shot pocket pistol.

25. Removable screw-on barrels were common in Europe, but not in the U.S.

26. English pocket pistol converted from flint lock to percussion.

27. Lindsay two-shot belt pistol with brass frame.

28. Bacon & Co. single-shot ring trigger pistol.

29. Allen bar hammer pistol. The mechanism was of the self-cocking type.

30. Massachusetts Arms Co. single-shot pocket pistol fitted with Maynard's tape primer mechanism.

31. Roll of Maynard's tape primers.

32. Lindsay two-shot belt pistol.

33. Unmarked .28 caliber single-shot breech-loading pocket pistol.

(Artifacts courtesy of Buffalo Bill Historical Center, Cody, Wyoming.)

LEFT: Wild Bill Hickok, photographed in Rolla, Missouri, c. 1864. His dandified dress seems out of place for a Civil War contract scout, but since he was paid five dollars a day, he could afford good clothing.

in the cow camps, railheads, and anywhere that a turn of a card could reap riches or despair. Perhaps the earliest and certainly most prosperous era of the Western gambler was the halcyon days of the steamboat. Romantics tend to think of the low-lying high-stacked riverboats, with their huge side or rear paddle wheels flashing through the waters of the Mississippi or Missouri rivers, as the golden age of travel. Reality was different. When Charles Dickens ventured upon an American steamboat in the early 1840s, he recalled that one tried to find accommodation aft, because the boilers were liable to burst forward. Underwater snares, sandbanks, and the occasional burst boiler were daily hazards, but it was a relatively inexpensive means of travel, provided one kept clear of the harpies, pimps, and of course the gamblers who plied the river.

The gambler has for long had a bad reputation. Steamboat gamblers were particularly well versed in tricks and schemes to divest the dudes and tenderfeet from their dollars. Even the suppliers of warlike implements lost no time in advertising

the fact that gamblers were an endangered species. The *Philadelphia Mirror* of October 10, 1836, published a "Notice to Gamblers and Other Sportsmen—Bowie knives and tomahawks sold here." Pistols and knives were the favored weapons. The revolver was not yet available, but Henry Derringer's .41 and .45 caliber pocket pistols certainly were, and the demand was such that they were widely copied. Produced in several sizes, the most popular was the .41 caliber pistol that was just five inches long. Loaded with loose black powder and a lead ball and fired by means of a percussion cap, it was deadly at close range. Carried in waistcoat pockets, coat sleeves, boot tops, or indeed anywhere convenient, secret but accessible to the user, its presence, or at least that of some kind of weapon, was comforting, and the

**BELOW: Hays City was founded in 1867 and sat on the Union Pacific Railroad. The first eight years of its existence were the most troubled in terms of gunfights and violence, but the influx of stable farming families in the 1870s brought more harmony.**

other players invariably were also "heeled." In later years, as a gesture of good faith, it was common for members of such games to disarm or at least place a token pistol on the table. What was hidden away, of course, only came to light in a crisis.

By the mid-1860s, with the movement west, cattle drives, gold fever, and advancing railroads, the gambling elite moved along. Mining camps were popular because the prospect of large amounts of gold "dust" lured many "sports" or "genteel

**BELOW: The Long Branch saloon (center, showing exterior) is almost as famous as Dodge City itself. But it bears little resemblance to the version that appeared regularly in Hollywood's *Gunsmoke*.**

loafers" to such places. And the more that arrived, the greater the prosperity, particularly among the saloon and brothel set where most of them congregated. Bodie, California, was a fine example. W. S. Bodey, who was a member of a party led by Terence Brodigan, first discovered gold there in 1859. According to the *Bodie Chronicle* of November 3, 1879, his find was accidental, following a run-in with some warlike Paiute Indians. Forced to take a different route, the party found a likely looking valley, and Bodey dug a prospect hole. When he turned up evidence of gold, everyone joined in. But it was 1877 before the real bonanza strike was made, and eventually an estimated $20 million worth of gold and silver was mined from the area. In the years between the discovery and the strike of 1877, the place simply ticked over, with a

population that rarely exceeded fifty. Back in the early 1860s, J. Ross Brown stumbled on the place, and in his *Adventures in the Apache Country*, he recalled that when he arrived at Bodie he found only two married miners, the remainder being without women. But instead of misery, he claimed that these "jolly miners were the happiest set of bachelors imaginable," spending their time perfecting all the arts and crafts usually performed by women, thereby "proving by the most direct positive evidence that woman is an unnecessary and expensive institution which ought to be abolished by law."

By the 1870s and until the place peaked as a mining town, perhaps only 10 percent of the population of Bodie were women, and many of those were prostitutes. Its rival, Aurora, was founded in 1860 and for a time boasted among its

ABOVE: Joseph "Rowdy Joe" Lowe in later years when he became almost respectable. Joe was known as a character all over the West. As was his one-time partner, the redoubtable "Rowdy Kate." The pair parted in 1876.

inhabitants Samuel L. Clemens, known to history as Mark Twain. Like Bodie, Aurora had its share of violence, saloons, gamblers, and the inevitable prostitutes. In general, the violence and eventual taming, civilizing, and growth in population experienced by the mining camps was very similar to the cattle towns. Although the demise of the mining camp was often total, the cow town prospered. There was, of course, one other major difference: the cowboy. Tough, hard-bitten, and interesting they may have been, but the old-time miners lacked the glamour associated with the cowboy, exemplified by his colorful dress, nomadic lifestyle, and, of course, his horse. That, combined with the danger met daily when branding, driving, and generally tending the awesome and totally unpredictable Texas longhorn, inspired an adulation that goes far to explain why the cow towns receive more than their share of attention.

The cattle shipping points were obvious targets for the "pasteboard pirates" and the "locusts of lechery." Abilene's launch into the cattle trade in 1867 did not start an immediate invasion of gamblers and others, but by 1870 they were well entrenched. The city council in 1871 imposed fines for gamblers and exacted license fees from those who provided them with accommodation. It was a situation that existed in all the cow towns. Newton's gamblers were well publicized. On September 17, 1871, the Topeka *Daily Commonwealth* noted that:

> There is a mania for gambling in Newton. The heart of every man who has been here long enough to dig down a little to the substrata of life, nestles the germ of this passion. In some it has bloomed into a full blown flower. These latter are mostly professionals, who sit on the percent side of the table. Most of them are well known all over the extreme west. Listen to their chat as they sit together after dinner or supper smoking their cigars and re-counting bygone experiences, and you will discover that they are well traveled, earnest men, thinkers in a rough sort of way, and invariably readers of human nature.

The editor of the Abilene *Chronicle,* however, found no reason to romanticize about gamblers. Rather, he sought to warn his readers of the dangers of gambling and the wicked element that promoted it. On June 1, 1871, he published an exchange item headed simply "Gambling," which listed some of the more common tricks. The article explained the games of roulette, rouge et noir, vingt et un, and poker. The tricks employed to cheat addicts (the "suckers") by the professional cardsharps ranged from simple to ingenious. Marked cards (that is with notches on the edge or other indications of their face value) and fixed roulette wheels abounded. Some cheats had small knee mirrors to "reflect" upon their opponent's hand during dealing. And the superstitious souls who liked to

sit in certain places, particularly with their backs against a wall, were often the victims of their own obsession. Instead of a real wall to lean against, it was sometimes a cunningly concealed partition behind which lurked an accomplice. A peephole enabled him to see that victim's cards, and by means of a prearranged signal (either a loose board upon which the gambler's foot rested or a wire tied to a foot) the hand was read and cheating commenced.

Many of the well-known cow-town figures gambled, some professionally. Benjamin ("Ben") Thompson gambled professionally for much of his life. He was born in Knottingley, Yorkshire, England, on November 2, 1843, and was the son of a mariner. His family, which included his

younger brother Billy, immigrated to the United States in the early 1850s where he was brought up in Texas, later achieving a reputation as a gunfighter and gambler.

Wyatt Earp, whose best-remembered exploit was the gunfight at the O.K. Corral, was involved in gambling from the early 1870s. In the 1880s in Tombstone, Arizona, he acquired an interest in the flourishing Oriental Saloon. He later owned several saloons in Idaho and was involved in

**BELOW: Ellsworth in 1879, looking very peaceful, having by then rid itself of the cattle trade. Those who had demanded the streets be made safer were, as is the way of these things, the first to feel nostalgic for the old days.**

mining ventures. In the wake of the Klondyke gold rush, Earp was active in the saloon business in Nome, Alaska. Earp was also accused in later life of being mixed up in various confidence games, but the evidence is not very clear. What is certain, however, is that gambling and the saloon business were passions of his.

Probably the best known of the gunfighters to become involved in the saloon and gambling business was Luke Short, whose "war" with Dodge City received nationwide publicity. It all began with the "wet" and "dry" debate in Kansas, following the Kansas state legislature's decision in 1880 to change the constitution so that it would seriously affect the drinking habits of the saloon set. Dodge City

## SHARPS'S COMPETITORS

Christian Sharps (1811–1874) established a tradition of excellence; his firearms were much admired both by the military and civilians alike. His many rivals sought to surpass him, but few did. By the late 1860s and early 1870s (when Sharps himself was no longer involved in rifle manufacture), a number of rival makers produced arms that appealed to the civilian market, in particular the buffalo hunters who were busy exterminating the Lords of the Plains in droves.

Remington, Ballard, and others vied for the lucrative market. Ballard produced a number of "hunting" rifles in calibers ranging from .32 to .44, which met with some success. But it was the Remington sporting and hunting rifles that proved to be Sharps's biggest rivals. Their calibers ranged from .40 to .50 with a powerful cartridge to match. No matter who the makers were, hunting or buffalo rifles were expensive, between $100 and $300 depending upon the maker and the quality. The addition of special sights or telescopic sights was an important

factor. Ammunition aroused as much controversy as the weapons themselves. Hunters "loaded their own" most of the time and paid special attention to the black powder used. The American powders tended to burn "hot and dry" and cake up the bore, whereas the English version made by Curtis & Harvey burned "moist."

1. Maynard .50 caliber rifle in fitted case with reloading tools, powder flask, and cartridges. Note second barrel. These were normally supplied in different calibers from .32 to .44, rim- or center-fire.

2. Cartridge box for the Maynard rifle.
3. Sturdy breech-loader by the Brown Mfg. Co.
4. Remington No. 1 Rolling Block sporting rifle. It was chambered for various calibers from .40 to .60; popular with hunters and plainsmen alike.
5. Remington-Hepburn rifle with pistol grip.
6. Fine example of Frank Wesson's two-trigger rifle.
7. The outside hammer Peabody hunting rifle appeared in calibers .44 to .45.
8. Remington Rolling Block short-range rifle in the "Light Baby Carbine" model.
9. Winchester single-shot rifle Model 1885 with a 20-inch round barrel.
10. Similar weapon fitted with 30-inch octagonal barrel. Both weapons have adjustable rear sights.
11. Fine Marlin-Ballard No. 2 sporting rifle in .38 center-fire.
12. .38 center-fire "shells" for the Marlin-Ballard.
(Artifacts courtesy of Buffalo Bill Historical Center, Cody, Wyoming.)

became the center of attention when the town council decided to implement some of the proposed reforms. Rival factions sprang up composed of prosaloon men (keepers and gamblers) generally called "the Gang," and the "Reformers," composed of antiliquor councilmen and, surprisingly, several saloon owners. These were more concerned with their public image in a political sense than any moral scruples.

The "Gang" included Bat Masterson, W. H. Harris, and the likes of Luke Short, whereas the "Reformers" counted among their membership the erstwhile mayor, Alonzo B. Webster, Mayor Lawrence E. Deger, and Mike Sutton, a lawyer. The "Reformers" alleged that the gang members were con men who were up to all manner of tricks. Their activities in effect deterred settlement. Webster had been elected mayor in 1881 and is reported to have put a stop to many of the so-called rackets, imposing certain quasi-moral restrictions. His successor Deger, elected in April 1883, was thought by some to be his "creature" and still guided by Webster.

Short went into partnership with W. H. Harris in the Long Branch saloon and within days was confronted by a new ordinance against prostitution—his "singer" was arrested and charged with soliciting. A run-in with a local policeman, during which shots were fired but no one was hurt, led to Luke's arrest, and within days he was told to leave town. This he did, but he headed for Topeka where he spoke to the press and had an audience with the governor.

Word also spread to the west that "Luke Short is in trouble," and a number of his friends announced that they would come to his assistance. The press had a field day. Dire warnings were given on what might happen if Wyatt Earp, Bat Masterson, Doc Holliday, Charlie Bassett, Rowdy Joe Lowe, Shotgun Collins, and others appeared on the city's streets. As it turned out, the city fathers capitulated when some of those characters showed up, and Luke was reinstated. But, had things gone badly for the council, the governor had been prepared to send in troops to restore order. In honor of the occasion, Short and his friends were photographed, and the picture was quickly dubbed "The Dodge City Peace Commission." In 1884, Short tried to sue the city of Dodge for throwing him out the previous year. It was settled out of court, and Short departed satisfied.

ABOVE: "Squirrel-tooth Alice," one of Dodge City's better-known prostitutes. Dressed very respectably, her attire reflects the far-reaching changes taking place within the city itself.

Bartholomew "Bat" Masterson (he later changed his name to William Barclay Masterson), the Canadian-born gambler, saloon owner, and prizefight enthusiast who became a newspaperman, served as a county sheriff in Kansas and later as a deputy U.S. marshal. He, too, enjoyed gambling and became an expert in both its tricks and potential. In later years he was to write at length on the characters that turned a card as easily as they pulled a trigger. But according to Arthur Chapman, writing in the New York *Herald-Tribune* of

January 3, 1930, on one occasion Bat himself was accused of cheating and came near having to prove his skill with a gun as well as his sleight of hand. Bat and his friend, one "Conk" Jones, fell out when Jones claimed that he had taken advantage of a young fellow with more money than sense. Mr. Chapman's informant was John L. Amos, who had been sharing a hotel room with Masterson and Jones:

He and Bat had come to a showdown in a poker game. The rest of the table had dropped out, Jones among them. Bat raked in the pot without showing his hand. The young fellow started to protest and then thought better of it. The play may have been alright, but it did not suit Jones. Conk leaned over and said. "Bat, don't ever make a play like that again when I'm around." I knew from the sound of Jones' voice and the look in his eyes, that he was trying to force Bat into a fight right-there. Bat laughed it off and Conk walked away, and apparently forgot the incident as the men remained on a friendly footing. Someone spoke about it afterwards, but Bat poo-poohed the idea of any trouble between Jones and himself. But knowing Jones as I did, I am certain the stage was set for a gun battle between experts for a few seconds that night.

Even James Butler "Wild Bill" Hickok is reputed to have run a gambling place. This was described in the press as a "hell" in Junction City during the late 1860s. He also built a saloon in Hays City, but soon disposed of it, having little interest in the problems that went into owning and running such places. In Abilene he indulged in the pastime in between his duties as city marshal, as he had done in Hays City when acting sheriff of Ellis County in 1869.

Once his gunfighting days were behind him, Wild Bill concentrated on gambling, and it was when playing poker at Deadwood in 1876 that he was murdered while holding a hand that was comprised of the ace of spades, the ace of clubs, the eight of clubs, the eight of spades, and a queen or jack of diamonds "kicker," today remembered as "the Deadman's Hand."

In later years, some claimed that Hickok was a poor gambler, but others believe that he was as canny as the next man when faced by would-be cheats. There is a story long in circulation that best explains Hickok's modus operandi. This version comes from the Ellis County Free Press of January 5, 1887, and was copied from the Chicago News. Headed "A Good Hand at Poker," it stated:

"Did you ever hear of Wild Bill's ace full?" asked a local manipulator of the cardboards. "The story may be old, but it's true . . . Wild Bill had a weakness for poker, and knew no more about it than a baby. The consequence was he was a picnic for the sports, and they fleeced him right and left. He was repeatedly warned that he was being robbed, but he always replied that he was able to take care of himself.

"One night he sat down to play with a fellow named McDonald, a fine-worker and expert. McDonald did as he pleased, and the scout found his pile getting smaller and smaller as the game progressed. As he lost he began to drink, and midnight found him in a state of intense but repressed excitement—a condition that made him one of the most dangerous men in the West. It was at this juncture that McDonald, smart gambler as he was, made his mistake. He should have quit. However, Wild Bill's apparent coolness deceived him.

"Finally, the scout seemed to get an unusual hand, and began to bet high and heavy. McDonald raised him back every time, until the top of the table was about out of sight. At last there was a call.

"'I've got three jacks,' said McDonald, throwing down his hand.

"'I have an ace full on sixes,' said Bill.

"'Ace full on sixes is good,' said McDonald, coolly turning over his opponent's cards, 'but I see only two aces and a six.'

"'Here is the other six!' suddenly roared Bill, whipping out a Navy revolver, 'and here'—drawing a bowie knife—'is the one spot.'

"'That hand is good,' said McDonald, blandly, arising slowly. 'Take the pot.'"

Some gamblers were extremely dangerous people, and among the genuine "good bad men" of the gambling fraternity was Joseph "Rowdy Joe" Lowe, one of the most interesting of the many lurid characters who ever turned a card or pulled a pint behind the bar of a saloon. Born in New York state in 1845, Joe grew up in Illinois and Missouri from where, in February 1865, he enlisted in Battery B of the Second (New) Missouri Regiment of Light Artillery. The Civil War was over before he really heard a shot fired in anger, but he remained in the regiment until December of that year, by which time he had served in the Powder River Indian Expedition that took him to Montana and back through Nebraska and Missouri. He appeared in Ellsworth in 1867 and was a typical roustabout and hanger-on. By 1869, however, he was involved in the saloon business and remained in it (and the lucrative dance hall trade) for most of his life. With his common-law wife Kate "Rowdy Kate" Lowe, whose real name and origin have so far eluded us, he ran gambling halls and "houses of ill fame" in Ellsworth, Newton, Wichita, and places in Texas and later in Colorado. He had shoot-outs with several individuals, but it was his feud with Edward T. "Red" Beard at Delano, across the river from Wichita, that is best remembered.

The pair were rival saloon owners and occupied space within yards of each other. On October 27, 1873, Red looked through the window of his dance house, and as Joe appeared at the window of his, Red took a shot at him with his Navy revolver. Red was drunk at the time, otherwise his aim might had been better. As it was, the slug grazed Joe's neck. Furious, Joe rushed over to complain.

The pair had a heated exchange and then both fired at each other. Red's shot went wild, but Joe's missed Red and passed across the bridge of bartender Billy Anderson's nose. This blinded him and robbed him of his sense of smell. Red and Joe then began stalking each other taking potshots before retreating to reload. Beard, in his drunken state, also shot one of his "girls" in the stomach, which did not endear him to his employees.

Shortly afterward, as Red was creeping about near the Chisholm Trail bridge, there came the thunderous report of a shotgun, and Red was found with one arm shattered and a ball in his hip. Lowe soon afterward gave himself up to Marshal Mike Meagher, later claiming that he remembered little of the fight since he, too, was drunk at the time. Joe was cleared of the killing but skipped the state rather than go on trial for his wounding of Anderson. Ironically, on February 11, 1899, Joe Lowe died unarmed and with his boots on following a row with a former policeman who shot him without allowing him any chance to defend himself.

Whatever the attitudes to gambling—and they varied considerably—the obsession with gambling was a major source of revenue in the cow towns and other places. Stuart Henry noted that luck in all things was paramount, and especially the "chumminess" between people who regarded luck as their guide. Few felt that it was sacrilegious to gamble. The gamblers who frequented the cattle towns did so only during the trail-driving season (May to October), moving on elsewhere for the winter months. Mining towns or those with more perennial activities could claim resident or itinerant gamblers. Of the more permanent characters, the Ellsworth *Reporter* of October 3, 1872, noted that the few Texans who stayed over when the season ended were subject to "the off-season doldrums":

Just at present his stock in trade is light. His bank roll, which last summer he flashed up on every occasion, now scarce ever sees the light of day . . . He makes no reckless bets, nor does he indulge in games whereof he does not understand . . . at the recollection of those past flush times he sighs and says, "d—n such a country as this, the Black Hills is the place for me." But after a second thought he takes it all back and concludes to wait for the cattle trade [to return].

Gambling, whether it was at cards, wagers, or the risks involved in driving cattle to market, represented status and a place in society, and to some it suggested power. Joseph G. McCoy, however, made it plain that bankruptcy could easily stare one in the face, and he should have known. For his founding of Abilene as the first direct shipping point of cattle east had been based upon an oral arrangement with the Union Pacific Railway Company, Eastern Division, for a return of five dollars per carload of cattle shipped. When the company changed its name to the Kansas Pacific Railway in March 1869, they reneged on the deal. Despite winning a lengthy court battle, McCoy was a broken man.

In his *Human Life* articles, Bat Masterson recalled that "gambling was not only the principal and best-paying industry of the town at the time, but it was also reckoned among its most respectable and . . . the elements of chance played a part, an important part . . . it was also reckoned . . . [to be] . . . respectable." Respectable or not, the potential for taxation was enormous. Gary L. Cunningham noted that the

LEFT: "Timberline," a noted Dodge City prostitute, still shows some of the good looks she had before dissipation, drink, and disease ruined her and many other such "soiled doves."

legal heritage of this action can be traced back to the city of New Orleans in 1823, when the law allowed the city to license six gaming establishments at the rate of $5,000 apiece. It was eventually repealed, but not before municipal income had benefited.

Abilene, however, imposed no such sum, preferring fees that worked in the form of fines. Individuals paid between five and ten dollars, plus costs, whereas proprietors of gambling establishments could expect to pay an average of twenty dollars or as much as seventy-five dollars per month. Further fines were imposed if the gambler got drunk or committed another misdemeanor, such as being caught carrying a "concealed weapon" in contravention of the state statutes; if proved, this always resulted in a fine.

In 1873, Wichita looked with a jaundiced eye on gambling and imposed severe penalties within the city itself. The council curtailed both the gambling and saloon-keeping fraternities' activities. The rot had begun to set in the previous year when it was reported that income from the gambling houses and places of prostitution had proved very lucrative. One irate gambler, Isaac Thayer, a former sheriff of Ellis County and a veteran of the Battle of Beecher Island, addressed a note of complaint to the city council in which he alleged that, having paid fifty dollars per month for permission to run a gambling establishment, he was now being asked to pay a further twenty-five. Thayer requested that the money be returned or offset against his next monthly payment. The outcome of that exchange is not known, but by

August 14, 1873, the *City Eagle* reported that "All gambling houses in the city have been closed. Quite a number had taken their tables and fixings and gone to the other side of the river where no fines will be imposed on them nor 'police!' arrest them." Across the river was Delano, which was not yet a part of the city and therefore was immune from city taxes.

Abilene's demise as a cattle town and the reforms that smote it months before the final season ended was not lost either on the press or the patrons of the gambling dens. In his *Chronicle* of July 27, 1871, V. P. Wilson described gamblers as "licentious and stealing characters who . . . crawled into this place in violation of the laws of the State and ordinances of the Town." He forgot to mention the lucrative fines and license fees exacted by McCoy's administration, probably because he and the mayor were at loggerheads over the rights and wrongs of the cattle trade and the money it brought to the region.

**Sisters in Sin**

Like the gamblers, saloon keepers, and the other flotsam and jetsam of the cow towns, prostitutes also played their part in creating a thriving community. The morally inclined may well have detested the harlots, but in an almost totally male dominated society, they performed a role that if nothing else sated passions in an atmosphere that always remained potentially violent.

While some towns accepted, willingly or otherwise, the existence of prostitution in their midst, others did not. In May 1870, the Board of Trustees of Abilene passed an ordinance authorizing the removal of brothel owners and "lewd women" from within corporate limits. By September, most of them had moved to St. Louis, Kansas City, even faraway Baxter Springs, but when the cattle season opened again in May the following year, they came flooding back in even greater numbers than before. Texas Street now housed

all the ingredients that made a cowboy's life even bearable. Ultimately, however, the permanent residents of Abilene made a stand, and Mayor McCoy ordered Marshal Hickok to supervise the removal of all the brothels to an area southeast of the city, known as "McCoy's Addition," much to the mayor's annoyance. By September 1871, fed up to the back teeth with heavy fines and other abuses that affected their lives (such as the revoking of licenses to run dance halls and to sell whiskey and brandy) and mindful of the fact that the cattle season was once more at an end, the inmates of McCoy's Addition finally moved on to new pastures.

James B. Hickok was one of a number of cow-town lawmen that had affairs or lived with known prostitutes. Other well-known figures also formed associations. Bat Masterson had several affairs, as did others, including the Earps. In their case, they went further: in Wichita in 1874 two of their women were charged with soliciting. According to the police court records, Bessie Earp, the wife of James, was fined for soliciting in May, and a similar charge was made against Sallie Earp, whose relationship to the brothers has not been clarified. Bessie and Sallie Earp were fined eight dollars and two dollars in court costs.

Wyatt Earp's involvement with women (he was married three times) has not received the same scrutiny as have his alleged gunfighting exploits, but one encounter with the notorious Frankie Bell, a well-known denizen of Dodge City's red light district, in July 1877 reached the ears of the press. According to the *Times* of the July 21, she had heaped "epithets upon the unoffending head of Mr. Earp [who was at that time on the police force] to such an extent as to provoke a slap . . . besides creating a disturbance of the quiet and dignity of the city, for which she received a night's lodging in the dog house and a reception at the police court next morning, the expense of which was about $20. Wyatt Earp was assessed the lowest limit of the law, one dollar."

With time, the declining cattle trade, the encroachment of

**LEFT: The Pearl Saloon in Abilene, in the early days before paved roads and sidewalks replaced the wooden shacks; by the end of the 1880s, the kerosene lamps would be replaced by gas or electric light.**

so-called civilization, and other restrictions, social changes in cow towns and mining camps were marked. Gambling, saloons, and prostitution still flourished, but their activities were much more low-key or pointedly ignored by the "better class of citizen" who rarely came into contact with such people. The late Lucile Stevens, who was born in Wichita just before the turn of the century, told this writer that as a small child she knew many of the old-timers who had founded the place and witnessed its growth into a respectable community. But the "other side of the tracks" and those who inhabited the place were never discussed. She then recalled that one Sunday, about 1905, she was returning from church with her mother and an aunt. For some reason they took a wrong turn, and their buggy passed a place outside of which sat a number of desperate looking women, in various stages of dress, who stared at them in amazement as they drove past. When, in all innocence, she asked her father who they were, he was furious. "Only years later," she recalled, "did I learn that those poor women were dance hall girls and prostitutes."

Mrs. Stevens also explained why documentation about the early days in the cow towns was lacking. Local fires (a common problem) were only partially responsible. The real culprits were the people who destroyed records, who did not wish their early participation in the founding of the city to be known. "They were more concerned with what it had become than what it had once been. People of that time were more concerned with what was happening in Washington or your Queen Victoria's court, and its social significance than the whereabouts of old city records and lurid stories about cowboys and gunfighters."

This was true, of course. George L. Cushman, the author of the first in-depth account of Abilene's period as a cow town, told this writer that in the early 1930s he had reason to visit the local fire station and was just in time to rescue many of the old city records for the period from the department's incinerator. Someone had decided that they were no longer needed. Fortunately, a large number of such records have survived. They indicate how cow towns and mining camps grew from tents, shacks, and muddy streets strewn with dung and debris, the inevitable saloons, dance halls, and brothels to the stores and other civilized enterprises that are part of its respectability and its life.

# THE JOHN BATTERSON
# STETSON HAT

The Stetson hat has become a defining motif of the cowboy, its classic lines evoking an age of tough men working beneath the sun, rain, and snows of the West. Its creator was one John Batterson Stetson, the son of a hatter, who was born in 1830 in Orange, New Jersey. His father instructed him in the arts of hat making, but the young Stetson was entering a bleak profession, renowned for its poor financial prospects. Following his father's death, John

Stetson worked for his brothers for a time before setting up his own hat-making company. However, a bout of tuberculosis convinced him that he needed a more stable career. He subsequently became the manager, then partner of a brick-producing factory in St. Joseph, Missouri, although this employment was terminated when the Missouri River flooded and destroyed the factory.

During the Civil War, Stetson, having failed to join the

**ABOVE AND RIGHT: Stetson hats were both stylish headwear suited for a trip into town and tough pieces of utility clothing. Stetsons worn in the South generally had taller crowns and wider brims than those worn in the cooler, more northerly climes.**

army on account of his poor health, went off gold prospecting in the Rocky Mountains. In 1872, he and a party of other men were caught out one night in a violent thunderstorm. They attempted to shelter beneath sections of animal skin, but they were utterly soaked. One of the men complained about the lack of good shelter material, and Stetson suddenly felt inspiration. Using his hat-making skills, he produced strong, waterproof material using the process of

"felting," which involves binding layers of fur together using a heating then cooling process. The result is a strong material resistant to most climatic conditions. Stetson fashioned the material into broad-brimmed hats for his colleagues to wear, and the men soon became dependent on their environmentally tough headgear.

Soon other gold prospectors were approaching Stetson for hats, and he sold his first one for five dollars. On the basis of his emerging success, Stetson moved east to Philadelphia to try and start up a new hat business there. He realized, however, that the East Coast urban fashions were not suited to his hat style, so he moved back out West where he targeted ranchmen with his Stetson hat. Made out of soft felt, the "Boss of the Plain"—as Stetson eventually named it—had a four-inch-deep brim, a four-inch crown, and came in a natural tan color. It had everything a cowboy could want from a hat. Its brim kept sun and rain off the head and shoulders. It could be turned upside down and used to carry oats or water to a horse or used as an improvised drinking vessel. The hat could fan flames into life or urge cattle into order. It also seemed almost indestructible.

Soon Stetson was selling thousands of hats each year at up to twenty dollars apiece, and the hat became popularized by everyone from the Texas Rangers to Buffalo Bill. By 1906, the year in which Stetson died, an astonishing two million hats were being made in his factory each year. Today, even in the modern age, Stetson hats still command respect among the people of America's West.

## Chapter Four

### BETWEEN GOOD AND EVIL:

# WESTERN LAW AND ORDER

The "Gunfight at the O.K. Corral" lasted about thirty seconds, and an estimated seventeen shots were fired. At the end, of the eight men who were involved, three were dead, three were badly wounded. Tombstone's relief when the Earps quit Arizona was reflected nationwide.

LEFT: Gunfighter, thief—and deputy marshal—"Big Steve" Long, lynched in Laramie City, 1867, by a group of vigilantes. The vigilante "committee" lynched at least three others. N. K. Boswell, a local rancher and later first sheriff of Albany County, then deputy United States marshal and warden of the territorial prison, was a leading member of the necktie party.

# LAW AND ORDER

The eternal struggle between good and evil—religious belief versus paganism, honor, integrity, and morality versus anarchy, dissipation, and other sins of the flesh—or corruption of morality set against a Western background has stirred passions for generations. The personal conflict between the "good" gunfighter and the "bad" gunman is a particular attraction, but the reality of the West was not a simple "good guys" and "bad guys" scenario. Rather, it was human endeavor to better itself in a harsh, sometimes hostile environment. It is a curious fact that, despite innumerable accounts of the lawlessness of the West, there is also the underlying belief that justice, law, and order would eventually triumph.

The reality of how the gunfighter spent his time, and the level of violence his life involved, are wide open to misunderstanding. Contrary to the way they are represented in many Western movies, gunfighters did not exist simply to move between gambling dens and gunfights, and killings were generally infrequent. Based on available evidence, as compiled by Bill O'Neal for *The Encyclopedia of Western Gunfighters* (University of Oklahoma Press, 1979), the top three murderers of the West were Jim Miller, Wes Hardin, and Bill Longley. Confirmed kills for these three men are twelve, eleven, and eleven, respectively, although Miller made a confession to having killed forty-four men just before he was executed. Miller, Hardin, and Longley were undoubtedly a trio of violent men, but some of the other great names of the Wild West had far less notches on their gunstocks. Billy the Kid killed four men (despite being in around twenty gunfights), as did Ben Thompson, Henry Brown, John Slaughter, Clay Allison, and Jim Courtright. The legendary Doc Holliday and Pat Garrett killed only two men apiece, while Bat Masterson only killed one. Wyatt Earp and the Sundance Kid, names synonymous with the gunfighter profession, possibly killed no one at all, although Garrett has five "possibles" in his statistics.

Figures such as these should make us cautious about classifying all the gunfighters as habitual and comfortable killers. Certainly they were hard men, but killing has rarely been a practice to take lightly, even among the tough. The average lifespan of the gunfighters is also revealing (again, O'Neal has done fascinating work in this regard, see page 7 of the *Encyclopedia*). The average age of a gunfighter who

ended his days violently—and this generally accounts for around 50 percent of those we classify as gunfighters—was thirty-five. The other 50 percent who managed to avoid the bullets lived to an average age of seventy, respectable even by today's standards. Although some gunfighters would compress much of their killing into a few short years, typically during an intense phase of feuding, many others would stretch out their shooting career over many years. We should therefore

acknowledge that, even among the criminal fraternity, murder was an infrequent event rather than a constant recourse.

So what did the gunfighters do with their lives when they weren't propping up a saloon bar, sitting at a table, chasing down a fugitive, or furthering a criminal career? Most gunfighters were, at least for substantial periods of their lives, in thoroughly conventional and legitimate employment.

LEFT: Pinkerton detective Bill Sayles. The Pinkertons were one of the most feared law enforcement agencies of the West, and here Sayles is pictured during the vigorous pursuit of the Wild Bunch. The Pinkerton agency later attracted hostility over its use of undercover agents when handling labor disputes for industrial clients.

Admittedly, O'Neal lists thirty-five gunfighters "employed" as hired gunmen, forty-five as cattle or horse rustlers, twenty-six as bandits, and twenty-four as gamblers. Yet these figures should not be interpreted as sole employment. Harvey Logan "Kid Curry," for example, worked as a rancher and horse breaker in addition to his spells as rustler, gunman, and armed robber. The infamous John Selman was variously a farmer, butcher, rancher, saloon keeper, soldier, and law officer in his fifty-six years. Although the jobs taken by the gunfighting fraternity could be specialized and unusual and include telegraph runner, irrigation manager, insurance executive, painter, dentist, whisky salesman, and actor, by far the largest source of employments were those jobs that dominated the lifestyle of the West: prospector, miner, clerk, saloon owner, farmer, rancher, cowboy, soldier (particularly during the Civil War), and laborer. However, out of the 255 gunfighters listed by O'Neal, a full 110 of them were at some time or other employed as law officers. More will be said about this

connection below, but what emerges is how easily an individual slipped between the worlds of law and order and criminality and chaos. Jim Miller, for example, was one of the West's worst murderers, but even he was accepted into the Texas Rangers for a period. Wyatt Earp was an intermittent law officer who had been arrested for stealing horses in Indian Territory and who was also thrown out of the Wichita police force for gambling (he was gambling and keeping fines taken from prostitutes). Nineteenth-century law officers

ABOVE: A portrait of Annie Rogers and Harvey Logan. Logan—better known by his nickname, "Kid Curry"—was one of the Wild Bunch's more vicious members. Unlike other gang figures such as Butch Cassidy, Logan had no compunction about shooting people.

LEFT: A rare photograph of Judge Roy Bean (with watch chain), "the Law West of the Pecos," outside his saloon at Langtry, Texas. His verdicts were very controversial and often delivered with gallows humor.

often worked without today's oversight from a governing body and in places where the rule of law was precarious. As such, it was little wonder that distinction between the lawman and the criminal could be blurred.

We should resist moral judgments, however. The lawman of the Wild West had to live in times very different than our own. By contemporary standards, it is daunting to consider a society where everyone might be armed, yet the West of the early and middle nineteenth century was such a place. Parts of it were populated and civilized, while other regions were regarded as near barbaric and hazardous. Consequently, it was accepted that those who lived in the less-populated regions were armed more for defense than offense. Another factor was the sheer distance between settlements or cities. Places sprang up simply because they were on the route of a well-known overland trail or because of the railroad, and well ahead of the advance of settlement.

## Enforcing the Law

People moving West created some of the conditions that favored the lawless element. Individuals reserved the right to settle disputes among themselves; problems with Indians, who naturally resisted white encroachment upon their lands, led to frequent disputes, and the U.S. Army had the thankless task of establishing lonely forts or posts simply to keep both sides apart. That this frequently failed is a matter of history, as is the fact that people resented interference by government

(they still do), so the establishment of law and order often lagged far behind settlement. Would-be emigrants naturally assumed that the law would ultimately follow on after them, and with it social, economic, and political developments to enhance their livelihood. Vigilantes were expedient but not the answer to the problem, and neither were squatters' rights associations, which had been formed to protect claims or embryonic settlements, for their sometimes-overzealous reactions failed to protect the bona fide claimants, which caused resentment. Therefore, the basic need of the ordinary folk was established community law and not anarchy. With time, territorial, district, and state courts took care of the problems, but mostly the individual had to fend for himself.

Responsible for building forts and posts across the country

**LEFT: Texas cowboys at work, their handguns displayed prominently on their hips. Note how the cowboy on the right has his gun arranged with the handle pointing forward, this facilitating a cross-body draw.**

**BELOW: A cattle drive in Colorado in the late nineteenth century. It remained the job of law enforcement officers to control such men when they hit the town after months on a long, lonely, and arduous trail.**

LEFT: Charles Behrer, a prominent member of the Montana vigilantes who broke up the notorious Plummer gang, was very active in the cleaning-up operation that broke the likes of George Ives.

BOTTOM LEFT: Alexander Davis, the celebrated "miners' judge," who on one occasion issued a warrant for the arrest of Jack Slade for upsetting a milk wagon. Slade, however, persuaded him to drop the charge.

to protect both red and white man, the army was also initially responsible for bringing law and order to the West. Sometimes martial law was all that stood between civilization and anarchy. The government established Indian agencies at many of these posts, appointing agents to keep Indians and whites from each other's throats. Keeping the peace on the frontier was essential, not only for the present but the future. The Indians suspected it, and the government knew it for a fact: whites would one day rule the roost, and if this could be achieved peaceably so much the better.

The law, like government, followed in the wake of emigration, and this resulted in sparsely populated areas relying to a lesser or greater extent upon individual policing.

**BELOW: A group of soldiers ride past Fort Bowie in Arizona. The fort was built in 1862 to control the nearby Apache Pass. Soldiers, as much as cowboys or gamblers, could be a source of trouble in the towns, particularly after the Civil War.**

Law and order within the United States was based on the old English legal system; despite numerous changes since, many features remain, especially in regard to officials. The sheriff and marshal still exist. In the United States, the sheriff would be an elected officer of a county responsible for maintaining peace and keeping order, attending court, guarding prisoners, serving processes, and executing judgments. A sheriff need not have any legal experience, his appointment being more political than professional. However, his salary would be paid by the county and,

**ABOVE: A movie poster glorifies the clean-cut image of the Western hero, while the girl whispers to him, "The cattle thieves are after you!" He doesn't look like a member of a lynch mob. The poster was printed and displayed in 1914 in Chicago.**

Even when territories were established, or granted statehood, the lack of railroads, proper trails, or other means of communication meant that communities or individuals took care of their own problems. The vigilantes of California and Montana were extremes dictated by demand at a time when the law was just not functioning or established. Vigilantes in other areas, such as those that influenced the running of Hays City, Kansas, in 1869, were more concerned with political power than maintaining law and order, so it is useful to understand how the American legal system of the time worked to appreciate its benefits and shortcomings.

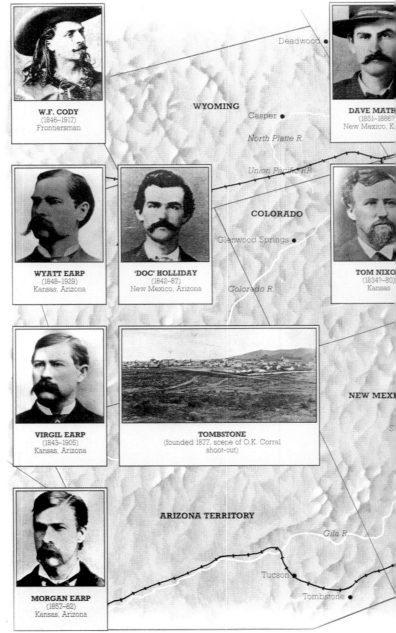

depending upon how much he was paid, dictated both the number of deputies he had and how much they were paid. His immediate subordinate was the under-sheriff (a term rarely used today), and a couple of deputies, one of whom acted as jailer. During troubled times, it was not unusual for extra deputies to be sworn in and then dismissed when no longer needed. Crime committed within the county came within his jurisdiction, and although he could invoke his authority within city limits he usually left that to the town police force.

The city council elected its own police force. The term "marshal" was still in use until recent years, but, even in the period of this present study, it was often coupled with the more grandiose title of "chief of police." The "marshal" in turn hired "constables" or "assistant marshals" at the discretion of the city council. Usually only two men were hired, but in most cow towns as many as five men might be taken on during the cattle season. The marshal was sworn to uphold the state laws, implement local ordinances, and generally keep the peace. They were rarely well paid. Tom

WILD BILL HICKOK
(1837–76)
Missouri, Kansas

TOM SMITH
(1840–70)
Wyoming, Kansas

BEN THOMPSON
(1843–84)
Texas, Kansas

JUDGE ISAAC PARKER
(1839–96)
Arkansas, Indian Territory

HECK THOMAS
(1850–1912)
Texas, Indian Territory

TEXAS RANGERS
(Indian fighters, lawmen 1823–61; reinstated 1874, and to present time)

ABOVE: Baz "Bass" N. Reeves, one of a number of black lawmen who worked for Judge Isaac Parker. The judge also employed Indians as deputy U.S. marshals. Some sixty-five black, red, and white marshals died in the territory.

Smith, Abilene's first marshal or chief of police (and one of the earliest recipients of the title in the cow-town era) was initially paid $150 per month, later raised to $225. Smith's immediate successor (following his murder in November 1870) was paid $150 to act in a caretaker capacity until a new man was chosen. Other places were not so generous. During the height of the cattle season, a marshal might be paid one hundred dollars or more a month, but once the season, ended he took a salary cut down to seventy-five, or perhaps fifty, dollars. Since the county sheriff and his deputies were paid a fixed rate by the county, if a city council paid below the norm, then a marshal's deputies fared even worse. This is rather ironic because it cost a council nothing to pay the police force whose salaries came out of monies extracted from fines or taxes imposed upon the gambling, saloon-keeping, and bawdy house "trade." Worse, the city fathers

ABOVE: Crawford Goldsby, better known as "Cherokee Bill." Bill was part Cherokee, part Mexican, part African American, and part white—a provocative mixture. He killed a number of men and was hanged at Parker's court in 1896.

even begrudged the amount spent on ammunition for the police force. A typical example can be found at Wichita where, in 1871, according to city records, a measly six dollars was allocated for each policeman. Seventy-five cents was

ABOVE: Ben Daniels, whose colorful and checkered career included a jail sentence for mule theft, service as a policeman in Dodge City, and as one of Teddy Roosevelt's infamous Rough Riders.

ABOVE: Christian Madsen, another of the "Three Guardsmen." Born in Denmark, he served in the Danish army before emigrating to the United States, where he served in the Fifth Cavalry and later as a lawman.

allowed either for a box of six paper or foil cartridges for a .36 or .44 caliber pistol, and a box of caps cost twenty cents. For powder, shot, and cartridges, $1.35 was admissible. One can only assume that they were expected to make every shot count or be personally liable for unauthorized discharges. Considering the restrictions placed upon the police, one can only wonder how the Texans could afford their all-too-frequent bouts of cowboy chaos.

Most town councils insisted that their police should conduct themselves properly. The previously mentioned Ellsworth "Ordinance No. 1" passed in April 1870 decreed that members of the police force found in brothels or gambling and drinking on duty would be fired. Other places had similar rules, for there was always the danger (so they thought) of their policemen being corrupted or bribed by the inmates.

Then there was the question of firearms in the hands of the police. Contrary to popular belief, police forces seldom shot it out with criminals then carried on as if nothing had happened. Rather, an officer might be hauled before a coroner's court and statements taken from the officer and from witnesses. Sometimes, of course, the coroner's court convened to examine the events that led to a policeman's death; this was accepted as a hazard of the job by those who undertook the task of policing a sometimes unpredictable population made up of large numbers of transients with scant regard for the law.

State police, as existed in Texas and other southern states following the Civil War, were more politically expedient than constitutional and were eventually replaced by local organizations—in the case of Texas by the reinstatement of the Texas Rangers in 1874.

### The United States Marshals

The U.S. marshal dominated local and county police forces. Created in 1789, the U.S. marshal was a presidential appointment ratified by congress. Between 1840 and 1900 he was elected to cover "districts," which could be states or territories. His main brief was to uphold the federal code of laws. Some of the larger states might have two marshals covering districts described as "Northern" or "Southern," but in most cases the appointment covered one state or territory. Some marshals had policing experience, but that was not essential. In fact, the idea of a U.S. marshal pursuing evildoers personally would probably horrify members of the judiciary. In the old days, some of them did actively get involved, but most of the actual fieldwork was delegated to the deputies.

Each marshal had an office deputy who took care of the paperwork. He in turn issued orders to the field deputies who were sworn in as *posse comitatus,* which translates as "power of the county." (The word "posse" suggests a crowd, but in fact it could be one man). Before 1896, when the United States government issued official commissions and paid a salary, only the office deputies were salaried; the

others were sworn in and, in return for serving subpoenas, warrants, and arresting individuals charged with federal crimes (robbing the mail, desertion from the army or the navy, stealing government stock, or murdering Indians on or off the reservation), they were paid a fee, plus mileage. This was two dollars per day, and the mileage was worked out at

**ABOVE: An Oklahoma Boomer is ejected from Indian territory by soldiers, his squatter family by his side. Such actions were generally not performed unless the person in question had been involved in criminal activity.**

**LEFT: A dissolute crowd of Boomers enter Oklahoma territory. "Boomers" were itinerant and transient railway workers on America's spreading railroad network. They had reputations for fighting and heavy drinking.**

about six or ten cents a mile while on active duty. The marshal himself received no salary—his reward was the office itself—but he did receive a proportion of the fees allowed against his deputies' claims. Before 1896, deputy U.S. marshals were eligible for state or territorial rewards; not so the marshal or his salaried office deputy. In 1869, for instance, Wild Bill Hickok arrested two Negro deserters from the Tenth Cavalry and lodged them in the jail at Fort Hays. He later received the reward for their capture. In some instances, however, promised rewards were withdrawn on a technicality or the recipient might have to share it with his assistants. The term "bountyhunter" was more aptly termed "manhunter" in the old days.

Those individuals who set out on manhunts were invariably either commissioned police officers or employees of railroads, express agencies, or well-known organizations such as Pinkerton. An exception, perhaps, was the "Nations" or Indian Territory—present-day Oklahoma.

In Indian Territory, law was aligned with tribal law of incumbent tribes. These laws applied only to individuals belonging to the nation or tribe where the alleged offense took place. It could be complicated, and the Indians had their own ideas about how justice should be carried out. Judge Isaac Parker, whose United States Court for the Western District of Arkansas until the late 1880s included the Indian Territory in its jurisdiction, employed a large number of deputy U.S. marshals, many of them black or Indian. In his interesting book *Black, Red, and Deadly*, Art T. Burton has told their (much neglected) story and emphasized the role such people as Baz "Bass" Reeves, an African American lawman, played in establishing law and order in the region. Both the black, white, and red marshals faced some of the roughest and toughest criminals on the continent, and if Parker's reputation as the "hanging judge" is anything to go by, they were all remarkably effective.

In other areas, however, local interpretation of the law depended very much upon the prevailing situation. The cow towns largely concerned themselves more with state rather than federal laws since they were of prior concern. Boosted by local ordinances, they generally worked. Yet even here there seems to be a belief that cow towns were without law,

**ABOVE: A long view of Wichita's Main Street, as seen in a wood engraving from 1874. Wichita's levels of violence increased with the arrival of the railroad in 1872, an event that brought Texas cattle drives to the town.**

doubtless a reference to a Wichita editor's exasperated comment that "anything goes in Wichita!"

When counties were established and cities were granted the right to elect their own government, the election or appointment of local police forces became commonplace. In essence, a town marshal or chief of police had no jurisdiction outside town limits; that was the province of the county sheriff. Since both were responsible for civil rather than federal crimes, the U.S. marshal for the state or territory took over that responsibility. He did not normally interfere in the matter of civil crime but if asked could provide deputies to assist.

The emphasis upon "frontier justice" as seen from the muzzle of a six-shooter is understandable. In the early days, the lack of jails and intimidation by the lawless to impede justice did emphasize the role that the gun played in bringing law and order to the frontier. As each place was founded, or gold and silver deposits encouraged mass migration and the birth of yet more "boom towns," attempts to bring law to such places proved difficult. Vigilante groups, regulators, and

RIGHT: Louis C. Harman, the city clerk of Dodge City in 1883, was also on the police force. He fell foul of Luke Short when he arrrested Luke's "singer." Luke shot at him twice and missed both times.

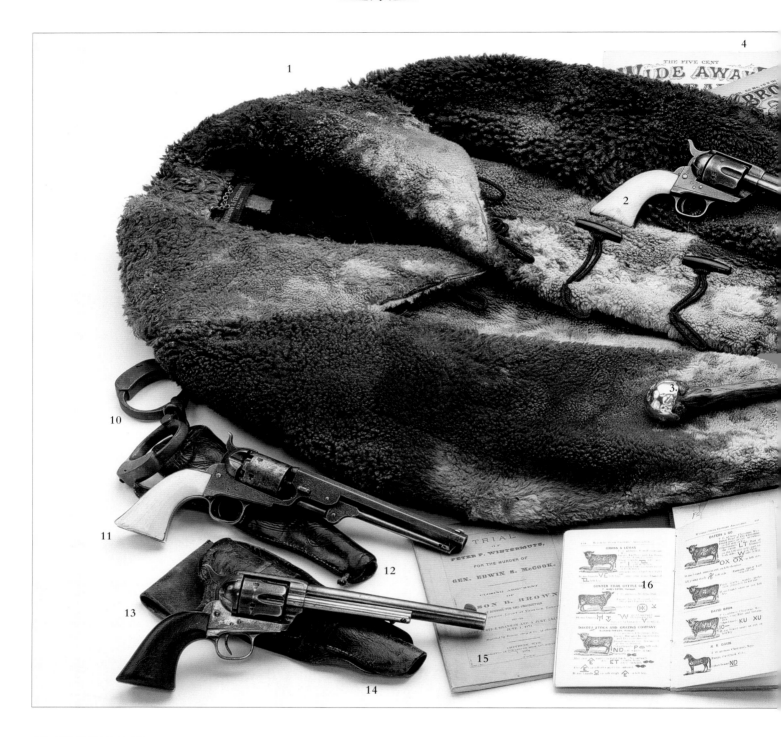

## "I AM THE LAW"

As should be clear from this book, lawmen—marshal, sheriff, constable, peace officers by any name—were tough and brutal men, many of whom had been on the other side of the law in earlier times or in other locations. They were as violent as the element they were hired to control. In early range wars, peace officers were often little more than hired assassins operating on instructions from the big ranchers. One of the artifacts above is a good example of how right and wrong was

not defined by the law and could be a matter of individual conscience. Asa Shinn Mercer, the author of *Banditti of the Plains* (17) had come to Wyoming to edit the *North West Live Stock Journal*, the official publication of the Wyoming Stock Growers Association (WSGA), which represented the monied interests intent on controlling the cattle industry. As the events of the Johnson County war unfolded, Mercer came to sympathize with the homesteaders and turned against the WSGA. The book reflects his prosettler view.

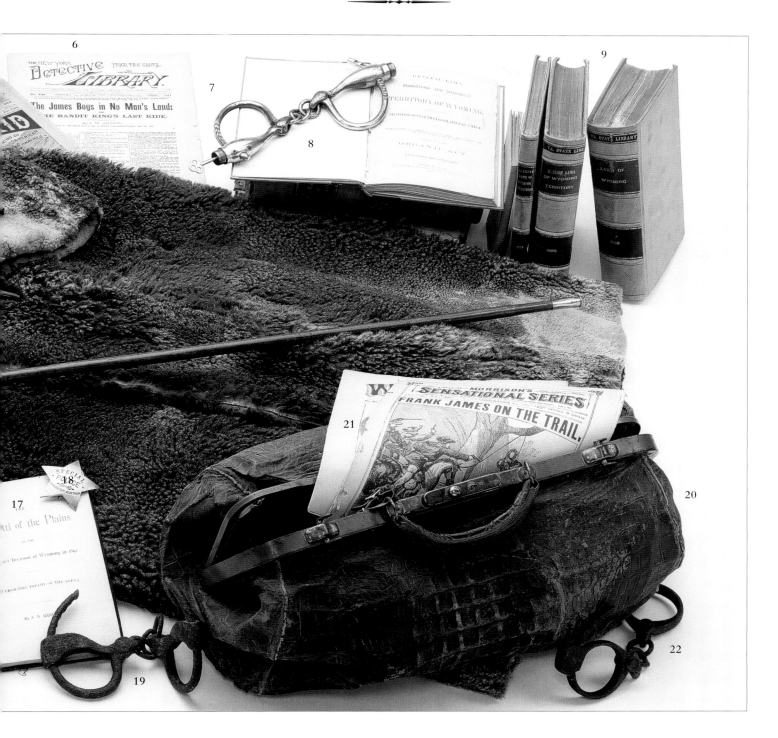

1. Wombat fur double-breasted overcoat worn by Henry Dahlem, first sheriff of Park County, Wyoming.
2. Colt single-action revolver used by Sheriff E. N. Wolf of Lampasas, Texas, 1884–1890. Wolf purchased the pistol in 1882 with a 7 1/2 in. barrel and cut it back to 4 5/8 in.
3. Coin silver-headed cane engraved "Col. Cody 'Buffalo Bill' to Jack Stilwell, Nov. 14, 1893." The tip of the cane is a brass .44–40 shell casing.
4–6. Contemporary sensationalist pulp papers.
7. Nickled iron handcuffs with key.
8, 9. Legal treatises: *The Compiled Laws of Wyoming*, 1887; *Revised Statutes of Wyoming*, 1887; *Laws of Wyoming*, 1869; and *Session Laws of Wyoming Territory*, 1879 and 1886.
10. Pair of metal handcuffs or restraints.
11. Colt Model 1851 Navy revolver, .36 caliber, engraved with ivory grips.
12. "Slim Jim" style leather holster for revolver above.

13. Colt single-action Army revolver carried by Marshal William Blunt of Emporia, Kansas. Note 7 1/2 in. barrel, .45 caliber.
14. Mexican double-loop leather holster for revolver above.
15. Pamphlet: *Trial of Peter P. Wintermule, Cheyenne, Wyoming*, 1874.
16. Brand book of the Wyoming Stock Growers' Association, 1885.
17. Book, *The Banditti of the Plains, or The Cattlemen's Invasion of Wyoming in 1892*, by A. S. Mercer.
18. Five-pointed nickel silver badge of the special police of Livingston, Montana, made by G. J. Mayer Company, Indianapolis, Indiana. (Courtesy of Old West Antiques, Cody, Wyoming.)
19. Pair of patent metal handcuffs.
20. Alligator hide traveling bag of Deputy Sheriff E. S. Hoops, Cody, c. 1890.
21. Dime novels: Morrison's Sensational Series.
22. Pair of metal handcuffs or restraints.
(Artifacts courtesy of the Buffalo Bill Historical Center, Cody, Wyoming.)

other "sin sifters" played a part, but it was not justice in a legal sense: hotheaded prejudice was no substitute for cold logic based on established principals. In general, lawlessness in the West was as much a result of a lack of law as a reaction by those opposed to it. The tradition of the lone avenger— righter of wrongs, a combination of the duelist and an executioner—has little place in reality, yet the role of the individual in establishing, implementing, or supervising the carrying out of legal requirements did play a part in the fight to bring calm out of chaos. Nowhere is that tradition better exemplified than in the years immediately following the Civil War, when unreconstructed rebels, disillusioned ex-guerrillas, and those sworn to uphold the law clashed head on. In its wake came the myths and fables that today inspire stories about the gunfighting lawmen whose exploits have thrilled generations.

Town marshals, or chiefs of police, were provided with deputies whose numbers were increased or decreased at the whim of the city council. During winter months it was not unusual for the marshal to be on his own, whereas once the cattle season started he could have as many as five deputies, some full-time, taken on to assist during a particularly busy period. In the 1870s, the cow towns had populations of perhaps 1,000 permanent residents, but during the cattle season this number could treble. Theophilus Little recalled in 1910 that in Abilene, in April 1871, there were approximately 500 people, but by June 1 there were about 7,000 of them sleeping in tents, filling hotels and boarding houses or simply "under blankets spread upon the prairie." Controlling such a mass of people required firmness and tact. Fortunately, the majority of them were well aware of their transient nature and were only concerned with enjoying themselves in the many saloons, gambling houses, and other places of entertainment.

Town marshals were also responsible for street cleaning as well as patrolling, although it is unlikely that they attended to these tasks themselves. They were also supposed to keep an eye out for blocked chimneys and other public nuisances, particularly stray dogs. In Abilene, the council allowed Marshal Hickok fifty cents for each stray dog he shot. History does not record if he personally carried out that task or assigned it to a deputy. On one occasion, however, he was called upon to shoot a maddened Texas longhorn that had escaped the pens and was careering along Texas Street. A set of horns from the animal are now on view at the Dickinson County Museum at Abilene, where they were placed by J. B. Edwards in 1940, shortly before his death.

Town police were also responsible for seeing that places of entertainment were properly supervised and trouble free. In the cattle towns and mining camps, however, this had its problems. Street patrols, spot checks, and the occasional arrest of a troublesome drunk were the norm. Only when things really got out of hand did the police call for assistance from the public. Usually, however, the presence of the police on the street kept things in check and proved comforting for those citizens who appreciated the economic advantage of the cattle trade but abhorred its evils.

In attempting to contain the violence and establish some form of law and order, city councils were faced with a problem. There were few so-called professional policemen available, so much reliance was placed upon men of reputation whose standing in the community inspired trust simply because they could quell the mob. As McCoy expressed it in what was thought to be a reference to Hickok: "no quiet-turned man could or would care to take the office of marshal, which jeopardized his life"; hence "the necessity of employing a desperado—one who feared nothing and would as soon shoot an offending subject as to look at him." It was far from ideal, but it was better than nothing. So began the era of the gunfighting town marshal.

## The Peacemakers

The man with a gun served to mar or motivate, and we have seen how the cowboy influenced or deterred growth. Now it was the turn of the peacekeepers, the men who more than any others inspired the legend of the gunfighter. The lone man facing down a mob of drunken Texas cowboys by sheer force of character or by the threat of his reputation as a killer

**ABOVE RIGHT: Thomas James "Bear River" Smith, who led the Union Pacific workers' riot at Bear River, Wyoming, in 1868. He is said to have served as a policeman in New York before coming West and later to Abilene.**

**LEFT: Baca Store, Socorro County, as seen in the twentieth century. Elfego Baca—lawman and gunfighter—ran the store in the 1880s before donning a mail-order badge and two pistols and proclaiming himself county sheriff.**

is the dominant image of the gunfighting lawman. The visual impact of Gary Cooper's almost single-handed fight against a band of killers in *High Noon* was good cinema, but it was not based upon fact. Any suggestion that the mob would overwhelm the police force would result in a rush of citizens anxious to help. Fortunately, that rarely happened, for citizens relied upon their police force to do the job they were paid for and most of the time they succeeded.

The job of lawman could carry as much political weight as legal authority, and many of those who joined the police rose to higher civic or political positions. A fine example of this sort of man is Elfego Baca. Baca was born in 1865 in Socorro, New Mexico. When he was seventeen, Francisco Baca, Elfego's father, was imprisoned in Los Lunos, New Mexico, for killing two men during a gunfight. Baca would

LEFT: Wild Bill Hickok photographed by A. P. Trott of Junction City in 1871. His presence in Abilene caused quite a stir, and he was considered to be one of the "sights" at the end of the trail.

eventually become a law enforcement officer, but as a youth his energies railed against the legal system—in February 1881 he actually broke his father out of prison. Nonetheless, by early 1883 Baca had adopted a new identity as a lawman. The term "lawman" should be applied loosely to Baca's early career; he seems simply to have pinned a homemade badge on himself and ridden into trouble carrying little official authority. Yet in January 1883, he made his first killing, shooting a member of a cowboy gang that had been terrorizing the town of Escondito.

In October 1884, Baca became a deputy in Socorro County overseeing the small community of San Francisco Plaza. During this year, animosity had grown between the Hispanic community and the Anglo-Americans over land rights and livestock rustling. Hence a potentially explosive situation arose when the Hispanic Baca received a request from a local saloon bar owner to apprehend the cowboy named Charlie McCarty. McCarty was a local hell-raiser given to firing off his guns for fun; he particularly enjoyed firing at the feet of Mexicans to make them "dance." Baca marched bravely up to McCarty (admittedly, McCarty was worse for drink, a fact which eased his arrest), took his revolver, and dragged him off to a nearby house where he was held by Baca and two other deputies.

Storm clouds soon began to gather. McCarty was an employee at the John B. Slaughter ranch nearby, and his coworkers were a bunch of hardened and violent men. Roughly a dozen of McCarty's associates soon gathered around the improvised prison and attempted to break in to free the prisoner. Baca replied by opening up with his rifle and his pistol. Although Baca did not hit anybody, Young Parnham, the foreman at the Slaughter ranch, was thrown from his horse. The horse subsequently toppled and crushed Parnham on the ground, and the man died of his wounds. Sobered by the incident, the parties negotiated the release of McCarty on agreement that he be tried for his crimes the next morning in a local saloon. The justice of the peace, William Wilson, fined McCarty five dollars to account for his part in Parnham's death.

Despite the outcome, Baca knew that he remained in danger. He holed up in a solid picket cabin even as a vengeful mob coalesced around Slaughter. The following morning, the mob set out to get Baca. All told, there were around forty people in the mob, and they included several constables deputized by Wilson to arrest Baca, including the cowboy William Hearne. The group descended upon Baca's hiding place, and Hearne stepped up and kicked the door. In response, Baca shot him twice in the stomach, the injuries being fatal.

What followed is now known as the "Frisco War." The group surrounded the cabin and began to pour hundreds of rounds into it. It was subsequently estimated that around 4,000 bullets were fired during the gunfight, although this figure is open to question. Certainly the superstructure of the cabin was totally riddled, but the floor level was recessed into the ground, and here Baca was able to hide from the flying bullets. Such was the intensity of fire that after the event a broomstick handle was found with eight individual bullet holes through it. Baca single-handedly held off the onslaught with his pistol despite, at one point, part of the roof collapsing in on his head after it had been set ablaze by flaming rags.

Nightfall came without any resolution, and the next morning the gang renewed their efforts to flush Baca out. One man even attempted to approach the cabin hiding behind an iron oven door, but an accurate pistol shot from Baca grazed his scalp, and he quickly retreated. Apart from Parnham, one other man had been killed in the "Frisco War," with another seriously wounded in the knee. Finally, Baca surrendered himself to Deputy Frank Rose after thirty-three hours of siege, and he was taken to Socorro County Courthouse jail on a charge of murder.

Baca's position in relation to the law during all these events is ambiguous, but in 1885 he was twice indicted and twice acquitted on the charge of murder. Subsequently, Baca had an impressive career, his ambition fueled by considerable vanity. He became the elected Socorro County clerk, a school superintendent, and ran his own detective agency. He also began to practice law and became an attorney, later exaggerating that he had defended nineteen men charged with murder, and each time took home the "not guilty" verdict. In 1905, Baca became the district attorney for

Socorro and Sierra Counties and later dabbled, generally unsuccessfully, in politics. Further work in law enforcement saw him kill again (he shot the Mexican revolutionary Celestino Otero in El Paso in 1915), but he himself lived out his natural life and died in Albuquerque in 1945.

Baca's experience shows how perilous and ill-defined was the lawman's position, and this was never truer than in violent towns such as Abilene. Abilene's experience of violence from 1867 to 1870 has already been mentioned, but with the appointment of Thomas J. "Bear River" Smith as her first marshal (or chief of police), aided by a couple of deputies, the lawless element soon realized that they had someone to contend with. Smith was born in 1830 in New York. Of Irish extraction, Smith was a solid Catholic and possibly worked for a time with the New York police force. However, in the mid-1860s Smith moved to Nebraska in the employ of the Union Pacific Railroad. Smith was a man moved by injustice. In 1868, by which year he was working in Wyoming (still in the rail industry), he led a group of railway workers to break out a friend of his whom, he felt, had been wrongly imprisoned in the local jail. The incident ended in a violent scuffle during which Smith was wounded. Nevertheless, his passion for righting wrongs persisted, and he was a marshal in various towns before becoming Abilene's chief of police in 1870.

Tom Smith proved to be an effective and courageous officer. In 1904, following the dedication of a memorial to him, Theodore C. Henry (elder brother of Stuart, the man who hired Smith), recalled that he would wade into a crowd of unruly cowboys using his fists to disarm them. Perhaps he did on occasion, but Smith, like his successor Wild Bill, wore his pistols prominently displayed at all times. Sober, a Texas cowboy was liable to do as he was told; with drink inside him, he was prone to react violently to authority. Stuart Henry noted that Smith and Hickok "feared this in cowboys more than anything. To guard against it Marshal Tom Smith rode or walked in the middle of Texas Street and Marshal Wild Bill kept his back to some wall."

Tom Smith proved so effective that the county sheriff, Joseph A. Cramer, who appointed him a deputy, sometimes asked for his services. It has also been reported (but not verified) that the then United States marshal for Kansas, Dana W. Houston, appointed him a deputy U.S. marshal. It was while acting on the behalf of Sheriff Cramer (who was terminally ill) that Tom Smith met his tragic end. He and a deputy, James H. McDonald, went to arrest a homesteader named Andrew McConnell, charged with murdering a man named John Shea. First reports had indicated that McConnell killed Shea in self-defense in a dispute over cattle on his land, but it later transpired that the shooting was a cold-blooded murder. Leaving McDonald with the horses, Smith advanced alone to the cabin where he told McConnell that he was under arrest. McConnell promptly drew a pistol and shot the marshal through his right lung. Smith fired back and grappled with him. Then Moses Miles, a near neighbor and McConnell's original alibi for the defense story, rushed up and struck Smith with a gun, knocking him to the ground. He then grabbed an ax and almost decapitated Smith.

Alerted by the shots, McDonald rushed toward the cabin but was beaten back by a fusillade of shots from both men. He returned fire and managed to wound Miles, shooting two of his fingers off. A bullet removed his hat; he then felt a hard blow to his chest and assumed he had been shot. It was later discovered that the ball had lodged in his pocket book! The two men then made good their escape on the officers' horses. McDonald raised the alarm, and a furious posse set off in pursuit. The pair were eventually captured and put on trial. To the disgust of Abilene's citizens, they received only long-term prison sentences instead of the rope that many believed they deserved. Thirty-four years later, the citizens dedicated a monument to Tom Smith, describing him as "A Fearless Hero of Frontier Days Who in Cowboy Chaos Established the Supremacy of Law."

Patrick Hand, a gunsmith, was appointed to succeed Smith and James McDonald, who was to prove himself a good officer and later achieve a good reputation in Newton, in turn replaced him. But despite his heroic attempt to

**RIGHT: A monument to one of the West's most colorful characters, Wild Bill Hickok. Hickok was described by a Black Hills newspaper as having the "resemblance of a buckskin bedecked mountain man" and his death was widely mourned.**

**ABOVE: The main street at Ellsworth early in 1872. The famous Drover's Cottage had just been erected following its removal from Abilene. The railroad was making provision for large cattle shipments.**

apprehend Smith's murderers, McDonald was shunned by some of the citizens who believed that he had deserted Tom in his hour of need. They ignored the fact that Smith was in part responsible for his own downfall. Had he ordered McDonald to accompany him to the cabin instead of waiting by the horses (a precaution any thinking officer would have taken), it is likely that he would have arrested McConnell without any trouble.

### A Terror to Evildoers

At Abilene's first municipal election on April 3, 1871, Joseph G. McCoy was elected mayor. One of his first tasks was to reorganize the police force and prepare the city for the imminent arrival of the first Texas herds of the season. His own personal dislike of McDonald ruled him out as a contender for the job as marshal (although he would remain on the force), and, since there were no others anxious for the job, McCoy sought an outsider. John B. Edwards in later years claimed that Wild Bill Hickok himself applied for the position, while Charles Gross asserted that it was at his suggestion that McCoy approach Hickok who was at the time living in Junction City, filling in his time as a deputy numerous accounts of the "hundreds" of bad men he had killed either in the line of duty or in personal combat. The fact that, by the time he became Abilene's marshal, Wild Bill's tally amounted to five known victims meant little to the press and public. As a result, during the eight months that he ruled the roost, Wild Bill had little trouble with the Texans. The townspeople never really got to know him except by reputation, yet most of them felt safe with him around, whereas the Texans found themselves outclassed and preferred to leave well enough alone. Nevertheless, Hickok never took any chances and made sure he kept clear of dark alleyways or other places where a would-be assassin could lurk.

Stuart Henry had made it clear that neither Smith nor Hickok trusted the Texans, and some are convinced that Hickok did not understand them, which may account for his reported animosity toward them. Certainly, he stood no nonsense, and there is a legendary account of him wading into a crowd of drunken cowboys and thrashing its leader. What may have some bearing on that yarn is a report published in the Kansas City *Journal of Commerce* on August 13, 1871, that alleged that he had hit a Texan over the head with the butt of his revolver and "stamped him in the face with his boot heel, inflicting a severe wound." The other Texans then informed Wild Bill that he would not be safe overnight, but they "mistook their man, as 'Wild Bill' is the last man to be driven away by such threats. At last accounts he was still there and unharmed. Such a marshal might do for such a place as Abilene, but for Kansas City we don't want him." The writer obviously did not understand the frontier tradition of "marking" an enemy, and neither was it made clear why Hickok attacked the Texan in the first place.

The council took full advantage of Hickok's presence. On their orders he arrested vagrants, closed down illicit gambling games, and, in the height of summer, following complaints from a large number of respectable ladies, he supervised the removal of the dance halls and brothels from Texas Street. The occupants viewed such a move with delight. Even when it came to a complete shutdown in September, Hickok and his deputies received little resistance, if any at all, from the denizens of the so-called McCoy's Addition.

U.S. marshal or gambling. In any event, Hickok arrived in Abilene about April 11, and on McCoy's personal recommendation the council "unanimously confirmed" the mayor's choice; on April 15, Hickok was appointed marshal, or chief of police of Abilene.

For most people, Hickok epitomizes the breed of gunfighting lawmen. What he may have lacked in professional expertise in such matters, he more than made up for it in presence and reputation. It was his reputation that counted for much during the eight months that he administered law and order in Abilene. Once news of his appointment got around, writers all across the West either extolled his reputation as a scout and "pistoleer" or invented

**LEFT: Isom Prentice "Print" Olive, one of Texas's most famous cattlemen. He fought hard to build his empire which, was hit by the blizzards of 1885–1886. He moved to Kansas and was murdered by Joe Sparrow in 1886.**

The curious who came to Abilene during the summer of 1871 simply to meet Wild Bill, "the hero of *Harper's Monthly*," were disappointed to find that he did not "have a man for breakfast" in true frontier tradition but was generally courteous, self-effacing, and quietly spoken.

Wild Bill's presence, aided by a number of policemen who obviously had faith in their boss, deterred most of the troublemakers, and it was October before he was finally compelled to use the pistols that had earned him such an awesome reputation.

RIGHT: James Masterson, the youngest of the famous brothers, whose gunfighting career surpassed Bat's. Jim was later involved in the arrest of the Doolin gang. He died from "galloping consumption" in 1895.

LEFT: James H. Kelley, generally called "Dog" on account of his love of the animal, was prominent in the saloon business in Dodge and later served as its mayor. A bullet meant for him killed the dance hall girl Dora Hand.

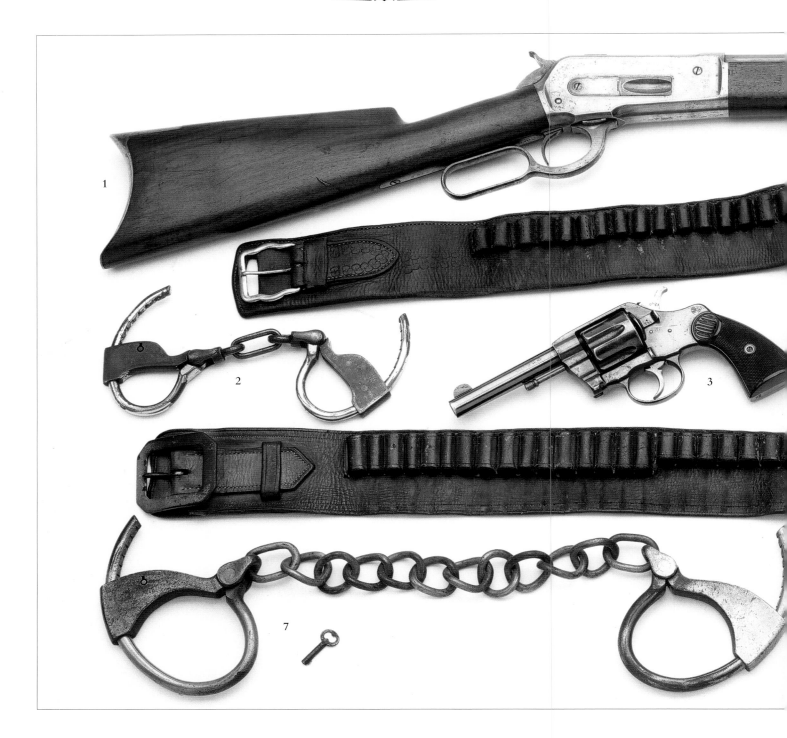

## FROM LAWMAN TO OUTLAW

The names of Doolin and Dalton, as we have noted, were notorious throughout Kansas and Oklahoma during the 1890s. The Daltons, originally on the side of the law (Frank had been killed in the line of duty in 1887, and Grat, Bob, and Emmett all wore badges briefly), became outlaws and were wanted men. Federal and state officers such as Ed Nix, Chris Madsen, Bill Tilghman, and Louis Eichoff were soon on their trail.

Emmett Dalton was the one brother to survive the deadly attempt to hold up two banks at the same time in Coffeyville, Kansas, in 1892. Badly injured, he spent some years in prison before being pardoned. He later moved to Hollywood and became a technical adviser for Westerns, a short-lived movie hero, a real estate agent, and an author of several books.

The lure of motion pictures that so attracted the likes of Buffalo Bill also interested men like Bill Tilghman, who actually took part in the film depicting the capture of the Bill

Doolin gang (rather like Audie Murphy, but without the acting talent or the Congressional Medal of Honor). Louis Eichoff helped bring law and order to Oklahoma Territory. Eichoff is almost forgotten today, but Chris Madsen's solid-gold presentation badge gives us some indication of the respect he earned among his peers. When Bill Doolin had the good sense to avoid involvement in the Dalton raid on Coffeyville, he continued to plague Oklahoma. Eichoff was one of the deputies ordered to bring him and his gang in.

1. Winchester model 1886, caliber .40-82, carried in pursuit of Bill Doolin's gang by Louis Eichoff.
2. Handcuffs of the 1890s.
3. Eichoff's Colt model 1889 double-action .41 caliber revolver.
4. Revolver holster and cartridge belt used to carry Eichoff's Colt .41.
5. Solid-gold badge inscribed "To Louis Eichoff U.S. Deputy Marshal from CM [Chris Madsen]." (Madsen was a former soldier who resigned from the service in 1891 to take up a post of deputy U.S. marshal in Oklahoma.)
6. Leg irons and key used in pursuit of the Doolin gang by Louis Eichoff.
7. Shackles and key used by Eichoff.
8. Revolver holster and belt that belonged to Emmett Dalton.
9. One of ten factory-engraved Colt .45s shipped to St. Louis from the factory with pearl grips. Emmett Dalton claimed that he and the Dalton gang armed themselves with these guns when they raided Coffeyville.
(Artifacts courtesy of Gene Autry Western Heritage Museum, Los Angeles.)

On October 5, a large number of Texans were in town, some of whom had remained to visit a local fair, others enjoying a final fling before returning home. As the excitement mounted and the Texans grew more lubricated and began massing on the streets carrying pistols, Hickok confronted them and advised them to disarm. He went into the Alamo saloon, and minutes later a shot was heard on the street. Hickok had been standing at the bar with Michael Williams, a former Kansas City bartender who had acted as a part-time jailer in the summer and later as a "special policeman" hired by the Novelty Theater. When the shot came, Hickok told Williams to stay where he was and headed for the front door. Outside, about fifty armed Texans led by Phil Coe, a gambler and owner of the Bull's Head Tavern, confronted him. Coe is reported to have had a grudge against Wild Bill; he told him that he had fired at a stray dog. But he still had his pistol in his hand, and it is claimed that he made a movement or a remark that prompted Hickok to draw his own pistols, according to an anonymous admirer writing for the *Chicago Tribune* in 1876, "as quick as thought." Both men were only eight feet apart. Coe fired twice; his first shot went through Hickok's coattails, and the second hit the ground between his legs. Hickok also fired twice, both shots hitting Coe in the stomach. He was then conscious of a figure rushing at him from the shadows, gun in hand—he fired twice more. Surrounded by a howling mob of drunken and

**LEFT: Benjamin "Ben" Thompson, who earned a reputation as a gunfighter and gambler. He was elected city marshal of Austin, Texas, but Ben's past and his association with gamblers finally caught up with him and he was murdered in 1884.**

**ABOVE RIGHT: John "King" Fisher, former rustler, cowboy, rancher, and later lawman and gunfighter. In later years he became a deputy sheriff. He was with Ben Thompson when he was murdered in March 1884.**

**RIGHT: William "Billy" Thompson, the homicidal brother of Ben. Ben had saved Billy's neck several times, and it was Ben who "treed" Wichita when Billy escaped after killing Sheriff Whitney in 1873.**

armed Texans, their shadows dancing in the light of the spluttering glare of kerosene lamps, he roared to them to back off. Only then did he see that the second man was Williams.

Old-timers (and some of the press) claimed that Hickok was visibly moved when he realized what had happened. He holstered his pistols, gently picked up his friend, and carried him into the Alamo and laid him on a billiard table. Then, with tears streaming down his face, he charged from the place and began pushing and shoving the crowd, ordering it to disperse. Within half an hour the place was deserted. Williams's death had a great effect upon Wild Bill, and it was widely reported that he paid for the funeral. As for Coe, he lingered for three days in great agony. It was even claimed that he was visited by a preacher, sent by Wild Bill, according to an eyewitness to the shooting reported in the local paper, "to pray with him and for him." Coe's body was shipped home to Texas for burial, and it was reported that Hickok's name was much vilified and that threats were made against his life.

Editor Wilson, who in the past had criticized the city council and its police force, decided that Hickok's actions during that night of chaos were commendable. He believed that Coe deserved what he got and warned other would-be troublemakers that, "there is no use in trying to override Wild Bill, the Marshal. His arrangements for policing the city are complete, and attempts to kill police officers or in any way create disturbance, must result in the loss of life on the part of violators of the law. We hope that all, strangers as well as

**RIGHT: Chauncey B. Whitney, the sheriff of Ellsworth County, gunned down by Billy Thompson on August 15, 1873. Whitney was one of the survivors of the Beecher Island fight in 1868 against the Indian Roman Nose.**

**BELOW: This Governor's Proclamation offering a reward of $500 was widely distributed, but copies of it are now rare. Despite the public outcry and the efforts to detain him, Billy Thompson managed to escape justice on a technicality in 1877.**

# GOVERNOR'S PROCLAMATION.

WHEREAS, C. B. Whitney, Sheriff of Ellsworth County, Kansas, was murdered in the said county of Ellsworth, on the 15th day of August, 1873, by one William Thompson, said Thompson being described as about six feet in height, 26 years of age, dark complexion, brown hair, gray eyes and erect form; and Whereas, the said William Thompson is now at large and a fugitive from justice;

NOW THEREFORE, know ye, that I, Thomas A. Osborn, Governor of the State of Kansas, in pursuance of law, do hereby offer a reward of FIVE HUNDRED DOLLARS for the arrest and conviction of the said William Thompson, for the crime above named.

**L. S.**

IN TESTIMONY WHEREOF, I have hereunto subscribed my name, and caused to be affixed the Great Seal of the State. Done at Topeka, this 22d day of August, 1873.

**THOMAS A. OSBORN.**

By the Governor:
**W. H. SMALLWOOD, Secretary of State.**

citizens, will aid by word and deed in maintaining peace and quietness."

Charles Gross, who got to know Wild Bill better than most, recalled late in life that when he was advised of the threats made against him, Hickok procured a shotgun that he adapted to his needs: the barrel was shortened to twelve inches, and it was loaded with heavy shot. A strap enabled it to be concealed beneath a coat. But Hickok never carried the weapon outside city limits.

Late in November, during a tram ride to Topeka, five Texans tried to attack Hickok, but he "circumvented" the parties and at pistol point ordered them to remain on the train when it left for Kansas City. On November 25, the Topeka *Daily Commonwealth* published an account of the event under the heading "Attempt to Kill Marshal Hickok," which was copied verbatim by the *Chronicle*, November 30.

Hickok's attempts at preventing further bloodshed were considered commendable, and he deserved the thanks of all law-abiding citizens throughout the state for "the safety of life and property at Abilene, which has been secured, more through his daring, than any other agency."

By December, however, the council had decided that it could no longer submit to the "evils" of the cattle trade (a public statement to that effect was issued in the following February), and neither did it have need for Mr. Hickok's expensive services. On December 13, Hickok and his deputies were dismissed, to be replaced by a temporary marshal hired for fifty dollars a month.

Abilene's demise as a cow town was welcomed by Newton and Ellsworth, which, together with Solomon, Salina, and Brookville, had vied with each other for the lucrative cattle trade.

The latter three towns, which had only received a small share of the market, are nowadays hardly remembered as cow towns, whereas Ellsworth, Newton, Wichita, Dodge City, and Caldwell share a place in folklore that ranks with Abilene.

**LEFT: The grave was quick to take people in the old West, either through violence or through disease. Pictured is an ornate carved-wood hearse, used in Miles City, Montana, from around 1880, to carry dead miners to the graveyards (those who could afford it).**

Ellsworth had been shipping cattle by rail since 1871, when it was reported by the Topeka *Daily Commonwealth* of July 16 that an estimated 35,000 head had been sent east. Founded in 1867, the place had achieved a reputation for violence that ranked with Hays City—itself only recently established and reputed to be so rough that citizens went armed all the time. By 1868, vigilante action had given way to established law and order, and with the arrival of the cattle trade proper in 1872, it took on its new role with ease. The Drover's Cottage

**BELOW: Dueling was not an uncommon way of settling disputes in the West. Pictured here are a fine pair of Colt 1851 dueling pistols with carved pearl handles. Unlike in the Western movies, duelists tended to take careful aim rather than a quick draw.**

in Abilene was dismantled and shipped to Ellsworth, where it became one of the sights and vied with the Grand Central Hotel for custom. Chauncey B. Whitney, who would soon leave office when elected county sheriff, headed the police force. He was succeeded by John L. Councell, who was later fired and in turn replaced by John "Brocky Jack" Norton, one of Hickok's deputies from Abilene whose poor reputation in Abilene had followed him to Ellsworth. Norton was later demoted but remained on the force. The new marshal, however, was Edward O. Hogue—a gutsy individual who did his job without fuss or fanfare.

Ellsworth's economy boomed during the latter part of 1872 and the early months of 1873. The saloon business in particular was a great source of income both to the

LEFT: The Webley Bulldog revolver would be easily concealed in a gunfighter's pocket. The whole weapon was only 5.5 inches long and came in .442, .45, and .32 calibers.

proprietors and the local tax collectors, so it was inevitable that the saloon would be the focus for trouble; the first real shoot-out of the cattle season occurred on July 27, 1872, when the notorious cattleman Isom Prentice "Print" Olive was shot by James Kenedy, the son of the Texas cattleman Miflin Kenedy, in the Ellsworth Billiard saloon.

On August 1, the Ellsworth *Reporter* described in graphic detail exactly what happened:

### The First Shot
### Two Men Wounded, No One Killed

Ellsworth, which has been remarkably quiet this season, had its first shooting affair this season last Saturday at about six o'clock, at the Ellsworth Billiard saloon. The room was full of "money changers" at the time, busily at work, and lookers on intently watching the games. Among others I. P. Olive was seated at a table playing cards. All of a sudden a shot was heard and sooner than we can write it, four more shots were fired. Kennedy [sic] came into the room, went behind the bar and taking a revolver walked up in front of Olive and fired at him telling him to "pass in his checks." Olive threw up his hands exclaiming "don't shoot." The second, third and fourth shot took effect, one entering the groin and making a bad wound, one in the thigh and the other in the hand.

Olive could not fire, though he was armed; but some one, it seems uncertain who, fired at Kennedy, hitting him in the hip, making only a flesh wound. The difficulty arose from a game of cards in the forenoon, Kennedy accusing Olive of unfair dealing. Olive replied in language that professionals cannot bear. The affair made considerable excitement. The wounded were taken in custody and cared for. Drs Duck & Fox extracted the bullet from Olive and a piece of his gold [watch] chain which was shot into the wound. It was feared that Olive would not survive, but the skill of the doctors saved him. Kennedy was removed to South Main Street and put under the charge of three policemen, but by the aid of friends he escaped during the night from the window and has not been heard of. All has been quiet since the affair and is likely to remain so.

The man who shot Kenedy in the hip was James "Nigger Jim" Kelly, Olive's trail boss, who had been outside on the veranda when the firing commenced. He shot through the open window and then rushed in to help his employer. Kenedy was the same individual who later shot and killed the dance hall girl Dora Hand at Dodge City, mistaking her for the mayor, James "Dog" Kelley, against whom he bore a grudge.

Ellsworth's violent reputation, earned in the 1860s, dogged him all through the cow-town era. The editor of the *Reporter* expressed local concern when, on August 14, 1873, he wrote:

LEFT: This businesslike pair of Wells Fargo "messengers" (stagecoach guards) are equipped not only with regulation shotguns but rifles as well. Note the heavily laden double cartridge belts.

RIGHT: Dodge City advises would-be troublemakers against carrying firearms but advertises a favorite "gunfight lubricant," "Prickly Ash," a popular alcoholic beverage made from that aromatic and bitter shrub.

We protest against so much arming by our police. It may be well enough for our marshal and his assistants to go armed, but one six-shooter is enough. It is too much to have to see double armed men walking our peaceful streets.

It is not probable that any of the shotted revolvers will hurt anyone, for these are not the days of '67 and all people know it. Don't let us by too big a show of deringers, lead strangers to imagine that order is only to be maintained by the use of them.

One pistol is enough and that should be concealed as much as possible.

A day later, the editor had cause to reflect on his words when perhaps the most infamous killing in Ellsworth's violent history took place, one that is still hotly debated. That summer of 1873 witnessed a national panic over the economy, and in Ellsworth its effect upon the cattle business was cause for alarm. An estimated 177,000 head of cattle were held in pens or pastured some miles from town awaiting shipment east. In the saloons, cowboys, drovers, and the inevitable gamblers sat and sweltered in the ninety-degree heat. The police force at that time consisted of Brocky Jack Norton, the marshal, Ed Hogue, and John "Happy Jack"

Morco, the latter a particularly obnoxious individual who offended fellow officers, citizens, and Texans alike. The Texans and the gamblers disliked Morco particularly. He had arrested Ben Thompson's brother Billy for alleged assault with a pistol, for which Billy was fined ten dollars plus fifteen dollars in court costs.

That morning, Ben Thompson had financed a friend, John Sterling, to enable him to take part in a high-stake monte game, with the promise of a percentage of any winnings and the return of his original stake. Sterling won more than $1,000 but was not anxious to return either the stake or advance a percentage of his winnings. This made Ben mad,

and he cornered Sterling in Nick Lentz's saloon. Sterling struck Ben in the face, but before Ben could retaliate, Morco forced himself between them and made Ben leave. Ben went straight to Brennan's saloon where he remained until Morco and Sterling, both of whom were heavily armed, appeared at the entrance of Brennan's and ordered him to come out. Knowing what would happen if he did, he ducked out the

**BELOW: Caldwell, Kansas, by the early 1880s was largely brick-built, but it still retained the crude unpaved streets of most Western towns. Already known for its violence, the cattle trade enhanced it.**

back door and into Jack New's place where he had left a pistol and a Winchester rifle. Billy then arrived, armed with Ben's fine English-made double-barreled shotgun (made by George Gibbs of Bristol). Having got himself "heeled," Ben decided to face his tormenters. Billy, who was liquored-up and staggering around, jerked one of the triggers of his shotgun and discharged a barrel. The shot just missed a

**BELOW: The Meagher brothers both served the law. But it was Mike (right) who earned a reputation as a peacekeeper—first at Wichita and later at Caldwell, where he was killed in a gunfight on December 17, 1881.**

couple of passing Texans. The brothers then walked toward the railroad intending to continue the fight and to do so without endangering local residents.

Hearing the shot, Sheriff Chauncey B. Whitney, a friend of the Thompson brothers, hurried to defuse the situation, persuading the pair to accompany him back to Brennan's. As Ben listened to him, he moved near the door, heard someone shout a warning, and turned to see Morco coming toward him, pistol in hand. Ben fired at him, the ball splitting the doorjamb of a local store. Morco ducked and ran inside.

At that moment, Whitney and Billy rushed into the street, Billy brandishing the shotgun. He staggered, turned, and

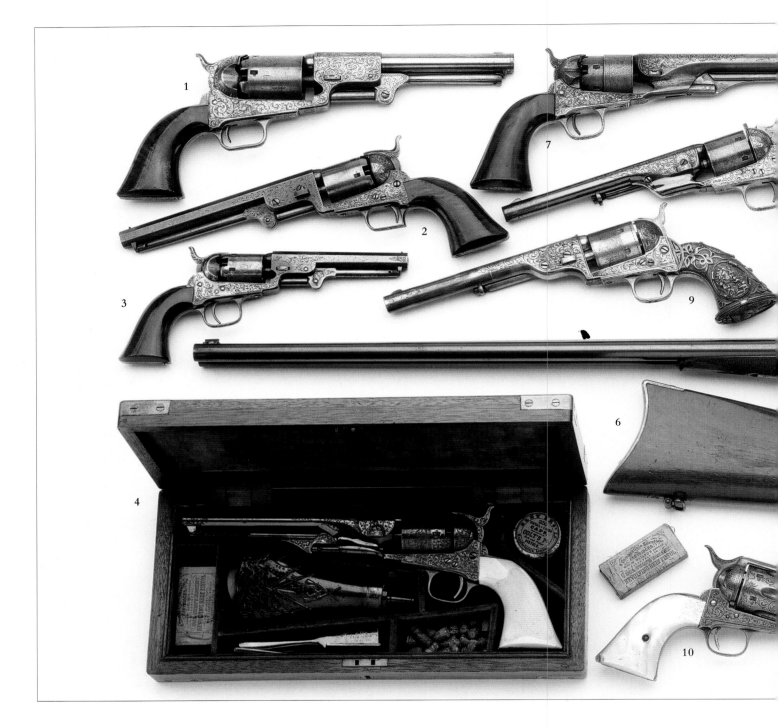

## ENGRAVED COLTS

Finely engraved and embellished Colts could be ordered directly from the factory or acquired from a number of independent artists. From early days, the Colt company offered engraving, inlaid precious metals, grips of ivory, pearl, or other exotic materials, special cases, and other features for an added fee. Sam Colt began a tradition of giving such firearms as a way of encouraging business and favors; in many circles an engraved Colt marked a person of stature.

1. Third model Dragoon revolver, .44 caliber, dated about 1851, scroll engraved. The revolver features a bust of George Washington, with deluxe walnut grips.
2. 1851 Navy revolver, featuring early vine-style engraving, about 1851, with walnut grips.
3. London pocket revolver, about 1855, London-style engraving, .31 caliber, special walnut grips.
4. Model 1861 Navy, .36 caliber cased revolver with checkered ivory grips, in the best engraving style of Gustave Young. This revolver was presented to banker William H. Cox by the Colt company.
5. Gold inlaid and engraved Colt double-barrel hammer rifle, serial number 33, embellished by Cuno A. Helfricht, about 1880, and known to have been used by California politician J. H. Budd.
6. Samuel Colt presentation 1851 Navy revolver with detachable canteen shoulder stock, engraved by Gustave Young. Special walnut stocks.

7. Model 1860 Colt Army .44 caliber revolver, about 1870. This one shipped in 1877 to Kittredge and Company of Cincinnati, Ohio.

8. Gustave Young engraved 1861 Navy, conversion to cartridge, ivory grips.

9. Gold and silver plated, L. D. Nimschke engraved Colt .44 caliber rimfire open top revolver with cast plated grips, made by Tiffany and Company, New York.

10. Deluxe engraved Colt frontier .44-40 caliber revolver embellished by Cuno Helfricht, about 1880, silver plated, engraved pearl grips, shown with the engraver's business card and an example of one of his engraving tools.

11. Engraver's sample gun, third model deringer, .41 caliber. This is a pattern or sample gun made by Cuno Helfricht in the 1870s.

12. Colt single-action Army "Sheriff's Model," scroll engraving by Cuno Helfricht, pearl grips, 1912.

13. Model 1902 automatic pistol, Cuno Helfricht engraved, pearl grips, nickel plating, sporting version of a military pistol.

14. This .38 caliber Model 1903 New Army & Navy double-action revolver was shipped as an army shooting prize to Captain John T. Thompson in 1903. Cuno Helfricht's full floral engraving is handsomely complemented by the checkered ivory grips.

15. Cased New Police double-action revolver, engraved by Helfricht, with ivory grips, and made about 1905.

16. Flat top target single-action army revolver engraved by William Gough, inlaid with gold and mounted with checkered ivory grips.

(Artifacts courtesy of Gene Autry Western Heritage Museum, Los Angeles.)

fired point blank at the sheriff. Whitney's scream of agony stopped the place dead. Several men ran up and tenderly picked up the injured man and carried him to his home. While he remained conscious, he repeated that it was an accident. He died in great agony on August 18.

Following the incident, Ben turned on his brother for shooting their friend, and he feared that he might not be able to keep the equally incensed mob at bay for long. Billy turned his whiskey-sodden gaze upon his brother and is reported to have mumbled that he would have shot if it had "been Jesus Christ." Ben did hold the town at bay while his brother escaped, and only agreed to surrender if the mayor disarmed Morco and friends. This was agreed, and he then surrendered to Ed Hogue. The disgusted mayor promptly fired the whole police force. In later years it was claimed that Wyatt Earp actually arrested Ben, but city records disprove that. In 1877, Billy Thompson was arrested and brought back to Ellsworth for trial but escaped justice on a technicality. Ben Thompson's devotion to his brother was legendary—he got him out of one scrape after another. Mean, vicious, vindictive, and totally unpredictable, Billy's survival was remarkable. E. D. Cowan's recollection of one incident in his life was typical. Writing on the "Happy Bad Men of the West" in the Denver *Daily News* of October 23, 1898, Cowan said:

A conspicuous example of his type was Bill Thompson, brother of that other Texas Thompson named Ben, who made considerable of a record as a pacifier at Austin before he was assassinated. Bill was laying off up in Colorado, after having had to slip across the Texas border between suns, when the historic double lynching of Frodsham and Stewart occurred at Leadville. Obedient to a request more imperative than polite, several hundred thugs, footpads, lot jumpers, burglars and assassins left Leadville the following morning and colonized thirty-five miles away at Buena Vista, the new temporary terminal of the South Park Railroad. They were soon joined by their kind in numbers from every quarter of the state. Highway robbery and every other sort of robbery and murder in the first degree became the pastime of the place . . .

But there was a happy bad man in the town, and it was Bill Thompson. He was elected mayor on the quiet by a backroom oligarchy. After the Texan had punctured the anatomy of a few of the worst bad men of Buena Vista, and satisfied everybody that he really enjoyed a good stand-up-and-shoot fight, the gaiety of the select society subsided, and in a few days he was the unchallenged despot of the town. Meanwhile robbery and crime increased.

Cowan related that a certain Colonel Amos C. Babcock loaned Billy fifty dollars when the railroad moved on and the inhabitants dispersed. Thompson was penniless and needed money to return home, where he had been assured he would not be charged with any offenses. Aware of Billy's nature, the colonel made the loan anonymously, but Billy learned who he was. Later, in Austin, when the colonel was trying to get a state capital loan for a project and he wished to involve Ben Thompson, he found it impossible to reach him, for it was concluded that those involved were "damn Yankees." His luck changed when he passed a saloon and bumped into a drunken Texan. It was Billy, who recognized him right away. By the next day Ben, too, was his friend and joined in his project.

Billy Thompson's eventual demise has so far escaped the record. Ben's widow heard it said that he was killed in a confrontation in or around Laredo, Texas, in the late 1880s. She had heard that Billy killed several Mexicans before he finally expired. Whatever the truth, few mourned him, unlike Ben, whose hearse was followed by sixty-two vehicles.

## From Guns to Gavels: The End of an Era

The gunfighter's role in settling the West was magnified by novelists, filmmakers, and others anxious to cash in on a burgeoning myth. We have already examined the role he played on both sides of the law, and shortly we will consider his role as a latter-day duelist. First, it is important to take a closer look at the weapons of his trade, primarily the pistol. The most popular weapon of the time was the single-action pistol. The principal instrument was the Colt, but

**RIGHT: Wild Bill Hickok from a family tintype, c. 1863–1864. Photographed when he was a contract scout for the Union Army, Hickok is dressed in the typical nondescript garb of the time, away from his more usual glamorous image.**

## COLT DERINGERS, POCKET PISTOLS

The development of Colt firearms was always characterized by the constant process of invention and improvement. Beginning in about 1869 the Colt company diversified, producing a great variety of single-shot pocket pistols, small pocket revolvers, double-action revolvers, and other products in addition to its line of shoulder arms. Small pocket pistols for self-defense were used by women and men, gamblers, gunmen, and lawmen.

1. First Model Deringer pistol, about 1870, .41 rimfire, engraved, handy as iron knuckles in a fist fight.
2. Second Model Deringer pistol, .42 rimfire caliber, made from 1870 to about 1890.
3. Third Model Deringer pistol, .41 caliber, manufactured about 1875–1912.
4. Open Top Pocket Model revolver, .22 caliber, 1875, seven shot cylinder.
5. New Line Pocket Model revolver, .22 caliber, nickel with pearl grips, 1876, back strap engraved "J.M. Foote, Jr."
6. New Line Pocket Model revolver, .32 caliber rimfire, 1880.
7. Model revolver, for the .38 caliber rimfire New Line, unfinished and stamped "M."
8. New Line revolver, .41 caliber rimfire, 1874, five shot cylinder.
9. New House model revolver .38 caliber centerfire, five shots, 1881.
10. Cloverleaf House model revolver, the first solid frame metallic cartridge revolver made by Colt. Four shots in .41 caliber, made in 1874.

11. New Police model revolver, .38 caliber centerfire with lanyard, 1882.

12. Model 1877 double-action Lightning revolver, .38 caliber, back strap engraved "Capt. Jack Crawford," used by this well-known scout and "poet laureate" of the plains.

13. Model 1877 double-action Lightning revolver, .41 caliber, blue finish with pearl grips.

14. Model 1877 double-action Lightning revolver, caliber .38, engraved with ivory grips, with longer barrel and attached ejector rod.

15. Factory model gun for the Model 1878 double-action revolver, this version a flat-top target gun, serial number M.

16. .38 caliber Long Colt cartridges, popular in several different models of revolvers.

17. Frontier double-action revolver, model 1878, .45 caliber, portions cut away at the factory to demonstrate the mechanism.

18. Short barrel "Sheriff"'s" model 1878 double-action in .45 caliber, unfinished factory model gun, serial number M.

19. Hammerless model 1878 double-action, an experimental version which did not go into production. Serial number 1.

20. Standard production 1878 double-action Frontier revolver, .45 caliber, 7¹/₂-inch barrel.

21. .44 Smith & Wesson cartridges.

22. Experimental prototype double-action revolver with swing-out cylinder, no serial number, patented 1884. Five years later Colt issued the first production swing-out cylinder revolver, a mechanism similar to many used in the West from 1889 to the present day.

(Artifacts courtesy of Gene Autry Western Heritage Museum, Los Angeles.)

Remington, Smith & Wesson, and others played a part in furthering the mystique of the gunslingers. Colt's Navy revolvers (both the so-called 1851 and 1861 models) proved to be among the most popular during the percussion era and were closely rivaled by Colt's New Model Army of 1860 and the several Remington Army and Navy pistols of the period. Accuracy varied, of course, and all sorts of claims have been made concerning one or the other of them, but Colt's .36 caliber 1851 Navy was probably the most accurate, even if it lacked the power of the heavy .44 models. While it amused some of the better-known pistol shots to fire at targets at one hundred yards or more, they were really only concerned with their accuracy at ranges of between five and fifteen feet, which was the normal distance when they were called upon to defend or make a reputation.

The romantic attachment of later generations to various guns and their alleged part in winning the West is not reflected in contemporary attitudes. Guns were regarded as necessary tools in the business of survival. Some weapons were more popular than others, but that was reflected in their practical as well as popular appeal. An article titled "Frontier Weapons" that appeared in the Wichita *Daily Eagle* October 11, 1884, reported that a correspondent had spent some time at El Paso, Texas, where he entered a large store that enjoyed a reputation for selling more firearms than any of its rivals. Wandering around the cases of glittering weapons, his attention was drawn to a young man of about twenty-three, whose appearance suggested that he was a cowboy. "He was dressed in approved frontier style, sombrero it would take three days to walk around the rim of, white handkerchief tied loosely round the neck, blue shirt, pants stuck in his boots, and large Mexican spurs upon his heels, jingling as he walked. He wished to buy a 'gun.'"

It was then explained in the "expressive and laconic tongue of the frontier" that a "gun" was a revolver. A rifle was called by the name of the maker, whereas a sporting weapon was generally called a "shotgun." The salesman directed the young fellow to a case containing a handsome revolver: "How would you like this? It is the newest thing out—a double-action forty-five." The cowboy shook his head. "Ain't worth a row of beans. No man 'cept a tenderfoot wants that kind of

RIGHT: William "Buffalo Bill" Cody was a legend within his own lifetime as well as in the generation following his death. The lithograph is entitled *Buffalo Bill the Scout* and was probably produced during the 1880s.

thing. Give me an old reliable all the time. Ye see a man that's used to the old style is apt to get fooled—not pull her off in time—and then he'll be laid out colder'n a wedge."

The reporter then noted that the cowboy was handed a single-action version of the same model, which he carefully examined, cocked, fired, and twirled around his forefinger, cocking and pulling the trigger as the butt returned to his hand. He decided to purchase the pistol and disappeared into the crowd. The storekeeper then claimed that few men could spin and cock a pistol with such skill—among them had been "Curly Bill" Brocius (who had pulled that stunt on Marshal White in Tombstone), Billy the Kid, Pat Garrett, and others, but Curly Bill had been the best. He might have added that a similar trick was claimed by John Wesley Hardin to have fooled Wild Bill; but it now appears that no one heard of that incident until Wes mentioned it in his *Life*.

By this time, the newspaperman was very interested in the sort of people who purchased weapons. He asked if many "Bulldog" type pistols were sold. The storekeeper told him that they were "chiefly bought by railroad laborers, tramps, and boys." The Bulldog owed its name to the British .450 five-shot Webley pistol of that name. Small and easily concealed, with its short barrel and heavy caliber, it was both handy and deadly. The storekeeper, who was probably more used to the innumerable "suicide specials" turned out in the East, damned the whole breed with faint praise: "The bulldog is a poor pistol, shoots wild, and can't be depended upon for over fifteen feet. The great trouble with all these pistols are that they are hard on the trigger. The boys get over this by having the catch filed down. The pistol of the cowboy is as fine on the trigger as were the hair-triggers of the old dueling days."

The storekeeper then introduced his by now fascinated listener to "a kind of shot-gun that has a limited use" and led him to the back of the store. Here were half a dozen shotguns that had been cut down so that the barrels were only two feet

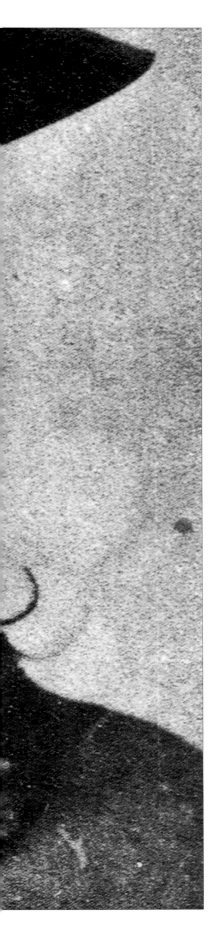

long. "These guns are prime favorites with sheriffs, deputy sheriffs, United States marshals and officers of the law generally, and when they get the drop on you with one of them it's a case of throw up your hands, no matter how much sand you may have got. They are handy, and you can stow them away under the seat of a buggy with ease. Wells-Fargo's messengers all carry them, and at a short range they beat rifles and six-shooters all to Hades." Suitably impressed, the correspondent remarked that there seemed to be fewer accidents with firearms in the West than in eastern states— extraordinary when it was appreciated that every man out West went armed. The storekeeper disagreed:

It is not. The men who are always handling firearms are the most careful with them. I'd like to see you point a pistol or shotgun at a cowboy, and he'd make you drop it so quick 'twould make your head swim. There used to be a good many accidents, though, a few years ago, when the boys were in the habit of carrying the full six loads in their guns, and trusting to the safety catch to avoid any danger. Sure as the gun dropped on the ground off she went. A number got shot this way. Now nearly every fellow carries one chamber empty with the hammer resting on it when, of course, no jar can discharge it. Some of the cowboys are regular dudes about pistols. Nothing will do them but gold and silver mounted and ivory handled weapons. Rich Mexicans are more given to this style of thing and even Americans. The truth is that nickle-plated [sic] and silver-plated revolvers are not the best on the plains. The reflection of the sun on the white metal surface of the barrel is fatal to accurate shooting.

The reference to self-inflicted wounds due to carelessness reminds us that even some of the better-known pistoleers had their moments. On January 9, 1876, Wyatt Earp, then a policeman on the Wichita force, was sitting in on a card game with some cronies when, according to the *Beacon* on January 12, an unusual event occurred:

Last Sunday night, while policeman Erp [sic] was sitting with two or three others in the back room of the Custom House saloon, his revolver slipped from its holster and in falling to the floor the hammer which was resting on the cap, is supposed to have struck the chair, causing a discharge of one of the barrels [chambers]. The ball

LEFT: William Frederick "Buffalo Bill" Cody in stage costume, in about 1873. He was never a "pistol fighter," but his interpretation of the Wild West in his stage and later exhibition days was influential in establishing the myths.

passed through his coat, struck the north wall then glanced off and passed out through the ceiling. It was a narrow escape and the occurrence got up a lively stampede from the room. One of the demoralized was under the impression that some one had fired through the window from the outside.

Mr. Earp evidently failed to heed his own alleged comments to his biographer Stuart N. Lake, who reported that he only loaded five shots in a six-shooter to "ensure against accidental discharge." Even more embarrassing was the predicament faced by Deputy Marshal Daniel Jones of Caldwell one evening in September 1879. The *Post* on September 25 reported what happened when, during the course of his duties, the deputy marshal found himself in desperate need to relieve himself:

It happened at one of Caldwell's fashionable hotels, and, like all other fashionable hotels, has two small rooms—over each door is an inscription by which a person may know whether he is to be admitted or not, but it being dark, and Dan's "business" qualifications not allowing him to stop, and read everything that is hung up entered. About this time a lady attempted to enter but was foiled by Dan turning an inside latch—the lady hastened away, but soon returned with the key—(this is not a romance)—locked, unlocked and relocked and finally left to return no more.

Now, as Dan's occupation calls him on the street he concluded that he might depart with safety, but imagine his feelings when he discovered that he had been locked in, but, as will be seen, Dan is equal to all emergencies, and began trying to extricate himself from his odorous prison. There is a seat in the room just opposite the door upon which Dan sat himself down, put his feet against the door, and with Heenan like strength pushed the door assunder, and at the same instant back went Dan's revolver down, down to the bottomless—after which a light was brought into requisition—it was fished up, a tub of water, barrel of soft soap and scrubbing-brush were readily used up and the pistol looks as natural as ever, and if the street gossip don't mention this we will never say a word about it to Dan.

One classic example of carelessness with a pistol occurred when a man from Emporia, Kansas, appeared in Newton, August 4, 1872. The editor of the Emporia *News* noted that

**LEFT: Transportation in early Deadwood was limited to oxcarts (as depicted) or the Cheyenne & Black Hills Stage Line coaches that plied between the Hills and Cheyenne. Shipments of gold dust were well guarded.**

one Dan Beckwith "accidentally shot himself with a small revolver in the right arm, while showing some boys how to use the weapon. It is believed that the arm will have to be amputated. Another warning to be careful in the handling of firearms."

The *Daily Eagle's* correspondent, used as he was to the general sight of hip holsters worn so that the butt of the pistol faced to the rear or forward for a "reverse" or a "cross-draw," was intrigued to learn that there was now available another kind of holster, and the clerk was anxious to show him. "Men who are used to the country either buy a caliber 41 or carry a 44 or 45 in a shoulder scabbard," he remarked. On being asked to elucidate, the clerk described it as a scabbard (holster) with a strap "passing over the right shoulder, and supports the pistol under your coat on the left side. It enables you to draw while a man is thinking that you are only looking for your handkerchief."

## Quick on the Draw

No gunfighter worthy of the name could ever be described as slow when it came to getting his gun into action. But so preoccupied were the old-time writers with the speed and accuracy attributed to the man-killers that little attention was paid to practicalities. Rather, they were more concerned with speed and notches on their guns than realities. Consequently, the careless reference to someone being fast on the draw is rarely questioned, particularly when it is inextricably linked with the gunfighter myth. But no gunfighter of the time, if asked to explain how he got his gun into action, would have described himself as fast. Fast to the inhabitants of the old West was an expression they might have used when referring to a loose woman or a town that was lax in morals or legal restraint. "I have seen many fast towns," declared John Wesley Hardin, "but I think Abilene beat them all." "Quick" was a term more commonly used, but even this emphasis on speed took second place to "the drop," seeking an advantage. Interviewed in 1865, Wild Bill Hickok is reported to have declared: "Whenever you get into a row be sure and not shoot too quick. Take time. I've known many a feller slip up for shootin' in a hurry." This emphasis upon accuracy rather than speed might appear to diminish the legendary prowess

of those old-timers, but not a bit of it. When they spoke of "taking time," it was the split second it took to make the decision to draw or take whatever evasive action might be required. In effect, the so-called fast draw was a reactional response and not speed, although an onlooker unversed in the finer points of gunplay might be excused for thinking that he was witnessing a quick draw. Writing in the *New York*

*Herald-Tribune* on January 3, 1930, Arthur Chapman described the lengths to which some of the old-time gunfighters were reputed to have gone in order to stay alive. Despite its fictional overtones, it makes interesting reading:

It was not magic which enabled Bat Masterson to produce some wizard-like effects with the draw. It was hard and unrelenting

practice. Just what it meant to acquire the degree of Doctor of the Draw at Dodge City in those days, was recently revealed to the writer of this article by John L. Amos, a prominent official of the Union Pacific Railroad at Salt Lake City. Mr. Amos, as a youth seeking adventure, found himself in the whirl that was Dodge City. His roommates were Masterson and "Conk" Jones. "Conk Jones was a wonderful gunfighter," said Mr. Amos. 'He did not gain the

**LEFT: Deadwood, Dakota Territory, about 1877. Founded in April 1876, it soon attracted a large population of would-be goldminers who flocked to the place once gold was discovered.**

prominence of many others, but I happen to know that for nerve and skill, he could not be beaten. He and Bat seemed to have taken a shine to me as a youngster. The only complaint I had against my roommates was that they were always practising gunplay. For at least an hour every day, they would practise with unloaded guns, draw and click, draw and click. Bat had a most peculiar way of carrying his revolver. It was tied on a string which was hung around his neck. He would reach inside his coat, and bring out the revolver, breaking the string in the same motion. Evidently it was a scheme he had developed himself. Masterson and Conk practised their gunplay in the room and generally, I was the target. I would hear a click behind me and would turn around to find that one of them had snapped his revolver at me. If I came in the door, perhaps both of them would go through the motion of drawing and firing at me as I entered. I liked both of them a lot, but finally I had to tell them that my nerves were going to pieces, and I would have to hand in my official resignation as their target.

"But no matter whether they aimed at me or at a bedpost, they would put in just so much time every day, perfecting themselves in the draw. And they never failed to inspect and clean their revolvers daily."

The suggestion that Bat Masterson carried a pistol on a piece of string slung around his neck that "broke" each time he drew his revolver makes no sense at all. Assuming he was armed with a .45 caliber Colt revolver, which when loaded weighed about three pounds, it would have taken more than a piece of string to hold that weight! But Chapman's yarn does serve to show how the mystique of speed played such a big part in the fast-draw myth. Curiously, little reliable evidence exists either to boost or deflate some of the stories that have been handed down concerning speed and skill. Wild Bill Hickok is generally regarded as the epitome of the Western gunfighter both in performance and accuracy, yet no authentic targets are on hand, although this writer has been advised of several that are claimed as such. One exhibited to me some years ago was an envelope that had been tacked to a tree and the postage stamp affixed to its center. There were six holes in the paper, two of which clipped the stamp. It was claimed that Hickok fired from ten yards. Unfortunately, it had not been signed or otherwise authenticated.

In 1865, Colonel George Ward Nichols met Hickok in Springfield, Missouri, and in the February 1867 issue of *Harper's New Monthly Magazine* claimed that Wild Bill offered to demonstrate his skill with his Colt Navy pistol, and proceeded to empty all six shoots at a signboard fifty yards away that included the letter "O." "In an off-hand way, and without sighting the pistol with his eye, he discharged the six shots of his revolver. I afterward saw that all the bullets had entered the circle." Bearing in mind that only weeks before, Hickok had put a pistol ball through one Dave Tutt's heart at "one hundred paces," such a feat does not seem unreasonable, except that Nichols weakens his case by suggesting that Hickok did not take aim. Similarly, in 1910, Bat Masterson reported a similar incident, only this time it took place at Kansas City, Missouri, and the distance was increased to one hundred yards. Expert pistol shots have no difficulty in hitting targets at one hundred yards with the Colt Navy pistol, but they do so with carefully aimed shots. Attention is also paid to the loading of each chamber. Nevertheless, neither the colonel nor Bat thought it necessary to explain how Wild Bill could discharge a pistol within city limits and escape a fine.

That Hickok was considered a good pistol shot is not in doubt. His contemporaries were in awe of his reaction to danger and his uncanny ability to hit targets, but even they agreed that some of the feats attributed to him were fictional. One acquaintance, W. E. Webb, who met him at Hays City in 1869, declared in his *Buffalo Land*, published in 1872: "I do not believe, for example, that he could hit a nickel across the street with a pistol-ball, any more than an Indian could do so with an arrow. These feats belong to romance. Bill is wonderfully handy with his pistols, however." To which Luther North added: "Wild Bill was a man of Iron Nerve and could shoot straight enough to hit a man in the right place when the man had a gun in his hand, and just between you and me, not many of the so called Bad Men could do that."

John Wesley Hardin was considered by many of his contemporaries to be a good pistol shot, and shortly before his death fired several shots into a card at close range and signed his name. But by his own words, he knew all the tricks of the trade and claimed to have fooled Wild Bill with the

RIGHT: The murder of Wild Bill Hickok by John "Jack" McCall on August 2, 1876, created a sensation. Then as now, tourists and others visited his grave, many of them carefully noting Charley Utter's moving epitaph.

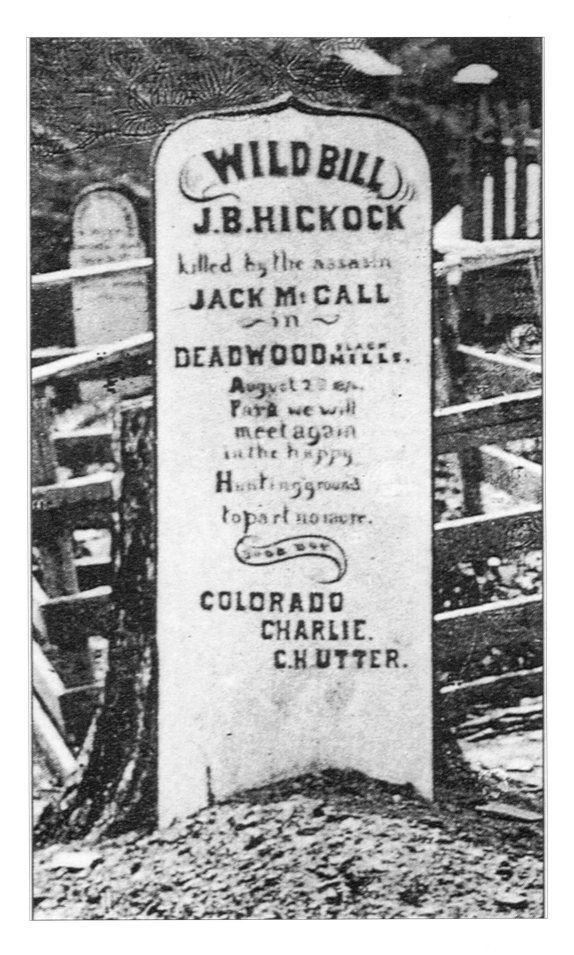

"roadagents" or "Curly Bill" spin back in 1871. Descriptions of it vary. Earlier we reported how a cowboy performed one version in an El Paso gun store—by spinning the barrel forward on the trigger finger and catching the butt and cocking the pistol as it came back to the hand. In the Hardin version, the pistol is offered butt first, but the index finger stays in the trigger guard. As the victim reaches for the butt, it is spun back into the hand, cocked, and "what are your favorite flowers?" The only problem with Hardin's story is that he says Hickok had two cocked pistols on him when he

**LEFT: John "Doc" Holliday appeared in a number of Western boom towns in their heyday, including Dodge City, Tucson, and Tombstone. Ravaged by alcoholism and tuberculosis, he died at thirty-six.**

**BELOW: Denizens of Dodge whose miscreant molars gave trouble could be "drilled" by Doc without suffering from lead poison. One wonders if there were any dissatisfied customers with nerve enough to complain.**

tried that trick. As Hickok reached for his pistol, he jumped back and cocked it. What is not explained is how Hickok could have two cocked pistols on Hardin and yet at the same time reach for his.

Topping the list of Texas "bad men" with a reputation for violence and as a shot was Ben Thompson, the British-born gambler-gunfighter. His cronies always maintained that Ben was a good shot and that had he and Wild Bill met face-to-face following Hickok's shoot-out with Ben's erstwhile partner Phil Coe in Abilene, the outcome would have been very close. But Ben was in Kansas City at the time, and any such speculation is academic. It does seem evident that he was a good shot and in 1879 took part in a shooting match against William "Buffalo Bill" Cody. Buffalo Bill at that time was touring with his Combination and, following a performance at Austin, Texas, he was introduced to Ben Thompson. We suspect that it was not a first-time meeting for either of them, for it is likely that they first met in Kansas. The *Austin Daily Statesman* of December 10, 1879, reported that "Buffalo Bill went out of town yesterday with Mr Ben Thompson and some other gentlemen, and he showed them

PHOTOGRAPHED FROM DODGE CITY TIMES, ISSUE OF JUNE 8, 1878

## DENTISTRY.

J. H. Holliday, Dentist, very respectfully offers his professional services to the citizens of Dodge City and surrounding country during the summer. Office at room No. 24, Dodge House. Where satisfaction is not given money will be refunded,

a little crack shooting. With Mr Thompson's rifle he struck six half dollars out of seven that were thrown up." Ben was impressed, as indeed were the others, for Cody's reputation on the plains as a rifle shot was second to none. But when it came to pistols, Cody was outclassed. Old-time plainsmen recalled that Buffalo Bill had never been any great shakes as a pistol shot, and although in later years he improved, there was a sneaking feeling in some quarters that much of his ring work was done with smoothbore pistols firing birdshot. True or not, he was man enough to admit that he had met his match with Ben. Proof of his admiration for the gunfighter came to light in 1881 when, according to the *Daily Statesman*, June 15, "Yesterday morning Marshal Thompson [Ben had been elected City Marshal and Chief of Police in the election held the previous December] received a very handsome present from Buffalo Bill . . . a costly target pistol manufactured by Stevens & Co. of Chicopee Falls, Massachusetts."

Following Ben Thompson's murder on March 11, 1884, his wife disposed of the pistol, which eventually ended up in the hands of a private collector who placed it on loan at the National Cowboy Hall of Fame, Oklahoma City. It is described as a target pistol chambered for the Colt .32 caliber center-fire cartridge, and it is fitted with a ten-inch barrel. Superbly engraved, with nickel-plating and a gold wash finish to the barrel and frame, the grips are made of pearl. The back strap bears the inscription, "Buffalo Bill to Ben Thompson." A similar weapon was also ordered which bears the back strap inscription "W. F. Cody." It was not uncommon for engraved pieces to be given as tokens of admiration.

In July 1880, when Ben's homicidal brother Billy got into trouble at Ogallala, Nebraska, and wounded a bartender who in turn wounded Billy, Ben asked Bat Masterson to get him out of trouble, and en route to Dodge City the pair stayed at Cody's ranch at North Platte.

Attitudes to gunfighting varied. Hickok was philosophical

**LEFT: David "Mysterious Dave" Mather photographed in Dodge City in 1883—note the "Assistant Marshal" band on his hat. To some Dave was a wicked man and a "killer of killers." His death remains a mystery.**

on the subject. He believed that no one could outrun a bullet, so if one was coming it was better to face it—an ironic comment considering his demise at the hands of a back-shooting coward. He also thought it better to aim for the body rather than anywhere else for the simple reason that if one shot a man "in the guts near the navel; you may not make a fatal shot, but he will get a shock that will paralyze his brain and arm so much that the fight is all over."

"The first man you kill," mused Jim Moon (whose real name was Henry Wilcoxon), "it goes pretty hard with you for a while, but after the second or third you don't mind knocking over one of these gunfighters any more than you would a sheep," he remarked to E. D. Cowan shortly before he was killed by Charley Wilson in Denver. "The man who pulls a gun on you when you have nothing in sight is a cur. All you need to do is walk right up to him, take it way and beat him over the head with it, so he won't try it again. Nearly all my men came for me. Of course, I went after some of them—had to." Cowan then described in his *Daily News* story of October 23, 1898, how Moon handled such encounters, one of them with "a bad man from Breckenridge":

Only a few weeks previously Moon, while seated with a friend and two women at a restaurant and having a rather merry time not objected to by the proprietor, was, according to his way of thinking, insulted by a lieutenant and officer of police. He beat both of them nearly to death with the chinaware and chairs, hurried his three companions into a hack, which he ordered driven to a half-way house outside the city limits, and held his impromptu block-house a week with a double-barreled shotgun against the combined police and the sheriff's force. He surrendered only when liberty was guaranteed him.

Shortly after, a bad man from Breckenridge pulled a six-shooter on Moon in a gambling room. He captured it and hit his assailant over the head with the butt. The blow knocked the Breckenridge killer down a flight of stairs and the body was taken to the morgue; the neck was found to have been broken. Moon was acquitted.

Then came Jim Moon's last attempt to brain or shoot a man with his pistol. A woman was at the bottom of the trouble. Clay Wilson was a mild-mannered, inert sort of a young fellow. Moon got entrance to his room one night and made him dance a jig in his

RIGHT: A haunting image of Dodge City and some of its inhabitants. Citizens of Dodge City were prohibited from carrying guns north of the nearby railroad line, but south of the tracks there was no such law.

night shirt while the .45-caliber bullets cut splinters out of the floor around his feet.

The following morning, Wilson put in his pocket a Colt sawed-off (presumably a large caliber pistol with a shortened barrel) which was the favorite weapon of the happy bad man. He went into the Arcade to take a drink. Moon was there and ordered him out. He obeyed but came back with the six-shooter in his hand. He fired twice before Moon grappled with him, both bullets plowing through the heart. With that strange vitality that is explicable in the deer when it bounds for hundreds of yards after having received a mortal wound but unaccountable in man, Moon fought for the possession of the six-shooter, which Wilson discharged a third time, the bullet again passing through the body. Moon did not quit the fight until a fourth bullet broke his neck.

Nothing in the annals of border tragedy is so remarkable as the last battle of Jim Moon, waged with animal-like instinct after he had been fatally shot. His own six-shooter was found in his coat pocket. Moon was large, alert, athletic, red-headed, and of course blue-eyed. Before settling in Colorado he disposed of some of the most troublesome junior bad men in Arizona.

Cowan's final comment on Moon's eyes is another tribute to the stereotype gunfighter. In more recent years, George D. Hendricks devoted a whole volume (*The Bad Man of the West*) to characteristics that set them apart. Out of fifty-seven so-called bad men examined, thirty-eight of them had blue or blue-gray eyes.

In contrast to Moon's violent reaction to what he considered to be personal insults, Cowan declared that "Bill Hickok was a finer type of the happy bad man than such as Jim Moon, because he was a genuine lover of law and order. When Wild Bill ruled in the name of good citizenship it fared ill with every pistol expert who undertook to run the town. His assassination at Deadwood was one of the most cowardly acts remembered in the mining camps," a view shared by many of Hickok's contemporaries. In Hays City,

**LEFT: Chalk Beeson poses for the camera with a magnificent bull. Beeson was the owner, for a time, of Dodge City's infamous Long Branch Saloon. At one point in Dodge, there was a saloon for every sixty-three members of the population.**

where Wild Bill lived for several years and for a brief period enforced the law, he was known and admired as a "law and order man." Anyone who let it be known that they "had it in for him" was advised to put up or shut up, for it was well known that Hickok usually hunted up those who made such threats. The *Hays City Sentinel* of February 2, 1877, added:

> The many tributes to his bravery, coolness, and generosity are not exaggerated. Bill was a quiet, peaceably disposed man—never boisterous and quarrelsome—and never starting a row. But when Bill was once convinced of an adequate cause for taking a hand in a row, there was always a funeral. This is where he differed from the generality of frontiersman. The ordinary ruffian, when involved in a row, would bluster around until, in the natural course of events, he would get shot; while Bill would perforate his opponent and then do his blustering at the funeral.

E. D. Cowan also described the demeanor and character of John Holliday, whose professional calling as a dentist earned him the title "Doc" on the frontier. It was said of him that he was "well drilled in the art of dentistry, but for those who doubted his ability, he would drill 'em for free." Born in Georgia in 1851, Holliday came from a genteel background but early in life had displayed characteristics that later led to his reputation as a killer. His already bad disposition was not helped when he contracted tuberculosis, which necessitated a life in a high, dry climate. Holliday's relationship with Wyatt Earp often proved an embarrassment both to Earp who had political as well as social ambitions and to his friends who were said to detest him. But it was Doc Holliday who stood by him when the Earp brothers fought it out at the O.K. Corral in 1881. His later involvement with the Earps after the murder of Morgan caused him most problems. Holliday was arrested on trumped-up charges in Denver in an attempt to get him extradited to Arizona. Cowan's version of what happened is informative if perhaps embroidered:

**RIGHT: Las Vegas, New Mexico. Depicted is the South East Plaza in 1881. Cattle wandered or lay in the streets, in what appears to be rural peace. But in the saloons and gambling halls, violence was never far away.**

To Holliday's record is accredited the breaking up, if not the extermination, of the Pimo [sic] county, Arizona, "rustlers," a class of murderous cattle thieves who prospered in New Mexico and Arizona until wiped out by the happy bad men [i.e. the O.K. Corral and the local rustlers]. Holliday was tried for murder in Pima County, whose official life at the time was dominated by the rustlers' conspiracy, and in spite of this adverse influence was acquitted. Tom

Fitch, of California, who defended him, told me that the witnesses for the prosecution were the best witnesses for the defense, since by their testimony it was clearly proved that Holliday killed all his men under fire, and with the odds often against him. He was incredibly swift and accurate with the six-shooter and ambidextrous. Given two men for objects, anywhere within the semi-circle he could hit both at the first discharge . . . After Holliday got free from the Pima County trials he made his way with all haste to Colorado. Under a trumped-up indictment a warrant was issued for his arrest and he was taken at Denver. The plot of the rustlers was to get him across the border of New Mexico and lynch him. Bat Masterson, who was greatly attached to Holliday, made a plea for assistance in the *Tribune* editorial rooms the night of the arrest. He submitted proof of the criminal design upon Holliday's life. Late as the hour was, I called on

LEFT: Tom Nixon's wife Cornelia and their son Howard Tracy, about 1877. Innuendo asserted that one of the reasons Nixon and Mather fell out was over her favors; but no evidence of a liaison has come to light.

RIGHT: Thomas C. Nixon, buffalo hunter, rancher, and lawman. His feud with Dave Mather finally led to bloodshed. Although fault lay on both sides, there were many who thought that Tom had been the aggressor.

Governor Pitkin and he agreed to order a public hearing of the requisition. The true motive of the arrest was sufficiently proved out of the mouth of the deputy sheriff. Governor Pitkin refused to grant the requisition, reprimanded the deputy sheriff, gently lectured Holliday as to the requirements of good citizenship in Colorado and dismissed him.

Whether Bat Masterson really liked Holliday or not is uncertain. His own assessment was that he had "a mean disposition and an ungovernable temper, and under the influence of liquor was a most dangerous man." But Bat, like many of Wyatt Earp's friends, tolerated Holliday simply because he was a friend of Earp's. Later, Masterson reported the incident involving Governor Pitkin in Human Life: "I was in Denver at the time, and managed to secure an audience with Governor Pitkin who, after listening to my statement in the matter, refused to honor the Arizona requisition for Holliday." Bat then declared: "I then had a

complaint sworn out against Holliday charging him with having committed a highway robbery in Pueblo, Colorado, and had him taken from Denver to Pueblo, where he was put under a nominal bond and released from custody. The charge of highway robbery made against Holliday, at this time, was nothing more than a subterfuge on my part to prevent him from being taken out of the state by the Arizona authorities, after Governor Pitkin went out of office, but the Colorado authorities did not know it at the time. Holliday always managed to have his case put off whenever it would come up for trial, and, by furnishing a new bond, in every instance would be released again."

Jack DeMattos, editor of an annotated version of Masterson's *Human Life* articles, discovered that the actual charge leveled against Doc was not highway robbery but "bunco," (a swindle, usually at cards). The case was continued indefinitely, which meant Holliday could not be extradited from the state.

**LEFT:** George Hoover erected the first saloon in Dodge in a sod hut June 17, 1872, thereby creating the place. He later became the town's first mayor and bank president. He died in 1914.

**RIGHT:** Orlando A. "Brick" Bond, who hailed from New York and settled in Dodge in 1872. He is credited with the deaths of 6,183 buffalo between 1874 and 1875. He joined with Nixon in the saloon business.

Doc Holiday's luck finally ran out. His pulmonary condition worsening, he went to Glenwood Springs, Colorado, seeking some relief, but galloping consumption set in and he died at ten on the morning of November 8, 1887, at the Hotel Glenwood. They buried him that afternoon in the Linwood Cemetery. He was thirty-six years old, but his ravaged body made him look like a man in his eighties.

David Allen "Mysterious Dave" Mather shared in demeanor and general behavior Holiday's antisocial characteristics. Born on August 10, 1851, the first of three sons born to Ulysses and Lydia Mather, he and his younger brother Josiah Wright Mather, born October 11, 1854, both made their way west. Josiah also became a noted figure in the West but he did not achieve anything like the reputation of

LEFT: Robert M. Wright, one of the early-day businessmen of Dodge whose book did much to publicize its status as the "cowboy capital" that is remembered to this day. He knew most of the famous frontier characters.

RIGHT: Patrick Sughrue. He and his twin brother Michael served as policemen during the hectic days of "cowboy chaos" in Dodge City. Pat later became sheriff of Ford County and Mike of Clark County.

his brother. Josiah was to die with his boots off at Grangeville, Idaho, on 18 April 1932. In their time, however, the Mather brothers were known as tough characters, and Dave was a particularly hard case. According to his biographer, Jack DeMattos, Dave Mather probably appeared out West post-1870. It is claimed that he had links with a gang of outlaws in Arkansas before moving on to achieve a notoriety in such places as Texas and Missouri. His first prominent mention, however, was in New Mexico, where he became mixed up in gambling and alleged crooked activities at Las Vegas. Here he met and became friends with several ex–Dodge City figures, including Doc Holliday. Mather was also ambitious. He applied for and was appointed as a deputy U.S. marshal. This appointment came at a time when he, together with others, was under suspicion for alleged involvement in stagecoach holdups and other robberies, but he was never indicted for any of those crimes. Instead, he was busily serving writs upon some of those with who he was alleged to be in cahoots.

Mather, however, is best remembered for his exploits in Dodge City where he settled in May 1883. His arrival coincided with the famous so-called Dodge City War between Luke Short and his partner William H. Harris and the town council over prostitution. Mather was not involved in that fracas. On June 1, 1883, he was appointed assistant city marshal and celebrated the event by having the only known photograph of himself made, which depicts him wearing a ribbon around his hat bearing the words "Assistant Marshal." He was also appointed as a deputy sheriff of Ford County. Not everyone, however, welcomed his appointment as an assistant marshal. One man even wrote a letter of complaint to the governor about Mather's behavior and inferred that the police force was intimidating the citizens. If any action was taken, it was not recorded, and Mather remained on the force. At that time, the marshal was Jack Bridges who was earning one hundred dollars per month, and his assistant seventy-five, which was good money. On July 6, the council boosted both the marshal's and the assistant marshal's salaries to $150 and $125 respectively, which prompted the Ford County *Globe* of July 24, 1883, to comment: "Dodge City pays her marshal $150 per month and the assistant marshal

$125 per month. Besides this, each of them is entitled to kill a cowboy or two each season." But both Bridges and Mather lost their jobs following the election of April 1884. The incoming mayor, George M. Hoover, himself an old-time saloon keeper and wholesale liquor dealer, replaced them with William M. "Bill" Tilghman as the new city marshal, and as his assistant he chose Thomas C. Nixon.

Dave Mather managed to retain his commission as a deputy sheriff, but he was increasingly concerned with local politics, which were in something of a turmoil when he joined the Democratic Party. The Kansas statutes that had introduced prohibition into the arena met with a mixed reaction. Added to this, Mather and a Texan friend named David Black had become proprietors of the Opera House saloon with the intention of turning it into a dance hall. This was much against the wishes of the new mayor and council and soon led to friction. To add insult to injury, Dave's rival and bitter enemy, Tom Nixon, not only had his old job but also, in partnership with Orlando A. "Brick" Bond, owned the Lady Gay saloon that they operated as a saloon-cum-dance hall. On May 22, the council passed legislation to forestall any plans by Mather and Black for a dance hall by passing Ordinance No. 83 that, in part, claimed that it would be unlawful for anyone to maintain in Dodge City "what is commonly known as a dance hall, or any other place where lewd women and men congregate for the purpose of dancing or otherwise."

For reasons not disclosed, Nixon's establishment was not touched. In reprisal, Mather and Black advertised in the Dodge City *Democrat* on June 7 that they intended to sell their beer for only "five cents a glass," which was less than half the going rate. Nixon and his cronies soon reacted: pressure was placed upon local liquor dealers and beer wholesalers, and the Opera House saloon soon dried up. On June 12, *The Times* reported a court ruling concerning potential jurors and the demon drink, which took a great swipe at the partners:

**RIGHT: Michael Sutton was a prominent lawyer in early-day Dodge City who acted for the defense in Dave Mather's trial. Once, in 1879, he assisted Sheriff Bat Masterson in the capture of horse thieves.**

A man who is engaged in selling liquors, or in any other unlawful business, is incompetent to act as a juror. This is a virtual disfranchisement of a large class of people in Dodge City, and if the rule was applied to the country, it would make a vast army of incompetents.

Little by little, prohibition is taking hold in this city. It may appear insignificant, but the 5 cent beer business lends to prohibition.

It soon became increasingly obvious to Mather and Black that Nixon was a leading light in their problems, and it would only be a matter of time before there was trouble. Black was not personally involved in the dispute between Mather and Nixon. Tom Nixon, like Mather, had a shrouded past. It is known that by 1870 he and his wife Cornelia and young family were living near Fort Dodge, where Tom had a local reputation as a buffalo hunter. He also owned a small ranch

but later set up in business in Dodge City repairing wagons. It was rumored that a woman was the cause of the friction between Nixon and Mather and that the saloon feud was a smoke screen. Some even claimed that there was a relationship between Mather and Cornelia Nixon.

This was all conjecture: the real reason (if it had nothing to do with the saloon feud) was never disclosed and would never be discovered later.

Tom Nixon made the first move; on July 18, 1884, as Mather stood in the doorway of his Opera House saloon, Nixon took a shot at him from the bottom of the porch stairs. The bullet missed Mather, who suffered only powder burns and the odd splinter.

Sheriff Pat Sughrue rushed up at the sound of the shot and promptly disarmed Nixon and took him over to the jail. Mather dismissed his wound as superficial, but protested that

LEFT: A famous street scene that was the basis for the present-day "Front Street" re-creation in Dodge City. Clearly visible is another street view of the Long Branch and Beatty & Kelley's saloon facing the tracks.

he had not been armed; Nixon claimed that he was and that he had only fired because he believed Dave was going for his gun. Mather said that he would not press charges, and many people expressed the opinion that the matter was far from over. Nixon was bound over in the sum of $800 to appear at the next term of court charged with "assault with intent to kill."

Robert M. Wright, a local merchant and the author of *Dodge City: The Cowboy Capital*, stated that Dave Mather was "said to be a very wicked man, a killer of killers. And it was and is an undoubted fact that Dave had more dead men to his credit, at that time, than any other man in the West." On July 21, 1884, yet another victim was added to his tally. Almost seventy-three hours after their first encounter, and ironically in approximately the same spot (but their positions were reversed), Dave Mather shot and killed Tom Nixon. *The Globe and Live Stock Journal* on July 22, under the heading "The Murder," declared that Mather shot Nixon at ten the previous evening as the assistant marshal was "on duty at the corner of Front Street and First Avenue."

The paper described how Mather "came down the stairs from his saloon and on his arrival at the foot he called to Nixon who was standing at the corner, and on Nixon turning around Mather commenced shooting at him, firing four shots, two of them striking him in the right side one on the left side and one passing through the left nipple, killing him instantly."

Mather was immediately placed under arrest, and a preliminary hearing was arranged for July 30 at the Ford County Courthouse at Dodge City. DeMattos unearthed the original court records, which contradict some of the published accounts of both the shooting and testimony.

Witnesses testified that Nixon was looking in on a game of cards when he was shot and was oblivious to his danger. When Mather called out "Tom," immediately followed by four shots, Nixon was heard to say, "Oh, I'm shot" or "I'm

**RIGHT: A well-appointed saloon in some Western cow town. In the early days of the nineteenth century, a saloon might be little more than a crude hut or even a tent, but eventually the massive profits from gambling created expensive establishments.**

killed," before collapsing. It was also claimed that he had turned to face whoever spoke just as the shots were fired. Nixon never had a chance to draw his own revolver. Following the shooting, Mather walked up the stairs to his saloon.

Witness Archie Franklin stated that "Nixon did not fall after the first shot. He fell between the second and third shots. Mather advanced after the first shot. I could not say that he shot Nixon at all after he was down."

Bat Masterson, who appeared on the scene moments after the shooting, testified that he was among the first to reach the body. He added:

> I was probably the first that took hold of him. He was lying on his right side and back, with his head south west, and his feet north east. His right hand was up and his left was on his left hip.
>
> This was about a minute after the last shot was fired. He had his revolver on. He was lying on it. It was in his scabbard [holster]. It looked as if it might have fallen partly out or been drawn partly out. I did not see any other weapons on him or in his hands.

Sheriff Pat Sughrue testified that Mather did the shooting with a Colt's .45-caliber pistol, but he did not "see the pistol while it was being shot."

In court the following day, July 31, the reporter for the Topeka *Daily Commonwealth* claimed that he was seated close to Mather. In his report, published on August 3, he described Dave as "calm and collected, and being unrestrained, the best observer of human nature could not have selected him as the man whose life was in jeopardy." Michael Sutton, a well-known lawyer in Dodge, acted for the defense and tried unsuccessfully to impeach one of the witnesses. Mather's attempt to obtain bail was denied, and he was placed in jail to await trial for first-degree murder.

Following some wrangling and legal hassle for a change of venue, the trial was finally fixed to take place at Kinsley, Kansas, on December 29. On December 31, the jury retired and twenty-seven minutes later rendered a "not guilty" verdict. The consensus of opinion on all sides seems to have been that Nixon was the aggressor and that Mather's actions were justifiable.

Dave Mather's subsequent career was fraught with scrapes, and his final disappearance only adds to the mystery surrounding him. A body found on the tracks of the Central Texas Railroad was thought to be that of Mysterious Dave; the dead man's identity was never disclosed, but the description matched Dave's. The Kingman, Kansas, *Courier* of May 21, 1886, described the body as that of a man aged about "thirty-five or forty-five years of age, with a long black moustache. There is a hole in the side of the head, the nature of which cannot be determined without a surgical examination, but it is believed to be a bullet wound. He had

near him two bottles of whiskey and some cigars." Curiously, DeMattos unearthed a document in the court records of Ford County that claims that Mather was driven out of Dodge under threat of death, but his ultimate fate remains a mystery. Yet, like Billy the Kid, Jesse James, and other notorious characters, stories of sightings continued to circulate long after the subject ceased to exist. Even Dave's own brother Josiah was later to confess that he had no idea what had happened to his brother or where he went after leaving Dodge. Josiah secretly hoped that "Mysterious Dave" would one day become "Prodigal Dave," but he never did.

## Sips, Slaps, and Shots

Personal disputes, feuds, and rows over wine, women, and cards beset frontier towns and settlements, and the outcome of such disputes invariably led to violence. Perhaps the most memorable of Dodge City's gunfights was that which took place between Levi Richardson and Frank "Cock-eyed Frank" Loving in the Long Branch saloon on April 5, 1879. This encounter had all the ingredients of the classic Western gunfight, but there was also a touch of graveyard humor about it, for as it turned out it was almost a farce. The Ford County *Globe* graphically described the fight on April 8:

**LEFT: The interior of the Long Branch Saloon in Dodge City. In place of television's Miss Kitty, one finds an all-male domain. The angle of the photograph clearly shows how much room was taken up by the bar.**

LEFT: Dallas Stoudenmire photographed when Marshal of El Paso (badge prominently displayed). He cuts a fine figure. No pistols show, for he carried them in specially made hip pockets. He also carried a "belly gun."

RIGHT: The Mexican jail at Paso del Norte in 1880. From here a number of Texans escaped after being jailed over the shooting of a peddler. They tried to cross the Rio Grande but were gunned down.

There is seldom witnessed in any civilized town or county such a sense as transpired at the Long Branch saloon, in this city, last Saturday evening, resulting in the killing of Levi Richardson, a well-known freighter, of this city, by a gambler named Frank Loving.

For several months Loving has been living with a woman toward whom Richardson seems to have cherished tender feelings, and on one or two occasions previous to this which resulted so fatally, they have quarreled and even come to blows. Richardson was a man who had lived for several years on the frontier, and though well liked in many respects, he had cultivated habits of bold and daring, which are always likely to get a man into trouble. Such a disposition as he possessed might be termed bravery by many, and indeed we believe he was the reverse of a coward. He was a hard working, industrious man, but young and strong and reckless.

Loving is a man of whom we know but very little. He is a gambler by profession; not much of a roudy [sic], but more of the cool and the desperate order, when he has a killing on hand. He is about 25 years old.

Both, or either of these men, we believe, might have avoided this shooting if either had possessed a desire to do so. But both being willing to risk their lives, each with confidence in himself, they fought because they wanted to fight. As stated in the evidence below, they met, one said "I don't believe you will fight." The other answered "try me and see," and immediately both drew murderous revolvers and at it they went, in a room filled with people, the leaden missives flying in all directions. Neither exhibited any sign of a desire to escape the other, and there is no telling how long the fight might have lasted had not Richardson been pierced with bullets and Loving's pistol left without a cartridge. Richardson was shot in the breast, through the side and through the right arm. It seems strange that Loving was not hit, except a slight scratch on the hand, as the two men were so close together that their pistols almost touched each other. Eleven shots were fired, six by Loving and five by Richardson. Richardson only lived a few moments after the shooting. Loving was placed in jail to await the verdict of the coroner's jury, which was "self defense," and he was released.

Richardson has no relatives in this vicinity. He was from Wisconsin. About twenty-eight years old.

Together will all the better class of our community we greatly regret this terrible affair. We do not believe it is a proper way to settle difficulties, and we are positive it is not according to any law, human or divine. But if men must continue to persist in settling their disputes with fire arms we would be in favor of the dueling system, which would not necessarily endanger the lives of those who might be passing up or down the street attending to their own business. We do not know that there is cause to censure the police, unless it be to urge upon them the necessity of strictly enforcing the ordinance preventing the carrying of concealed weapons. Neither of these men had a right to carry such weapons. Gamblers, as a class, are desperate men. They consider it necessary in their business that they keep up their fighting reputations, and never take a bluff. On no account should they be allowed to carry deadly weapons . . .

The *Globe* cited several witnesses. Adam Jackson, the bartender in the Long Branch, claimed that Richardson was on his way out of the saloon when Loving came in:

Loving sat down on the hazard table. Richardson came and sat near him on the same table. Then Loving immediately got up, making some remark to Richardson, could not understand what it was,

**RIGHT: The Overland Building, corner of El Paso and Overland Street. The Texas Rangers headquartered here when in town, and it was to where George Campbell was carried. He died there the next morning.**

Richardson was sitting on the table at the time, and Loving standing up. Loving says to Richardson: "If you have anything to say about me why don't you come and say it to my face like a gentleman, and not to my back, you dam[n] son of a bitch." Richardson then stood up and said: "You wouldn't fight anything you dam[n]—" could not hear the rest. Loving said "you try me and see." Richardson pulled his pistol first, and Loving also drew a pistol. Three or four shots were fired when Richardson fell by the billiard table. Richardson did not fire after he fell. He fell on his hands and knees. No shots were fired after Richardson fell. No persons were shooting except the two mentioned. Loving's pistol snapped twice and I think Richardson shot twice before Loving's pistol was discharged.

City Marshal Charles E. Bassett testified that when the shooting started he was at Beatty & Kelley's Saloon. He ran to the Long Branch and was on time to witness the remarkable sight of both men running around the billiard table, then the stove, shooting at each other:

I got as far as the stove when the shooting had about ended. I caught Loving's pistol. Think there was two shots fired after I got into the room, and positive there was one Loving fired that shot, to the best of my knowledge. Did not see Richardson fire any shot, and did not see him have a pistol. I examined the pistol which was shown me as the one Richardson had. It contained five empty shells, Richardson fell while I was there. Whether he was shot before or after I came in am unable to say. I think the shots fired after I came in were fired by Loving at Richardson. Richardson fell immediately after the shot I heard. Did not see any other person shoot at Richardson. Did not see Duffey take Richardson's pistol. Do not know whether Loving knew that Richardson's pistol had been taken away from him. There was considerable smoke in the room. Loving's pistol was a Remington, No. 44 and was empty after the shooting.

"Duffey" was William Duffey, who testified that Loving fell at one point and he imagined that he had been shot. He then grabbed Richardson's pistol and recalled that there "might have been a shot fired by one or the other while we were scuffling." He added that he was not sure if Richardson had been shot or not, "but I think he had, as he was weak and I handled him easily." He also stated that he thought that Loving was unaware that he had disarmed Richardson.

Bassett's reference to Loving's pistol as a "Remington, No. 44" is confusing. It seems that the marshal was referring to its caliber—.44 Remington—rather than the weapon's serial number. Possibly it was the New Model Army revolver of 1875 that was chambered for the .44 Remington cartridge, or perhaps it was one of the thousands of original 1863 New Model Army percussion revolvers that the company began converting to center-fire ammunition during the early 1870s. Of greater significance, of course, is the extraordinary fact that two men, bent upon killing each other, could run around a billiard table and a stove in a crowded saloon, firing wildly. And that those shots that missed either antagonist also missed

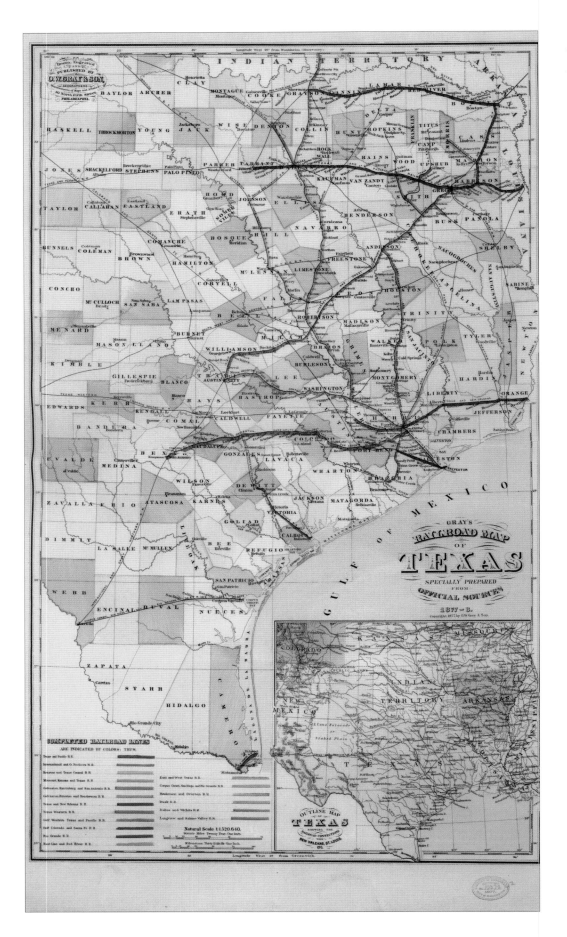

LEFT: Gray's railroad map of Texas, printed around 1888. The map clearly indicates how the railroad network opened the state up to commerce and settlement. Work on the first railroads in Texas began in 1851, and by 1880 there were over 2,500 miles of track in the state.

anyone else. But both men dispelled the vision of the cool, calm gunfighter of legend. Indeed, they let emotion rather than their heads rule the day.

It was an outcome that surprised men versed not only in the art of gunplay but familiar with both combatants. The coroner's jury's verdict was unanimous: "The said Levi Richardson came to his death by a bullet wound from a pistol fired by Frank Loving in self defense." Loving's own career following that fight was short-lived. He was killed in Trinidad, Colorado, in 1882 by John "Jack" Allen, who himself had been forced out of Dodge in 1876 following a row with some Texans.

Texas witnessed a lot of violence, and it also exported a number of noted gun-toters. On home ground, however, the state still harbored a number of hard cases. El Paso, scene of several shoot-outs, paid host to several that are testimony to the reactions of men bent upon jealous revenge.

On April 14, 1885, the city found itself virtually without law when the city marshal and the county sheriff, accompanied by deputies, were attending a murder trial in Presidio County. The marshal left Charles M. "Buck" Linn in charge. Linn, a former Texas Ranger, was at that time in charge of the city jail. Buck was regarded as a man to be depended upon just so long as he remained sober, but when drunk he was described as "crazy."

Unfortunately, that was the night he chose to hit the bottle, and when he heard that Sam Gillespie, a friend of a man he is reported to have pistol-whipped, was demanding that Buck be locked up and tried by a grand jury, he was furious. He sent word to Gillespie that he would shoot him on sight; Sam prudently armed himself and hid in a convenient doorway to wait, but Linn saw him and hesitated, then turned and hurried into the Gem saloon, where he bumped into an old crony named William P. Raynor. Described by some as "the best-dressed bad man in Texas," Raynor was an interesting character. By profession a gambler, he had also been employed as a collector of customs at Clinton, Texas, and later served for a brief period on the El Paso police force. He was well versed—as was Linn—in the finer points of gunplay.

Raynor, generally popular with most people, had a reputation for interfering in other people's affairs, and before

long the pair were showing the effects of several hours of drinking in various saloons.

George Look, an early-day resident of El Paso who in later years compiled a personal memoir, recalled that the pair had a row in the Gem saloon with Bob Cahill, a young faro dealer. After Linn and Raynor parted, Look warned that there might be trouble, particularly when it became clear that both men had been having their drinks "charged up on ice" when their money ran out.

The peace of what appeared to be a quiet enough evening was abruptly shattered as Raynor suddenly appeared at the entrance of a theater that adjoined the main barroom of the Gem. The entertainment of soldiers relaxing on furlough was sharply curtailed by Raynor bawling out: "Where is that son of a bitch who came to town tonight?"

Most of the troopers hit the floor immediately; others escaped via the exit. At that moment, Raynor noted that Look and the saloon's proprietor were themselves seated in the audience. Confused and embarrassed, he holstered his pistol, removed his hat, and bowed his way out. "Excuse me, gentlemen—excuse me," he apologized and was gone. Whoever it was that Raynor was looking for kept silent and hidden.

According to his biographer, Wyatt Earp was present on that occasion visiting his friend Lou Rickabaugh. This account claims that Raynor had tried to provoke Wyatt into a fight, which he declined. Raynor then started to insult a man standing at the bar sporting a white hat. Raynor's taunts ceased when the man known as Robert "Cowboy Bob" Rennick assured him that he was unarmed.

Disgusted, Raynor left the bar, leaving Rennick fuming. His reputation had been insulted, and he determined to get even. He walked across to the faro dealer and asked to borrow a pistol, stating that he would not be imposed on. The dealer shook his head: "Have no trouble—go on out." Ignoring him, Rennick reached into the drawer and grabbed the dealer's pistol.

It was just as well for him that he did, for the door burst open and Raynor rushed in, firing wildly. Rennick, with remarkable coolness, dropped to one knee, cocked the pistol, and holding it firmly in both hands, opened fire, cocked, and fired again, hitting Raynor first in the shoulder and then in his stomach. Raynor, dazed and numbed by the shock of the heavy lead slugs, continued to shoot, ruining a billiard table with his final shots before turning away and staggering into the street where he clambered on to a passing streetcar and collapsed across a seat.

Passengers heard him mumble that his mother should be informed that he had "died game."

RIGHT: This photograph of George Campbell and Jim Manning was made in 1881. George had no quarrel with the Mannings. Rather, he kept in with them, as he did others among the sporting set. His ivory-stocked Colt .45 is worn butt forward as was still common at the time. The pistol still exists and is now owned by a member of his family. Its serial number is 22459, which means it was manufactured in 1875.

LEFT: George W. Campbell photographed in Ironton, Ohio, in 1877, aged twenty-seven. The plate was made during a trip to his home. Largely ignored by historians, George was highly regarded by his contemporaries.

Rennick appeared in the doorway of the Gem, but he took no further action. What is more, he followed George Look's advice and left town, slipping over the border to Ciudad Juarez.

Furious at the demise of his partner, Linn searched every saloon for the hapless Cahill, convinced that the faro dealer with whom he and Raynor had rowed earlier in the evening was responsible. Stuart Lake has credited Wyatt Earp with the advice to the worried Cahill, who was no gunfighter, to get

himself "heeled," to have his gun cocked, and not to shoot until he was ready. He advised him, too, to aim low, for the belly.

When Linn eventually burst through the door of Cahill's saloon, gun in his hand, the denouement was swift. Responding to Linn's opening fire deliberately and with great coolness, Cahill aimed his pistol and fired twice. If Wyatt Earp really had advised him, it worked. One ball struck Linn in the heart, and he was dead before he hit the floor,

ironically almost exactly where Raynor had earlier been shot. It was now Cahill's turn to flee across the border, where he joined Rennick.

Raynor lived for several days. Some reports claimed that Rennick had expressed the wish that someone should have killed him years ago but hastily added that "if Bill gets well, what I said don't go." Soon after Raynor's death, Rennick and Cahill returned to El Paso where they were acquitted on a plea of self-defense.

**LEFT: One way to settle a dispute in earlier times, but one with the same moral code as any later Western gunfight, at least on one side. This duel, fought along "European" lines in theory, occurred in 1804 in Weehawken, New Jersey, between Federalist politician Alexander Hamilton and former Vice President Aaron Burr (the duel was the result of character attacks in the newspapers). Hamilton had no intention of actually firing, but Burr shot him without hesitation. Hamilton died two days later.**

El Paso also witnessed the exploits of one of Texas's most publicized peace officers and a man who, but for the demon drink, might well have joined the ranks of the immortals. Dallas Stoudenmire was not a native Texan but a Southerner nonetheless, having been born at Aberfoil, Alabama, on December 11, 1845. He came from a large family and is reported to have joined the Confederate Army in 1862, surviving the war despite several severe wounds. Having tried a stint as a farmer near Columbus, Texas, he finally took the plunge and enlisted in Company A of the Frontier Battalion of the Texas Rangers.

Stoudenmire's service papers describe him as being six feet two inches tall, with hazel eyes auburn hair, and others recalled that he had a broad, pale face and a "granite jaw." As a Ranger, he proved very effective, but there were those who were concerned about his attitude. Utterly fearless, Stoudenmire, if provoked or convinced that he was right, could kill without compunction—characteristics judged by some to be necessary when upholding the law in a lawless society but by others to suggest a mad dog on a leash.

When Stoudenmire arrived there in 1881, El Paso was a curious mixture of old and new. Its proximity to Mexico (Paso del Norte, later to be renamed Ciudad Juarez, was separated from El Paso by the Rio Grande river) and the anti-Mexican attitude of many of its predominantly white population, boosted by the fact that there was little law enforcement, created problems on both sides of the river.

Stoudenmire at that time was marshal of Socorro, New Mexico, where his reputation with a gun was already known. Since leaving the Rangers he had been involved in several shoot-outs, some on a personal basis and the others in an official capacity. His brother-in-law, Doc Cummings, was the proprietor of the Globe restaurant in El Paso and is believed to have been responsible for persuading Dallas to come to the place.

Just prior to Stoudenmire's arrival there had been a dispute with Mexicans over the shooting of a Mexican peddler by Americans, some of who had escaped back across the border. Others had been captured and jailed. Aided by some friendly prostitutes, the men had been helped to escape but had been killed by a Mexican armed with a rifle as they struggled through the water to escape. This led to a revenge attack by some of El Paso's citizens, but the locals were more concerned with establishing law and order within city limits.

Among the early peace officers appointed by the city council was George W. Campbell, a native of Greenup County, Kentucky, who was born December 23, 1850, and went west in the middle 1870s, eventually arriving in Texas where he served for a time as a deputy sheriff. Later, on the recommendation of the Texas Rangers, he was appointed marshal of El Paso on December 1, 1880. But Campbell, like his predecessors and his successors, had problems with the local mayor, Solomon Schutz, who seems to have run things pretty much his own way. When Mexicans were arrested, he sought to drop the charges. In his biography of Campbell, *El Paso Lawman*, Fred R. Egloff suggests that this was because Schutz did not wish to upset his Mexican customers on both sides of the border. There is some suggestion that to supplement his income, Campbell "shook down" the local gamblers and brothel keepers. Word was that the Rangers intervened and Campbell resigned, but in effect the Rangers had interceded to assist Campbell. He actually left office when he and the mayor fell out over the nonpayment of back pay and expenses. His departure from office led to a wave of lawlessness that involved the Rangers.

Dallas Stoudenmire became marshal of El Paso on April 11, 1881, following the forced resignation of his predecessor, Bill Johnson, whom many considered to be an alcoholic. Within days of Stoudenmire's appointment, there was a

**BELOW: The old Greene County courthouse at Springfield, Missouri, about 1865. From this point Dave Tutt stepped out to meet Wild Bill for the last time. A chance shot or deadly accuracy at one hundred paces ended his career.**

RIGHT: The original print of this photograph of Wild Bill is a *carte-de-visite* by Wilbur Blakeslee of Mendota, IIllinois, where Hickok appeared in 1869, en route from the Plains to his mother's home at nearby Troy Grove.

major upset between the Mexicans and Americans. A number of Mexican cattle had been driven across the border and were found on John Hale's ranch. It was alleged that he and the Manning brothers, Frank and Jim, were involved with him. The mayor, anxious to keep in with his Mexican customers, gave them the right to carry arms on Texas soil, which caused an uproar.

On the way to the Hale ranch, some of the Mexicans were ambushed and murdered. Once news of this reached Mexico, more armed men came over and Gus Krempkau, a Spanish-speaking constable in El Paso, was called in to act as an interpreter. An inquest was opened and adjourned, and the Mexicans recrossed the border bearing their dead. But behind them they left a simmering resentment both over the deaths and the decision to allow so many armed Mexicans into the area.

Fred Egloff learned much of Campbell's part in El Paso's early history from his family and surviving correspondence. He also discovered that Campbell's hometown newspaper carried an account of what happened to George Campbell following the inquest, and it gives us another insight into the activities of Dallas Stoudenmire. George's brother Abe visited El Paso to learn more of his brother's death, and in May 1881 the Ashland *Independent* carried a letter from him that gave a résumé of the cause and the outcome. His report disclosed a campaign to blacken characters or distort the facts. Tradition asserts that following the inquest Campbell was drunk and yelling that Stoudenmire should have arrested the Mexicans. When Krempkau appeared on the street, Campbell abused him, but Gus ignored the tirade.

At that moment John Hale, the worse for liquor, leaped to his feet, drew his pistol, ran at Krempkau, ordered Campbell out of the way, and shot Krempkau through the lungs. Realizing his action, Hale jumped behind a pillar. At that moment, Stoudenmire arrived, took in the situation, and opened fire, killing an innocent Mexican bystander. But his next shot hit Hale right between the eyes. Campbell meanwhile was yelling that he was not involved.

The dying Krempkau pulled his pistol, cocked it, and put a ball through Campbell's wrist, forcing him to change his pistol to his left hand; Gus's next shot hit him in the foot,

Stoudenmire then joined in and brought Campbell down, who in his dying moment accused the marshal of murdering him.

The Rangers, who had stood by during the shooting, later stated that they believed that Stoudenmire had had the situation under control. The *Independent* article, however, gives us reason for doubt:

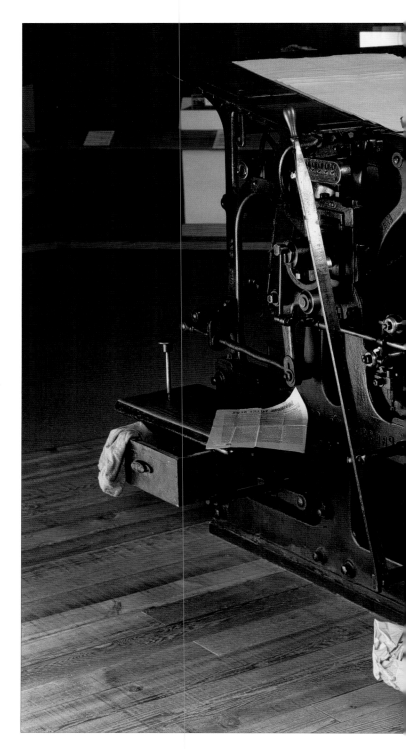

When reviewing the events that led to the shooting, Abe admitted that there was evidence of a dispute between Campbell and Krempkau, but that Campbell had been trying to avoid gunplay, especially when Hale interceded and opened fire. It was Krempkau or Hale who hit Campbell in the foot, and Stoudenmire who hit him in the arm, after he had shot the innocent Mexican and then blown Hale's brains out. As Campbell tried to grasp his pistol with his left hand Stoudenmire shot him again. "This was about six o'clock, P.M. and he died about five o'clock the next morning. He was perfectly rational up to the second before he died. He made his dying declaration in the presence of the State's Attorney, in which he stated the facts as I have given them above. Said that he did not want to have any difficulty, and that he understood Knowcamp [Krempkau] to accept the explanation."

**LEFT: The printing press was a vital tool for disseminating news (and many myths) about the lives and adventures of the gunfighters. Here is the Babcock steam-driven press that printed the *Cody Enterprise* newspaper for the town of Cody, Wyoming. By 1880, the technology allowed the newspaper editors to add photo engravings and half tones.**

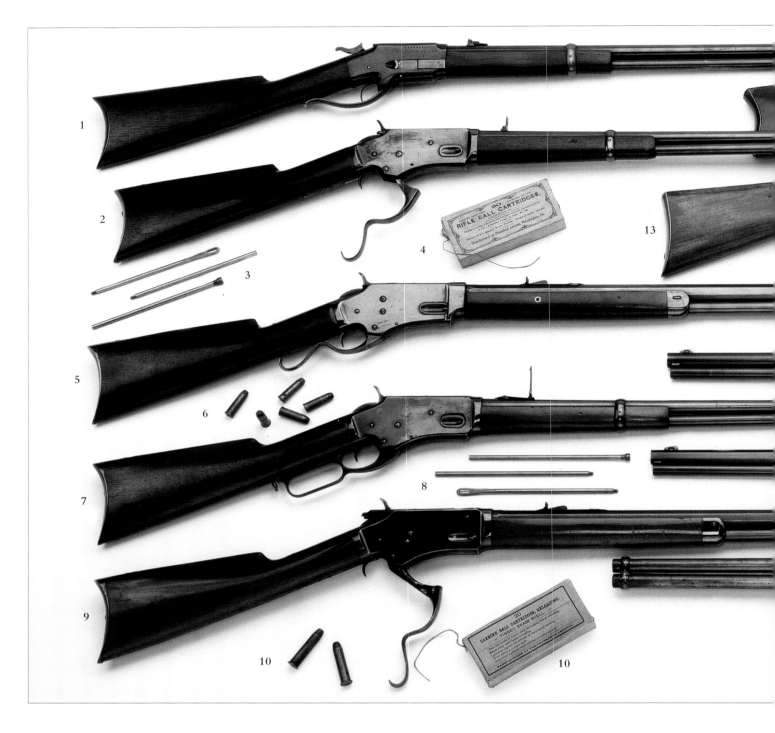

## BURGESS, WHITNEY VARIANTS

Andrew Burgess was a prolific inventor who, in 1873 and 1875, patented a lever action for rifles that also included features patented by G. W. Morse in 1856. He contracted with Eli Whitney Jr. (whose company had made Sam Colt's Walker pistols back in 1847) to produce a magazine lever-rifle that competed with the Winchester. The venture was not a success, and in the mid-1880s Colt also manufactured an improved Burgess lever-action rifle. Tradition has it that Winchester

threatened to produce revolvers if Colt continued to manufacture the Burgess. Production stopped. Whitney, however, did produce other lever-action weapons, notably the Whitney-Kennedy series (one such was owned by Billy the Kid).

The Whitney range of lever-action rifles was designed for frontier or sporting rather than military use, and an estimated 20,000 such rifles were made. Like the Winchester arms, the carbine version had a 20-inch barrel and the rifle a 24-inch

barrel. The company also produced several bolt-action models designed for military use, but none was purchased by the Ordnance Department, though a number of these latter arms reportedly found favor in Central and South America.

1. Whitney-Burgess carbine in .40 caliber.
2. Whitney-Kennedy lever-action carbine showing the "S" lever on early models.
3. Three-part cleaning rod for the above carbine.
4. A box of .45 caliber "Rifle Cartridges."
5. A Whitney-Burgess-Morse lever-action rifle in .44 caliber.
6. Its ammunition. Cartridges were called "shells" out West.
7. Whitney-Kennedy carbine fitted with a full loop lever.
8. Cleaning rod for the above weapon.
9. Whitney-Kennedy rifle in .40-60 caliber.
10. .40-60 cartridges for the above rifle.
11. Whitney-Scharf lever-action hunting rifle, sold in .32-20, .38-40, and .44-40 calibers.
12. Hunting rifle cartridges.
13. Another version of the sporting rifle.
14. Government "loads."
15. Typical Stetson-type broad-brimmed hat.
16. Colt-Burgess lever-action rifle.
17. Cleaning rod for the Colt-Burgess rifle.
18. Colt Lightning slide-operated rifle. Colt produced a number of variants.
19. Remington-Keene magazine bolt-action rifle in .45-79 caliber.
(Artifacts courtesy of Buffalo Bill Historical Center, Cody, Wyoming.)

Follow-up reports in the Western press further confused the issue, and there are a number of unanswered questions. Egloff raises the point that Dallas was not charged with murder, which may have been because the mayor and council were anxious to get rid of Campbell, so they backed their own man, Stoudenmire.

Dallas Stoudenmire continued in office, where his presence and reputation kept the lid on. His armament was a pair of .44 Smith & Wesson .44 caliber No. 3 "American" pistols, silver-plated and ivory stocked, which he carried in specially made leather-lined hip pockets. He also carried a "belly gun," a .44 Richards-Mason conversion of the Colt 1860 Army revolver, the barrel cut down to about two inches.

Late in the evening of April 17, Bill Johnson tried to ambush Stoudenmire as he and Cummings took an evening stroll, but was himself shot dead by both men. Eight bullets were found in his body. Others are reported to have joined in but missed. For his part, Stoudenmire blamed the Manning family but could not prove it. His handling of the situation in El Paso met with general approval, but the strain began to tell and he took to drink. Soon after, he married, and during his absence on honeymoon, James B. Gillett, a deputy marshal, took over (the same Gillett who later made a name for himself as a Texas Ranger). Cummings made the mistake of falling out with the Mannings and was shot dead in a saloon fight.

On his return, Stoudenmire declared open war on the Mannings. The city council interceded and persuaded both sides to make peace, but the strain took its toll and Dallas again took to drink. He ultimately resigned, his place being taken by Gillett. On September 18, 1882, Dallas decided the time had come to have a showdown with the Mannings,

claiming that they had put the word out that he wanted a fight. He found two of the brothers in the Coliseum, Jim standing beside the bar and Felix (known as "Doc") playing billiards. Brother Frank was summoned. "Doc" and Dallas got into a shouting match. Walt Jones, who had accompanied Dallas to make sure there were no problems, tried to intervene. Dallas pushed him aside—a fatal mistake. "Doc" pulled his .44 double-action and fired, the ball smashing into Stoudenmire's pocket book. Again Manning fired, and this time he hit Dallas in the left breast. Now severely wounded, Dallas managed to draw one of his own pistols and shot Manning in the right arm above the elbow, causing him to drop his pistol. Pluckily, Manning threw himself against Dallas before he could fire a second time, and, locked together, the pair staggered about in a *danse macabre* until they fell into the street. At that point, Jim Manning arrived armed

with a .45. His first shot thudded harmlessly into the barber's pole, but he took careful aim for the second one and blew Stoudenmire's brains out. Doc Manning, free from Stoudenmire's embrace, grabbed one of his pistols and started to beat the now lifeless body on the head before he was finally pulled off.

The inquest found that Jim Manning acted in self-defense to protect his "unarmed" brother, and no further action was taken. Old-timers, however, were adamant in their view: a bullet may have been the instrument, but it was alcohol that destroyed Dallas Stoudenmire. He was considered to be a man who, in better times, had deserved his good reputation.

### "Walk 'n' Draw"

Tradition asserts that gunfighters approached gunfights in the manner of duelists—face-to-face and firing on a given signal or on the command of one of them. This oversimplification has remained a constant feature of film and fiction for more than a century. Few Hollywood-style gunfights took place, and those that did were not quite as the storytellers might wish. Perhaps the one gunfight that best illustrates the face-to-face "walk 'n' draw" encounter took place at Springfield, Missouri, on Friday, July 21, 1865, between Wild Bill Hickok and Davis K. Tutt. The pair were reported to have been friends for some time but had fallen out the day before over a game of cards. Both men believed that they were in the right and were prepared to back their opinions with pistols if necessary.

Although James Butler Hickok was generally known in southwest Missouri and parts of Arkansas as "Wild Bill," he had yet to establish the reputation he eventually achieved on the Plains. He won the name of "Wild Bill" as a result of his activities during the Civil War as a Union Army scout, detective, and spy. He was admired by most of the officers for whom he worked and had a number of friends within the city. Tutt, on the other hand, was not well known and even

LEFT: Ellsworth in 1879 was beginning to lose its "shacks and tents" image and assume respectability denied it during the hectic 1860s and its cow-town period. Still dominant are the railroad tracks dividing the place.

today is obscure. In his youth, Dave became embroiled in the Tutt-Everett feud that clouded the horizon for some years and led to his own father's death. When the Civil War broke out, the family were living in Yellville, Arkansas. Here, Dave enlisted in the First Regiment, McBride's Brigade, Arkansas (Confederate) Infantry, early in 1862.

Military records indicate that Dave served only one year with the regiment before being detached to the quartermaster's department as a brigade wagon master in 1863. Confederate military records (such as exist) contain no further information. The questions then are: when did he meet Hickok, and where? It was understood that the pair had been acquainted for some years, which suggests either that Dave changed sides or got to know Hickok when the latter was himself working behind enemy lines. Hickok also spent some time at Yellville, which might explain the connection. Early in 1865, Dave brought his mother, a sister, and a half brother to Springfield, which would suggest late pro-Union sympathies on their part.

The fateful card game that led to the pair falling out took place in the old Lyon House or Southern Hotel. Tutt is reported to have lost a lot of money to Wild Bill, and he reminded Hickok of a forty-dollar debt he owed him for a horse trade. Hickok paid up, but when Tutt said he still owed him thirty-five dollars from a previous game, Wild Bill claimed it was only twenty-five. Dave then reached across the

RIGHT: This photograph of Tombstone was made by C. S. Fly in about 1885. But for the O.K. Corral fight in 1881, Tombstone might have been abandoned years ago. It is now a tourist attraction.

table and picked up Hickok's prized Waltham watch, said to have been a present from his mother. In later years, the Tutt family was to claim that the watch was in fact Dave's, and it was Hickok who picked it up.

This conflicts with the evidence given at the trial and penned by Colonel Albert Barnitz, post commander in Springfield, on the day of the shooting. Tutt made it known that he would wear the watch next day on Public Square, despite Wild Bill's suggestion that this was an unhealthy decision.

Accounts of what happened on July 21 are as numerous as the allegations that led to the shoot-out, but the simple facts are that at about six in the evening, as Hickok walked on to

the square from the direction of the Lyon House, Tutt appeared beside the courthouse. Both men pulled their pistols and, while still on the move, opened fire. Colonel George Ward Nichols, who first publicized the fight nationwide in an article on Wild Bill published in *Harper's New Monthly Magazine* for February 1867, gave the distance between them as both "fifty paces" and "fifty yards," a distance that dispels much of the mystique of a face-to-face conflict. Nevertheless, within hours of the shoot-out, Colonel Barnitz, who witnessed the fight from the balcony of the Lyon House where he had his headquarters, wrote in his journal that both men "fired simultaneously, as it appeared to me, at a distance of about 100 paces. 'Tut' [sic] was shot directly through the

chest." Colonel Barnitz also confirmed that the fight was over cards and that Tutt had provoked Hickok.

It says much for Hickok's marksmanship that he could hit a moving target (and one that was firing back) at such a distance with an awesome accuracy. The pistol he used has been a controversy in itself. Some writers have claimed that he shot Tutt with a .44 Colt Dragoon and actually rested it on a hitching post to steady his aim. Others alleged that the pistol was a .32 caliber Smith & Wesson No. 2 Army revolver.

The actual weapon was a .36 caliber Colt's Navy pistol: Wild Bill carried two of them, worn butts forward in holsters attached to a military belt. Colonel Nichols also noted that his waist was "girthed by a belt which held two of Colt's Navy revolvers." The recent discovery of a photograph made at the time clearly shows Wild Bill with his Navy pistols, worn as described.

Some have dismissed Hickok's heart shot at such a distance as luck, and they may be right, but they do an injustice to the

**LEFT: Richard Gird at left, Al Shieffelin, center, and Ed Shieffelin at the right, photographed some time after Ed discovered the silver outcropping that led to a silver strike and eventually the settlement of Tombstone.**

LEFT: Ed Schieffelin, whose discovery of silver led to the establishment of Tombstone, dressed in a wool shirt, neckerchief, sombrero, kneeboots, and armed with a Sharps, looks the part of a typical prospector.

pistol. Despite the reams of nonsense written about both marksmanship and the miraculous accuracy of the old-time gunfighters, the real answer lay in their pistols. The Navy was sighted in for about sixty yards but in the hands of an expert it is accurate up to about two hundred yards, that is to say with carefully aimed shots. The ball itself has been known to go as far as six hundred yards, but at that distance would be totally ineffective. The only drawback to the Navy (and weapons of like caliber) was its comparatively small size (equivalent to the modern .38) and limited stopping power. This problem was encountered in India during the Mutiny of 1857 when maddened Sepoys sometimes took all six bullets from a Navy before expiring, by which time they had occasionally cut down the pistoleer. To rectify this problem, Colt's London Agency shipped out a large number of Dragoons, and these, in company with the big .442 Adams pistols (and a limited number of the company's .50 caliber Dragoon pistols), proved to be very effective. Even out West, it was claimed that when used in combat with Indians the Colt Dragoon was the preferred weapon. Nevertheless, the West produced a few situations where the smaller calibered pistols failed to work. As a result, close encounters of the revolver kind were often fatal.

Following the Tutt fight, Barnitz had Hickok arrested and handed over to the civilian authorities, and he was promptly charged with murder, later reduced to manslaughter. On August 5, Hickok went on trial. The judge went to great lengths to explain the law in respect of self-defense, and how it was not a plea if the defendant had intimated that he was prepared to fight rather than avoid any conflict. He also dismissed testimony, which repeated hearsay claims that Tutt had threatened Hickok. The jury, however, decided that Hickok did act in self-defense and acquitted him.

Reaction among the citizens was mixed. Barnitz advised his wife that opinion was equally divided between Hickok and Tutt, but the press was adamant that street shoot-outs had to be discouraged. On August 10, the *Missouri Weekly Patriot* complained that the jury only took ten minutes to reach a verdict, but that the "general dissatisfaction felt by the citizens of this place with the verdict in no way attaches to our able and efficient Circuit attorney, nor to the Court . . . Those

who censure the jury for what they regarded as a disregard of their obligations to the public interest, and a proper respect for their oaths, should remember that they are partly to blame themselves."

The editor then went on to suggest that the citizens of the town were "shocked and terrified" at the thought that a man could arm himself and lie in wait for his victim, with the connivance of cronies anxious to see bloodshed, yet failed to "express the horror and disgust they felt, not from indifference, but from fear and timidity." This comment must have come as a surprise not only to Hickok (who like many others had walked around the place for several years armed with one or two revolvers and other weapons) but also to those citizens who had endured four years of war without feeling terrorized by the sight of armed men.

Within months of the shooting, whatever animosity there might have been disappeared. Hickok became the focus of much attention, and his write-up in *Harper's* not only gave him nationwide fame but also established the tradition of the Western gunman's role as a latter-day duelist.

Understandably, gunfights were never welcomed in populated areas, and while it was also true that such drastic action was an expedient means of ridding the place of unwanted or dangerous individuals, its effect could be demoralizing and certainly dangerous to others if the shooting got out of hand. In an environment where most people either went armed or had access to pistols or other weapons, there was always the danger of community shoot-outs. Both cattle towns and other boomtowns addressed this problem very early. Ordinances against the use and carrying of firearms within city limits were passed but frequently ignored. In 1868, a year after it was founded, Ellsworth, already worried by the violence in its midst that threatened to engulf the place (a fact that was almost gleefully publicized in the newspapers of rival townships), feared the worst. But it was 1870 before it got around to tackling the problem in

**RIGHT: The Cochise County courthouse, built in 1882. Courthouses began to be constructed throughout the United States from the end of the eighteenth century—before that, any meeting place might be used to dispense justice.**

LEFT: John P. Clum, Indian agent, with some of his Apache scouts at the San Carlos reservation. As editor of the *Tombstone Epitaph,* he supported the Earps and remained a lifelong friend of Wyatt Earp.

earnest. On April 1, "Ordinance No. 1" included a section devoted to firearms, with particular attention to places where their use was strictly prohibited. The ordinance was very specific in its definition of just where the inhabitants of Ellsworth could or could not "burst a cap and burn powder." Other towns tried similar legislation with varying results. Only when the cow-town era ended did they claim any real success, by which time the age of the six-shooter was also a thing of the past. Meanwhile, fines took care of most of those who would rather pay up than disarm. It was an ongoing problem, however, and one that was not helped by individuals who, perhaps dismissed from the police force for some reason or other, willfully disobeyed the roles and continued to carry arms.

John "Happy Jack" Morco, whose activities during the disturbances at Ellsworth led to the death of Chauncey Whitney at the hands of Billy Thompson, was generally regarded as an obnoxious individual and was particularly "hated" by the Texans. His demeanor was such that most of the people he encountered shunned him, which is perhaps why some wag named him "Happy Jack." One wonders why such a character should have been employed by the police force in the first place, but few cow towns were that fussy when they feared "cowboy chaos" and leaped at someone who might be tough enough to stand up to them. Following his dismissal from the police force, Morco went to Salina but returned to the city where he paraded about attached to a pair of "ivory-handled" six-shooters. His presence was unwelcome, and he was advised to disarm or leave town. Morco chose to stay, which was a mistake on his part.

Following some quite disastrous appointments to the police force following the Thompson brothers' episode, J. Charles Brown, a former farm boy from Illinois who had proved himself an able assistant marshal, was elected city marshal of Ellsworth. He was very familiar with Morco's personality and had been personally involved in a dispute over the two pistols that he carried. It was claimed that when Jack left Ellsworth following his dismissal from the police force on August 27, he took with him a pair of pistols valued at one hundred dollars, which belonged to

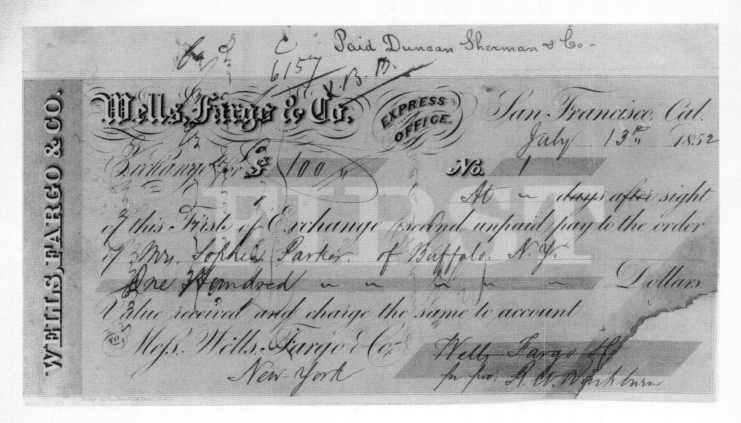

# THE WELLS FARGO
# COMPANY

The historian of the West, Leon Claire Metz, has written that, "without Wells Fargo, the West would not have nearly been so wild." The claim seems warranted, for the presence of the Wells Fargo stagecoaches and railroad carriages inspired some of the greatest armed robberies of the nineteenth century. The company was founded in March 1852, principally by Henry Wells and William Fargo, and was based in San Francisco. Initially it specialized in express delivery, transferring mail and valuables (it was a major carrier for the gold mines, transporting both gold and wages) throughout the burgeoning Western settlements and to the urban centers in the east. It quickly diversified into providing direct banking services, including the issue of bank drafts and the sale of gold dust to the U.S. Mint.

The key to the Wells Fargo business was speed, and any available means was used to transfer its lucrative packages, including pony rider, steamboat, and stagecoach. From 1858,

its distribution system was centralized into the Overland Mail Company, a fusion of Wells Fargo coaches with the other prominent express operators. Wells Fargo also later controlled the western reaches of the Pony Express.

The stagecoaches in particular were targets for robbers and bandits. The classic four-wheeled, six-horse Concord coach, so called because it was built in Concord, New Hampshire, was a transportation system both durable and elegant. Under the driver's seat was the object of the bandits' attention, the Wells Fargo treasure box made of pine and oak, reinforced with iron straps. The box itself could weigh up to 150 pounds. Protecting each stagecoach would be a company

**ABOVE: A Wells Fargo check dated July 13, 1852, for the payment of one hundred dollars to a Mrs. Sophie Parker of Buffalo, New York. The company is still providing personal banking services today, over 150 years after it was founded.**

shotgun messenger. This individual would ride the coach carrying a shotgun, usually with its barrel sawn down to around ten to fourteen inches and loaded up with heavy 00 buckshot.

Dozens of Wells Fargo coaches were robbed at gunpoint (the gunman Black Bart alone stripped twenty-seven stagecoaches of their valuables), and security became a headline issue for the company. Wells Fargo was soon employing large numbers of detectives and law officers for the protection of its assets and the apprehension of robbers. This increased with the move into railroad delivery in the late 1860s. The company shifted much of its business onto the railroads with the opening of transcontinental lines in 1869. The railroads enabled Wells Fargo to serve customers from the Pacific to the Atlantic coast, with routes stretching from New York to California. They also exposed the company to the train robbers, including such notorious figures as Butch Cassidy and his Hole-in-the-Wall gang. Increased security on board the trains—including, in some instances, armed posses ready to dismount on horse from cattle cars and give chase to the bandits—steadily limited the viability of train robberies.

Wells Fargo changed management in 1901 and moved its headquarters to New York but continued its growth. By 1910 it had a network of 6,000 destinations, increasing to 10,000 by 1918. It remains a thriving company to this day, known as much for its part in the mythology of the American West as for its commercial strength.

**BELOW AND RIGHT:** Wells Fargo offices spread across the United States, their viability ensured by the spread of the railways. The poster indicates something of the company's geographical reach and hints at their great financial power in the nineteenth century.

## WELLS, FARGO & CO.
# BANKERS
### AND
# EXCHANGE DEALERS.

**W. F. & CO.,**

In connection with their EXPRESS BUSINESS, will also transact a general

**BANKING, EXCHANGE AND COLLECTION BUSINESS.**
GENERAL AND SPECIAL DEPOSITS RECEIVED.
*COLLECTIONS AND REMITTANCES*
Made in all parts of California, Oregon, the Atlantic States and Europe, with promptness and dispatch.

**GOLD DUST, GOLD AND SILVER COIN, AND BULLION,**
BOUGHT AND SOLD.
Money advanced on GOLD DUST deposited, for transmission or coinage.

**SIGHT EXCHANGE**
ON NEW YORK AND BOSTON, FOR SALE AT CURRENT RATES.
**DRAFTS**
ALSO DRAWN PAYABLE AT THE FOLLOWING PLACES, VIZ:

| | |
|---|---|
| ALBANY, NEW YORK, | HAMILTON, OHIO. |
| TROY, "  " | SPRINGFIELD, " |
| UTICA, "  " | CINCINNATI, "  " |
| SYRACUSE, "  " | LOUISVILLE, KENTUCKY, |
| OSWEGO, "  " | DETROIT, MICHIGAN, |
| AUBURN, "  " | JACKSON, " |
| GENEVA, "  " | ANN ARBOR, " |
| ROCHESTER, "  " | KALAMAZOO, " |
| LOCKPORT, "  " | NILES, " |
| BUFFALO, "  " | ADRIAN, " |
| BINGHATON, "  " | MONROE, " |
| OWEGO, "  " | CHICAGO, ILLINOIS, |
| ELMIRA, "  " | GALENA, " |
| CORNING, "  " | LASALLE, " |
| ERIE, PENNSYLVANIA, | PEORIA, " |
| PITTSBURG, " | ALTON. " |
| HARTFORD, CONNECTICUT, | ST. LOUIS, MISSOURI, |
| NEW HAVEN, " | MILWAUKEE, WISCONSIN, |
| CLEVELAND, OHIO, | SHEBOYGAN, " |
| SANDUSKY, " | RACINE, " |
| TOLEDO, " | KENOSHA, " |
| MANSFIELD, " | MONTREAL, CANADA EAST, |
| NEWARK, " | QUEBEC, "  " |
| ZANESVILLE, " | HAMILTON, "  WEST, |
| COLUMBUS, " | TORONTO, "  " |
| DAYTON, | |

**WELLS, FARGO & CO.**
NO. 114 MONTGOMERY STREET,
SAN FRANCISCO.

## FREIGHT & EXPRESS

The Pony Express and Wells Fargo and Company carried a major part of the mail and valuable cargo over a short period of time and captured the imagination of the world. Less glamorous were the plodding ox and mule trains of many smaller companies that pulled the heavy freight—bars, mirrors, and pianos for the saloons, cast-iron stoves, nails, and equipment for hardware stores, and plows and other tools for farmers, miners, and tradesmen. Every commodity except raw

materials had to be shipped west. Transportation, like every other endeavor in the West, was perilous. Cargo had to be hauled hundreds of miles through inhospitable terrain, often through rapidly changing climate. The drivers had to contend with hostile Indians and of course, the white bandit. The individuals who brought material to the West played no small part in the establishment of civilization, and their exploits are largely unsung today. William H. Russell was one of the most respected businessmen in Missouri. His career had earned him

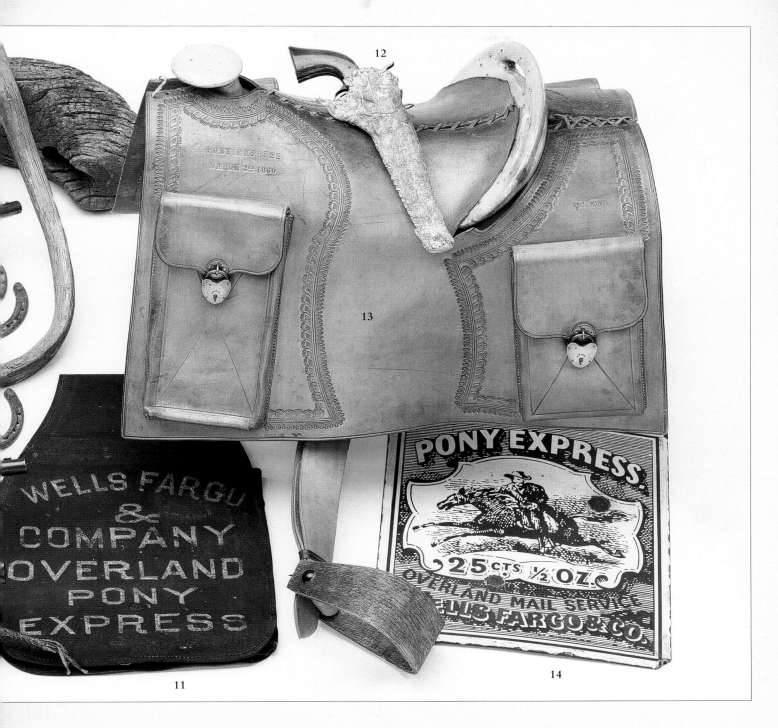

the title of "Napoleon of the West" and afforded him the ability to live in high style. The Pony Express freight man built a twenty-room mansion, but like so many others, his fortune was lost, and when he died in 1872 he was penniless.

1. Wooden yoke for oxen, and ox bow, one of two on each yoke..
2. Driver's bullwhip.
3. Wooden grease or lubricant bucket for wagon wheels and axles.
4. Wood iron-bound Wells Fargo strong box.
5. Breech-loading side hammer double-barrel shotgun made by J. B. Clabrough and Bro., London, 12 gauge.
6. Sharps New Model 1859 carbine with special order 15-in. barrel, .52 caliber, for Wells Fargo, for protection of coaches.
7. Breech-loading side hammer double-barrel shotgun with short barrels made by Rhode Island Field Gun Company, 12 gauge. Stock marked "Adams Express Co., No. 10, Denver, Colo."
8. Brass base shot shells for 12-gauge shotgun.
9. Iron and wood wagon jack.
10. Iron mule shoes.
11. Painted canvas saddle bags used by Wells Fargo and Company Overland Pony Express.
12. Whitney Navy revolver, .36 caliber, in open top "Slim Jim" holster.
13. Pony Express saddle with *mochila*, which fitted over the saddle and had four locked compartments intergral to the body.
14. Metal advertisement for Pony Express.

John Good. A telegram was dispatched to Salina, and when the train on which Morco was traveling stopped at the depot, the police boarded it and arrested him. Good and Brown followed and gave some testimony before returning to Ellsworth. Morco pleaded that the pistols were his, and without them his life would be worthless, for he had made many enemies among the Texans. Before returning to Ellsworth, Brown advised Jack to keep on the move and away from Ellsworth, but for reasons best known to himself, Morco followed on the next train.

When word reached police headquarters that Morco was back, armed and boasting that he would "make away" with anyone who upset him, Marshal Brown realized that he had trouble on his hands. On the evening of September 4, Brown confronted Morco and ordered him to disarm. Morco refused. Some reports have him offering resistance to arrest, others that he tried to draw his pistols on the marshal, but the outcome was that Brown shot him through the heart.

Most people viewed Morco's death with a sense of relief. His wife, from whom he had been separated for some years, happened to be in town with a theatrical troupe when he died, and she stated that he had a habit of boosting his own image. Of the twelve men he claimed to have killed, his wife said she only knew of four, and they were men who had come to her assistance when he was beating her up in a drunken rage.

Any feelings of remorse Marshal Brown might have had following the shooting of Happy Jack was swiftly dispelled by the editor of the Ellsworth *Reporter* who remarked on September 11, 1873:"Happy Jack is gone, and considering his manner of going, we can think of him only as 'Poor Jack!'"

The Coroner's inquest over the body of "Happy Jack" decided that "John Morco came to his death from the effects of two bullet wounds, discharged from a six-shooter in the hands of Chas. Brown, a police officer of the city of Ellsworth, in self defense, while in discharge of his duty, and was justified in the act."

Gunfights between "consenting adults" or outlaws and lawmen were considered the norm, but when politics came into it, it also invoked factions. Such a situation existed in Tombstone, Arizona, when the Earps, Clantons, and McLaurys swapped lead outside the O.K. Corral to settle a dispute that was to become the most famous gunfight of them all.

In 1877, Edward L. Schieffelin discovered a rich silver outcropping in the San Pedro Valley, some seventy miles southeast of Tucson, Arizona Territory. Legend asserts that when Ed, his brother Al, and a close friend named Richard Gird started prospecting, some prophesied that all they would find would be tombstones. True or not, that was the name given to the Tombstone Mining District and ultimately to the town that sprang up. It attracted all kinds of people: would-be miners, gamblers, prostitutes, speculators, and a breed of men who get little attention in the history books but whose activities often led to conflict. These were the land or town-site speculators.

In more recent years, the differences between individuals and the eternal battles between "cowboy rustlers" and the ranchers has also focused attention upon those who engaged in land grabs. Tombstone seems to have had its fill of them.

By 1881, Tombstone had a population of about 10,000 people. Following disputes with the land grabbers, the populace had been granted incorporation and the town was the seat of the newly created Cochise County. It also boasted two newspapers, the *Tombstone Epitaph* and the *Nuggett*. Despite these apparent signs of civilization, the lawlessness in and around the place was known nationwide and, following the gunfight at the O.K. Corral, President Chester Arthur in 1882 threatened the place with martial law. But all this was in the future when Wyatt Earp and his brothers, Virgil and James, arrived there on December 1, 1879. Virgil, who had achieved some fame as a policeman, had been appointed as a deputy U.S. marshal for the Tombstone area in November by the U.S. marshal for Arizona Territory, Crawley P. Dake. If Virgil was the real leader of the Earp clan, it was Wyatt who dominated it.

Wyatt Earp's cattle town experiences were such that he was well known in Kansas but not elsewhere, and some indication of his current reputation can be gleaned from comments in the Kansas press following his resignation from the Dodge City police force in September 1879. He went first to Las Vegas and from there to Tombstone. The *Ford County Globe* of March 30, 1880, reported that Wyatt had recently sold a mine in Tombstone for "thirty thousand dollars. The mine is called the 'Cooper Lode' and is not worked at present owing to the quality of foul air that has accumulated in the shaft." Earp was then joined by other ex-Dodgeites. He soon established himself in the community. He found employment with Wells Fargo & Company as a shotgun messenger and was later appointed a deputy sheriff of Pima County. Soon, the Earp clan was joined by Doc Holliday and assorted wives and mistresses, and later by Morgan Earp, considered by many to be the "hothead" of the family.

In Tombstone, Wyatt also had an "interest" in the Oriental saloon and a faro table at its rival, the Eagle brewery. The Earps soon made their presence felt and they were also aware of the undercurrent of political pull that existed in the place, although there is no evidence of their involvement in anything but local politics, where Wyatt had put himself up as a candidate for sheriff. Unfortunately, the Democrat John Behan won, which did not sit well with the Republican Wyatt, a state of affairs that had repercussions later.

On a broader front, however, there was the matter of local attitudes both to people and the law. The local ranchers resented the influx of people lured to the area by gold and silver, and for their part, the denizens of the gambling halls and saloons detested the ranchers and their belief that they owned Arizona. This led to a deep distrust and the threat of violence. The Earp faction was right in the middle, for besides Wyatt's role as a deputy sheriff (he served for a brief period), Virgil was city marshal. This led to open conflict with the notorious Clantons and McLaurys, whose combined rancher-rustler activities were the talk of the territory. Yet they continued to obtain government contracts to feed the reservation Apaches (some alleged that the cattle for this purpose had been stolen from Mexicans).

Old Man Clanton, head of the clan, was a formidable character and had fathered three sons: Joseph Isiah "Ike," Phineas, and the youngest, Billy. The McLaurys consisted of Robert, Thomas, and William Roland "Frank." Allied with both families was William C. Claiborne.

The Earps had little contact with the "rustlers" until Wyatt lost a prized horse. He learned that Billy Clanton had it, but when challenged he admitted it was a mistake. However, when six mules disappeared from an Army post and Virgil was called in his capacity as a deputy U.S. marshal to track them down, things heated up. Accompanied by Wyatt and a squad of soldiers, the posse discovered the animals at the McLaury ranch where they were about to obliterate the

**LEFT: John Behan and his wife. Behan generally disliked the Earps, who believed he was hindering rather than helping when he tried to stop them from arresting the Clanton-McLaury faction at the corral.**

## WYATT EARP

Endless debates have been conducted about what kind of guns were used by Wyatt Earp and his associates. Unfortunately, there is often an absence of clear evidence and specific weapons promoted, as Earp guns often lack clear proof of their pedigrees. Some factors are certain. The preferred handgun was Colt, either in percussion or (post–1873) the single-action Army or Peacemaker. Reliable and well enough made to withstand rough usage, it has been claimed that some lawmen (Earp included) "buffaloed" would-be troublemakers by hitting them over the head or alongside the ear with the barrel.

Stuart Lake's biography of Earp established the story that Wyatt carried a Colt with an extralong barrel, the "Buntline special." Lake claimed that in 1876 Ned Buntline went to Dodge City and presented Earp, Bat Masterson, Neal Brown, Charles Bassett, and Bill Tilghman with "Specials," complete with detachable carbine stocks.

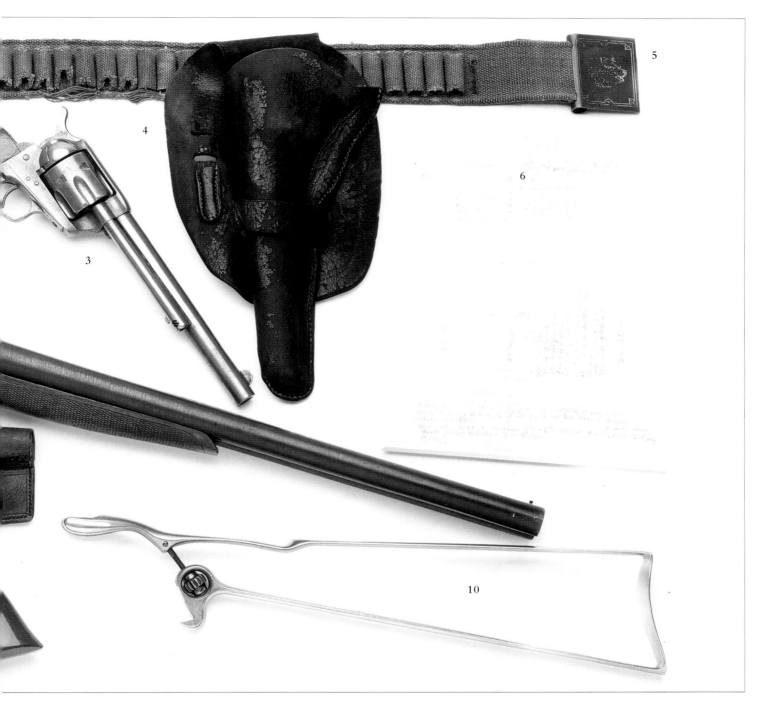

The Colt company did and still does make Peacemakers with long barrels, but there is no conclusive evidence to suggest that Buntline (or anyone else outside of Kansas) had heard of Wyatt Earp in 1876. Research by W. B. Shillingberg (*Wyatt Earp & the "Buntline Special" Myth*) established that in 1929, Mr. Lake was shown such a pistol and was so taken with it that he decided to equip his hero with a special pistol.

1. Colt single-action .45 used by Doc Holliday. He told his nephew he carried this throughout his Western adventures.

2. Colt single-action .45 used by Wells Fargo detective Fred Dodge who claimed that Wyatt Earp borrowed the gun at the time Curly Bill Brocius was killed.

3. Colt single-action .44-40 used by John Clum while editor of the *Tombstone Epitaph* and during the capture of Geronimo.

4. Holster for Clum's Colt, purchased by him at Spangenburg gunsmith shop in Tombstone.

5. Web cartridge belt used by John Clum.

6. Diagram of Tombstone gunfight drawn by Wyatt Earp in later years.

7. Double-barrel shotgun reportedly used by Wyatt Earp to kill Frank Stilwell, one of the killers of Morgan Earp.

8. Factory holster for a long barrel Colt single-action.

9. Colt single-action .45 with extralong 16-inch barrel, adjustable rear sight.

10. Detachable shoulder stock for the long barrel Colt.

(Artifacts courtesy of Gene Autry Western Heritage Museum, Los Angeles.)

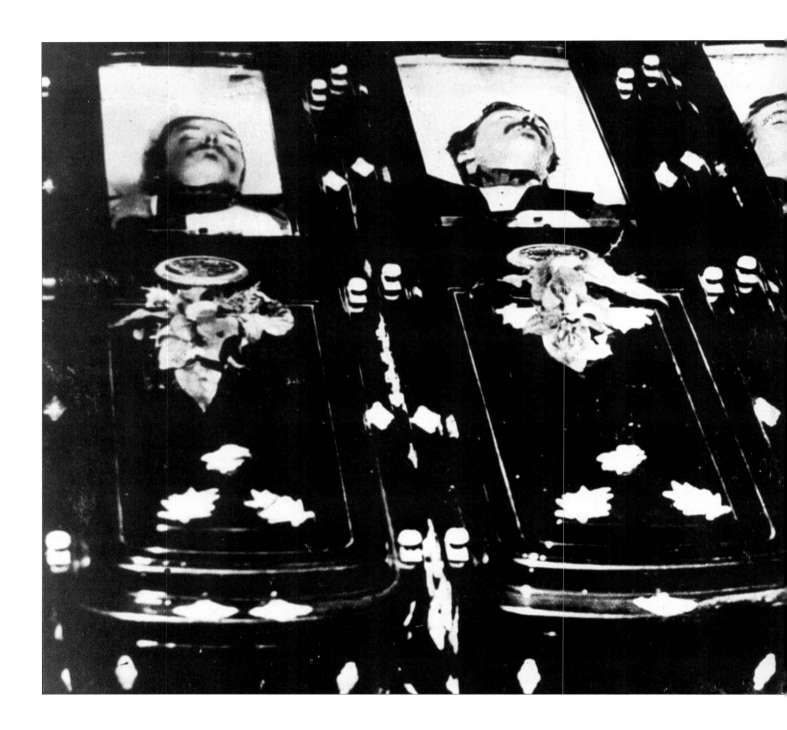

U.S. brands. Faced with the threat of prosecution, a trial, and a possible trip to the state penitentiary, the McLaurys agreed to return the mules and pay restitution to the army. Unfortunately, soon after the posse left, "rustlers" turned up and drove the mules off. This sort of behavior, the robbing of stagecoaches and the appearance of Clantons and McLaurys as posse members, did not lead to good relations. Matters were not improved either when it was rumored that Doc Holliday had also been engaged in stagecoach robbery, but

this was not proved. To further complicate matters, Virgil upset county sheriff Behan when, in his capacity as a deputy U.S. marshal, he arrested two of his deputies, Frank Stillwell and Pete Spence, charging them with robbing stagecoaches.

Frank McLaury confronted Morgan Earp on the street one day. McLaury suggested that they shoot it out, but Earp declined. Then, on October 25, Ike Clanton fell foul of Holliday at a lunch counter in a saloon. Ike tried to back off, but Doc was "on the prod." "Hey, you damn son of a bitch

LEFT: The McLaurys and Billy Clanton laid out in ornate glass-topped coffins. Some contemporary reports described them as having been "murdered on the streets of Tombstone," which annoyed the Earps.

election, and any reward monies would go to Ike. When this alleged arrangement became public, Ike claimed he had been set up, so there was no love lost on either side. Consequently, Ike was very unhappy when Holliday challenged him. Then Morgan appeared and Ike all but ran out of the saloon, begging both men not to shoot him in the back. "Go and get heeled," Doc yelled after him.

On the morning of October 26, Ike appeared on the streets looking the worse for wear following a night of cards and boozing. Still in an alcoholic haze, he began mouthing threats against the Earps, and when he got his hands on a six-shooter and a rifle, someone thoughtfully suggested Wyatt should know. Wyatt promptly sought out Virgil, and together they searched for Ike. They found him in an alley and grabbed his rifle, and as he went for his six-shooter, Virgil pulled it from Ike's hand and struck him over the head with it. Ike collapsed to his knees, shaking his head. Virgil then placed him under arrest "for carrying arms within city limits," and the brothers dragged him before the court. Here he was fined twenty-five dollars for the offense. The Earps offered to pay his fine if he would fight, but he declined, saying that he did not need encouragement; he would find them anywhere at any time and all he needed was "four feet of ground."

Outside the courthouse, Wyatt entered into a shouting match with Tom McLaury that ended when Wyatt smacked Tom on the side of his head with the barrel of his pistol. Leaving the dazed and bleeding McLaury in the street, the Earps walked away. War had now been declared; everyone knew it was only a matter of time before shouts would lead to shots. Advised that the combined Clanton and McLaury gang had stationed themselves down at the O.K. Corral, the Earps knew that the showdown had come. Hearing of the situation, Doc Holliday hastily joined them, arming himself with his favorite shotgun, made by W. W. Greener of Birmingham, England. (Recently, however, it has been claimed that Doc carried a cut-down Meteor 10 gauge, which he called his "street howitzer.")

In his capacity as city marshal, Virgil was duty bound to avoid bloodshed if possible, but it is doubtful if that thought really crossed his mind.

cowboy," he called out, "go get a gun and get to work." He added a few other choice insults and claimed that Ike had been making threats against himself and his friends, which Ike denied. Ike, apparently, had also been accused of playing one side against the other, and it was rumored that Wyatt, when he had learned that Old Man Clanton had died and Ike was now head of the family, had tried to bribe Ike into divulging the names of the stage robbers. Wyatt, it was claimed, thought this information would help him in his bid for sheriff in the next

**RIGHT: Tombstone's own version of "Boot Hill." (The first one was at Hays City, but the most famous one was at Dodge City.) In more recent years, some spurious epitaphs have appeared on the site to add "color."**

Sheriff John Behan heard of the pending fracas as he sat in a barber's chair on Allen Street and hurried over to Hafford's saloon where the Earps were preparing themselves, urging Virgil to disarm rather than shoot it out. Virgil gave him no such assurance, and Behan declared that he would disarm them himself. On the corner of Fremont Street, Behan met Frank McLaury, who assured the sheriff that he did not want a fight, but neither would he disarm.

The pair then set off toward Fly's Photographic Gallery, which was adjacent to the corral. There, Behan was assured by both Ike Clanton and Tom McLaury that neither was armed. In desperation, Behan urged the others to give up their arms. "Only if you disarm the Earps," Frank McLaury said, Billy Clanton said he was anxious to go home, and Billy Claiborne declared that he had been trying to get them to leave town. Behan had almost talked them into accompanying him to his office when the Earps and Holliday appeared at the end of the street, walking in line abreast. "Stay here," he said, and hurried to meet them.

"For God's sake, don't go down there," he begged. Virgil stared hard at him and then pushed him aside. "I'm going to disarm them," he said, and the four men moved forward. Behan yelled at them to go back but, he was ignored. Virgil, well aware that the situation could erupt into violence, had appointed his brothers and Holliday as deputy city marshals. Some historians think that Virgil genuinely wanted to disarm the men at the corral, but others believe that Wyatt was determined that there would be a showdown.

In dress and manner, the four Earps exemplified the typical gunfighter: wide-brimmed, low-crowned black hats and long "Prince Albert" frock coats. Wyatt was armed not with a Colt .45 (or the mythical "Buntline Special") but a .44 Smith & Wesson New Model No. 3 American that had been presented to him by John P. Clum, editor of the *Epitaph*. In place of a conventional belt and holster he had instructed his tailor to line one of the pockets of his coat with canvas and to wax-rub it so that the pistol would not snag and could be removed in a hurry. The others carried conventional .45 Colt "Peacemakers."

As the Earps approached, the Clantons and McLaurys grouped themselves on Fremont Street, almost directly in front of Fly's home and gallery, and on open ground rather than inside the O.K. Corral as some have claimed. When the two factions were about eighty feet apart, silence fell, broken only when Billy Claiborne suddenly fled to Fly's home, where he was joined by Behan.

John Behan was later to testify that Wyatt Earp started the fight by calling out: "You sons of bitches, you have been looking for a fight, and now you can have it." Wyatt, however, maintained that Virgil first ordered them to give up their guns, and when Billy Clanton and Frank McLaury went for their pistols, Virgil yelled, "Hold, I don't mean that; I have come to disarm you." Billy Clanton then shouted, "Don't shoot me, I don't want to fight." Tom McLaury promptly opened his coat to show that he was not armed and shouted out to that effect.

Wyatt Earp was to claim that Behan had told them that he had disarmed the men, but the sight of pistols in the hands of Frank McLaury and Billy Clanton convinced him that they were all armed, so he opened fire. Ignoring Billy, he shot Frank, whom he regarded as the deadliest of the gang. Two shots were fired almost in unison: Wyatt shot at Frank and Billy Clanton shot at Wyatt. "I don't know which shot was fired first. We fired almost together. The fight then became general," Wyatt later stated in evidence. Virgil then ordered them back to the street where Holliday had stationed himself. Ike Clanton took the opportunity to rush up to Wyatt and grab his left arm. Realizing that he was unarmed, Earp told him to fight or run. Ike ran, narrowly escaping a blast from Holliday's shotgun.

Wyatt's first shot hit Frank McLaury in the stomach, but he managed to get one shot off before staggering off toward the street. Tom McLaury then dragged his brother's Winchester from its saddle scabbard and took cover behind the terrified horse. Morgan, meanwhile, had managed to put a pistol ball into Billy Clanton's right wrist and another in his chest. The boy staggered back against Fly's gallery and tried desperately to use his pistol with the other hand. At that moment, Frank's horse bolted, exposing Tom McLaury to Holliday, who fired his second barrel into him, almost knocking him off his feet. As his waistcoat became bloodied, Tom screamed in great agony, staggered into Fremont Street, and died.

Virgil, surprisingly, had not yet fired a shot, but he received a ball in the calf of his leg, which knocked him to the ground. Billy Clanton was still a threat. Frank McLaury somehow raised himself up and fired at Doc Holliday, who had tossed aside his shotgun and pulled his nickel-plated six-shooter. Both men fired together. Doc missed, but Frank's shot nicked Doc's hip, removing a piece of skin and a part of his pistol holster. Morgan, too, had problems; Billy Clanton, with his last shot, managed to put a ball in his shoulder and was promptly shot by Wyatt. A sudden silence descended over the scene. Dust and white-gray smoke from the black powder ammunition drifted slowly in the breeze. From his house came Camillus Fly, brandishing a Henry rifle. When no one made any moves, he lowered the gun and knelt down beside the still breathing Billy Clanton. Gently he removed the six-shooter from the boy's hand. Billy's last mumbled words were: "Give me some more cartridges."

The "Gunfight at the O.K. Corral" lasted about thirty seconds, and an estimated seventeen shots were fired. At the end, of the eight men who had been involved, three were dead, three were badly wounded, and only two of them escaped without a scratch—Wyatt Earp and Ike Clanton, who turned coward and ran. It had a number of repercussions. A preliminary examination before a magistrate proved to be unsatisfactory insofar as the populace were concerned. Sheriff Behan and Ike Clanton swore out a warrant for the arrest of the Earps, and a hearing was had before Justice of the Peace Wells Spicer. After listening to all the evidence (which took thirty days), Spicer criticized Virgil's actions in deputizing his brothers and Holliday, even though he conceded that the "social climate" gave him little choice. He decided that there was insufficient evidence to charge the Earps and Holliday with murder and ordered their release.

Across the state, however, opinion then, as now, was mixed. The acting attorney general, Samuel F. Phillips, described Virgil as being "more disposed to quarrel than to cooperate with local authority." Dake, however, resisted official attempts to get Virgil fired and pointed out that although the Earps had not been acting in a federal capacity, they had nevertheless rid the territory of three out of five members of the "cowboy [rustler] element." The press also contained plaudits and a lot of condemnation of the Earps. But closer to home, other forces were at work.

Parties not entirely connected with the Clanton-McLaury faction made attempts on the lives of the Earps following the

## PLAINS INDIANS FIREARMS

Some gunfighters were Indian killers of course, but some were their protectors, ostensibly at least, working as peace officers in the Indian Territory, where killing an Indian was a federal offense, along with robbing the mail, desertion from the army, and stealing government stock.

Indian firearms are readily identifiable by use of brass-tack decoration, their hard-used condition, and their use of rawhide to effect rudimentary repairs. The Indians lacked the

maintenance skills to service the arms properly, most of which, if they were metallic cartridge repeating rifles and revolvers, had been taken from enemies and not bought or traded. Some Indians used breech-loading weapons as muzzle-loaders with loose powder and ball when ammunition was unavailable. Indian firearms, because of hard use, are very scarce, and few survive today. They are very much collector's items. Chiefs, rather than warriors, had first claim on weapons taken from the whites.

1. Crow chief's staff.
2. Flintlock pistol, made from cut-down trade musket, .50 caliber.
3. Colt Model 1851 Navy revolver with brass tack repair, .36 caliber.
4. Crow rifle scabbard, hand-tanned buffalo hide.
5. Unmarked percussion .45 caliber single-shot rifle. Note rawhide repairs around lock area and rear of barrel.
6. Sioux ammunition pouch with beaded decoration.
7. Santee Sioux rifle scabbard, hand-tanned smoked deerskin.
8. Percussion single-shot trade rifle, with brass tack decoration on stock, probably .45 caliber.
9. U.S. Model 1841 percussion rifle.
10. Northern plains ammunition pouch, buckskin or elk hide.
11. Flintlock trade musket.
12. Crow ammunition pouch
13. Cheyenne or Santee Sioux ammunition pouch, possibly elk hide.
14. Sioux Ghost Dance pouch.
15. Crow rifle scabbard.
16. Ballard breech-loading sporting rifle, with altered fore stock and brass-tack decoration.
17. Winchester Model 1866 carbine, with brass tack design.
18. Oglala Sioux rifle scabbard, hand-tanned elk hide.

shootings. Morgan was murdered in a saloon; Virgil was maimed by a shotgun blast. The blame for Morgan's murder was laid at the door of Pete Spence and Frank Stilwell, both of whom may have been in the employ of the land grabbers whose activities remained hidden for years. Regardless of the cause, Wyatt shot Stilwell at Tucson and later killed a man associated with Spence at a camp in the Dragoon Mountains.

Tombstone's relief when the Earps quit Arizona was reflected nationwide. The controversy surrounding that O.K. Corral fight has never subsided. But if nothing else, it graphically illustrates the dangers to any community when law and order either does not exist or is manipulated for other purposes. Most people prefer the gavel to the gun.

**Deadwood: A Study in Lawlessness**

Throughout this book we have tripped through many places teetering on the edge of anarchy—Abilene, Dodge City, El Paso, Tombstone. Another town that must take equal ranking is Deadwood, South Dakota. Deadwood has come to represent all that was lawless about the West. Kicking against

the town's gunfights, prostitution, heavy drinking, and theft, however, was the periodic attempt to restore the rule of law. The success of each attempt was very much down to the quality and personal grit of the character behind the lawman's badge.

Deadwood was born out of the gold rush. The forested Black Hills of South Dakota was the territory of the Lakota Sioux, a fearsome warrior tribe. Despite some white American explorations for gold in the area in the 1830s and 1850s, all of which were repelled by the Lakota, in 1868 the

United States government declared that the Black Hills would become part of the Great Sioux Reservation. This status would ultimately be as much of a curse to the Indians as a blessing. For when gold miners and settlers finally began to pour into the area and founded the town of Deadwood around 1876, the new arrivals actually had no land rights, and so essentially they lived outside of the law, with all the implications for degenerative behavior that implies.

During the early 1870s, the rumors about gold in the Black Hills strengthened, and at the same time the government's commitment to maintain the integrity of the Indian reservation weakened considerably. In 1874, George Armstrong Custer lit the fuse of settlement when, as part of a government-backed exploration, he attested to the presence of large gold resources in the Black Hills area. His observations were accurate—during the next half century, over three million tons of gold would be mined from the area. Armstrong's finds precipitated a stampede of gold miners into the Black Hills, aided by outlandish claims in the newspapers and magazines about the wealth to be had and the ease with which it could be acquired. In 1876 Deadwood was founded. It was one of several towns created to accommodate the rushing influx of miners, tens of thousands of whom poured into the region from across the United States with the hopes of making their fortune. Deadwood itself was a sprawling collection of shacks, houses, crude stores, saloons, and other assorted premises straggling throughout the narrow canyon of Deadwood creek. It was a place almost without law, its location in Indian territory putting it beyond the reach of federal authority (in fact, during the 1870s and 1880s many murders went unreported through concern that the federal authorities might actually become interested in policing the settlement if there were constant reports of killing). Soon Deadwood was experiencing one or two murders every single day. The writer John Ames, in *The Real Deadwood* (Chamberlain

**LEFT: A U.S. paymaster coach, seen here on Deadwood Road to Fort Meade in 1888. Stagecoaches were intensely vulnerable to ambush, hence the two guards, one of whom sits at the front of the coach with his rifle. The other would likely sit to the rear.**

Bros., 2004), has calculated that about 10 percent of the Deadwood population were meeting violent deaths each year, and he points out that if a proportionate murder rate were applied to New York, then the city would be experiencing 700,000 killings each year.

So why was Deadwood so unusually brutal? First and foremost, the limited or absent presence of the law—a fact which in itself attracted many wanted criminals to seek anonymity in Deadwood—combined with the inverse presence of gold made for a climate of theft, suspicion, and violent competition. There were undoubtedly huge commercial gains to be made from gold mining—over $1 million worth of gold was extracted in June and July of 1876 alone—but the serious money was concentrated in the hands of the larger enterprises. These used more intensive methods of mining over larger areas, whereas most miners were individuals who mined a fairly small pocket of territory, living by its side in a tent or a rudimentary shack. Such people, especially in the early days of the gold rush, could make good money when compared to, say, laboring or farming vocations. A typical haul of gold dust translated into a wage of around twenty-five or thirty-five dollars per day, compared against a typical monthly wage of around fifty dollars for working on the railroads or as a cowboy.

However, set against this income was the exorbitant cost of living in Deadwood, particularly the unusually high food costs. Fresh food, especially fruit and vegetables, was mainly imported into Deadwood to a captive market, and prices skyrocketed. A dozen eggs could sell for over a dollar, and flour cost 600 percent its usual price. These costs ruthlessly slashed into gold profits and made the diet of most miners unhealthy and spartan. Hunger and poor living conditions doubtless fueled much of Deadwood's violence, and as gold pickings became leaner in the late 1800s, desperation drove men to armed thievery as a way of making up the monthly income (many men had left families behind out east and had to send regular money back home).

Yet there were plenty more compounding factors that sent Deadwood into a spiral of violence. Gambling and prostitution were Deadwood's principal service industries, concentrated in a saloon district that became known as the

"Badlands." As we have seen throughout this book, gambling and violence were natural bedfellows in the West, but the lack of law enforcement in Deadwood enabled gambling-related killings to escalate to virtual wartime casualty levels. Furthermore, many of the residents of Deadwood were veterans of the Union or Confederate armies, and they

3562. Deadwood and Delaware S
Deadwood, S. Dak.
Photo and copyright by Grabill,

brought with them much of the bitterness and thirst for revenge engendered by four years of Civil War. Other catalysts for violence in Deadwood included racial hatred, fights over women (there was only one woman for every two hundred men in Deadwood, and those women were mostly prostitutes), industrial disputes over poor working conditions, and plain boredom. Whatever the case, it would be a brave man who attempted to impose law and order on the Deadwood society.

One such man was Seth Bullock, Deadwood's principal lawman for over forty years. Bullock was born in Sandwich, Ontario, in 1847. After a childhood under the strict discipline

LEFT: Deadwood and Delaware smelting works at Deadwood, 1890. New smelting processes using cyanide enabled Deadwood to experience a temporary revival of its gold extraction from the Black Hills in the 1880s, a boom that lasted until around 1914.

of his father, a retired British major, Bullock moved out to Montana in 1867 and eventually came to involve himself heavily in Republican Party politics in the state. His gift to the future was implementing the 1872 Yellowstone Act, making the Yellowstone National Park a vast protected wilderness. The following year, he became sheriff of Montana Territory in Lewis and Clark County, and on August 1, 1876, he arrived in Deadwood. His purpose there was commercial —having been impressed by the news of the gold rush, he set up a hardware store in the town with his partner, Sol Star.

Bullock was quickly impressed by Deadwood's brooding air of violence, sending his wife and daughter back to safety in Michigan. Furthermore, the day after his arrival, August 2, 1876, Wild Bill Hickok headed down to the Number Ten Saloon for a game of poker.

Hickok hadn't been long in Deadwood, but the town had already had its effect on his humanity. Gone were the days of flamboyance and his time as a law enforcer; instead, world-weariness, gambling, and drink replaced them. He began his game that afternoon with luck against him, and by late afternoon he had even borrowed money off the bartender to keep himself in play. At 4:10 p.m., Jack McCall, a drifter who had possibly lost some money to Hickok in an earlier game, simply stepped up and shot Hickok through the back of the head, the bullet exiting Hickok's face and embedding itself in the arm of another player. (It was later discovered the bullet that killed Hickok was the only functioning round in McCall's revolver.)

The death of such a legendary frontiersman shook even the iron hearts of Deadwood. There was an upsurging desire for someone, or some organization, to bring order to Deadwood, and one Isaac Brown was elected Miner's Sheriff on August 5. However, on August 20, Brown and several other townsfolk were killed in an Indian attack outside Deadwood, so a new figure of authority was needed. After several months of establishing himself as a model citizen, Bullock was appointed to the job in March 1877, the position being authorized by the governor of Dakota territory.

Bullock would be a dominant force for good in Deadwood for over forty years, and he must have been a man of formidable character. Contemporary accounts refer to Bullock as a man of iron integrity and a tough-as-dirt personality. He had an unusually penetrating stare, a clean-cut yet strong appearance, and a preference for resolving disputes without resorting to gunfire. For example, in one instance in 1877, some thirty miners rioted and took over their mine in protest over working conditions. Bullock simply had burning sulfur dropped into the mineshafts, thus flushing the miners out into the open where they were promptly arrested without any bloodshed.

Prisoner numbers in Bullock's first year of office speak of his efficiency in the sheriff's role. On July 16, 1877, the county jail had seventeen prisoners, but only four weeks later that figure had risen to twenty-nine inmates. He also formed militia companies to give his personal authority the clout of numbers and firepower, and using these and his handpicked group of deputies, he was able to break up organized criminal gangs as well as tackle the Native American tribes in the woodlands surrounding the settlement.

Bullock lost his reelection to sheriff in the fall of 1877, but instead became deputy U.S. marshal of the territory. This was not his sole employment—he developed commercial enterprises in mining and ranching—but the constancy of his presence ensured that Deadwood steadily slipped into the fold of law by the end of the nineteenth century, the blood-red days of the "Badlands" becoming nothing more than a memory.

## With Their Boots On

In the period that witnessed the westward movement, the mining ventures, the railroads, the Indian wars, and the immortalizing of the cowboy, the ubiquitous "man-killer" or "gunfighter" achieved a notoriety of his own. But few of those who became famous lived to a ripe old age. Some, like Edward Masterson, Tom Nixon, and Tom Smith died in the line of duty, while others, such as Hickok, Stoudenmire, and the likes of Jesse James and Billy the Kid, were murdered

**LEFT: There were other Boot Hills, this one at Virginia City, Montana Territory. It appears sparsely populated, but it was a constant reminder to gunfighters of their own and others' mortality.**

either because of their reputations or for financial or personal gain. Of those that survived, perhaps Wyatt Earp was one of the few who, in old age, was lifted from obscurity to become "heroic," not for what he actually did but for what he symbolized. As early as March 8, 1879, the *Dodge City Globe* had forecast both the end of the cattle trade and a determined effort to "civilize" the West:

> There is a class, still a large one . . . which looks with horror upon the approach of manners, customs and ideas tending to drive out the "frontier" characteristics of Dodge. They look with profound contempt upon a town whose police officers are not walking arsenals. They look back with regret to the time when "a drink was a quarter and a cigar two bits." They are not such bad fellows after all; but they do not long for a quiet life. They are not so many as they were. Some have lately felt the cordon of grangers pressing upon them and they have flitted; some to [Las] Vegas, some to Silver Cliff, and some to Leadville.

The message was plain: change was inevitable. By the middle 1880s, police forces were being issued with uniforms. In effect, the West had adopted an Eastern appearance. The change was subtle but significant. And as its "wildness" retreated, so did the frontier image. Gone were the familiar broad-brimmed hat, white shirt, open waistcoat, and one or a pair of pistols openly displayed. Indeed, were such characters to be seen by the turn of the century, many people would have been alarmed.

Only later, when those who lived through the era grew old and reminiscent about the old days, was there any regret for their passing.

Today, of course, the man with the large hat and prominently displayed pistols is the image most people cherish, or at least find irresistibly exciting, of what to them was indeed the Age of the Gunfighters. The final chapter in this book looks in greater detail at the death-dealing hardware.

# GAMBLING
# IN THE WEST

For good and (mainly) ill, gambling was integral to the life of the West. The spread of peoples westward across the U.S. during the nineteenth century necessitated centers of entertainment for the masses, particularly in those places with heavy concentrations of working men, such as mining towns, army forts, railheads, and cow towns. Most of the early gambling saloons were very rudimentary, being little more than drinking halls fitted out with an odd faro table. However, gambling establishments quickly flourished into major corporate enterprises, fueled by thousands of individuals who gambled professionally, in addition to the millions who gambled occasionally.

From the 1840s to the early 1860s, the Mississippi River was the focal point for American gamblers. Cities such as New Orleans and St. Louis offered a high density of

**ABOVE AND RIGHT:** *Frank Leslie's Illustrated Newspaper* brought to life the intrigue of gambling, including scenes of a prayer meeting outside a Springfield, Ohio, saloon (above), a gambler being shot (top right) and an 1870 card game (bottom right).

gambling establishments, while the river itself was home to gambling aboard riverboats. R. K. DeArment's article "No Sure Bet: Gambling on the Frontier" (*Wild West*, April 2005) explains that in the pre–Civil War period there were around 600–800 professional gamblers working on the river alone. However, the gold rush and the development of the cow towns drew gambling farther out west, and by 1850 San Francisco was an epicenter for Western gambling to rival anything in the East. Towns such as Deadwood, Abilene and Tombstone also came to thrive on gambling. John Ames in *The Real Deadwood* has pointed to the enormous profitability of some establishments, such as the infamous Gem Theater run by Al Swearengen: "On a typical night Swearengen took in $5,000—and some nights the take reached $10,000. These amounts were huge in 1876, when a typical family might have to survive on about $600 dollars or less annually."

The main gambling games of the mid- to late nineteenth century were card games. By far the most popular around the mid-nineteenth century was faro, a fairly simple game of chance betting that, in the hands of an experienced player, could net big rewards—one Mississippi gambler, Charles Cora, won $85,000 in six months playing faro. The other big card game of midcentury was vingt-et-un, which evolved into blackjack. Poker began to make its takeover of the gambling world during the 1870s, and by the end of the nineteenth century had nudged faro from its position as the most popular card game.

The end of the century saw many gambling establishments turning their last cards. Witnessing the ruin of countless individuals and the violence that accompanied gambling culture, American society turned against the gambling world. Women's movements were particularly vocal and influential in attacking gambling, and alongside prohibitions passed against alcohol, state legislatures steadily closed down many gambling establishments (Nevada being a notable exception). By 1907, a headline from a newspaper in Arizona territory declared that "The Tiger Is Dying," the "tiger" reference being another label for faro, but the headline could have been adapted to almost any other gambling game.

Only in the second half of the twentieth century did (legal) gambling see a resurgence in the United States. But this time around, it was without the constant threat of gunplay.

# Chapter Five

## TOOLS OF THE TRADE:

# GUNS OF THE WEST

The age of the gunfighter was built upon a sequence of revolutions in firearms technology—the percussion cap, the revolver, and the unitary cartridge. Without these developments, the era of the convenient personal firearm would not have been possible.

LEFT: Frederic Remington's *The Flight (A Sage Brush Pioneer)*. Illustrator, painter, sculptor, and writer, Remington (1861–1909) created this dramatic scene in 1895. Above all others, it was Remington who captured the life of the Western frontier.

# THE PERCUSSION AGE

The firearms revolution of the Wild West began in about 1800 across the other side of the Atlantic, in rural Scotland. In the countryside of Aberdeenshire, the Reverend Alexander John Forsyth of Belhelvie, an avid hunter, was becoming increasingly maddened with his flintlock firearms. By 1803, the year of the Louisiana Purchase, the flintlock was already a venerable piece of firearms history. Its origins lay in an earlier mechanism, the snaphaunce lock, which made its appearance in the mid-sixteenth century. The snaphaunce weapon (the word derives from the Dutch phrase *schnapp hahn*, "pecking cock") was fired by a spring-loaded arm driving a piece of flint against a steel set above a priming pan. The sparks from the resulting collision ignited the black powder in the pan, the flame being directed through a vent hole to ignite the main powder charge in the barrel.

The flintlock that emerged around the beginning of the seventeenth century improved upon the snaphaunce by combining the striker plate and the pan cover in one, the falling of the flint lifting the pan cover and exposing its powder.

Pan covers were essential to keep the gunpowder in a loaded weapon relatively dry. The snaphaunce had initially featured a hand-operated pan cover (it had to be manually swung open before firing), and later the cover was mechanically hinged to lift at the same time as the trigger was pulled. The virtue of the flintlock was its relative mechanical simplicity, its greater reliability over previous lock systems, and its production-cost benefits.

Despite the respected history of the flintlock, Forsyth was troubled by its "hang fire"—the delay between the pulling of the trigger and the ignition of the main charge. The flintlock's hang fire could be so pronounced that the sparks of the flint striking the steel and the fizzle of the pan powder could give an alert prey a half-second warning of the shot, enough time for it to escape. What was required was a faster mode of ignition, and it was to this task that Forsyth set his mind.

Forsyth found his solution in the work of English chemist Edward Howard. In 1799, Howard had been conducting experiments with fulminates, explosively volatile compounds produced by dissolving metals in acids. One of his discoveries, fulminate of mercury, could be detonated by impact alone, and this caught the Forsyth's attention. In 1805, Forsyth was successful in utilizing fulminate of mercury in a new kind of ignition system for firearms. Having stabilized the compound using potassium chlorate, which also had the side effect of increasing the power of detonation, he designed

BELOW:The Mortimer Dueling Pistol, 1800 (left), and the Rigby Overcoat Pocket Pistol, 1818 (right), both from England. The Rigby fired a lead ball of 12 bore—i.e., twelve bullets aggregated one pound of lead—and would have been a formidable arm at close quarters.

a pivoted magazine, known as a "scent-bottle lock" after its shape, that could present small amounts of the fulminate under a "hammer," essentially a modified cock. The hammer struck the compound upon firing, and the flame took the usual route through a vent hole to the powder charge.

Little did Forsyth know it, but he had laid the foundations for modern small arms. The near-instantaneous detonation of the fulminate of mercury meant that the time lag between trigger pull and the ejection of bullet or shot was now negligible. Forysth's new lock, however, had limited impact on the emergent west of the United States. In the United States, the flintlock would remain the primary weapon of civilian and military service for the first two decades of the nineteenth century. Indeed, conservatism within the American military meant that flintlocks were the mainstay of infantry firepower until the time of the Civil War. However, the true significance of Forsyth's invention was that it contributed to the development of percussion-cap weapons.

**ABOVE: Flintlock firearms persisted in the West well into the nineteenth century, despite the advent of percussion weapons. This handsome pair of flintlocks dates from 1857.**

The problem of Forsyth's lock was that it still involved loose powder with all its accompanying impracticalities and unpredictable performance. Subsequent arms designers quickly sought ways to either solidify or contain the fulminate to make it more "user-friendly." Building on Forysth's work, British gun makers such as Joseph Manton, Thomas Cartmell, and Samuel Nock formed the fulminate into solid disks or pellets using gum arabic as a binding agent, the pellets being placed into a cup atop the vent where they would be struck by the hammer. While promising in principle, the fulminate pellets were awkward to handle and prone to crumbling, and Forsyth attempted to improve on the system by sandwiching the pellets at regular intervals between two strips of paper or linen, the pellets being

## AMERICAN GUN-MAKING SHOP

The earliest known depiction of an American firearms manufactory dates to about 1820. The reconstructed colonial gunshop depicted here may be a little earlier (probably 1800–1810) and is typical of a three- or four-man operation where there was a distinct division of labor. An individual had a specific talent, be it as a lock maker, barrel forger, stock maker, or gun fitter. Each practiced his trade, turning over his finished product to the master for final fitting and assembly. There was no such concept as interchangeability at this time, each firearm being an individually crafted piece. Such a shop would also do a thriving business repairing and upgrading obsolete arms such as the flintlock pistol of about 1800–1820, the Model 1777 and Model 1795 flintlock muskets shown in

the window. Note the stock blanks, the rough-cast brass trigger guards, and the complete lack of mechanical power.

Technology did not follow the pioneers and settlers from east to west immediately. Settlements often served as dumping grounds for obsolate military arms and crude sporting pieces. Eventually, rifled firearms became more readily available, and as the flintlock era gave way to the percussion ignition system, firearms makers along the Mississippi caught up. A great gunsmithing center evolved in St. Louis, one of the primary jumping-off points for the West. Military requirements energized development with the adoption of a reduced-bore rifled musket in 1855. With the rimfire metallic cartridge, modern firearms had arrived, mostly to serve the needs of western mobilization.

advanced one at a time onto the nipple. Tape-primed percussion-lock weapons would have limited impact. Although in the United States, Dr. Edward Maynard's Model 1855 Pistol-Carbine enjoyed some commercial and military success using tape priming.

A different direction to tape priming was taken by Joseph Manton in 1818, who placed a small amount of priming powder into a thin copper tube. The tube was placed into a vent in the side of gun, and when the trigger was pulled, the hammer would crush the exposed top section of the tube against a protruding peg, detonating the tube's contents and starting the process of main-charge ignition. Gun makers such as the Milanese Giuseppe Colsole and English Charles Lancaster used the detonating tube in several weapons, but it was soon superseded by arguably the greatest invention in firearms history, the percussion cap.

Crediting the invention of the percussion cap is a historical minefield, there being numerous competing claims. The protagonists are Englishmen Joseph Manton and John Day and the artist Joshua Shaw, who immigrated to the United States in 1817. Shaw is said to have conceived of the percussion cap in 1814 and he obtained a U.S. patent for the invention in 1822, well before Manton took out British patent 7965 for the same idea in 1839, although he was using the system before then. Whatever the derivation, the percussion cap quite simply consisted of a small copper "hat" containing the fulminate. The cap was placed onto a specially designed nipple beneath the hammer, a vent running from the nipple through to the chamber. When the gun was fired,

**BELOW: The percussion-cap pistol changed the face of firearms technology. Top is a British percussion dueling pistol made by Manton, and similar weapons were exported from the United Kingdom to the United States in the nineteenth century. Below is a Deringer pistol, shown with a can of Hicks percussion caps.**

the hammer detonated the cap, the flash of which in turn ignited the main charge. Although the percussion cap might have seemed an incremental step onward from previous fulminate ignition systems, it was actually a revolution in firearms. Nowhere would the revolution be felt more keenly than in the Wild West.

## The Revolver

While the percussion-lock system would have an equal application to rifle technologies, it was in the field of handgun technology that it most transformed the world of the gunfighter. The "profession" of gunfighter was not possible with flintlock firearms. While a prearranged duel could be fought with flintlock pistols, the weapons were not suited to easy concealment (the bulky hammer, frizzen, and pan would catch on clothing), and transportation while loaded could result in lost priming powder. The percussion cap brought smaller, slimmer weapons and more reliable ignition, both positives for the gunfighter. More importantly, however, it inaugurated the defining handgun of the Western world—the revolver.

An enterprising young man from Hartford, Connecticut, created the true modern revolver. Samuel Colt, however, did not claim to have invented the revolver but simply to have perfected a working, reliable investment. The revolver principle had been around for over a century by the time Colt started his experiments. The late eighteenth century

saw the emergence of flintlock "pepperbox" pistols, which had multiple barrels each with its own pan and frizzen. After firing one barrel, the user would manually rotate the barrel set to align the next barrel. Pepperboxes would remain in use until the 1850s, utilizing percussion ignition to keep them relevant. A major boost to pepperbox popularity was the introduction of hammer- or trigger-powered rotation of the barrel group. A few "single-action" pepperboxes (meaning the barrels were rotated and aligned for firing by the cocking

TOP: Samuel Colt's development of the revolving breech firearm made possible the world of the gunfighter. Colt estalished his own manufactory in 1848, having achieved financial success with the Walker Colt revolver.

ABOVE: Allen & Thurby pepperbox revolver, 1837. The pepperbox handguns were precursors to the revolver; pulling the trigger rotated the entire barrel group.

**ABOVE: Five-chambered flintlock revolver by Elisha Collier, an American living in London, from about 1818.**

**RIGHT: A break-down drawing used by Colt to take out his first patents in England and France in 1835.**

of the hammer) were present during the eighteenth century, and in 1814 the gun maker Elisha Collier of Boston produced one of the first practical U.S. models. In 1836, Benjamin and Barton Darling took out a U.S. patent on a single-action percussion pepperbox, and in 1837 their rival Ethan Allen patented a "double-action" system (the barrels were rotated and the hammer cocked purely by trigger pull).

In the West, the pepperboxes had a respectable popularity with some civilian users, but they were not a gunfighter's weapon. Pepperboxes were extremely heavy and cumbersome to use. Allen's double-action weapon required a defiantly heavy trigger pull to perform its many mechanical operations and so had poor accuracy. Furthermore, there were many occasions of use when the flash from a hammer-struck percussion cap jumped across to fire adjacent barrels, this resulting in a disastrous multibarrel explosion.

Then along came Samuel Colt. In later life Colt spread the story that the idea for the revolver had come from his time as a cabin boy aboard the Corvo, the movement of the ship's wheel inspiring the revolver concept. The tale, while colorful, was more a publicity story than fact, and it is most likely that Colt derived his inspiration from mentally modifying existing designs. (In many ways his ratchet mechanism for rotating the cylinder is very similar to that used on a flintlock revolver designed by John Daft in the seventeenth century.) What is not in doubt is that Colt began the mass arming of the citizens of the United States.

Colt's revolver was structured around three main parts: 1) a handle, hammer, and trigger group that formed the frame of the revolver; 2) a removable octagonal barrel unit fitted to the front of the frame; and 3) the cylinder, its revolution powered by a pawl attached to the hammer. Loading the revolver involved removing the barrel and cylinder (the barrel was quickly removed by using a simple key), inserting paper cartridges into each chamber from the front, capping each separate nipple with a percussion cap, then reassembling the weapon. Colt also supplied a second cylinder with the pistol that could be preloaded for a quick cylinder exchange.

Colt's first revolver was a dramatic improvement over earlier designs owing to the quality and precision of the machining, its safety (the cylinder was locked in place by a lever bolt when ready to fire to ensure the correct alignment between barrel and chamber), and its general balance and accuracy. It had an initially shaky production history. Colt's first prototype, built by gunsmith Anson Chase of Hartford, Connecticut, in 1831 (this prototype was actually a revolver rifle), blew up during testing on account of percussion-cap flashover detonating all the chambers at once. Setting the nipples within deep recesses solved this problem, and the next batch of models—this time made by John Pearson of Baltimore—worked well.

Following a number of setbacks and a lack of money, Colt eventually sailed to England, where he patented his invention in 1835. In February 1836, he also patented his arms in the

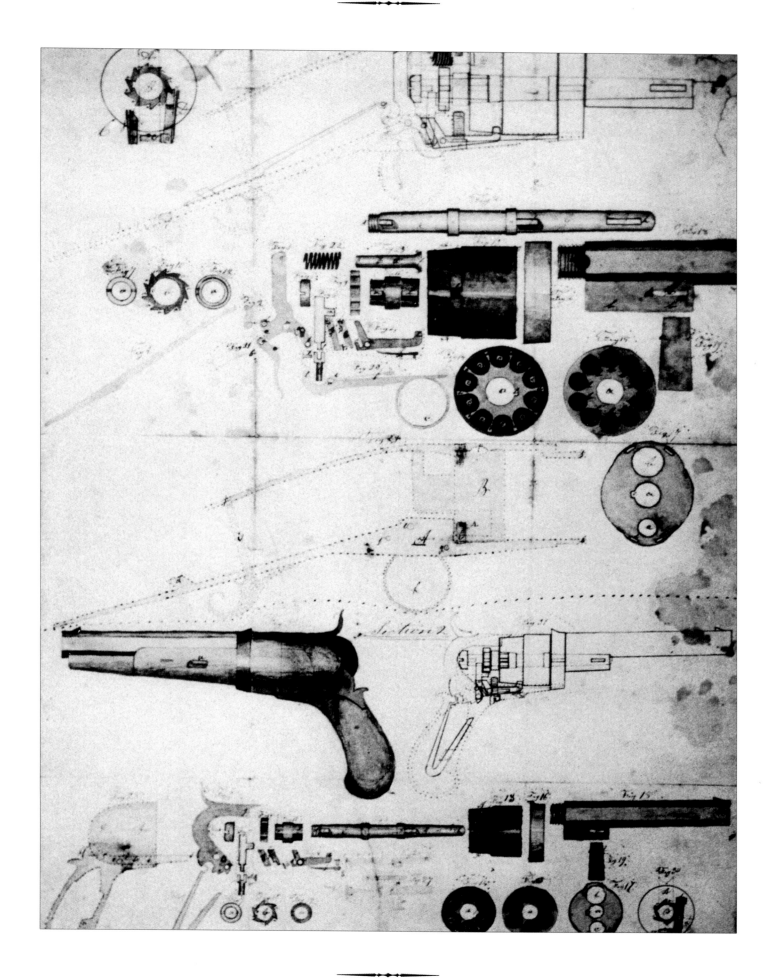

## SAM COLT'S REVOLVERS

Prior to the 1830s a practical and reliable repeating firearm was not available for hunters, soldiers, sportsmen, or gunmen. Although "repeating arms" had been known in various forms since the sixteenth century, they all lacked reliability. Collier's revolving flintlock pistols and long arms proved to be the first step toward "revolving arms," but ignition was a stumbling block. The invention of the percussion cap changed all that. And when Samuel Colt patented his revolver in 1835, he opened the floodgates to a whole new concept. Someone remarked that "God created man, but Sam Colt made them equal!" Others referred to "Judge Colt and his jury of six."

Colt's revolvers were much in demand both in the West and other parts of the country. By the early 1850s, he had established a factory in England. His mass-production methods revolutionized gun making on both sides of the Atlantic and led to changes in other industries. His involvement with the Patent Arms Manufacturing Company, Paterson, New Jersey,

which, with outside capital, manufactured his pistols and long arms, led to their adoption in Texas and usage by the U.S. Army. When the Paterson venture failed, Colt, as mentioned elsewhere, secured government contracts in 1847 during the war with Mexico. He later set up a factory in Hartford, Connecticut, from where his arms were in demand worldwide.

1. Colt prototype revolver with folding bayonet, made by blacksmith John Pearson about 1834-1835.
2. Colt first-model ring-lever revolving rifle, Paterson, about 1837.

3. "Texas" Paterson Colt revolver, .36 caliber, about 1838-1840.
4. Model 1839 Paterson revolving shotgun, serial number 138.
5. Cased Paterson belt-model revolver with accessories, about 1838-1840.
6. Soup tureen, about 1855, bearing Sam Colt's coat of arms.
7. Sam Colt's calling or business card, 1850s.
8. Silver cigar stand made for Sam Colt by New York silversmith William Adams, 1855.
9. Second Dragoon revolver in cutaway.
10. Engraved 1851 Navy revolver given to the Governor of Kansas at a time when violence characterized confrontations between pro- and antislavery forces.
11. Stock certificate for the Patent Arms Manufacturing Company.
12. Following the death of her husband, Mrs. Colt celebrated her husband's life with the publication of *Armsmear* (1866).
(Artifacts courtesy of Gene Autry Western Heritage Museum, Los Angeles.)

United States—the British patent had to be granted before the U.S. patent because the British government would not accept a patent application for a weapon already patented in the United States. On March 5, Colt signed contracts with some New York capitalists, who formed the Patent Arms Manufacturing Company of Paterson, New Jersey, to produce his revolving breeched rifles and revolvers.

By the late 1830s, Colt had sold a number of his revolving rifled muskets to the U.S. government, and the Republic of Texas purchased some pistols. By 1844, many of them had been issued to the Texas Rangers, who used them to good effect against Comanche Indians. This was a turning point: where once the Indians had had the upper hand and were able to send off a dozen arrows while the whites struggled to load their single-shot arms, Colt's five-shot pistols were a distinct advantage. In the hands of the Texas Rangers, they proved to be formidable weapons.

**Colt Pistols on the Pecos**

It seems fitting that the first civilian force to appreciate Colt's revolver should be the Texas Rangers. Formed originally in 1823 to provide some protection for outlying settlements against Indians in what was still Mexican territory, by the 1840s, when Texas was a republic, the Rangers were already earning a tremendous reputation. They never had a uniform as such and in the early days dressed casually. In appearance some resembled the "desperadoes" that they fought, but they proved their worth up against hostile Comanches, whose own reputation as the finest light cavalry on the Plains was entirely justified.

In his classic works *The Texas Rangers* and *The Great Plains*, Walter Prescott Webb not only paid tribute to the work of these men but also pinpointed the moment when the revolver really came into its own. In 1839, the Texas government purchased 180 holster-size .36-caliber Colt-Paterson pistols from Colt. At that time, "holster" denoted weapons intended to be carried in "saddle holsters" rather than on the belt. These five-shot nine-inch-barreled pistols, together with 180 rifles, were originally intended for naval use. By 1840, however, many of these arms had been issued to the Rangers. It was an inspired decision; for perhaps the

first time, the mounted soldier or Ranger was a match for his Indian opponent. Armed with a bow that shot flint- or steel-tipped arrows and backed by a fourteen-foot lance, the Comanche was a daunting figure. However, as was reported by the *Telegraph and Register* of April 17, 1844, a company of "Western Rangers, under the command of the gallant Captain [Jack] Hays . . . are sent out by turns to scout the country in every direction. The men are well armed, and are probably the most happy, jovial and hearty set of men in all Texas." One of those riders was Samuel Walker, who was later to play an important part in redesigning Colt's pistol. In 1846, he described to Colt an incident that was publicized as far away as England:

> The pistols which you made for the Texas Navy have been in use by the Rangers for three years . . . In the Summer of 1844 Col. J.C. Hays with 15 men fought about 80 Camanche [sic] Indians, boldly attacking them upon their own ground, killing & wounding about half their number . . . Without your pistols we would not have had the confidence to have undertaken such daring adventures.

Such a reputation in the hands of renowned individuals like the Texas Rangers was music to Sam Colt's ears, but before he could make full use of such accolades, he received a severe

ABOVE: **Colt's arms factory in Paterson, New Jersey, which was active from 1835. The initial Patent Arms Manufacturing Company, however, was not a financial success, and the company went into liquidation in 1842.**

setback. A lack of government orders and certain defects in the arms themselves caused the Patent Arms Manufacturing Company to fail. Colt refused to give up, continuing his experiments with arms and other projects. Then, in 1846, the worsening relationship between the United States and Mexico came to a head. The Republic of Texas, established following the defeat of Santa Anna, maintained a precarious amnesty with Mexico, but it was deemed only a matter of time before the two fought each other. A partial solution was reached in 1845 when, with mutual agreement, Texas was annexed by the United States. But on May 8, 1846, American and Mexican forces clashed in what is remembered as the Battle of Palo Alto, and they were at war. It lasted for two years before a peace treaty was signed in February 1848, at which time California became a territory of the United States.

In the opening months of the war, the few Paterson pistols in military hands proved themselves equal to the task, and demands for more revolvers convinced the government that the arm was of practical value, but none was readily available. When Colt learned that Captain Samuel Walker, who had been newly commissioned into the United States Mounted Rifles Regiment, had publicly praised his pistols, he wrote to him pointing out that with a military contract he could produce revolvers for the war. He also asked the captain for an honest opinion of the Paterson pistol and his ideas for improvements. Colt also offered to supply 1,000 pistols for twenty-five dollars each, reducing the cost with every thousand pistols ordered. Walker, on orders from the adjutant general's office, had been dispatched to Fort McHenry to establish a recruiting base, so he was easily able to visit Colt. The pair met and thrashed out the faults in the existing design.

On December 7, 1846, Walker managed to get an interview with President James K. Polk, who in turn introduced him to Secretary of War William L. Marcy. Marcy listened to Walker, who probably produced an existing Colt Paterson pistol, noting the proposed improvements. Despite objections from the ordnance department, Marcy approved a contract with Colt that was drawn up on January 6, 1847. Walker warned Colt that both their reputations were on the

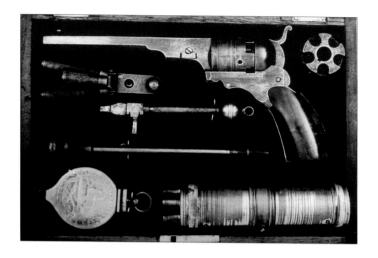

ABOVE: A fine .36 caliber Paterson Colt belt model in its original case with all the accessories that a new owner would receive, including spare cylinder and cleaning tools.

BELOW: Captain Samuel H. Walker was an important figure in the development of Colt firearms. A combat veteran of the U.S. Army and Texas Rangers, Walker suggested improvements to Colt's Paterson pistol in the 1840s, and in turn gained vital government contracts for Colt.

line and he had to meet his contractual obligations. Colt set to work and persuaded Eli Whitney Jr., of New Haven, Connecticut, to manufacture the pistols at his Whitneyville plant and the Sheffield steelmakers, Naylor & Company, through their Boston agents, supplied the raw materials.

The pistol that was finally accepted was a massive thing. Weighing four pounds nine ounces, it was a six-shot .44-caliber weapon with a nine-inch barrel that could be loaded with up to fifty-seven grains of black powder (forty grains was the recommended load) that could push a 140-grain lead

**LEFT: Eli Whitney Jr. is a seminal figure in the history of American industrial processes. Whitney's use of assembly-line machine technologies to produce Colt pistols laid down techniques for many future types of mass-production systems.**

**BELOW: Men of the Texas Rangers Frontier Battalion, Company D, proudly display their Winchester .44-40 Model 73 rifles, one of the defining firearms of the West.**

ball at an estimated muzzle velocity of between 1,300 to 1,500 feet per second. The Walker Colt also featured a lever rammer beneath the barrel that enabled the cylinder to be reloaded in situ rather than requiring removal. A number of the pistols blew up through faults in manufacture, but they proved their worth in action, and in anticipation of more contracts, Colt had Whitney manufacture a further one hundred pistols for civilian use.

Sadly, Walker, who had played a large part in the design and acceptance of the "Colt-Walker" revolver, was killed in action during the war.

One legacy of the Mexican War was the reaction of the Rangers and soldiers who had been armed with the new Colt revolvers. Some refused to surrender them or claimed that they had been lost in action or simply blown up. Captain John Williams, writing in May 1848, from Vera Cruz, Mexico, advised Washington that only 191 of the 280 new pistols issued to the Texas Rangers under Colonel Jack Hays's command had been handed in. Of this number, only eighty-two were serviceable. Unknown to him, perhaps, some of the missing arms had fallen into Mexican hands, but the message was plain: the day of the pistol fighter had arrived. With the money Colt received from his military contract, he was able to set up a pistol manufactory in Hartford.

Further government contracts followed, and in 1848 Colt redesigned the Walker pistol and produced the first of his "Dragoon" or "Holster" weapons now generally known as the Model of 1848.

The weight was reduced by seven ounces, and the barrel shortened to seven and a half inches. Several pocket pistols were also designed and produced, but it was the appearance in 1850 of a weapon tentatively called the New Ranger Size Pistol that attracted most attention, for this particular pistol surely more than any other of its time inspired the age of the gunfighter.

**BELOW: The Colt Patent Fire Arms Manufacturing Company in Hartford, Connecticut. The factory was established in 1847, and manufacture of certain parts was subcontracted out to gun makers such as Remington.**

## SINGLE- & DOUBLE-ACTION REVOLVERS

During Sam Colt's lifetime, all his pistols were single-actions. He experimented with self-cocking (by pulling the trigger and cocking and firing the hammer in one motion) but decided it was unreliable. Between 1850 and 1870, others followed his example, and the accompanying group of arms indicates how closely they followed Colt. A number of makers used top straps instead of the open frame, but in other respects copied Colt's basic design.

1. Belts varied in width. By the mid-1870s, cartridge loops were common. Before then most people carried saddlebags or ammunition pouches.
2. .36 caliber Whitney Navy pistol (s.n. 14457) that rivaled both Colt and Remington; well made and popular.
3. The pistol's original holster.
4. Whitney five-shot, .31 caliber pocket model. On both the Navy and Pocket pistols, the cylinder pin was attached to the rammer and held in place by a pin through the frame.
5. The Walch ten-shot .31 pocket pistol.
6. Massachusetts Arms Co.'s licensed copy of the British Beaumont-Adams .31 pocket pistol.
7. The MAC's version of the Beaumont-Adams Army Model in .44 caliber. A number of these were purchased by the Confederacy.
8. Remington-Beals Army pocket revolver.
9. Box of .31 caliber combustible cartridges.

10. Allen & Wheelock's center hammer Army revolver in .44 caliber.
11. Allen & Wheelock's center hammer pocket revolver in .28 caliber.
12. Six .44 caliber combustible cartridges for the Colt 1860 Army revolver.
13. MAC's Maynard primed belt revolver, .31 caliber.
14. Maynard's cap primers.
15. Springfield Arms Co. pocket revolver in .28 caliber.
16. Remington-Rider double-action New Model belt revolver (1863) in .36 caliber.
17. Remington New Model pocket revolver (1863) in .31 caliber.
18. IXL revolver believed made before 1857, based upon the British Adams.
19. Box of British-made Joyce percussion caps.
20. Another version of the IXL revolver. B. J. Hart of New York is often credited with their manufacture.
21. Another version of the IXL.
22. James Warner revolver.

23. Cooper double-action Navy revolver with a rebated cylinder; .36 caliber, five-shot.
24. Cooper five-shot .31 double-action pocket pistol.
25. Cooper pocket model; note close resemblance to Colt's pistols.
26. Combustible pistol cartridges. Sold in packs of six but larger quantities were available. Most civilians had reserves of loose powder, ball, and caps.
27. Pettengill's double-action hammerless Army pistol; six-shot, .44 caliber.
28. Manhattan's five-shot .36 caliber "Navy" pistol that some confused with Colt's pistols.
29. Metropolitan Arms Co.'s copy of Colt's 1861 Navy.
30. Manhattan 6-inch barreled Navy pistol.
31. Manhattan .31 caliber five-shot pocket pistol.
32. Union Arms Company pocket pistol with fluted cylinder.
33. Hopkins & Allen pocket pistol.
(Artifacts courtesy of Buffalo Bill Historical Center, Cody, Wyoming.)

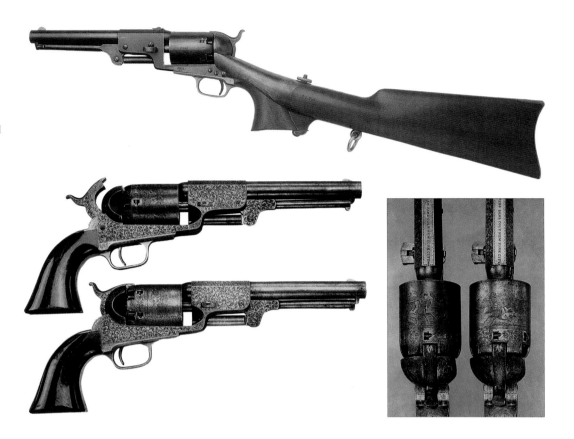

RIGHT: A group of highly collectable Colt pistols. The pair of Third Model Dragoon Percussion revolvers (engraving detail inset) would command in excess of $150,000 at auction. The other firearm is also a Third Model Dragoon, with detachable shoulder stock.

The new revolver was a six-shot .36-caliber weapon with a seven-and-one-half-inch octagonal barrel, an overall length of thirteen inches, and a weight of two pounds ten ounces. Around the cylinder was a die-rolled engraving depicting a battle between Texan and Mexican ships in 1843. The United States Board of Ordnance tested the new pistol and was impressed. On a single day's trial, it was fired 1,500 times and cleaned only once. Penetration tests on pine boards were equally impressive. The chambers were loaded with twenty grains of powder (the chamber could accept thirty grains) and the eighty-three-grain conical bullets pierced six pine boards set one inch apart. Its accuracy was applauded, but the board was more concerned with recoil, especially how it might affect a mounted horseman. Very shortly afterward, the "Ranger" title was dropped and substituted by "Belt" or "Navy" pistol, a factory definition. The military and public preferred the "Navy" tag, by which it was immortalized.

## Rivals

Colt's revolvers were certainly the dominant handguns in the United States in the mid-1800s, but they were not without their rivals. There emerged one particular area of competition: the battle between the single-action and the double-action revolvers. Until the 1870s, the majority of American-made revolvers were single action. Yet as early as 1851 the Englishman Robert Adams had patented a "self-cocking" revolver, utilizing an action that had been available for some time in the pepperboxes. Simply by pulling the trigger, the hammer was cocked and fired in one movement, and at the same time the cylinder was turned to bring a new chamber in line with the barrel—its Colt rivals had to be thumb-cocked for each shot.

The Adams revolver offered other potential advantages over the Colts. First, it was stronger, the whole of the pistol frame being machined from a single piece of metal, this producing a "top-strap" extending over the cylinder, whereas the top of the Colt cylinder was exposed. The Adams cylinder was removed simply by withdrawing a pin, the cylinder dropping out into the hand to be loaded in the same manner as the Colt.

Colt and Adams displayed their respective firearms in the Great Exhibition held in London in 1851, and the virtues and vices of each weapon were hotly debated. In terms of accuracy shooting, the Colt had the edge, single-action shooting requiring only a light trigger pull to drop the hammer. However, in fast combat situations (combat reports came in from Britain's many colonial wars), the Adams was a reassuring man-stopper, its double action ensuring a rapid switch between targets while its powerful .49-inch round had unquestionable killing power.

In 1855, a Lieutenant Beaumont of the Royal Engineers patented a modification to the Adams pistol that enabled it to be fired either as a double- or single-action. These weapons, known as Beaumont-Adams revolvers, were formidable competitors to the Colt. The Adams weapons denied Colt total market dominance in Britain, and Colt was eventually forced to close a British factory, although worldwide Colt sales remained strong. Beaumont-Adams revolvers were also produced in the United States either under license or as simple copies, with the main producer being the Massachusetts Arms Company.

The Beaumont-Adams revolvers, however, were not the only challengers to face Colt. With its patent expiration in 1857, Colt suddenly faced a rash of quality firearms appearing on the market. In 1860, Eliphalet Remington of New York began producing the .44 New Model Army and .36 Navy revolvers designed by Fordyce Beals. The former was a large, strong, reliable weapon with a "top-strap" frame that enjoyed decent popularity during the Civil War, it and

the Navy model being second only in usage to Colt's weapons. The New Model Army was a single-action weapon, although Remington introduced two more compact double-action weapons in the late 1850s. Another competitor to Colt was the Starr Arms Company in Yonkers, New York. Starr made a variety of single- and double-action weapons between the late 1850s and late 1860s. The Starr weapons sold well with the United States military, and by 1866 Starr had achieved sales of 48,000 pistols to federal customers alone.

Yet the competition to Colt must not be overstated, and the terrible years of the Civil War (1861–1865) truly defined them as the market leaders in muzzle-loading percussion

**LEFT: Competitors of Colt. The top gun is the British Adams .32 Pocket Revolver (featuring the Brazier rammer), and the bottom is the Remington Army Model 1863.**

**ABOVE: Colt recognized that the 1851 "Exhibition of the Works and Industry of All Nations," held at the Crystal Palace, London, was a great export marketing opportunity. Adams was there too, but Colt had the best gun stand.**

revolvers. Colt produced a new generation of revolvers, including the compact .31-caliber Little Dragoon pocket pistols and the superb .36-caliber Model 1851 Navy, that achieved sales of 41,000 units to the United Kingdom alone. In 1860 and 1861, Colt issued the .44 New Army Model and an improved .36 Navy Model, both of which became Civil War mainstays. The Army Colt alone formed 40 percent of Union handgun purchases during the war. The Civil War period saw an estimated total of around 750,000 handguns sold to both civilian and military markets, and it was a boom time for many gun makers. Yet those manufacturers who specialized in muzzle-loading percussion-cap weapons during these years would quickly face a new challenge. By the 1850s, a revolutionary type of ammunition system was entering use that remains dominant to this day.

**Enter the Breechloader**

As refined as percussion-cap weapons became during the nineteenth century, there was no denying that they retained some of the functional awkwardness of the flintlock. Loading a weapon with loose powder and ball, or even with a paper cartridge and a percussion cap, was a fussy and time-consuming process, and an alarmingly tardy business when one's life was threatened in combat.

Experiments with unitary cartridges—systems where the primer, powder, and ball are combined in a single unit—began in earnest in the second decade of the nineteenth century and ran in tandem with attempts to achieve efficient breechloading weapons. In 1812, the Swiss gun maker Johannes Pauly created a breechloading sporting rifle that was loaded with a paper cartridge featuring a brass head containing the priming mixture, this being detonated by the action of a firing pin. Twenty years later, the Frenchman Casimir Lefaucheaux moved much closer to a practical cartridge system when he developed the pin-fire cartridge. Like modern cartridges, this consisted of a brass case holding the primer, charge, and bullet. Each cartridge, however, had a pin affixed, the pin projecting out from the gun via a chamber slot when the cartridge was loaded. On pulling the trigger of Lefaucheaux's gun, the hammer fell onto the pin, which was in turn driven against the percussion cap to begin detonation. Further refinements of the new cartridge/

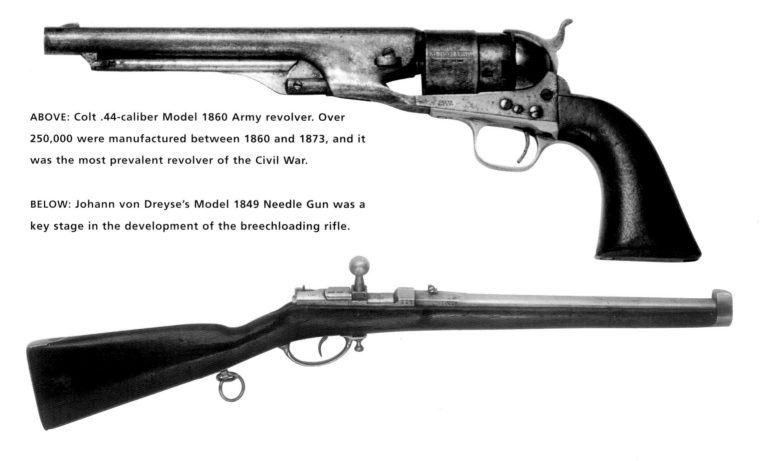

ABOVE: Colt .44-caliber Model 1860 Army revolver. Over 250,000 were manufactured between 1860 and 1873, and it was the most prevalent revolver of the Civil War.

BELOW: Johann von Dreyse's Model 1849 Needle Gun was a key stage in the development of the breechloading rifle.

**LEFT: Daniel Wesson was born in 1825. His older brother, Edwin, was a gunsmith, and Daniel began his gun making career with him in 1842.**

**FAR LEFT: Horace Smith was seventeen years older than Dan Wesson and began his working life in the Springfield Armory.**

loading system were soon forthcoming, the most significant being the work of the Prussian Johann Nikolas von Dreyse in the 1840s. Dreyse created the famous "Needle Gun" bolt-action rifle, which used a form of unitary cartridge, mostly made of cardboard, fired by the impact of a long firing pin that pierced the base of the cartridge and struck a cap positioned just behind the bullet itself.

More will be said about the development of rifles later, but in terms of revolver evolution, the first major step away from the percussion-cap system began with the invention of the rimfire cartridge by the Frenchman Louis Flobert. Flobert, building on the work of Bernard Houllier, created his cartridge in 1849. It consisted of little more than a percussion cap topped with a bullet, the powder being set in the rim of the "cartridge." The new round became known as the Bulletted Breech Cap, and in the United States, Flobert's invention did reasonably well, despite the low velocity of the bullet (it relied purely on the priming compound for propulsion). However, two American gun makers sought to improve on the design, and in so doing, the names of Horace Smith and Daniel Wesson would become firearms legends.

Smith and Wesson made the era of the gunfighter possible by creating the true breechloading cartridge revolver. First, they built on Flobert's work to produce an effective metallic cartridge that contained a charge of powder in addition to the priming compound, the latter being contained in a hollow rim formed around the base of the cartridge. The cartridge was detonated by the hammer striking the rim and crushing a section of it against the rear edge of the chamber. The brass walls of the cartridge expanded at the moment of firing to create a gas-tight seal against the chamber, thus ensuring that the entire force of propellant detonation was directed forward behind the bullet. Their second important action was their purchase of U.S. Patent 12608, originally taken out in 1855 by former Colt employee Rollin White. White had taken out a speculative patent on a revolver that featured a cylinder with fully bored-out chambers loaded from the rear with cartridges. With this patent in their hands, Smith and Wesson bided their time and waited for Colt's patent on the revolver to expire in 1857.

## Smith and Wesson

Smith and Wesson's first rimfire, unitary cartridge breechloading revolver emerged in 1858 as the .22 seven-shot rimfire Model No.1. The two gun makers had by this stage already been involved with the ongoing refinement of Walter Hunt's "Volitional Repeater" gun, a repeating rifle that fired .38-caliber bullets with the powder actually located in the base of the bullet itself. From 1854, Smith and Wesson, with gun maker Courtland Palmer (who had purchased the patents to Hunt's weapon), made repeating rifles and pistols along the lines of Hunt's repeater, and Daniel Wesson improved on the ammunition by placing priming powder in the base of the bullet rather than black powder, so the bullet

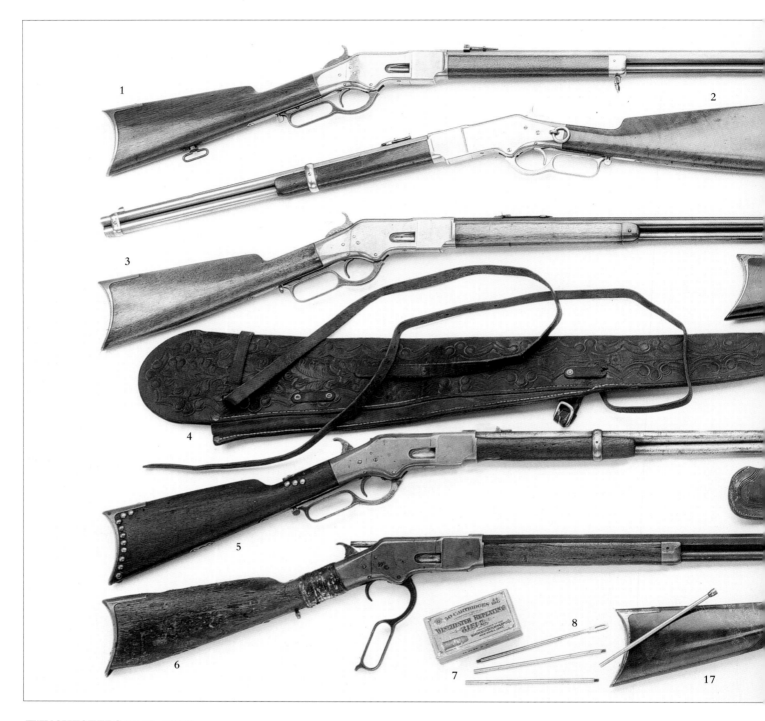

## WINCHESTERS 1866–1873

The legendary Winchester rifle owed its origin to the early Smith and Wesson and later Volcanic arms. But by the mid-1860s it was a much-improved version. The Model of 1866 (called the Yellow Boy on account of its brass receiver) could be loaded with fifteen cartridges. By far the most popular model was the standard rifle with a twenty-four-inch octagonal barrel (the carbine had a twenty-inch round barrel). Early advertisements for the Model 1866 made much of the fact that

an expert shot could empty the magazine in fifteen seconds; if loaded at that speed, sixty shots a minute was possible. By the late 1860s, however, rimfire ammunition for rifles and other large arms was in decline. With the center-fire cartridge came a new and improved Winchester—the legendary Model of 1873.

Winchester improved the mechanism and replaced the brass receiver with an iron one. The new .44-40 cartridge (.44 caliber backed by forty grains of powder) was a great improvement, but it did not impress the ordnance: it was a pistol round, and the

army wanted a much more powerful cartridge. The civilian market, however, welcomed the new cartridge, and in 1878 Colt chambered some of their Peacemakers and double-action Army pistols in .44–40, which were marked "Frontier Six-Shooter."

1. A fine Winchester Model 1866, .44 caliber, with 24-inch octagonal barrel and sling swivels.
2. Carbine version with a saddle ring and a round 20-inch barrel.
3. Some Model '66 rifles were made with round barrels on request.
4. Fine hand-carved leather scabbards were prized.

5. This Model 1866 was once Indian-owned—note typical brass-tack design.
6. Model 1866, with broken stock repaired with wet rawhide strips.
7. An original box of 50 .44–100 rifle cartridges.
8. Cleaning rod for the '73 shown in 17.
9. The cocking action of the Winchester; note how the breech pin cocks the hammer as the lever drops.
10. Spent cartridges.
11. Some original "shells" for Winchester '73.
12. Two-part cleaning rod.
13. Typical 1873 carbine with the round barrel and saddle ring.
14. A '73 with a round barrel and fitted with a shortened magazine.
15. Fine '73 carbine.
16. Typical saddle scabbard for a Winchester rifle.
17. Winchester target rifle with additional sights set behind the hammer.
(Artifacts courtesy of Buffalo Bill Historical Center, Cody, Wyoming.)

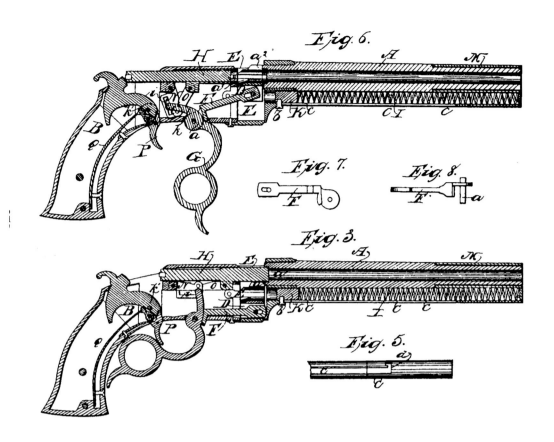

No. 10,535.

H. SMITH & D. B. WESSON
MAGAZINE FIREARM.
Patented Feb. 14, 1854.

2 Sheets—Sheet 2.

**ABOVE:** Smith and Wesson patent drawings (patent no. 10,535) for a "magazine firearm" operated by the Volcanic system of lever action.

**BELOW:** Patent drawings (dated August 8, 1854) for a Smith and Wesson cartridge, an improved version of Flobert's percussion-cap cartridge.

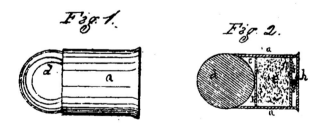

no longer required a separate percussion cap to be fired. However, in 1855 Smith and Wesson sold the rights to the Volitional Repeater to the Volcanic Repeating Arms Company (more on them later) and switched their attentions to their new rimfire revolvers.

The first Smith and Wesson revolver was of a "tip-up" variety. The gun frame was hinged just above the front edge of the cylinder, allowing the barrel to be swung upward when a spring catch below the cylinder was disengaged. With the barrel out of the way, the cylinder could be removed for reloading. It was a single-action weapon and was far faster to reload than the existing percussion-cap Colts. Its one major problem was the small-caliber low-powered round. Rimfire cartridges require soft cases to allow the rims to be crushed by the falling hammer, and this generally prevents them from taking heavy loadings.

Smith and Wesson persisted with their tip-up revolvers until 1869, when another fundamental shift in cartridge technology occurred—the development of the center-fire cartridge. Center-fire cartridges started to emerge with the designs of people such as Dreyse and Pauly (mentioned above), and others, including Englishmen Joseph Rigby and Charles Lancaster. Lancaster has a good claim to be the inventor of the true center-fire cartridge, having produced a brass shotgun cartridge in 1854 that featured a percussion cap located centrally in the base of the cartridge. The design of center-fire cartridges was improved by English army officer Colonel Edward Mounier Boxer and by Union Army officer

LEFT: A .22-caliber Smith and Wesson Tip-Up Revolver, for those who wanted a handgun that was easily concealed in a pocket or, for women, a handbag.

ABOVE: The Smith and Wesson .44-40 New Model No. 3 (here fitted with a target sight). Sales of the weapon were disappointing, and many were converted to the .44 Russian cartridge. In this form it had improved success.

Colonel Hiram Berdan (Berdan modified the cartridge so that the anvil against which the primer was struck was manufactured as an integral part of the cartridge itself).

Having manufactured 270,000 rimfire revolvers—putting a major dent in Colt's market share—in 1868 Smith and Wesson launched a .44-center-fire cartridge revolver, looking to counteract the commercial effects of the expiration of their own revolver patent. The new gun was .44 Model No. 3. Unlike earlier rimfire weapons, the gun's barrel was hinged in front of the trigger, allowing the rear of the chamber to be exposed and reloaded in situ. Furthermore, the gun featured a spring-loaded star plate in the center of the cylinder that engaged with the rims of the cartridges. When the barrel was broken, the star plate was automatically driven outward to eject all the spent casings in one action. Credit for the ejector system goes to one W .C. Dodge, an American gun maker

who sold the U.S. patent rights to Smith and Wesson in 1865.

The Model No. 3 was a true gunfighter's gun. It was quick to load, and its .44 bullet had all the stopping power a shooter could need. One of Smith and Wesson's famous early advocates was Buffalo Bill Cody. In fact, Cody's handling of the No.3 so impressed representatives of the Russian military during a visit to the United States in 1869 that Russia subsequently placed an order for 215,704 Smith and Wesson revolvers, the model being designated No. 3 Russian Model. The Russian Model had some crucial differences to the "American" Model (as it became subsequently known). The Russian Model was shorter, being twelve inches in length as opposed to the American's 13.38 inches. The American Model's 218-grain bullet was powerful, but it had a slightly loose fit in the bore that impaired accuracy over fifty yards. Russian modifications tightened up the bullet, bringing the muzzle velocity up to 750 feet per second as opposed to the American's 650 feet per second. Accuracy was also improved in the Russian Model.

Although the Russian Model was in many ways superior, the American Model still enjoyed respectable domestic sales, the U.S. Army ordering 1,000 in 1870. However, field experience with the initial Model 3 was not good, and Smith and Wesson had to make several sequences of improvements to bring it up to snuff. While they were doing so, most of the company's efforts were channeled into fulfilling its Russian contract, ultimately to its detriment. For while Smith and Wesson were churning out export revolvers by the thousands, Colt was creeping back with a firearm that would become synonymous with the Wild West gunfighter.

### Colt's Peacemaker

With Smith and Wesson's patents expired, Colt—now without Samuel Colt, who had died January 10, 1862—

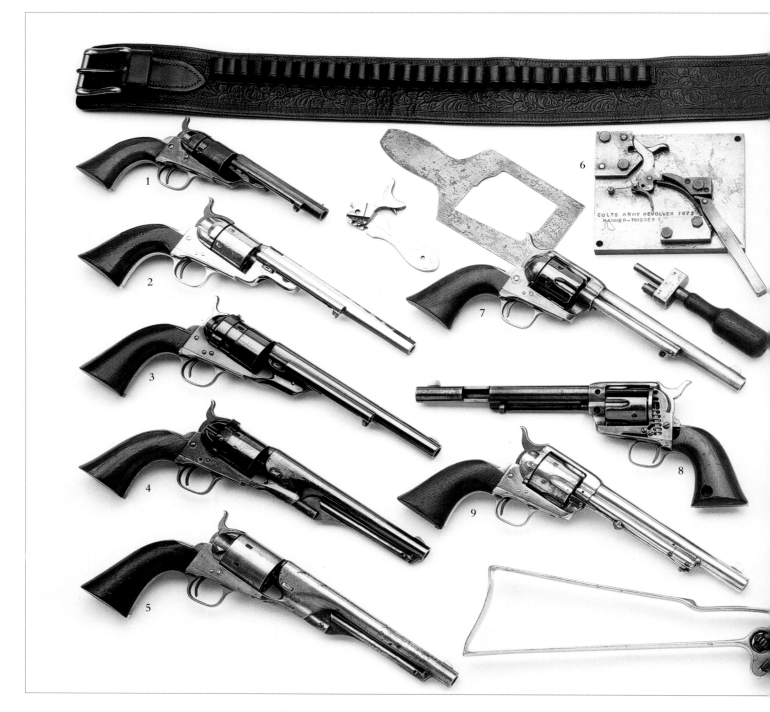

## THE COLT SINGLE-ACTION ARMY

Few firearms were as easily identified with the gunfighter and the settlement of the West as the Colt single-action Army revolver. Even its nicknames convey ideas of frontier lawmen and gunmen. Known variously as the Peacemaker, the Frontier Six-Shooter, the Thumb Buster, and the Hog Leg, this gun was popularly used and relied on by men and women on both sides of the law, and by both civilians and the military after its first release in 1872.

1. Model 1862 pocket Navy revolver, .36 caliber center-fire, c. 1873.
2. Model 1851 Navy conversion from .36 caliber percussion to .38 caliber rimfire, about 1873.
3. Richards-Mason Colt conversion revolver.
4. Thuer conversion of Model 1861 Navy revolver from percussion to front loading, tapered brass-cased cartridge, caliber .36, c. 1869.
5. Experimental .44 rimfire Colt cartridge revolver, c. 1868–1869.
6. Gauges used for initial manufacture of the Colt single-action Army revolver, 1872–1874.
7. Serial number 1, "s" Colt single-action Army, the first manufactured in 1872, shipped to England for promotional purposes.
8. Factory cutaway single-action, .45, showing internal mechanism.
9. Experimental .45 caliber single-action with automatic cartridge extractor.
10. Typical, inexpensive machine-embossed holster and belt for single-action Army Colt.

11. Gold-plated, pearl steer head grips, with silver inlaid name on the back strap, "Albert W. Bonds."

12. Box for .45 Colt cartridges, made by Remington-U.M.C.

13. Brass-cased .44 Smith & Wesson cartridges.

14. Nickel-plated, ivory-gripped Colt single-action .45 known to collectors as the "Sheriff's" model; was manufactured without the cartridge ejector.

15. Carved Mexican eagles on ivory grips were especially popular south of the border where the Colt single-action Army .45 became a weapon of choice.

16. Although available in many barrel lengths, the 4³/₄-inch model such as this .45 nickel-finished version was among the most popular of the single-action Colts.

17. Colt single-actions with detachable shoulder stocks and extralong barrels could be ordered from the factory. This was the first made in 1876.

18. Wells Fargo Express ordered a number of these .45 Colts for use by security personnel in 1909.

19. The same weapon proved reliable for Adams Express Company.

20. A .45 caliber Colt, factory ivory grips decorated with carving.

21. Second in popularity to the .45, the .44-40 received wide use.

22. With longer curved grips and special target sights, the Bisley model single-action gained popularity in England and the United States.

23. With fixed sights and custom finish and grips, the Bisley also saw use in the West.

24. Standard Bisley model with fixed sights and 5½-inch barrel.

(Artifacts courtesy of Gene Autry Western Heritage Museum, Los Angeles.)

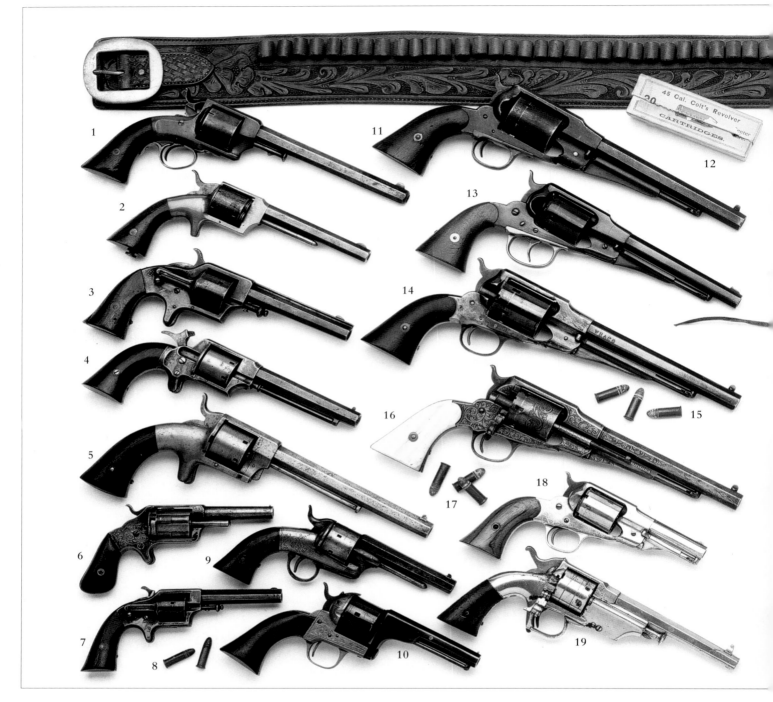

## COLT'S CARTRIDGE COMPETITORS

Among the numerous cartridge revolvers that appeared in the 1870s, when the Rollin White patent for bored-through cylinders expired, were a number that proved to be serious rivals to Colt's New Model Army Revolver, the Peacemaker. During ordnance tests, however, what the Colt lacked in manufacturing precision it more than made up for in reliability in rough handling, which made it an ideal weapon for military and frontier use.

1. Prescott single-action six-shot Navy revolver in .38 caliber rimfire.
2. Pond pocket or belt pistol.
3. Merwin and Bray pocket pistol.
4. Uhlinger pocket revolver (sometimes credited to W. L. Grant), .32 rimfire.
5. Bacon's Navy revolver, six-shot .38 rimfire.
6. Brooklyn Firearms Co.'s "Slocum" pocket pistol in .32 rimfire.
7. Eagle Arms Company cup-primed pocket revolver.
8. Two .22 caliber cartridges.
9. Bacon's .32 caliber rimfire pocket pistol. Short-lived because of infringement of Smith & Wesson's rights to bored-through cylinders.
10. Moore's "Seven-Shooter" .32 caliber rimfire pocket revolver.
11. Remington New Model Army 1863 converted from percussion to cartridge.
12. Box of .45 caliber ammunition from Colt's Army revolver.
13. Remington double-action New Model belt pistol.

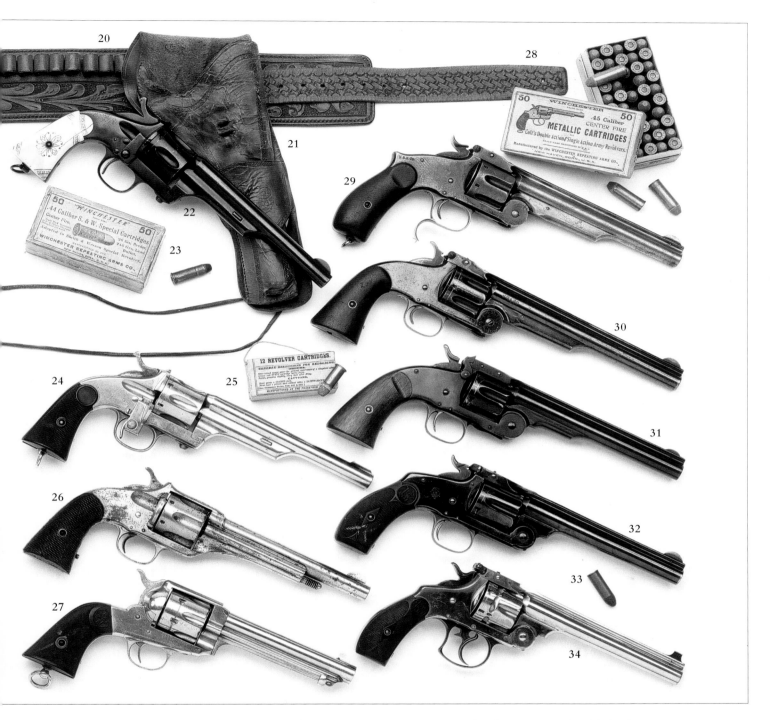

14. Remington New Model Army pistol converted to metallic cartridge.

15. Three .44 Remington cartridges.

16. A factory conversion of the 1863 Army revolver, engraved and fitted with ivory stocks.

17. Further Remington rounds.

18. Remington's No. 2 pocket revolver.

19. Allen and Wheelock's center hammer lip-fire revolver. Notches were cut into the rear of the chambers to allow the hammer to strike the cartridge "lips."

20. Belts complete with cartridge loops became common by the late 1870s. This ornate version is quite late.

21. The holster may not be contemporary to the belt, but it is of the type in common usage then.

22. Merwin and Hulbert's open-top Army revolver. This well-made pistol, beaten by the Colt Peacemaker in trials, was popular out West.

23. Box of reloadable cartridges made at the government's Frankford Arsenal.

24. Merwin and Hulbert's Army pistol, nickel-plated.

25. Government-made cartridges.

26. Merwin and Hulbert's Army pistol with top strap.

27. Remington Model 1890 single-action Army revolver. About 2,000 of these were made.

28. Box of Winchester-made cartridges for Colt's .45 double- and single-action Army revolvers.

29. Smith & Wesson's No. 3 Model Army pistol in .44 caliber "Russian." So-called because of special ammunition ordered by the Russians.

30. Smith and Wesson No. 3 American 1 Model.

31. Schofield version of the Model No. 3 with improved barrel latch.

32. Smith and Wesson New Model No. 3 revolver in .44 Russian caliber.

33. .44 Russian cartridge.

34. Smith and Wesson's .44 double-action 1881 "Frontier" revolver.

(Artifacts courtesy of Buffalo Bill Historical Center, Cody, Wyoming.)

**ABOVE: Colt New Line pocket revolvers were produced in a wide range of calibers, from .22 to .41 (the revolver pictured was the latter). They were rimfire weapons with solid iron frames.**

**LEFT: The .44-caliber Colt Frontier/Peacemaker, one of the most successful handguns of all time. It combined a reliable single action with capable stopping power.**

thundered back into the market with the Model 1873 .45 Single Action, more commonly known by the names Peacemaker, Frontier, and Army. Colt had produced its first cartridge revolver in 1871, the .41 caliber four-shot House Pistol, followed by a series of New Line Pocket Revolvers in various calibers.

Colt was feeling its way into the breechloading pistol market with these weapons, but none achieved the status of the Peacemaker.

The M1873 was a .45-caliber six-shot solid-frame revolver. As its full name suggested, it was a single-action-only revolver. The revolver was loaded and unloaded via a hinged loading gate, which sat over the upper-right-hand chamber. With the hammer at half cock, the cylinder could be rotated and the chambers loaded individually through the gate—if there were empty cases in the cylinder, these were ejected using an integral spring-loaded ejector rod that was aligned with the loading gate.

The M1873 was not a perfect weapon—several of its parts, particularly the ejector and the cylinder pin, were prone to break or malfunction—but overall the gun was a rugged and powerful man stopper. It became a standard U.S. Army handgun from July 1873 and a massive seller to civilian markets. All users appreciated the Peacemaker's ability to keep firing through improvised control of the hammer even if individual parts were broken, and the gun also had a pleasant feel in the hand and an ease of aim, qualities that made the gun the archetypal gunfighter's weapon. It was also a sound weapon for military acquisition, and the U.S. Army purchased 36,000 between 1873 and 1892.

Peacemakers were owned by many of the Wild West's most famous gunslingers and lawmen, and there is an interesting letter written by Bat Masterson to Colt on July 24, 1885. Masterson purchased a total of eight Peacemakers from Colt between 1879 and 1885, and his letter describes a customization request:

Gents,

Please send me one of your nickel plated short .45 caliber revolvers. It is for my own use and for that reason I would like to have a little extra paines taken with it. I am willing to pay extra for extra work. Make it very easy on trigger and have the front sight a little higher than the ordinary pistol of this kind. Put in a gutta percha [a natural latex acquired from the Isonandra Gutta tree] handle and send it as soon as possible. Have the barrel about the same length that the ejecting rod is.

Truly yours,

W. B. Masterson

The request is interesting because it shows that accurate aiming was a priority for those who depended on their pistol for fighting work, contrary to the popular impression of gunfighters as slinging their gun from the hip.

The Peacemaker took a large proportion of the American handgun market while Smith and Wesson were slaving earnestly to fulfill its huge Russian contract. That contract was actually as much of a curse for Smith and Wesson as a blessing, for when it came to its close in the late 1870s, Colt had truly established itself as the domestic market leader. Competition against both companies came from the likes of Remington. In 1875, Remington introduced its first cartridge revolver, a single-action .44 handgun modified from the earlier New Model Army revolver. For personal protection purchases, small-caliber "pocket pistols" from the likes of Forehand Arms, Iver Johnson, and Harrington and Richardson took another section of the market. These weapons were usually rimfire .22, .32, and .38 calibers and were suited to those who appreciated a concealed weapon, or the gunfighter who wanted a backup.

However, from the late 1870s onward, the emergent battleground in handgun manufacture was the double-action cartridge weapon, a competition fueled by the fact that European export markets tended to prefer the double-action gun to its single-action counterpart. Both Colt and Smith and Wesson launched double-action guns at similar times. In 1877 Colt began production of the "Lightning" and the "Thunderer," these being the same gun in different calibers, .38 and .41 calibers respectively. (The Thunderer was one of Billy the Kid's favored handguns.) These revolvers continued Colt's ascendancy, with a total of 166,000 pieces sold between 1877 and 1909. Inevitably, Colt also brought out a double-action version of the Peacemaker, known as the Frontier Double Action. The U.S. Army snapped up the new weapon, which would remain in active service somewhere in the U.S. military until the early 1900s. Smith and Wesson introduced its own double-action revolvers from 1879, mainly a range of .32 and .38-caliber weapons, with a .44-caliber gun joining the catalog from 1881. The Smith and Wesson double-action revolvers were produced in enormous quantities—over 900,000 by the end of the twentieth century's first decade.

## The Perfection of the Revolver

By the early 1880s, the gunfighter of the Wild West had a choice of weapons truly suited to his violent age. Colt, Smith and Wesson, and Remington were producing superb single- and double-action revolvers in a variety of calibers from .22 to .45, providing accurate killing fire at ranges of around sixty yards. It was Colt, however, that brought the nineteenth century's final major innovation to revolver design.

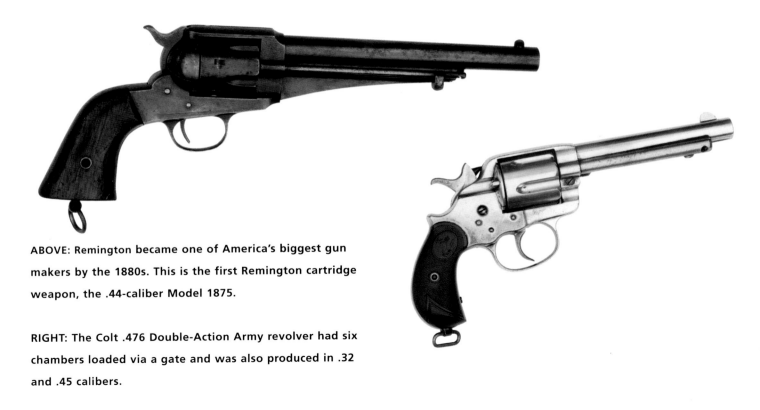

**ABOVE: Remington became one of America's biggest gun makers by the 1880s. This is the first Remington cartridge weapon, the .44-caliber Model 1875.**

**RIGHT: The Colt .476 Double-Action Army revolver had six chambers loaded via a gate and was also produced in .32 and .45 calibers.**

## WINCHESTER'S 1876–1886

Faced with the military's rejection of the Model 1873 because if its ammunition, Winchester produced a modified version known as the Model of 1876. This had a receiver able to accept the pressures generated by the government's .45-70 cartridge, which was two inches long—almost twice the length of the standard .44-40 round. In fact, the Model 1876 could accept a .45-75 cartridge with a bullet weight of 350 grains, which was more powerful than the government version. The rifle never

achieved the fame of the '73, but it was adopted by the Northwest Mounted Police and, like its predecessor, enjoyed a frontier reputation.

The prolific arms designer John M. Browning, whose brilliant designs would enhance Colt's and other companies' reputations, completely redesigned the Winchester rifle Model of 1886, the most powerful of them all. Chambered for .45-90, it also appeared in .50-110-300 Express, which proved to be a very popular caliber. The Browning-inspired Models of 1887,

9

10

11

12

13

14

15

16

1892, and 1894 also met with great success, and the keen-eyed will have noted that most Winchesters featured in Westerns are either 1892 or 1894 models, rather than the legendary '73. Many gunfighters and plainsmen carried a Winchester. The Model 1873 and the 1886 were used by buffalo hunters, but most hunters preferred the larger-calibered rifles.

1. Superficially similar to the Model '73, the '76 has an enlarged receiver and bigger loading-slot plate.
2. Cartridges for the Model 1876.
3. Like the '73, some Model '76s were sold with short magazines.

4. Serial no. 45569 is a nice example of a Model 1876 carbine.
5. Serial no. 40330 in contrast is a fully-blued rifle.
6. A fine pair of lady's buckskin gauntlets.
7. Serial no. 10018 is a '76 with a checkered pistol stock and target sights.
8. Two .43-70 cartridges for the Model 1876.
9. The Browning-designed '86 rifle: big improvement on earlier models.
10. Similar weapon, with choice wood pistol stock and target sights.
11. Note long "shell" case.
12. "As new" carbine version of the Model 1886 (s.n. 84841).
13. The short magazine '86 rifle (s.n. 57909).
14. High-powered cartridges for the Model 1886.
15. Silver-embossed hand-tooled rifle scabbard for the Model 1886.
16. Model '86 carbine with a ring that allows it to be slung over a saddle or shoulder.
(Artifacts courtesy of Buffalo Bill Historical Center, Cody, Wyoming.)

By the late nineteenth century, the one remaining awkwardness about American revolvers tended to be reloading. The Colt side-gate/ejector-rod method of reloading was cumbersome and even dangerous if the user was under mortal pressure. For Smith and Wesson, the break-open design allowed for faster reloading, but mechanical problems tended to result from wear and tear on the spring

Before turning to consider rifles, a journey through the handguns of the Wild West would be incomplete without some comment on a gun type very different from the revolvers but just as integral to the gunfighter's story. In 1807, Philadelphia gunsmith Henry Deringer produced a single-shot, muzzle-loaded percussion pistol, its dimensions small enough to allow it to be slipped into a jacket or trouser

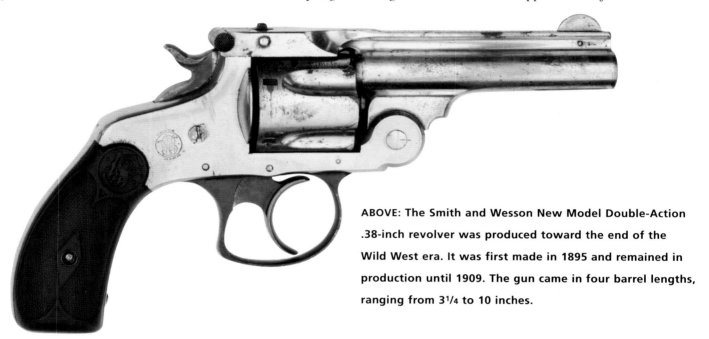

ABOVE: **The Smith and Wesson New Model Double-Action .38-inch revolver was produced toward the end of the Wild West era. It was first made in 1895 and remained in production until 1909. The gun came in four barrel lengths, ranging from 3¼ to 10 inches.**

catch. In 1888, Colt produced its Model 1889 Double Action New Navy Revolver, which featured a radical solution to the problem. The solution possibly built upon the work of European gun makers such as the Italian Captain A. Albini, who had patented a side-opening cylinder revolver in 1869. The cylinder of the New Navy was held on its axial pin on a pivoting arm that was secured to the gun's frame. The arm allowed the cylinder, when released by a thumb catch, to swing out to the side of the frame to expose all the chambers. A star extractor ensured a rapid emptying of the gun, and the lack of need for an ejector rod meant new cartridges could be quickly inserted and the cylinder snapped back into the frame. Although break-open revolvers persisted in the United States and Europe well into the twentieth century, the side-opening gun was gradually to take to advantage. All the major American manufacturers gradually moved to producing side-opening guns as the sun set on the last days of the Wild West.

pocket. Thus was born a whole series of derringer-type weapons (for an explanation of the variant double-r spelling, see page 246). Derringers were not the only type of pocket pistol, as diminutive revolvers were produced by most of the major U.S. gun manufacturers during the nineteenth century. However, the derringer came to be the preferred stow-away weapon for gamblers, gunfighters, and the West's criminal fraternity. Despite the popular impression that the men of the Wild West went everywhere with their revolvers, many establishment, town, and city ordnances prohibited carrying firearms. For those who felt naked without some form of weapon, the derringer could be slipped into pocket, bag, or ankle holster with no outward visible sign.

Derringers came in a wide variety of makes and models. A breechloading derringer was first produced and patented by Daniel Moore in 1861, the weapon being single-shot .41-caliber rimfire. The derringer established its notoriety when one was used by John Wilkes Booth to assassinate

ABOVE: The Model 1853 Pattern Enfield rifle was a British-produced weapon that saw considerable use in the Civil War and afterward in the hands of hunters. It was a sturdy percussion-lock weapon in .577 caliber.

President Abraham Lincoln in 1865, and these compact weapons subsequently became synonymous with underhanded violence.

## Rifles

Rifles are not quite as central to our story as revolvers; even so, a good rifle was an integral part of a gunfighter's personal armory during the nineteenth century. A rifle was particularly vital for those who spent time traveling through the American wilderness, the open range demanding greater reach from a firearm than the short-range revolver could supply. However well made a nineteenth-century revolver, it was an intrinsically inaccurate weapon after about fifty yards; by the end of the century rifles were comfortably hitting targets at 700 yards plus.

As in Europe, the United States persisted with muzzle-loading rifles well into the 1860s and 1870s. During the Civil War, for example, Union and Confederate soldiers employed some 820,000 British Enfield Rifle Musket Model 1853, in combat, 670,000 Springfield Model 1861 percussion-cap muzzle-loaders, and a variety of other muzzle-loaders from major and minor manufacturers. The accuracy and range of muzzle-loaders had increased dramatically with the standardization of rifling during the 1830s and also the improvement in ammunition types. The introduction of the Minié bullet—so named after its inventor, French Captain Claude-Étienne Minié—took the effective range of the muzzle-loaders out to over 500 yards. The Minié was a conical-cylindrical bullet with a cavity in its base; the cavity expanded on firing and gave the bullet a solid grip on the rifling. However, there was no getting away from the fact that muzzle-loading was a time-consuming process and dramatically limited available firepower both for the cowboy and the soldier.

## Breechloading Rifles

By the 1850s, breechloading rifles had made their way into American usage from Europe. A failed early experiment that laid the foundations for the redoubtable Winchester was the Volcanic lever-action rifle. The origins of the Volcanic weapon have already been described above, the gun beginning its journey in Walter Hunt's "Volitional Repeater." Smith and Wesson allied an improved version of Hunt's "Rocket Ball" ammunition system with a refined version of his lever-operated tubular magazine system to create a series of Volcanic rifles and pistols, a label given by an article on the weapons in *Scientific America*.

The Volcanic Repeating Fire Arms Company was established in late 1855. Volcanic produced a range of carbines in .38 caliber, the shortness of the Rocket Ball–type ammunition allowing for a very high magazine capacity—some of the carbines were thirty-shot models. Reloading was accomplished simply by the oscillation of the under-lever between each shot, the action of which also ejected the spent cartridge casing.

However, the ballistic performance of the ammunition was disappointing, and Volcanic went bankrupt in 1857. Crucially for future arms development, its assets were sold to one of its principal shareholders, Oliver Winchester, who formed the New Haven Arms Company.

Winchester, a haberdasher by trade, hired Benjamin Tyler Henry to make the Volcanic rifle a viable commercial proposition. Henry kept the defining tubular underbarrel magazine and underlever action—though he dramatically improved the mechanical reliability of both—but replaced the Rocket Ball with a .44-caliber rimfire round. The Henry rifle was launched on the eve of the Civil War, which slightly muted sales. Still, some 10,000 Henry rifles found their way

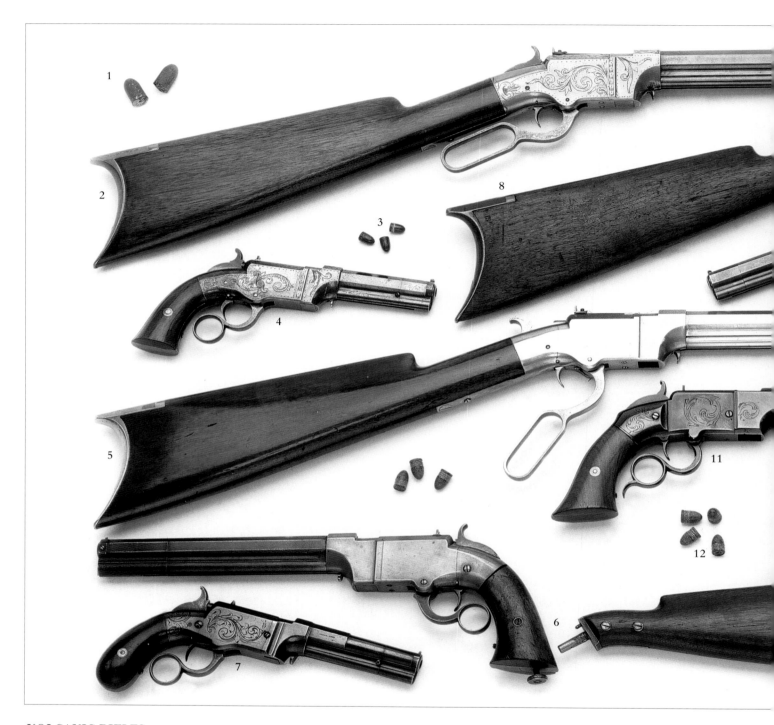

## VOLCANIC RIFLES

The so-called Volcanic magazine rifles and pistols were really a development of earlier pistols produced by Smith and Wesson in the early 1850s. These .30- and .38-caliber pistols (and a few very rarely encountered arms in .44) were unique. They were cartridge weapons at a time when the percussion system was in general use. Unfortunately, the cartridge, consisting of a hollow-nosed bullet that contained its own propellant, was not reliable; it was later replaced by an improved rimfire version. By

that time, Smith and Wesson had incorporated the company into Volcanic Arms and concentrated on other ventures.

As for the Volcanic pistols and rifles, they enjoyed a limited popularity, and in 1857 Col. Charles Hay, in command of the British Army's School of Musketry in Hythe, put the Volcanic through some severe tests. An expert shot, using the long-barreled version with a stock he was able to hit an eight-inch bull's-eye at 300 yards, placing nine bullets into the ring and two into the bull's-eye. And firing offhand at one hundred

yards, he had also hit the bull's-eye with a pistol. At the time that Col. Hay was experimenting with the Volcanic, Oliver Winchester purchased the company and renamed it the New Haven Arms Company. He appointed B. Tyler Henry to manage it, and his modifications to the mechanism and the ammunition culminated in the Henry rifle. But the Volcanic rifles were viewed as milestones in arms manufacture.

1. Pair of Hunt's patented caliber .54 "rocket balls."
2. Volcanic caliber .38 (.41 cartridge), 30 shot carbine (s.n. 88).
3. Trio of Volcanic No. 2 (caliber .41) bullets.
4. Volcanic caliber .30 (.31 cartridge), 6 shot pistol (s.n. 1340).
5. Volcanic caliber .38 (.41 cartridge), 25 shot carbine (s.n. 82).
6. Volcanic caliber .38 (.41 cartridge), 10 shot pistol-carbine (s.n. 1342).
7. Smith and Wesson caliber .30 (.31 cartridge), 6 shot pistol (s.n. 44).
8. Volcanic caliber .38 (.41 cartridge), 20 shot carbine (s.n. 1).
9. Volcanic caliber .30 (.31 cartridge), 6 shot pistol (s.n. 1868).
10. Volcanic caliber .38 (.41 cartridge), 10 shot pistol (s.n. 1159).
11. Smith and Wesson caliber .38 (.41 cartridge), 10 shot pistol.
12. Box of 200 No. 2 (caliber .41) Volcanic cartridges.
13. Volcanic caliber .30 (.31 cartridge), 10 shot target pistol (s.n. 1999).
14. Volcanic caliber .38 (.41 cartridge), 10 shot pistol (s.n. 1528).
15. Volcanic caliber .38 (.41 cartridge), 10 shot pistol (s.n. 1161).
16. Volcanic caliber .38 (.41 cartridge), 8 shot pistol (s.n. 822).
(Artifacts courtesy of Buffalo Bill Historical Center, Cody, Wyoming.)

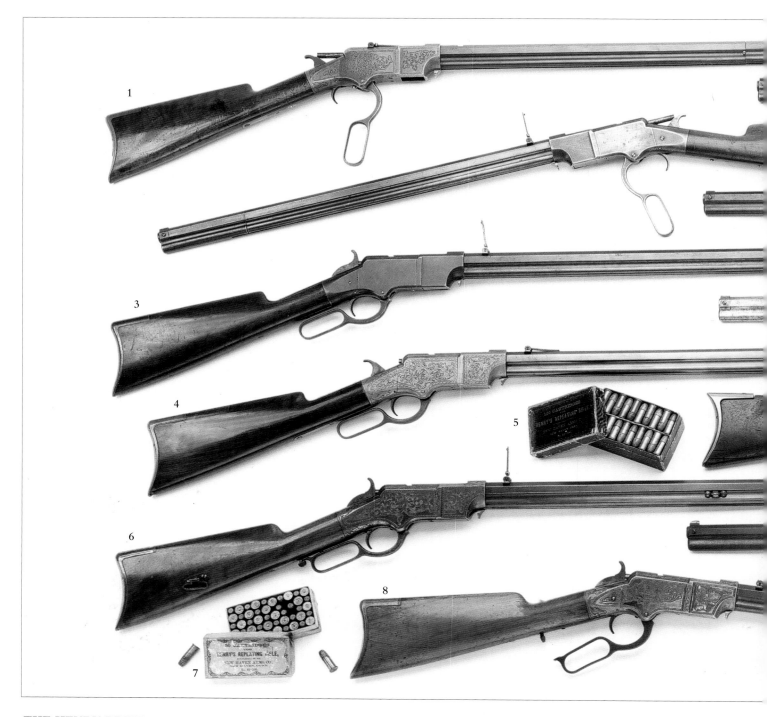

## THE HENRY RIFLE

The Henry rifle was a derivative of the Smith and Wesson/Volcanic arms. Henry's modification of the action and improved cartridge revolutionized the concept. It consisted of a brass casing with the propellant in its base and a 216-grain bullet and twenty-five grains of powder. This "rimfire" proved successful and was modified several times. Ordnance tests were encouraging, and it was claimed that at 400 yards the bullet could embed itself five inches into a wooden target.

The U.S. government was slow in accepting the Henry rifle, but by 1863 a large number of them had been issued to volunteer and state troops. Kansas in particular took to the Henry. It was reported in 1863 that Gen. James Blunt's bodyguards were to be armed with "Henry's Volcanic repeating rifles and two revolvers and will be mounted on picked horses." The Henry was fitted with a tubular magazine that could hold sixteen rounds. Its only drawback was its price: in October 1862 it was listed at forty-two dollars, the

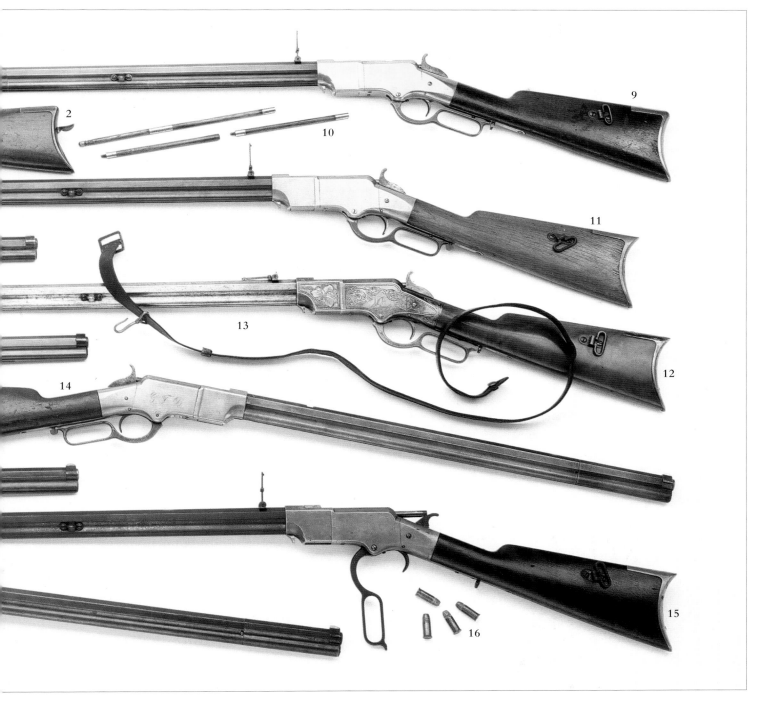

ammunition at ten dollars per thousand. Even the dealers failed to get a good discount, but demand was sufficient to keep the company busy. A major weakness was its exposed magazine spring, which meant loading from the muzzle end. In 1866 this was rectified by placing a slot in the side of the receiver and spring pressure from the muzzle end. Too late for the Henry, it was incorporated in its successor, the Winchester model 1866.

1. An early brass-frame Henry rifle (s.n. 14).
2. Iron frame Henry rifle, levered for loading.

3. Iron frame Henry rifle (s.n. 155).
4. Early production (rounded butt), engraved Henry rifle (s.n. 172).
5. Box of early caliber .44 Henry rimfire cartridges.
6. Early production brass-frame, silver-plated Henry (s.n. 2115).
7. Box of post–Civil War caliber .44 Henry rimfire cartridges.
8. Early production brass-frame, silver-plated, engraved Henry rifle.
9. Early production brass-frame Henry military rifle (s.n. 2928).
10. Four-piece wooden cleaning rod stored in the butt trap of Henry rifles.
11. Later (crescent butt) brass-frame Henry military rifle (s.n. 6734).
12. Later production silver-plated Henry military rifle (s.n. 7001).
13. Leather sling for Henry military rifle.
14. Later production brass-frame Henry military rifle (s.n. 9120).
15. Later production brass-frame Henry military rifle (s.n. 12832).
16. Quartet of caliber .44 Henry flat–nosed cartridges.
(Artifacts courtesy of Buffalo Bill Historical Center, Cody, Wyoming.)

into military use during the war, with thousands more going to private individuals who appreciated the gun's magazine capacity (sixteen rounds) and its reach—U.S. Army Ordinance Department tests showed that it was capable of five-inch penetration into wood at 400 yards.

On the downside, the tubular magazine was prone to malfunction from dirt ingress and its front-loading system was awkward. In 1866 Winchester gave his name to the Henry rifle and improved the magazine operation significantly, giving it a more convenient refill from the receiver end. The lever action was also simplified and made more robust.

Further refinements were introduced with the Winchester 1873, including a switch to the more powerful .44-40 centerfire round, this model being, alongside the Peacemaker revolver, one of the most recognizable firearms of the American West. (Colt made a variation of the Peacemaker in .44-40 Winchester caliber to allow the user to use a single ammunition type for rifle and sidearm, such was the popularity of the Winchester.)

The Winchester rifles were very much civilian weapons, the U.S. Army selecting the Springfield rifle (see below) then, from 1892, the Krag Jorgensen rifle. The '73 was forty-two inches long, fed from a fifteen-round magazine, had a realistic sight range of up to 600 yards, and fired a twenty-grain bullet capable of taking down man and beast with little problem.

Cowboys loved it as a superb saddle gun, it slipping easily into a saddle holster. For the same reasons, the Native Americans also embraced the gun; they gave it the nickname Yellow Boy owing to its golden receiver finish. Such was the quality of the Winchester that Buffalo Bill Cody wrote to Winchester in 1875 to declare:

**TOP: Oliver Winchester ran several businesses before turning his interest to firearms around 1856. The following year he became a major shareholder in the Volcanic arms company.**

**RIGHT: Geronimo (far right) is pictured with a .45-70 trapdoor Springfield. Two of the men hold the popular Winchester 73.**

I have been using and have thoroughly tested your latest improved rifle [the Model 1873]. I pronounce your improved Winchester the boss. Believe me you have the most complete rifle ever made.

Total production for the 1873 came to 720,610, making it the most prolific commercial rifle in the West, adored by cowboys, criminals, and lawmen alike.

## Other breechloading rifles

The Winchester may have been a "complete" rifle, but it was not the only rifle destined for significant usage in the Wild West. During the 1850s and 1860s several other popular breechloaders entered the hands of civilian and military

users, the most famous being the Spencer carbine and the Sharps rifle.

Christopher Spencer, a gun maker from Connecticut, patented the .52-caliber rimfire Spencer carbine in 1860. It was a lever-action weapon that actually predated the Henry, the lever enabling the ammunition feed from a seven-round tubular magazine that was inserted into the stock.

In a sense, the Spencer was one of the earliest weapons to be fed from a detachable magazine, as the user could carry preloaded tubes instead of refilling the empty magazine every time.

The Spencer was accepted for Navy service in 1860, but the U.S. Army's chief of ordnance rejected it for infantry service in preference for the 1861 U.S. Rifle Musket. President Abraham Lincoln himself tested the Spencer rifle in August 1863 and was so impressed with its accuracy, high rate of fire, and accessible field-stripping procedure that he personally forced a reversal of policy in the U.S. Army.

An initial order for 10,000 was the tip of the iceberg, and in total Spencer sold 94,196 carbines and 12,471 rifles to the U.S. Army between 1861 and 1866, during which time the

Spencer gave murderous service in the Civil War. Such were the volumes produced that, inevitably, thousands remained in civilian use after the war.

Another rifle famed during the Civil War era and subsequently was the Sharps Rifle designed by Christian Sharps. Sharps's original 1851 single-shot rifle used a patented breechblock that was moved up and down by a lever action on the trigger guard. With the trigger guard pushed down, the breechblock was loaded with a linen cartridge, the base of which was shorn off by the breechblock, thus exposing the powder, when the trigger guard was returned against the stock. Initially the gun was fired via a pellet primer system, although from 1859 it used a standard percussion cap.

**ABOVE: A Sharps New Model Carbine, showing the backsight in the elevated position. A skilled hunter could attempt to hit a large target, such as a buffalo, at ranges of up to 1,000 yards, although half that range was more practical.**

The advantage of the Sharps rifle was that its action was extremely robust, strong enough to handle the large .52 and .56 calibers of the early weapons. Sharps rifles were also highly accurate, a quality that led to their usage by Colonel Hiram Berdan's infamous 1st U.S. Sharpshooters. (Berdan personally demonstrated a head-shot to a man-sized target at 600 yards in front of President Abraham Lincoln in September 1861.)

The Sharps rifle gave seminal service during the Civil War, and by the 1870s Sharps was producing a powerful range of hunting rifles using metallic cartridges. Out on the range, a series of percussion-fired "Plains" rifles were developed, these being heavy-caliber long-range weapons purposely designed for the hunting of buffalo and other big game. Plains rifles could reach up to .60 inches in caliber (though were more typically .40–.50-caliber). The Sharps Model 1874 was a typical plains rifle. Its .45-caliber bullet—which weighed an enormous 550 grains—was propelled by a 120-grain load out to ranges of 1,000 yards. The hunter Billy Dixon used a Plains

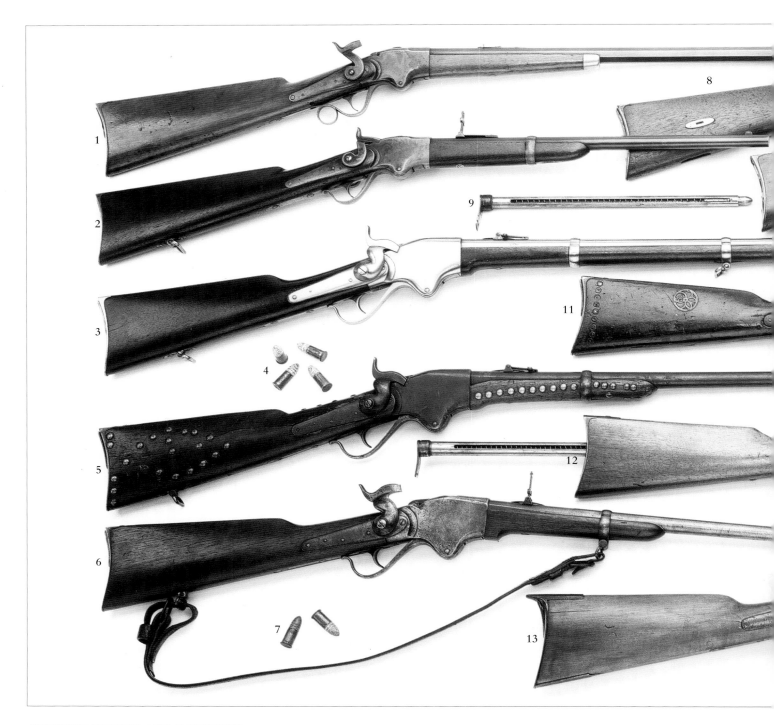

## SPENCER RIFLES AND CARBINES

According to the 1864 report by Brigadier James W. Ripley, Chief of Ordnance to the Secretary of War, the Spencer rifles and carbines were the cheapest, most durable, and most efficient of the many arms at the time in use by the Union forces. Its reputation among cavalry regiments was unchallenged. This seven-shot weapon, fitted with a Blakeslee quick-loader, was designed so that the ammunition was contained in a tube set into the stock. It took a matter of seconds to remove a tube and replace it. More than 90,000 carbines were purchased during the war and, following the conflict, the Spencer enjoyed a great frontier reputation. In 1865, the company introduced a .50-caliber version, complete with a magazine cut-off that enabled it to be used as a single-shot weapon if required. The Spencer was issued to various cavalry regiments, including the Seventh.

What the Spencer lacked in magazine capacity compared with the Winchester, it made up for by being easier to carry

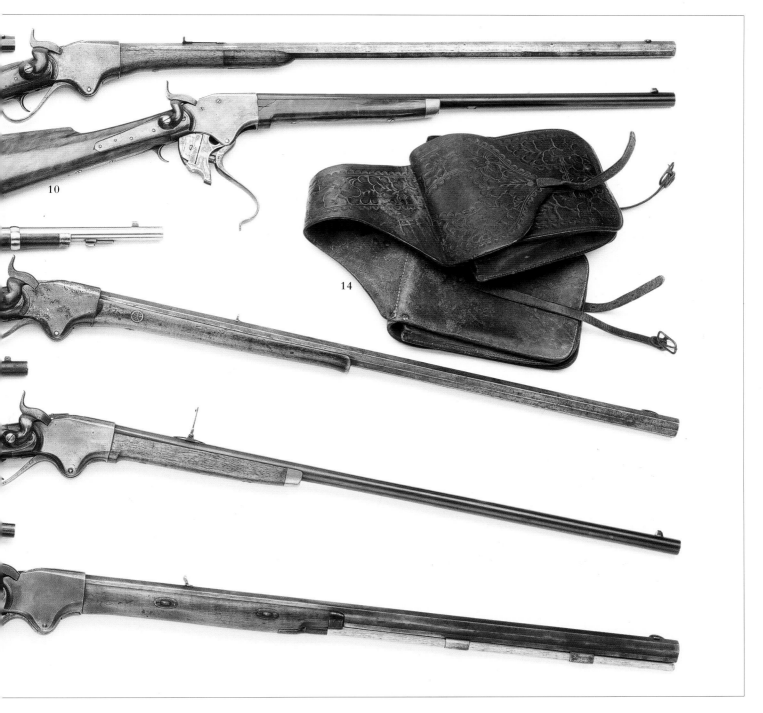

and faster to load. In 1874 the Spencer was superseded by the Springfield Model 1873, a single-shot carbine in .45-70 caliber capable of firing twelve or thirteen rounds a minute. Poor ammunition and lack of proper means of removing jammed cases led to the disaster at the Little Bighorn. Had the Spencer been used, it may well have saved lives.

1. Spencer caliber .36 light sporting rifle (s.n. 15).
2. Spencer caliber .44 light carbine (s.n. 5)
3. Spencer U.S. Navy contract caliber .36-56 military rifle (s.n. 121)
4. Four rounds of Spencer caliber .56-52 rimfire ammunition.

5. Spencer U.S. Army caliber .56-56 military carbine (s.n. 30670), carried at the battle of the Little Bighorn by a Cheyenne warrior.
6. Spencer U.S. Army Model 1865 caliber .56-50 military carbine (s.n. 5909).
7. Spencer caliber .56-56 rimfire cartridges.
8. Spencer caliber .56-46 sporting rifle (s.n. 17444).
9. Seven round tubular magazine for Spencer rifles and carbines.
10. Spencer caliber .38 prototype sporting rifle (no s.n.).
11. Spencer caliber .56-50 carbine (s.n. obliterated), rebarreled to a sporting rifle.
12. Spencer caliber .56-46 sporting rifle (no s.n.).
13. Spencer caliber .56-56 carbine (s.n. 35862), rebarreled to caliber .56-50 by John Gemmer of St. Louis under S. Hawken's stamp.
14. Pair of typical Western saddlebags, which might carry loose ammunition.

(Artifacts courtesy of Buffalo Bill Historical Center, Cody, Wyoming.)

rifle to shoot and kill an Indian on horseback at a range later measured at 1,538 yards. One important effect of the Plains rifles upon American social and natural history was that they facilitated the almost total destruction of the American buffalo herds. The killing of the buffalo was unprecedented ecological slaughter sanctioned on commercial grounds (hides and meat) and also political grounds, in that the destruction of the buffalo deprived the Native Americans of its primary source of meat and so forced them into compliance with government policy. The Sharps was not the only Plains rifle, although it was the most successful during the 1860s. Major competition against Sharps came from the likes of Martin-Ballard and particularly from Remington.

## The Rise of Gun Ownership

The nineteenth century saw a dramatic shift in the nature of gun ownership in the United States. Before 1850, only about 10 percent of the U.S. population owned a firearm. Certainly until the 1830s, guns tended to be classed more as luxury products or as requisite purchases for subsistence or commercial hunters. Even the famed militias were often only partially armed. In 1830, for example, a census of American militias recorded that there were 1,128,594 militia members but only 359,055 available weapons. Furthermore, a high percentage of these weapons were not serviceable, being old muskets. What gun ownership that existed was most concentrated on the frontier and in the American South.

Murder statistics for the period 1800 to 1845 are also revealing. During this period only around 15 percent of murders were committed with a firearm, with beatings and stranglings accounting for 40 percent and stabbings around 25 percent. However, by 1860—the intervening period seeing the widespread distribution of new revolver technologies—gun murders had risen to around 35 percent and by the end of the century to around 50 percent. (Statistical data taken from Jan E. Dizard, et al., eds., *Guns in America: A Reader*, New York University Press, 1999.)

How do we account for this surge in gun-related murders? Leaving aside the complex social changes that occurred in nineteenth century, considered in the preceding chapters, the simplest explanation is a massive rise in gun ownership. By the 1850s, gun manufacture had changed from a handcrafting tradition, where gun makers produced several dozen guns at best each year, to an assembly-line industry. Although Henry Ford is often credited with creating the modern production line, true credit arguably must go to Eli Whitney Jr., to whom Colt contracted out production of his revolvers during the 1840s. Before Whitney, the component parts of guns tended to be assembled at different locations before being delivered to a central workshop where the complex process of fitting would take place. Whitney rationalized this process, placing all the workers in one building, each working on a specific part of the manufacturing process.

This setup allowed for a much greater speed of production, aided by precision lathing processes that turned out uniform wood and metal parts requiring no great skill to fit together. The acceleration of production figures attests to the success of these methods as well as the growth of the gun companies themselves. The government's Springfield Armory produced 14,770 weapons between 1821 and 1830. By contrast, between 1860 and 1870 the same armory—rising to the demand of the Civil War—outputted 90,992 firearms.

The Civil War was undoubtedly the major catalyst for the surge in gun ownership during the nineteenth century. A rise had begun earlier, particularly from the 1840s, when gun companies became more sophisticated in promoting firearm ownership to an emerging middle class. However, the Civil War pushed guns into the hands of millions of American men, and once the war was over they either didn't want to relinquish their guns or sought to purchase new weapons. Indeed, many gun companies in the aftermath of the war heavily promoted the concept of personal security through gun ownership, and so were able to maintain strong sales in the antebellum period.

The debate on the consequences and reality of American gun culture continues to this day. What is undeniable is that the nineteenth century saw guns woven into the very fabric of American consciousness, (and indeed, into the American Constitution) and today those men who followed the "way of the gun" have become some of the most enduring heroes and villains, not only of American popular culture, but of the whole world's.

LEFT: Wyatt Earp, photographed looking out over the Colorado River a few years before his death on January 13, 1920. Gold prospector, saloon keeper, racehorse breeder, and boxing referee (for a fight between Bob Fitzimmons and Tom Sharkey in 1895), Wyatt Earp was famous for a few other exploits and modes of employment. What does he remember most vividly? Is it the murder of his brother Morgan? Is it the Coeur D'Alene gold rush? The O.K. Corral? Or perhaps it is emigrating to California at sixteen to work as a teamster with brother Virgil, before all the gunplay.

# INDEX

# ACKNOWLEDGMENTS

T = Top; B = Bottom; R=Right; L=Left

All images courtesy of Chrysalis Image Library apart from the following images:

© Museum of Fine Arts, Houston, Texas, USA/**Bridgeman Art Library**: 396–397

© H. Armstrong Roberts/**CORBIS**; Front Cover. © Bettmann/CORBIS: 64 and 356
© Ali Meyer/CORBIS; 399

© **"Just Gunfighters" Living-History Group**, www.justgunfighters.com: 108 and 109

**Library of Congress Prints and Photographs Division Washington, D.C 20540**:
14 [LC-USZ62-57524], 33T [LC-USZ62-26949], 49 [LC-USZ62-4049], 54 [LC-USZ62-109398], 58-59T [PAN US GEOG-Kansas no.7 (E size)], 84B [LC-USZ62-42836], 115 [LC-USZ62-134452], 116L [DAG no.233], 165 [LC-USZC4-2730], 172 [LC-USZC4-5217], 173, 175 [LC-DIG-ggbain-02286], 182 [LC-USZC2-762], 189R [LC-USZ62-2050], 239 [LC-USZ62-105004], 274TL [LC-USZC4-2488], 278-279 [LC-USZ62-110999], 279R [LC-USZ62-97956], 280 [LC-USZ62-87441], 284 [HABS, NM, 27-SOCO, 1], 289 [LC-USZ62-46192], 315 [LC-USZC4-6424], 390-1 [LC-DIG-ppmsc-02672], 394 [LC-USZ62-121647], 395B [LC-USZ62-14131], 395T [LC-USZ62-64798]

**Library of Congress and Map Division Washington, D.C 20540-4650**:
352 [G4031.P3 1877. G7 TIL]

Chrysalis Books Group Plc is committed to respecting the intellectual property rights of others. We have therefore taken all reasonable efforts to ensure that the reproduction of all content on these pages is done with the full consent of copyright owners. If you are aware of any unintentional omissions, please contact the company directly so that any necessary corrections may be made for future editions.